THE SULTAN'S YEMEN

THE SULTAN'S YEMEN

Nineteenth-Century Challenges to Ottoman Rule

Caesar E. Farah

I.B.Tauris
London · New York

Published in 2002 by I.B. Tauris & Co Ltd
6 Salem Road, London W2 4BU
175 Fifth Avenue, New York NY 10010
www.ibtauris.com

In the United States of America and Canada distributed by
Palgrave Macmillan a division of St. Martin's Press
175 Fifth Avenue, New York NY 10010

The Library of Ottoman Studies
Volume 1

ISBN 186064 767 7

A full CIP record for this book is available from the British Library
A full CIP record is available from the Library of Congress

Library of Congress Catalog Card Number: available

Copy-edited and laser-set by Oxford Publishing Services, Oxford
Printed and bound in Great Britain by MPG Books Ltd, Bodmin

Contents

Preface

The main focus of this study is on Ottoman efforts to maintain sovereignty over Yemen, which were constantly being challenged from within and without. Most data used to research this study are derived from Ottoman officer accounts and from the Başbakanlık Arşivi (Prime Minister's Archives) in Istanbul, Turkey. The various collections consulted are listed under Yıldız Tasnifi (sultan's palace collection) in the bibliography at the end of this book. For Ottoman accounts of their travails in Yemen I relied heavily on the Ottoman documents housed in the Prime Minister's Archives in Istanbul and on documents listed in a special collection entitled 'Yemen Meselesi' (The Problem of Yemen). The few available first-hand accounts by observers and Yemeni authors were consulted to achieve a balanced understanding of the forces at work in Yemen in the nineteenth century. On Britain's role in Arabia, I consulted reports from the Bombay government, which had jurisdiction over the Residency at Aden for most of the period under consideration, housed in the India Office Library in London, and Foreign Office reports to and from the field, principally Constantinople (Istanbul), and official transactions with the Ottoman government housed in the Public Records Office. The Foreign Office archives of the German Republic at Bonn and whatever documentation could be found in the principal library of Ṣan'ā', Yemen, were also consulted.

The newspapers, Arabic, Ottoman and Western language journals, and the range of other material consulted, including secondary sources, are listed in the bibliography.

I owe a debt of gratitude to the Bayazit library of Istanbul University for allowing me access to their Ottoman newspapers and pamphlets; and to the librarians, researchers and director, Dr Ekmeleddin Ihsanoğlu, of the Office of Islamic Conference's Research Centre for Islamic History, Art and Culture in the Yıldız Palace of Istanbul. Credit is due also to the librarians of the Belediye Kütüphanesi of Istanbul, to the Jaffet library of the American University of Beirut for similar support, and of the Assad library in Damascus for facilitating access to

Arabic material relating to this period of Yemen's history. The Yemeni Centre for Study and Research in Ṣan‘ā’ provided ground support to inspect various sites in the north and centre of Yemen, though the south was inaccessible at that time. Rector of the University of Ṣan‘ā’ and director of the Yemeni Study and Research Institute Dr ‘Abd al-‘Aziz Maqālih generously made a driver and vehicle available to me. Dr Yūsuf ‘Abdallah, head of the Department of Antiquities, offered the services of a graduate student to help locate the various places in Yemen included in the text.

The problem of how to treat transliterations of names and places was resolved by using the modern Turkish form for the Ottoman names of Ottoman government officials derived from Arabic, which most were. I employed the preferred Library of Congress method of transcription for the names of Arab leaders, chiefs and places in Yemen. Some exceptions were made because of the frequency of occurrence in English reports, namely Hodeida in lieu of Ḥudaydah, Mocha in lieu of al-Mukhā'. While Ṣan‘ā’ is the present designation for the capital of the country, English scholars of the region prefer direct transliteration from the Arabic, in other words Ṣan‘ā’. There are a number of towns and localities, as well as tribal units, referred to in Ottoman documentation that could not be located, even on an Ottoman map of the period, hence the need to extrapolate using the logical Arabic pronunciation.

The mode used for dates according to the Islamic calendar is that of the modern Turkish abbreviation for each month, as follows:

	Arabic	Turkish
M	Muharram	Muharrem
S	Safar	Safer
Ra	Rabī‘ al-Awwal	Rebiyülevvel
R	Rabī‘ al-Thāni	Rebiyülâhır
Ca	Jumāda al-Awwal	Cemaziyelevvel
C	Jumāda al-Ākhar	Cemaziyelâhır
B	Rajab	Recep
Ş	Sha‘bān	Şaban
N	Ramadān	Ramazan
L	Shawwāl	Şevval
Za	Dhu ‘l-Qa‘dah	Zilkade
Z	Dhu ‘l-Hijjah	Zilhicca

The funding agencies that enabled me to undertake research in the field, for which I am most grateful, are the Institute of Turkish Studies in Washington, DC, the Fulbright Hays' programme of the Department of Education, and the Grant-in-Aid of Research Program of the Graduate School of the University of Minnesota. In addition, I wish to express my gratitude to my wife Dr Irmgad Farah for her various contributions both in the field and at home. I wish to thank the archivists and librarians for the logistical support they gave me in locating various documents and studies both in published and manuscript form and to acknowledge the valuable contributions and input of my associate Hisham Abdul Khalek.

Introduction

Outsiders have been attracted to Yemen since before the Christian era, for it witnessed the rise of the earliest civilizations, Sabaean and Himyarite, which thrived on trade and agriculture. The early Greeks, then the Romans and other neighbours coveted its wealth and tried unsuccessfully to gain access to its rich spices, such as frankincense and myrrh. It was a land inhabited predominantly by tribal Arabs who adhered to no central authority. A tribal organization headed by a *shaykh* or chief who made decisions and meted out justice was the predominant administrative unit. A number of local dynastic rulers arose in the Islamic era, including the Ayyubids, Tahirids and Rasulids who managed at one time or another to unite the land. Missionaries sent out by the Prophet Muhammad himself were the first to convert the tribes to Islam. Once the country was fully Islamized, the two main branches, Sunni and Shīʻah, gained dominance among the Yemenis, the former in the highlands, and the latter in the south and lowlands. In the tenth century Zayd, a grandson of the Prophet, gained a number of converts to his brand of Shīʻah preaching and his followers took on his name; shortly thereafter Ismāʻīl, another grandson, acquired powerful followers in Yemen. The two did not only live in close proximity to each other but soon became serious rivals for dominance in the highlands. The Sunni adhered to the Shāfiʻi rite, which was predominant in the Egyptian and Syrian regions. They inhabited the southern highlands and the coastal region known as the Tihāmah or lowlands. Not only Greeks and Romans but also Abyssinians and Persians sought to control the spice trade and gain dominance over Yemen, but their presence was short lived.

Apart from a brief spell of Judaism at the beginning of the Islamic era, the people were originally pagan in religious adherence. Yemen and Oman were the first places to convert as a result of preaching in the days of the Prophet by his nephew Jaʻfar and his early followers. As a consequence, one of his descendants, Zayd, gained the upper hand and the sect known as Zaydi evolved and expanded to the point that Zayd's descendants provided the imams or rulers of Yemen right down until the beginning of the republican era in the mid-twentieth century. Another of the Prophet's grandsons, Isma'īl, and his followers managed to spread his version of Islam in the Yemeni highlands. Shortly thereafter two major branches of Shi'ism became deadly rivals, each having converted some of the most powerful tribes among highland Yemenis.

Historically, the country had been impervious to outside invasions. The Mamluks of Egypt controlled the land from the thirteenth to the sixteenth century when the Ottomans displaced them. Indeed, the conqueror, Selim I (1512–60) had been declared the 'protector of the two holy shrines' in Damascus in December 1516, before he finally defeated the feisty Mamluk sultan in Cairo the following month. Henceforth it was left to the Ottomans to carry on the task of protecting the Arabian Peninsula.

Soon after displacing the Mamluks, the Ottomans confronted the Portuguese in the lower Red Sea and Indian Ocean. At one time, in the 1540s, the Portuguese sailed right up to Jiddah in an attempt to capture and destroy the holy cities. The British finally displaced them as masters of the Indian Ocean and, by the nineteenth century, had established harbours in Yemen, first at Mocha and then, when chased out by an Ottoman agent, at Aden, over which, by a combination of ruse and force, they gained possession in 1839. This posed an additional problem for the Ottomans. Continual foreign intrigues and manoeuvres to gain access to the region's commerce, especially coffee in the Yemeni highlands, which the Dutch had first controlled in the seventeenth century, led to competition that ended, here as elsewhere, with the imperial powers challenging one another for commercial dominance and the British prevailing.

Once the British had chased the French out of India and had gained full control of the subcontinent, they became obsessed with protecting the route to India through Arabian waters — the Persian Gulf and the Red Sea through the Bāb al-Mandab. In 1817 they sought to install themselves at Mocha, the terminus of the coffee trade prior to overseas shipment. When a local chieftain checkmated their manoeuvres, they tried again in 1821, this time seeking control of Aden. This they achieved by luring an unsuspecting chieftain into their fold through his signing an agreement he could not read. This occasioned a long struggle by the chieftain's relatives and other nearby chiefs to check English attempts to expand upwards into the highlands for political and commercial purposes. When local chiefs became unable or unwilling to confront the superior military power of the English, they succumbed to signing more agreements, often under duress, which allowed the English to extend their sphere of influence into what has become known in recent years as South Yemen and which they were forced to leave fewer than 100 years later. Prior to their departure they entrusted surrogates among the *sharīf*s[1] of the lowlands to protect their sovereign rights against a challenge by the British who, since 1839, had become entrenched in the Aden region and were seeking to control trade with the highlands. The imams dominated the highlands and were independent. In the nineteenth century, intrigues by foreign powers, this time Italy and Britain, compelled the Ottomans to reassert themselves administratively and militarily in Yemen.

The Ottomans' return to Yemen in the mid-nineteenth century was occasioned by the same considerations that had brought them to the land for the first time during the last third of the sixteenth century, namely the perceived threat of Western imperialism generated by the Portuguese in the sixteenth century and by the British in the early nineteenth. Both powers had designs on the land for a range of reasons — commercial and religious for the Portuguese, political and commercial for the English. Though not the only part of the Muslim world threatened by imperial ambitions, it was particularly threatening in that it was so close to Islam's holiest sites, Mecca and Medina.

In the nineteenth century, the English sought to circle the Arabian Peninsula with bases and spheres of influence. They had started the process in the eighteenth century when the Portuguese were chased out of Oman and they drew up their first treaty with an Arab chieftain of the Arabian Peninsula. This enabled them to impose their influence and control over the land access to the Gulf of Oman and, by extension, the Persian Gulf, which culminated in their gaining control over strategic Kuwait at the beginning of the twentieth century.

Fearing this English push to the north (*drang nach norden*), in 1849 the Ottomans returned to Yemen to consolidate their sovereign right over the area. This they had achieved by conquest in 1569 when Sinan Paşa had been compelled to mount an expedition into the Yemeni highlands to check the rebellion of the then Imam al-Muṭṭahar ibn Sharaf al-Dīn (1558–73), which was inconclusive, obliging the Ottoman commander to enter into a peace arrangement with the imam.[2]

The same circumstance occasioned the launch of this campaign as the one that had led the Ottomans to take charge of the Arabian south in 1538, namely the Mamluks had handed them responsibility for the land's defence and protection, a period of rule that lasted only until 1635. They wanted to discourage local chieftains from succumbing to the sorts of temptations imperial powers offered in general and the arrival of the Portuguese had shown in particular. They also wanted to stabilize a society divided by tribal, sectarian and demographic factions. This, however, they failed to sustain because, within a century (in 1635), they found themselves retreating from the land, leaving its control to local rulers. A period of stability and prosperity ensued, however, which lasted until the rise of the Wahhabi movement in Nejd and which, with its strict fundamentalism, represented a different kind of threat to Ottoman domination.

When Ottoman surrogate chiefs lost control of the lowlands in the mid-nineteenth century and rival families were fighting for domination of the highlands over the imamate, the Ottomans returned to defend their sovereignty militarily. Having set up headquarters in the city of Zabīd in the Tihāmah, they spread their direct domination over the rest of the coastal area from ʻAsīr to the area bordering the English controlled land in the south, beyond the port city of Mocha.

When the struggle for domination among imams and claimants to the office intensified in the highlands, al-Hādi Ghālib ibn al-Mutawakkil Muḥammad (1850–51) persuaded the Ottomans, who recognized his claim, to provide him with the military support he needed to put down his rivals. They had attempted to control the highlands in 1849, but Ghālib's rival had treacherously repelled the expedition. Meanwhile, the Ottoman forces concentrated on pacifying the ʻAsīri region where its chieftain had been carrying on a feud with the legitimately recognized administrator of the Tihāmah.

Having successfully pacified the lower region, Ahmed Muhtâr Paşa, commandant of the Ottoman army, responded to the imam's urgent plea to lead his forces to Ṣanʻā', the administrative centre of the highlands, where he was warmly welcomed. This did not last because the imam's rivals mounted a resistance against him and his Ottoman supporters, and rebellions sprung up in most of the Zaydi lands from the south to the north. Ottoman forces were engaged to put down the rebellions and attempts were made to reorganize and stabilize the administrative structure of the land and to inject order into the operation. Their main aims were to pacify the opposing tribes, enlist them in the service of the state as local officials and tax collectors and introduce justice into the court system, which was neither uniform nor evenly applied. The Tanzimat era and its liberalizing decrees based on Western models sat uneasily with the Shi'ite Zaydis; in fact, even the Sunni Shāfi'is saw them as compromising decrees of the Sharī'ah.

The cost of pacifying the land kept mounting. It reached unbearable levels for the central government in Istanbul, which over nearly half a century had constantly to mobilize troops to combat insurgents at a cost that overtaxed an already bankrupted central treasury with little local revenue available to counteract some of the expenses. In that they mobilized mostly Syrian battalions to do the job until almost the last phase of the war, the task was not easy for the Ottomans. The soldiers were often unpaid, ill-clothed, under-equipped, and short on supplies and living allowances, and this made for demoralization and mutinies. Moreover, many sympathized with their fellow Yemeni Arabs, indeed to the extent even of passing on intelligence to the imam and his lieutenants.

To compound Ottoman woes, Sultan Abdülhamid II (1876–1908) had been inaccurately informed about the true state of affairs in Yemen. This was because many of the officials sent out to govern or administer had been ill-prepared for the task. Consequently, there were lapses in proper administrative procedures, recourse by some to self-enrichment through extortion, improper tax levies and harsh collection methods. At times even the army was employed to collect taxes, thus depriving the local chiefs, who had been appointed to do the job, of their fair share of levies, the state of its income and the imam of his due.

When the sultan learned of Yemen's problems, he tried to appease the inhabitants by sending out numerous commissions of inquiry, but their findings rarely reflected the true nature of Yemeni disaffection, which merely intensified the struggles and attacks on Ottoman forces. By the turn of the century the insurgence had become widespread. The 'Asīris, under the leadership of an outsider who claimed to be the Mahdi after espousing the Wahhābi doctrine of a strict Islam grounded in the Sharī'ah, the fundamental law of the faith, joined the forces of rebellion in Yemen. However, they were also fighting for their independence because Wahhābism and Zaydism represented the ideologies of two disparate sectarian trends. One had strict fundamentalist Sunni roots; the other, though also following basic Islamic teachings, inclined slightly towards the Shi'ite sect, from which it was derived and whose imams followed the Shi'ite notion of leadership, which emphasized their descent from the house of the Prophet through 'Ali ibn abi Ṭālib and his martyred son Ḥusayn.

Yemen, moreover, was full of Sayyids who claimed descent from 'Ali through his son Ḥasan and who had for centuries constituted a powerful and dominant class in the land. Indeed, one argument used to explain their alleged mistreatment at the hands of contemptuous Turkish administrators is that the rulers had reneged on a promise the conqueror Sultan Selim I had extended to them to honour their status and privileges as descendants of the Prophet Muḥammad.

The sultan tried his best to accommodate the legitimate demands of the Zaydi Yemenis who insisted on being administered according to the Sharī'ah's decrees guided strictly by the teachings of the Qur'ān, the holy book of Islam. Western observers posited that the rising against legitimate authority was due less to religious disagreements than to political manoeuvrings among Yemeni Zaydite factions to gain leadership of the flock. Autonomy, not independence is what they sought, as was clearly illustrated in the final agreement concluded between the government and the imam in 1911, which still left matters of defence and protection to Ottoman forces.

Technically, the Ottomans still ruled Yemen. In fact, they even consolidated their landholdings, extending direct authority over hitherto British-controlled Aden and the nine-district area adjoining it at the commencement of the First World War until they lost control at the end of the war and Yemen became independent under the leadership of the last imam to confront them in seven years of fighting (1904–11), namely Yaḥya Ḥamīd al-Dīn (1904–48).

In this book the aim is to recount, in considerable detail, the whole range of Ottoman involvement from the threatening incursions of British then Italian forces in the south and the Red Sea, the rebellions the Italians (more than the British) abetted through shipping arms to the imam's forces and to the Ottoman navy's desperate attempts to stop the smuggling of weapons into the highlands, often under the auspices of the powerful and defiant Zarānīq tribes of the Tihāmah. It is true that the British at times sympathized more with the Yemenis than with the Ottomans, which tended to increase friction between them in the neighbourhood of Ta'izz, centre of the administration in the south. However, it was not in the British interest to have a Yemen consolidated under the rule of the imam next door to them. They reached a political *modus vivendi* with the Ottomans, which held up to the formal delimitation of the border separating the districts under their influence from the Ottoman administered territory to the north.

Foreign, Ottoman and Arab correspondents reported regularly on events in Yemen. The progress of the insurrection and the mishandling of Yemeni affairs aroused considerable interest in Istanbul, London and Berlin — the Germans were on particularly friendly terms with Sultan Abdülhamid and supportive of his request to purchase arms. Indeed, Krupp Industries made available on a trial basis a number of its new weapons, especially the rapid-fire rifles and cannons for combat in the rugged terrain of Yemen, as well as speedy torpedo boats to prevent smuggling in the Red Sea.

The growing interest and concern of the principal European powers — England, Germany and Italy — led to a number of surreptitious expeditions ostensibly to see how the state of affairs might be redressed, but in effect to spy on the country as it deteriorated from bad to worse. The Ottomans referred to them as spies and often they were indeed spies. Nevertheless, some of their observations, which were usually accurate, are available as additional and interesting supportive data.

The revolution that ended Abülhamid's rule in 1909 ushered in an administration of unseasoned and uncomprehending Young Turks who, instead of living up to their commitment to equality and justice as decreed by their purported ideals, succumbed to the hot-headed newly designated Minister of the Interior Talaat Beg (later Paşa)'s formula for settlement of the Yemeni problem — first smash the rebellion militarily and then decide on what sort of administrative changes will lead to a settlement. By pursuing such a policy, which disregarded the Ottoman constitution's reconstituted provisions and the decisions of the Chamber of Deputies (Mebusan) and ministerial counsels, Talaat only prolonged the agony and suffering of Ottoman troops in the field.

In the end the counsels of the Chamber prevailed, and Sultan Abdülhamid's replacement, Mehmet Reşat, inherited the task of making peace with the imam. By then, Talaat had lost his voice in the final decision and in the agreement to which it led (in 1911), which did indeed usher in, however brief the period, an almost complete Yemeni loyalty to the Ottoman state in its waning days of hegemony in Arabia.

The period in question is heavily weighted towards rebellion and military activities, but unfortunately such was the reality on the ground.

Conscious attempts have been made to take into account social, economic and legal issues arising from the rebellions to the extent that they prolonged or curtailed the course of rebellion, for there were short periods of respite during which negotiations were undertaken to reach a settlement between the Ottoman government and the Yemeni leaders of the insurrection. While I consider the role of the 'Asīri uprising under Ibn Idris, claimant to the *mahdi*ship after he immigrated to that region from the Maghreb, it is only to the extent that it affected the course of the struggle next door in the Tihāmah. The full story of that uprising is left to another study.

A pressing issue that was never fully resolved in the decades of strife was how to improve the agricultural productivity of the land so as to raise incomes and revenues for both the inhabitants and the state. A related issue had to do with collecting customs duties, which the merchants and shipping companies would often evade by avoiding Yemeni ports where customs were collected to unload their goods in ports under British control where lower, if any, fees were paid. In addition, trafficking in illegal trade, however illicit it was, greatly reduced the state's potential income. Ottoman facilities for regulating and monitoring such traffic were simply inadequate and, given the shallowness of the entrance to Hodeida's harbour, it was not the most suitable port for docking ships, especially since heavy winds tended to blow the sailing dhows and *sunbūq*s off course before they could make their way to the docking facilities.

Moreover, their defence facilities were woefully inadequate. Smugglers who had travelled on Italian boats from ports on the African side of the Red Sea would be chased into Ottoman waters as hot-headed captains bombarded Yemeni facilities, like Midi, and the Ottomans would fail either to curtail or to contain the marauding by sea of the largely Zarānīq pirates.

Efforts to end rebellion and secure a fair administration for Yemen failed time and again. This was partly because the rugged terrain favoured the Zaydi rebels and partly because, after nearly five decades of trying to suppress an ongoing revolt led by the imams of the Zaydi highlands (who enjoyed the backing of their ulema because they saw the imam as fighting to establish the Islamic Sharī'ah as the basic law for legislation and administration), the heavy toll in men, materials and money made it impossible for the Ottomans to gain the upper hand.

With both sides finally exhausted after having invested heavily in asserting their claims, a final truce was achieved in 1911 at Da''ān. It ushered in a period of calm and stability during which the Ottomans preserved their sovereign rights and the imam honoured his commitment of loyalty. This lasted until the end of the Ottoman presence, which vanished shortly after the First World War.

Map of the Middle East

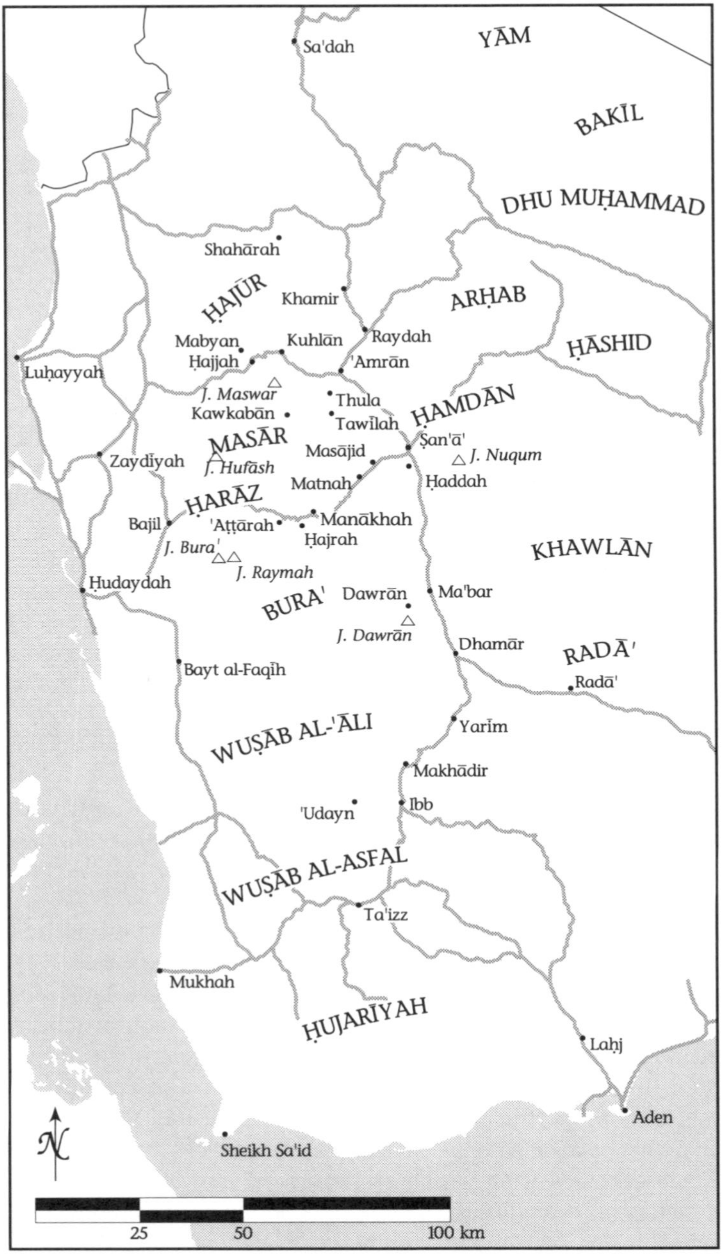
YĀM
Sa'dah
BAKĪL
DHU MUḤAMMAD
Shahārah
ḤAJŪR
Khamir
ARḤAB
Raydah
ḤĀSHID
Mabyan
Kuhlān
Ḥajjah
'Amrān
Luḥayyah
J. Maswar
Thula
Kawkabān
Tawīlah
ḤAMDĀN
MASĀR
Ṣan'ā'
J. Nuqum
Masājid
Zaydīyah
J. Hufāsh
Matnah
Ḥaddah
ḤARĀZ
Bajil
'Aṭṭārah
Manākhah
Ḥajrah
KHAWLĀN
J. Bura'
J. Raymah
Ḥudaydah
Dawrān
Ma'bar
BURA'
J. Dawrān
Dhamār
RADĀ'
Radā'
Bayt al-Faqīh
Yarīm
WUṢĀB AL-'ĀLI
Makhādir
'Udayn
Ibb
WUṢĀB AL-ASFAL
Ta'izz
Mukhah
ḤUJARĪYAH
Laḥj
Aden
N
Sheikh Sa'id
25
50
100 km

1. Anglo–Ottoman Confrontation at Mocha, 1817–22

The Ottomans had been physically absent from Yemen for a century and a half. In this chapter I focus on the events that impelled their return. At no time did they abdicate their sovereign rights over the land, for Yemenis still looked to them and their agents for protection. This was all the more compelling after the English began to intrude on the southern region and intimidate helpless *shaykh*s ruling there into yielding to their territorial demands. The intrusion set the tone also for their return physically to the land to alleviate the fears of the custodians of the sacred shrines of Islam, who had suspected the foreign powers' motives ever since the Portuguese first invaded the Red Sea in the mid-sixteenth century determined to bomb Mecca itself.[1]

English intrusion in the early nineteenth century posed a new challenge to Ottoman sovereignty, which led to the earliest confrontation. The focus here is on details and the effect of this first altercation between the English and Ottoman surrogate governor in the south, which forced them to give up their plans to implant themselves at Mocha, the port city through which coffee beans were exported. Anglo–Ottoman confrontation in Yemen began with an incident in Mocha in 1817. Mocha's significance lies in its strategic location at the lower entrance to the Red Sea. Before the capture of Aden, it was the main port for British trade linked with Bombay. It served also as the principal supply station for British vessels operating in the Red Sea and as the main outlet for trade with the Yemen.

Trade contracts with Mocha can be traced back to 1628 when the first factory was established there to trade in the coffee bean that bears its name. It first appears in the trade lists of the East India Company in

1660.[2] Records show that throughout the eighteenth century Mocha provided the most revenue of all Yemeni ports.[3] However, its fortunes were radically transformed a century later when it was described as 'a dead-alive, mouldering town whose trade as a port for coffee and hides has been killed by excessive taxation in the past and by its proximity to Aden ... the coffee that bears its name is shipped from Aden or Hodeida'.[4]

British interest first in Mocha and later in Aden was bound to arouse Ottoman concern, particularly following the bombardment of Mocha in 1820. Almost from the start, the Ottoman authorities viewed British demands in southern Arabia through the Bombay government as part of a broader design to deny them the exercise of full sovereign rights in a land considered sacred to them as Muslims. Suspicions of British motives coupled with local resentment of the Anglo–Indian trader led to what the British described as 'an outrageous attack' on the factory at Mocha in July 1817. The local *dola*, agent of the imam of Ṣan'ā', was accused of manhandling Lieutenant Dominetti of the Bombay Marine and Resident of the British East India Company at Mocha together with his companions. The Bombay government decided to take advantage of the crisis to make demands that would have granted them greater extra-territorial rights than hitherto enjoyed. When the local authorities refused, the British responded with a naval bombardment of Mocha on 4 December 1820, eliminating in the process the port's protective gun emplacement at both ends of its semi-circular harbour. The imam's government yielded and agreed to terms, including dismissal of officials that the British deemed obnoxious. John Richard Lumley, the squadron's commander, sailed back to Bombay on board the *Topaze* and the four accompanying cruisers.[5] William Bruce, Bombay's agent at Mocha, was charged with extracting a formal treaty from the imam embodying the concessions he was compelled to make. His *wakil* (deputy), Fatḥallah, and members of the Mocha council carried on the negotiations on his part. Captain Bruce himself served as official agent of the Bombay and, by extension, of the British government.

The treaty's opening clause stated that Lieutenant Robson, acting Resident, would attend to the imam's wishes 'regarding the public service'. The Resident would be permitted a guard of 30 men — equal in strength to those allowed to British agents in Baghdad, Basra and Bushire. He was allowed to ride on horseback through all gates of Mocha and was given access to outlying regions as well. The Residency was to have a plot of land on which to raise the British flag, and another to serve as a burial ground for its non-Muslim dependents. More importantly, the treaty recognized the Resident's right to travel to Ṣan'ā' to communicate directly with the imam on matters of common interest.

Provisions in the treaty relating to commerce improved the British position. Item 5 exempted British vessels from paying the anchorage charge of 400 Austrian crowns per vessel whether cargo was landed or not. Item 6 extended exemption privileges to all dependents of the British Crown, including Anglo-Indians, the merchants of Surat trading under the British flag and even Indians themselves. They were to be protected by the Resident and only the Muslims among them who opted for it were to have their disputes heard according to the provisions of the Islamic *Sharī'ah*. The enforcement of decisions, including punishment, was to be the prerogative of the Resident. Item 7 lowered the rate of customs duty levied from 3½ to 2¼ per cent, the amount then being levied on French trade.[6]

Needless to say, neither the imam nor his agent at Mocha entered into this treaty arrangement voluntarily, and the resentment generated by what they regarded as coercion was discernible in the resistance to the British efforts to enforce its provisions.

This exploitation of the incident was the climax of longstanding efforts to secure a firm foothold in this strategic port. The Bombay government was determined to obtain from the imam of Ṣan'ā' 'on whom the government of India is dependent', a public submission and apology, punishment of offenders, the removal of the 'offending *dola*', and indemnification for losses sustained by the East India Company and its personnel in the plundering of the factory at Mocha. The governor general had approved all this in Council and authorized the dispatch of the naval squadron under the command of Captain Lumley who set sail on board the *Topaze* on 19 November 1820. Captain Bruce, the Resident at Bushire in southwest Persia was empowered to conduct negotiations with representatives of the imam on behalf of the Bombay government. Bombardment of Mocha followed the imam's refusal to submit to their demands.[7]

News of the events at Mocha created 'a strong sensation at Constantinople' and the company was asked for an explanation.[8] The sultan's government informed the British ambassador, Viscount Strangford, that they regarded the assault on Mocha as an expression of British designs on Yemen as a whole. Strangford demanded an explanation of the 'circumstances, which may have excited suspicions of the Porte respecting the views of the British Government at Mocha'. In a preliminary response from the secretary of the India Board he was told that there were complaints that the Mocha government was unable to 'preserve the tranquillity of the country and that the detachment at Mocha had only a few rounds of ammunition', hence the landing of men and additional munitions of war. The secretary denied that the Board entertained 'aggrandizement in the Arabian Gulf ... and that we were about to erect facts to promote them'.[9]

Within a week, the Board had an explanation for the action taken at Mocha. London, Cairo and Istanbul sought it. The viceroy of Egypt was the first to receive news of what was seen as premeditated provocation on the part of the Resident aimed at justifying the action taken.

Objections appeared to relate first to the methods employed in provoking authorities at Mocha and second to the provisions of the treaty extracted as a result thereof. In the first set of complaints, the Resident was accused of housing 60 armed men and causing loud music to be played every morning and evening. His obtaining 200 tents, a number of large chests containing gunpowder, bullets and other munitions unloaded by vessels recently arrived from Bombay aroused suspicion that he planned to close the Bāb al-Mandab. He was accused of trying to bribe the imam of Ṣan'ā' with 100,000 *piastre*s annually in order to permit the British to extend their authority over Muslim and non-Muslim subjects. On turning down the offer, the Resident allegedly gathered a force with the intention of travelling to Aden to propose that its ruler join hands with the British against Mocha and the imam.

The India government categorically rejected the accusations and sent word to assure both Muḥammad 'Alī, viceroy of Egypt, and the sultan's government that it entertained no design on the interior of Yemen and did not intend to violate the sacred territory of Mecca as alleged. Furthermore, it had not sought jurisdiction over Mocha by purchase or attempted to raise the tribes around Aden against either the imam or the sultan. The Board then arranged for a letter to be addressed by the government of Bombay through the secret committee of the East India Company to London for transmission to Cairo and Istanbul explaining the several topics and assuring the Sublime Porte that the India government sought neither aggrandizement nor to encroach upon the sultan's authority over his dependencies in Yemen.[10]

Confusion and suspicion over the terms of the treaty allegedly stemmed from what was left out of the Arabic version of the English original. The *dola* had called the Resident's attention to the omissions in August 1821. He also complained of the lack of payment for a permit to allow the factory's Hindu broker to return to India.[11] The Resident in turn displayed open anxiety over the *dola*'s ability to contain bedouins, threatening to cut off water supplies from the well and circumscribe 'the insolent behaviour of the authorities'. This is why he asked for more armed men and ammunition. That he should ask for broad powers to adjudicate disputes was due to 'the litigious nature of the narratives'. The permanent stationing of a naval cruiser at Mocha was deemed necessary to protect British trade, particularly since the chief of the Yām tribe might attempt to spread 'his depredations' to Mocha.

In addition to the official areas of dispute there were also personal ones. It appears that the *dola* had repeatedly put pressure on the Resident to arrange loans for him, up to 5000 crowns, to liquidate the cost of goods purchased from Surat. In the end he yielded to the *dola*'s demands and turned over the sum to him without obtaining authorization from Bombay. Not wishing to act without explicit instructions from Bombay, the Resident wrote for specific answers to questions posed.

Francis Warden, secretary of the government of Bombay, replied on 6 September 1821 cautioning the Resident against compromising the factory's objectives in his transactions with the imam's government. This was all the more important because already consideration was being given to the eventual transferring of the post to Aden or some other place beyond the imam's territorial reach. He was asked to minimize complaints by not exempting brokers from the payment of duty if they were not in the immediate service of the company. All ships visiting Mocha must have their register and passes scrutinized to determine which ones were entitled to exemption from duty charges.

With regard to his role as adjudicator, he was told to exercise judgement and restraint, particularly when British subjects residing at Mocha did not initiate the complaints. Disputes involving natives were to be dealt with by the court of justice at Mocha. If a British subject was involved with a native then the Resident could enforce judgement either through his own guard or through the administration of the *dola*. The governor could not sanction fees for punishment; but if the guilty party happened to be a British subject, the Council could confine him until he was returned to the Residency. Authority was given for a cruiser to be stationed in the Red Sea both to protect trade and to dispatch messages, but not in ordinary duty. The Resident finally was enjoined against making loans to the *dola* to avoid setting a precedent, particularly when no advantage could be perceived from him.

To improve relations with the *dola*'s administration, the Resident dismissed the Indian *munshi*, Sayyid Ḥusayn, from the position he had occupied by appointment of Captain Robson and retained under Captain Bruce because of what was interpreted as obnoxious behaviour on his part towards the local authorities and his ignorance of the country and its surrounding states. He was immediately returned to India.

While the imam took note of the treaty between his government and Bruce as agent of the British government, he sent a deputy to seek clarification of certain provisions. The imam was also concerned over the assaults of the Yām tribe and their control of Zabīd after they had plundered Luḥayyah on the Red Sea coast. It was 20 days before he learned of the fall of Zabīd, although the town was only a three-day journey from Ṣan'ā'. The letter[12] borne by the deputy informed the Resident that he intended to establish his authority over the entire Tihāmah and of his impending visit to him at Mocha.

After delivering two Arabian horses to the Resident as a gift from the imam, his Hindu agent handed another letter to the broker[13] requesting a loan of 20,000 Yemeni crowns to defray the cost of an expedition he was about to lead against the Yām, who were still in control of Zabīd. The broker notified the Resident of the imam's request stating that he regarded the loan as a private matter and wished to refuse it, provided the company would offer him protection against the imam's anticipated wrath. Since the Resident had already instructed the company to adhere to matters of commerce only and transmit the intelligence of a political nature, he informed the broker that he would not get involved in the imam's concerns.[14]

Meanwhile, reactions from Istanbul were reaching London and being forwarded to India. Muḥammad 'Alī's agents in Yemen told the Ottoman authorities that foreign intruders' ambitions were about to defile the land of Islam. In a secret dispatch to the governor in council at Bombay, the secretary of state for foreign affairs conveyed messages contained in Lord Strangford's dispatches from Istanbul about the sultan's government's concern 'relative to certain proceedings of the resident at Mocha ... not less offensive to the religious feelings than injurious to the political rights and interests of the state'.[15]

Three dispatches from Rüstem Ağa, Muḥammad 'Alī's agent at Mocha, whom the Viceroy of Egypt described as merely a customs agent, fanned the Porte's indignation. The Reis Efendi summed them up as stating that the India government had adopted a hostile view towards the sultan's authority and rights of sovereignty in Yemen through its agent at Mocha, the Resident, who was also accused of encouraging tribal Arabs to revolt and offering the imam 100,000 *piastre*s a year to become a dependency of the government of India.

In relaying this information to the Marquis of Londonderry the foreign secretary, Strangford, informed him that the sultan's government attached much importance to the country that held the holiest cities of Islam. He also relayed to him the tenor of a prescript from the *Divan* (council of ministers) in which the sultan purportedly described the India government to be 'as faithless and as ambitious as that of Russia', insisting he would not yield an inch of the territory 'which has been sanctified by the footsteps of the Prophet'. He enclosed in his dispatch to India a résumé of the letters from Rüstem Ağa.

The résumé referred to a host of complaints about offensive conduct by the men the Resident housed, about arms and ammunition brought in illegally and, in addition, about chains imported from Bombay allegedly for blocking the straits of Bāb al-Mandab. The complaining customs agent suspected British motives and aims at Mocha when they refused inspection of the cargo unloaded, followed by the monetary offer to the imam, and efforts to remove residents from Bombay, Banyans and Ismā'īlīs from the jurisdiction of the Mocha courts in treating them as British rather than residents subject to Islamic law, despite repeated assertions by the imam that he would not tolerate Muslims being subject to non-Islamic law.[16]

On the basis of these reports the Reis Efendi[17] relayed to Strangford the Porte's demand that the British government openly disavow the conduct of its agent in Mocha and formally acknowledge that the country belonged to the Ottoman Empire and was subject in its totality to Ottoman jurisdiction. In the note delivered to the ambassador by the Reis Efendi, the British government was called upon not to compromise friendly ties with the sultan's government.[18]

In transmitting this intelligence to London, Lord Strangford warned that the Mocha affair could have a most serious effect on British influence and credit at Constantinople. He stated further that 'the strongest feelings of the Sultan and of his ministers have been called into action by the powerful appeals which have been lately addressed to them by the Turkish authorities, as well as religious as political, on the subject of the proceedings at Moka'.[19]

The Sharīf of Mecca, Muḥammad Ibn 'Awn, was alleged to have also written in a long dispatch to the mufti at Istanbul alluding similarly to the 'insults' that were reportedly being offered by the English to the '*Sacred Territory*' (*sic*) in the 'highest colours'. Since the mufti communicated '*directly*' (*sic*) with the sultan, the latter issued a prescript stating that 'if the English are to range themselves among the enemies of the Ottoman government [he] will yield to the decree of Providence but would not suffer the birth land of the Prophet to be defiled.'[20]

The sultan's government was of the opinion that deliberately provocative action at Mocha by the British was for the purpose of forcing a change in terms of the commercial agreements, which, at the time of its conclusion, were satisfactory to both sides. The note embodying this opinion went on to state that British traffic with the imam of Ṣan'ā', offering him tents and a pavilion for gifts, illicitly importing guns and ammunition for use in arousing tribesmen against Ottoman authority, and deliberately being rowdy, all of which 'suggest a line of conduct not presently understood, and so near to the land of the Kaaba … an insult to our religion and to all Moslems'.[21]

Lord Strangford's dispatches stated also that Muḥammad 'Alī had decided to take up the affair as a political question and that he was protesting strongly, viewing it as an affront to the sultan's sovereign rights and authority in Yemen. Strangford was unconvinced, on the other hand, that the viceroy was venting meaningless indignation to ward off suspicion from himself by seizing upon this opportunity to demonstrate his loyalty 'at so cheap a rate … knowing that his allegiance is suspect by the Sultan'.[22]

The ambassador himself was not fully informed about what had transpired at Mocha. He requested background information from Consul General Henry Salt stationed at Alexandria and details of Rüstem Ağa's three letters that had caused a major stir in both Cairo and Istanbul. In his reply of 16 August 1822, Salt stated that, following the bombardment of Mocha, a treaty was concluded with the imam of Ṣan'ā' recognizing, among other things, the Resident's right to have up to 40 *sipahi*s (mounted guards), similar to concessions made to other British consular officials and agents at Baghdad and Bushire. The sounding of drums at sunrise, dinner and sunset, which offended the Muslims of the town, was in accord with the practice of the guard everywhere. The tents were offered as gifts, but only one to the imam; the other was for his vizier. The large base, which Rüstem alleged housed cannon, actually housed wine and other provisions, including furniture for the Residency. Captain Hutchinson, then Resident, had them inspected at his own house according to Salt's report and the imam's agents were reportedly satisfied. He did not deny that three to four guns were unloaded and housed in the Residency's magazine; indeed, so was the steel cable alluded to earlier; but the latter was not for the purpose of blocking the straits at Bāb al-Mandab as alleged, a ridiculous feat considering the distance; rather it was for the cruiser *Antilope* when it returned from Cosseir.

The above information was based primarily on oral reports made to Salt by Captain Thompson of the 17th Light Dragoons and 'another gentleman lately from Moka'. But at the heart of the disagreement between the Resident and the native administration at Mocha was the issue relating to jurisdiction. The imam's representative insisted on trying all disputes involving non-British subjects, dependents of the factory and the Banyans according to Islamic law while the Resident was demanding they be judged in all matters by the Resident himself according to the capitulations respected by the Ottoman government.

Judging by Captain Hutchinson's impressions of the imam and his administration, one could scarcely anticipate a cordial resolution of differences. He accused the government of 'bad faith and rapacity'; the *dola* in his opinion 'was too engaged in the debauchery of his own harem to attend the business in government'. Yet, by his own confession, much of the difficulty was occasioned by the confusion over interpretation of the last article of the treaty.

On the other points of the accusations levelled against him, the Resident admitted that he had gone to Aden and made an offer of presents to the 'Sultan of that petty kingdom', but that was by order of his own government. He saw no fault in that, for the sultan was regarded as 'a perfectly independent prince, long united in the strictest friendship with the English'. Hutchinson argued, moreover, that when he first called upon the Sultan of Laḥj in 1810, the latter urged the British to establish a commercial factory next door at Aden. Now, in view of the difficulties in their relationships with the imam's government at Mocha, it was very probable that 'if the imam's government does not fulfil its engagements, the Factory will be removed from Moka and established in Aden'. This was the main reason for his trip to Aden, which aroused the suspicions of the Ottoman Porte.

As far as Hutchinson was concerned, both the imam of Ṣan'ā' and the 'chief of Aden' were independent princes, 'so it is not necessary to have the consent of the Porte to any arrangements that the India government may please to establish with these countries'. This was also the position of the governor general, the Marquis of Hastings and Montsuart Elphinstone, governor of Bombay, who was the one to authorize the blockade of Mocha in revenge for what was termed 'the atrocious conduct of the *dola*' in imprisoning and beating the Resident, digging up the corpse of the British surgeon and giving it to the dogs, and other acts of maltreatment.

Such conduct called for exemplary retribution, and the government of India argued this had been done with the utmost delicacy towards the Sublime Porte. Hastings allegedly informed Muḥammad 'Alī of his intentions to blockade Mocha and assured him at the same time of his specific intentions, regretting later the extremities engaged in by the expeditionary force sent to Mocha. Assuming it was a mistake, it could be explained, he submitted, in terms of the inexplicit orders to Elphinstone who was allegedly absent from Bombay when the harsh orders were issued to the commander of the expedition. Hutchinson also registered his annoyance with Muḥammad 'Alī for sending Rüstem Ağa's letters on to Istanbul in view of what he termed the good relations that had hitherto existed between the Egyptian viceroy and the British. He blamed it on 'a certain Efendi of considerable talent from Constantinople who has been in the service of the Pasha for a year and a half' without naming the person.[23]

Consul General Salt took up the matter with Muḥammad 'Alī in person and was assured by him that the originator of the reports from Mocha (Rüstem Ağa) was not his agent in Yemen, but rather the customs house master at Jiddah who ostensibly transmitted the remarks of 'unspecified' agents at Mocha. The viceroy seized upon this opportunity to inform Salt that the sultan's government for some time had been urging him to take control of the ports along the Red Sea as far south as Aden and that he might have to do so yet. In reply, Salt voiced the opinion that the India government might be happier to see the Ottoman government take direct control of these ports rather than see them 'fall into the hands of local Barbarians'. However, in this dispatch to Strangford, Salt stated 'I don't believe that the India govt. [sic] would want them [Ottomans] to take over Aden though; it is too strong a post, and too near Bombay to leave it in the hands of any first-rate power [Egypt], that might hereafter join with, or become our Enemy.'[24]

The explanations the India government ultimately forwarded to Istanbul via London and Alexandria did not appear to alleviate the Porte's concern over the Bombay government's motives and ambition in that strategic corner of the Arab Peninsula. The Reis Efendi communicated the minister's reaction to Strangford and hinted rather strongly that the ambassador himself might have been misled by the information he had received from agents at Mocha and the Bombay government, which he singled out as the proper defendant in this instance. The note he delivered on behalf of the sultan's government stated, among other things, that:

> We could not for a moment entertain the supposition that you have sanctioned any measures which could justly subject the British government in India to the suspicion of entertaining any project of territorial aggrandizement in the Arabian Gulf, but we are anxious nevertheless for details from you concerning every proceeding that has taken place at Moka since the establishment of the Residency at that Port.[25]

The secretary of state for foreign affairs relayed the communications received from Strangford about the happenings at Mocha and embodying the views of the sultan's government to all appropriate quarters at Bombay and Mocha. The Porte's interpretation of the affairs as 'not less offensive to the religious feelings than injurious to the political rights and interests of the state' particularly perturbed him. He requested the Bombay government to submit information that would remove 'the bad implications', together with a cogent and full explanation of the hostilities prevailing at Mocha between the British agent and the imam's representatives there. He also wanted a detailed account of the arrangements concluded with them. He asked for the explanations the Bombay government had submitted to be forwarded directly to him.[26]

In India the board acknowledged all communications forwarded by London and promised to conduct a full inquiry into the circumstances occasioning the Sublime Porte's concern about happenings at Mocha.

The explanations submitted subsequently were unconvincing. Most of the blame for misunderstanding was placed on omissions in the translation of the original treaty from English to Arabic rather than on the British Resident's improprieties. The India government admitted having insisted on the provision stipulated in Article 6, only to learn later that Captain Bruce had ostensibly gained the concession they wished independently. The imam of Ṣan'ā' himself allegedly made that concession. It seems strange, indeed, that the concession should appear in English but not in Arabic, the imam's only language. This was attributed to an oversight, not to any deliberate attempt to prevent the imam's government from realizing what it had agreed to.

Other explanations proffered indicated that the provision relating to the payment of duty would apply only to British merchants and not to others trading under the British flag. The Arabic version of the treaty was blamed for making it appear that all those under the Resident's jurisdiction would be governed by his terms. In fact, the Bombay government had insisted that only dependents of the factory, English and Hindu, were to enjoy the same consideration and immunity.[27]

With regard to the rest of the complaints, the Bombay government was at a loss to provide adequate answers. In fact it failed to address the key enquiry, namely how to explain those happenings 'which may have excited the suspicions of the Porte respecting the views of the British government at Mocha?'[28]

Weak as it might have seemed, the foreign office forwarded Bombay's explanation to Constantinople with the necessary copies to Alexandria for the enlightenment of the Egyptian viceroy who demonstrated open concern for what had transpired and equal interest in learning the results of the inquiry. Needless to say, Bombay's arguments failed to alleviate the Porte's suspicions and scepticism, but it was prepared to accept assurances from the British government that they did not entertain any territorial aggrandizement in southern Arabia. The matter thus was allowed to settle.

Sultan Maḥmūd was about to embark on full-scale plans for modernization, particularly of his armed forces, and in this he needed the goodwill of Europe. The episode was attributed to misunderstanding; the whole 'unpleasant business' was blamed on Rüstem Ağa having conveyed wrong information to Muḥammad 'Alī and then an unnamed zealot, who excited unduly the concern of the Ottoman sultan and his government, passing it on to Constantinople.[29]

Thus ended the first phase of Anglo–Ottoman confrontation in Yemen and while the agents of the sultan were able to contain the English and prevent their expansion for the time being this was only the beginning of what was to become an ongoing struggle.

2. Gaining a Foothold at Aden, 1825–40

The focus here is on the strategy the British pursued to acquire a permanent foothold in southwest Arabia following their failure to make Mocha in the Tihāmah their base. I show how the Ottoman viceroy of Egypt, Muḥammad 'Alī, became the unwitting instrument of British policy while ostensibly on a mission on behalf of his sovereign, the sultan, to suppress revolts and tribal defiance of legitimate authority that invited foreign intervention.

The lack of firm Ottoman control over the political scene in Yemen and the indigenous tribes' endless rivalries clearly helped British attempts since 1770 to establish a firm base in this strategic corner of Arabia. Exploiting this turmoil, the British, through the India government, first wrested a treaty agreement from the imam of Ṣan'ā', permitting them a foothold in Mocha; and, when unable to secure their position there, they extracted a similar agreement from the Sultan of Laḥj, enabling them to consolidate a position on the isthmus of Aden. Both agreements were of dubious legality, at least as viewed from the Ottoman position. At first the British sought to justify their presence by casting aspersions on Ottoman legal claims to sovereignty; but researchers in the Foreign Office archives could only come up with data supporting Ottoman *de jure* possession of Yemen.[1]

The sovereign rights of the Ottomans were acquired by conquest in 1539 during the sultanate of Süleiman the Magnificent and reinforced by Sinan Paşa (grand admiral of the Ottoman navy) in 1569.[2] Upon withdrawing from south Arabia, Sinan entrusted the administration of the lowlands (Tihāmah) from the port of Mocha to the port of Hodeida to the Imam of Ṣan'ā', who in turn appointed the Sharīf of Abu 'Arīsh as overseer. Sinan himself chose this ancient centre of Islamic learning as the administrative headquarters of the Tihāmah.

By their own accounts, the Ottomans did not attempt to establish direct rule in Yemen because of the great distances separating it from Istanbul, the capital. The *vali* of Hijaz acted as the liaison person with the Sublime Porte. Through such benevolent neglect, the *sharīf*s of Abu ‘Arīsh succeeded in time to exercise nearly independent rule over the lowlands, in full defiance of the imam’s administrative prerogatives. The imam and also often the chieftains of neighbouring ‘Asīr refused to accept the *sharīf*s’ authority and disputes, rivalries and bloody feuds ensued. Turmoil and confusion dominated the history of this region.[3] When matters got critical, the imam could only refer them to Istanbul for resolution.

The Ottomans had tolerated the establishment of trading stations in Mocha in the latter part of the eighteenth century, provided the maritime powers of Europe confined their activities to the port region. When the British found it necessary to strike up close relations with neighbouring chieftains and the imam of Ṣan‘ā’, they only served to awaken suspicion in Ottoman circles, particularly when the British argued the need to intervene on the grounds of being harassed by unfriendly local officials and chieftains. To eliminate such pretexts, the Sublime Porte authorized Muḥammad ‘Alī to pacify the region. The viceroy was already engaged on a mission to suppress Wahhābi defiance of Ottoman rule in Nejd. The Wahhābis had a strong following among the chiefs of ‘Asīr, an immediate neighbour of Yemen, and the ‘Asīris in turn were allied to Sharīf Ḥammūd of Abu ‘Arīsh. All were Wahhābis or sympathizers. Thus, Muḥammad ‘Alī had cause to move his military operations south. He also had the sultan’s orders.[4]

Sharīf Ḥammūd of Abu ‘Arīsh had allied himself with the Wahhābis in return for their acknowledging his rule over the Tihāmah. With reinforcements from Egypt under the command of Mîr-i mirân Halil Paşa, Mîr-i mirân Arnavut Paşa, officer in command in Jiddah, moved to avenge the defeat of his underling, Cum'a Ağa (*mutasallim* in ‘Qunagh’) by Ḥammūd and his allies. Meanwhile, Ḥammūd died and was succeeded by his young son Aḥmad, who teamed up with Ḥasan ibn Khālid of the Saud clan and set out to recapture Dir‘īyah, the Saud family’s home base, from the viceroy’s troops. Halil Paşa, who had set out from Mecca in Ṣafar 1234 (December 1818) met them, and at Mahāyil they defeated Aḥmad and scattered his troops. In pursuing them the Egyptian forces marched on to Abu ‘Arīsh. Aḥmad surrendered and was exiled. Then the Egyptian expedition set out to rebuild the fortresses of the Tihāmah (at Abu ‘Arīsh, Jāzān, Hodeida, Luḥayyah,

Zabīd, and Bayt al-Faqīh). All the areas the *sharīfs* had previously administered were restored to the imam's jurisdiction. The imam in return promised to deliver coffee to the imperial kitchens, as in the past.

The imperial government had serious reservations about the imams of Ṣan'ā'. Their rapacity and cruel handling of the tribes had alienated them from the lowlanders and accounted for much of the turmoil and lawlessness characterizing tribal relations in the two preceding centuries. The tribes specifically singled out for criticism were, in many respects, the most powerful: Dhu Muḥammad, Dhū Ḥusayn, Ḥāshid, Bakīl, and Yām.[5] All fought for dominion over the northern regions of Yemen. Ottoman observers felt they had to be dealt with strictly. Inhabitants of the coastal cities were equally interested in their being chastised. The merchants had suffered from their marauding and the populace from their raids. All assisted in financing the rebuilding of fortifications to keep them out. Often these were the very tribes who took orders from the imam of Ṣan'ā'.[6]

British merchants operating predominantly out of Indian ports had urged their government to take steps to secure their operations at Mocha. Attempts to do so through treaty relations with the imam bore little fruit, for it was the Sharīf of Abu 'Arīsh whom they had to circumvent and he did not take kindly to such measures. The British expected reprieve in Muḥammad 'Alī's expedition; while they had opposed an earlier expedition, they were not disposed to do the same in 1825, particularly when the Sublime Porte had ordered it.[7]

Remaining doubtful about their operation at Mocha, however, especially following a sharp dispute with the imam of Ṣan'ā' in 1828, the British began to cast about for an alternative site. Aden proved particularly attractive for the next location of a factory. Commanding an exploratory naval expedition on behalf of the India government, Captain Hutchinson was authorized to 'enter into a Convention with the Sovereign of Aden, arranging the terms on which the British Residency should be received at that place in the event it became necessary to remove it from the dominions of the Imaum of Sennaa [*sic*]'.[8]

The British were particularly anxious to secure Aden for their factory following the spread of rumours that Muḥammad 'Alī planned to occupy the isthmus, the strategic importance of which was discovered in 1829 when coal was transported to Aden from Mocha to provision the first steamer (the *Hugh Lindsay*) on its way to Suez from India.[9]

Muḥammad 'Alī did not seriously entertain the idea of establishing a military presence in Yemen until 1833 following a rebellion in Hijaz. Planned or not, the rebellion provided him with the pretext to march his troops into Yemen. It began in June 1832 when a high-ranking Circassian slave by the name of Muḥammad Ağa, alias Türkçe Bilmez ('Knows no Turkish'), hitherto considered a loyal follower of the viceroy, revolted with his Albanian followers in Mecca because they had not received pay for several months. All 2000 of them (horse and foot) marched to Jiddah where they seized the treasury and confiscated equipment and supplies. In December 1832 they set sail in warships they had commandeered for the Tihāmah. The rebels quickly occupied the coastal cities of Mocha and Hodeida, and the land in between as well. Discontented Arab tribes of the bordering region joined them.[10] Bilmez concluded an agreement with 'Ali ibn Mukhtār, an 'Asīri chief, offering, in return for support, to share with him the revenue of the region, which had not been collected owing to the absence of an official administrator. The Circassian, however, had incurred greater expenses than anticipated, so he defaulted on his agreement with 'Ali. When queried by British observers, Bilmez alleged that he rebelled because he felt he would soon depose Sultan Muḥammad 'Alī, and now he had an opportunity to prove his loyalty and usefulness to the Ottoman government. He anticipated as reward the governorship of the Hijaz.

The possibility of a prior understanding between the viceroy, his subordinate Bilmez, and the British concerning operations in Yemen is seen in reports from Consul General Campbell. According to these, Muḥammad 'Alī suggested to Campbell early in 1833 that he might send an expedition to Yemen to chastise Bilmez and rescue Ṣan'ā' from anarchy. If Bilmez's rebellion were staged, then a perfect pretext for immediate involvement would be ready-made. The facility with which Bilmez moved from Mecca to Jiddah to Yemen can only lend credence to this notion. Campbell's willingness to cooperate with the viceroy was further increased by news from Yemen that in the midst of the turmoil British commerce was suffering. It was reported that United States ships were taking away nearly all the coffee of Mocha to the detriment of British commerce.

Turning control over to Muḥammad 'Alī was not without its risks; while the viceroy controlling both sides of the Red Sea would facilitate British commerce (as Moresby reported to Campbell and the latter reported to Palmerston), the British might be acquiescing to a formidable territorial concentration in the hands of a powerful *vali* who might not always be friendly to British interests. It was presumed that once he was fully in control, Muḥammad 'Alī would annex the Yemen administration to the Hijaz, where his nephew Küçük Ibrāhīm governed. The sultan's government had invested Ibrāhīm with that office as a reward for suppressing the Wahhābis. Despite misgivings, Palmerston yielded to Campbell's argument that the viceroy's control of both sides of the Red Sea would only aid the shipping of the India government and he gave his blessing to the viceroy's expedition.[11] To quiet the Sublime Porte's anxieties, Campbell recommended that Palmerston's government reassure the Ottomans that the British considered Yemen an integral part of Ottoman territory and, administratively, an appendage of the *vilayet* of Hijaz.[12]

Meanwhile, reports from Captain Moresby, who commanded the India government's survey ship *Benares*, indicated that Bilmez's forces were concentrated in Mocha, where they meant to await the viceroy's troops. Moresby's letter from Jiddah of 26 June 1833 painted a bleak picture: the imam had died and with him the last semblance of order; Bilmez was detaining Surat ships at Mocha; and commerce was deplorable and its revival could be assured only if Muḥammad 'Alī took possession of Yemen. Even then it would not be an easy task — the viceroy would have to contend not only with the rebels but also with an interior of Yemen torn by the civil wars precipitated by the feuding brothers of the deceased imam, none of whom enjoyed much force, power or strong backing. Meanwhile, 'Ali ibn Mukhtār, the disgruntled 'Asīri chief, had gathered up his fighting men and laid siege to Bilmez at Mocha after seizing the entire area surrounding the port town.

Muḥammad 'Alī's navy recaptured or destroyed the vessels Bilmez had commandeered. Losses and defections had reduced the rebel force to between 1200 and 1500 men, of whom most were stationed either at Mocha or at Aden. The viceroy was most eager to dislodge the rebels from the fortress at Aden lest they convert the town into a piratical stronghold preying on Egyptian shipping in the Red Sea. To reinforce the siege of Mocha, Muḥammad 'Alī ordered a regiment of infantry (3200 men), a cavalry unit (400), and an artillery unit of 200 men with six field pieces and two mortars to be dispatched from Alexandria. Campbell urged the commanding officer of the expedition to take all necessary steps to ensure the safety of British subjects at Mocha.[13] The viceroy's nephew Aḥmad, who also served as minister of war, left for Yemen with an additional 2400 regular and 1200 irregular cavalry (chiefly

Anatolian), with 400 artillerymen. A caravan of 450 camels transported their baggage overland, while the men left by sea, 'all in good order'.[14]

Alerted by the alliance between the 'Asīri Wahhābis and Bilmez, the viceroy selected one of the 12 'Asīri chiefs detained in Egypt following the suppression of the Wahhābi uprising, bestowed upon him a pelisse of honour and dispatched him along with Aḥmad to Yemen. Muḥammad 'Alī counted on the 'Asīri Shaykh Muḥammad al-Dāsin to draw support away from Bilmez. He allocated over 1000 purses of nine-*piastre* gold pieces (a total equalling MT$ 60,000) to purchase the 'Asīris' support, promising him not to punish those who had allied themselves with Bilmez should they abandon him.

The Tihāmah's inhabitants were jubilant at the sight of the Egyptian expedition. For nearly two years the 'Asīris had visited upon them a variety of suffering and privation. Merchants had been plundered and the possessions of all carried away by land and sea. No one was able to ward off the 'Asīris' rapacious marauding. Rich and poor alike scrambled to get out. Neither Bilmez nor his deputy 'Abd al-Raḥmān, who served as *muḥāfiz* (guardian) of Bāb al-Sāḥil (at Bāb al-Mandab), spared foreign merchants. While the 'Asīris' marauding had commenced when Bilmez was in charge, it intensified after he fled — following negotiations with the 'Asīri chieftain Lāḥiq ibn Aḥmad Zaydāni whereby, in exchange for 2000 *riyāl*s (or perhaps only 200), he agreed to hand over Mocha. Bilmez arranged with one of his trusted deputies to open the gates of the town after he himself was safely on board a British vessel heading for Bombay — a scheme he had hatched with Anglo-Indians.[15]

While Bilmez's fate after reaching Bombay is shrouded in mystery,[16] that of the Egyptian expedition is not. It fared less well than anticipated during the whole of 1834. The Bombay government showed its concern by dispatching Captain Haines to Socotra in October of that year to investigate the purchase of that island to serve as a possible alternate coaling station. He was also asked to scout and map the Hadramawt coast.

Exasperated by the turmoil and by his inability to contain it, the imam of Ṣan'ā' reportedly offered to deliver up his country to the Egyptians, but his subjects refused to support that decision.[17] Elsewhere the war went on without a clear indication of the outcome. The key port cities of Luḥayyah and Hodeida were heavily garrisoned and Egyptian forces decided to await the reinforcements dispatched by Muḥammad

'Alī. It was not the Yemenis who posed a military problem for the Egyptians, as both high- and lowlanders were willing to accept reasonable terms; rather it was the 'Asīris and their allies among the Yemenis who put up the fierce resistance. The expedition suffered severe attrition, losing camels and horses because of insufficient provisioning. Local supplies proved both expensive and difficult to acquire. Morale fell drastically, particularly when the fierce 'Asīris outwitted the Egyptians several times in key battles. The troops captured the capital of 'Asīr, but the surrounding country remained in the hands of defiant Shaykh 'Ā'id ibn Mur'i, the recognized chief of the land. Three lowland provinces were captured, but not the key cities of Abu 'Arīsh, Saba', Bishr, or Banihahr. Reports reaching the viceroy clearly indicated that more men, material and money would be needed.[18]

The viceroy was too deeply committed to abandon the expedition and leave Yemen to the 'Asīris and their Wahhābi supporters. With 'Abd al-Raḥmān, *muḥāfız* of Bāb al-Sāḥil, killed by the 'Asīris, the last official connection with Cairo was broken. The viceroy nevertheless resolved to continue the fight. Mîr-i mirân Amin Beg headed land reinforcements and Kapudan Hafız the new sea units that were dispatched to relieve the exhausted troops. Küçük Ibrahim Hafız was put in charge of the entire expedition, which had now expanded by 2400 more men arriving via Suez and Jiddah and further financed by an extra 40,000 Austrian dollars. The money sent along earlier to buy the 'Asīris' loyalty appeared to have little impact; indeed, al-Dāsin was suspected of secretly working with the rebels.[19]

The operations in the Tihāmah brought some results. Maḥmūd Beg and a detachment of troops assisted by a bedouin force led by Ḥusayn ibn Ḥaydar captured the fort commanding the water supply to Hodeida on 15 January 1835. Four days later the governor, Maḥmūd ibn Mufassa, surrendered to the Egyptians at the local merchants' urging in order to prevent the city from being subjected to the looting that would have taken place had it been captured later. Mocha itself was placed under the command of Ḥusayn, as a reward for his cooperation with the Egyptians; but with the approach of Maḥmūd Beg, being uncertain of his status vis-à-vis the Egyptian commander, he fled the city on 24 January. Left unattended, Mocha was temporarily held by the captain of an Egyptian vessel and a handful of men who quickly secured the customs house gate and battery and hoisted the Egyptian flag.[20]

However, while Egyptian troops were successful in the Tihāmah, they fared less well in the highlands. Indeed, they suffered a number of serious reverses. The 'Asīris, led by those termed in Cairo Rijāl al-Ma' (men of the tribe of that name), who had once been held hostage by the viceroy and were known for their unflinching fierceness in battle, lured Küçük Ibrahim into their mountain fastness by pretending to flee his advance and inflicted heavy losses on the Egyptians. Once again Muḥammad 'Alī sent reinforcements, a further 2400 (a regiment) commanded by a former minister of war, Hurşid Paşa. He was convinced that his nephew had shown little skill or acumen in handling the 'Asīris. The campaign proved costly both in men and materials. The Rijāl al-Ma' and their fighters had inflicted heavy losses on the Egyptians. Both Küçük Ibrahim and the Sharīf of Mecca, who had accompanied him on the expedition, were among those who fled for their lives. Many Egyptian fugitives wandered about aimlessly in the desert and perished. A strong column of 'Asīris marched on to al-Ḥaṣā, a small port where the Egyptians had built a fort and were accustomed to receiving provisions, and captured it with its depot. Unaware of its capture, Egyptian vessels sailed unsuspectingly into the port and were taken; their crews and passengers were massacred.[21]

The campaign was fast becoming a major drain on the viceroy's treasury.[22] Another 100,000 MT dollars were sent in the escort of 50 cavalry to Suez. To raise the sum he had sold cotton at Alexandria on the understanding that he would be paid in either Spanish gold doubloons or Austrian dollars, the currency in use in Yemen.[23] However, in the year 1837 fresh troops under more competent command finally turned the tide of the war. Not only were the port cities of Mocha, Luḥayyah and Hodeida all recaptured, but interior centres such as Ta'izz and Ḥujarīyah as well. Stability returned momentarily to both Tihāmah and the highlands, for which the relieved inhabitants were grateful to Muḥammad 'Alī.[24]

However, no sooner did the sultan's government breathe a sigh of relief over the pacification of Yemen at last than it learned that the British were about to capitalize on the situation to implant themselves at Aden in keeping with plans that had been in the offing for some time. This news did not sit well with Muḥammad 'Alī, who had hoped to offset his huge campaign expenditures by tapping the customs resources of Yemeni port cities, including Aden. Moreover, he viewed Aden's location as important for the defence of south Arabia and the security of his hold on that area. The Hijaz was already a financial burden on him and on the sultan's government as well, for its revenues never provided for even its basic administrative expenses.

The India government had long since resolved to make Aden its outpost in place of Mocha, which already had proved both unstable and untenable. Besides Aden, which the sultan of neighbouring Laḥj who had managed to maintain a posture of independence vis-à-vis the imam of Ṣan'ā' ruled at this time, appeared far more suitable as a commercial and supply point.

Captain Haines of the India Marines already had detailed the advantages of Aden over other cities in his exploratory reports. James McKenzie of the Bengal Lancers had reported to the Foreign Office in London that Muḥammad 'Alī was planning to occupy Aden once he had suppressed the 'Asīris, and he urged the British to authorize the occupation of the isthmus before the viceroy could. He regarded Aden as a necessary port for establishing a British commercial presence in that corner of Arabia. As the India government opposed a lasting Egyptian presence in the Tihāmah, it was prepared to take steps to deprive Muḥammad 'Alī of control of Aden. Besides, it did not want the viceroy to be that close to Bombay. The strategic location of Aden halfway between Suez and Bombay did not go unnoticed by the India government, nor did the fact that it could provide British shipping with an excellent port facility. With the advent of steam transportation, it was an ideal coaling station as well.[25]

To justify its acquisition of Aden, London began to work through the India government to discredit the imam of Ṣan'ā' and, by extension, the Ottoman government's legitimate claims to Aden. They had recourse to books on geography and Palmerston instructed Campbell to tell Muḥammad 'Alī that rumours reaching London alluded to his designs on Aden — not to mention those 'upon Muscat and Baghdad'.[26] Concern was intensified by Muḥammad 'Alī's successful campaigns in Nejd and Yemen where, despite heavy costs in men, money and materials, he had succeeded in suppressing the Wahhābis and 'Asīris.[27]

In preparing the ground for the takeover of Aden before the Egyptians could occupy it, Rear Admiral Sir C. Malcolm Kirk, superintendent of the Indian navy, told the government of Bombay that 'both the Arabian and Abyssinian coasts of the Gulf of Aden were becoming very unsafe [because of] the depredations committed on trading vessels.' Furthermore, he reported that the 'Sultan of Aden had shown himself to be little better than a common marauder, permitting the plunder of ships driven on the coast, and, in some cases, sharing in the profits of these outrages'.[28] An incident involving the *Doria Dowlut*, a Madras vessel belonging to an Indian family that was wrecked off Aden in a storm in January 1837, provided a more specific pretext. It was alleged that the sultan had failed to prevent it being looted. The Bombay government asked the India government's approval to use this incident to demand satisfaction from the Sultan of Aden. It was followed with a proposal to the Court of Directors in London that permission be granted to take possession of the port of Aden in compensation for 'the insults offered by its ruler to the British flag'.[29]

Captain Haines was directed to proceed to Aden to accomplish this objective.[30] After obtaining satisfaction in the form of compensation for the loss sustained by the wrecked *Doria Dowlut*, he proceeded to 'negotiate' the transfer of Aden from the sultan's to the India government's control. He demanded both the port of Aden and the adjacent promontory, offering in exchange a meagre annual payment of 8700 Austrian dollars. Subsequent developments affirm the suspicion of scholars that the negotiations were conducted under the guns of his naval force and that the sultan, hardly able to understand the instrument presented to him for signing, was clearly intimidated; for no sooner had he signed the document of transfer than his own infuriated sons plotted to seize Haines before he could carry it back to Bombay. According to reports reaching Admiral Kirk, Haines apparently wanted to keep the negotiations secret, just between himself and the sultan, but 'he like a silly man trusted the whole to six merchants who soon dispensed it throughout the town.'[31]

Word reached Küçük Ibrahim that the British were surreptitiously manoeuvring to acquire Aden by any means. He made enquiries, only to get word back from Haines that he himself now controlled Aden by virtue of an instrument of transfer from the sultan. Haines also warned Ibrahim not to interfere.[32] Muḥammad 'Alī demanded clarification from Campbell and was told that the Bombay government considered Aden an independent power and could treat with its sultan if it wished. Exasperated by the whole Yemen affair, the viceroy was ready to withdraw and so he informed Campbell, but he made it clear that he would not allow Aden to lapse into foreign hands unless it could be shown that the imam of Ṣan'ā' did not exercise rightful jurisdiction over it. Thus, contrary to what the agents of the Bombay government reported, Muḥammad 'Alī did not acquiesce in the transfer of Aden.[33] He would allow the British to have a coaling station there, but no ruling rights; and this only after he had subjugated the rest of the country surrounding Aden.

After having encouraged Muḥammad 'Alī to undertake the expedition to Yemen, Campbell, on instruction from his government, was now urging him to withdraw.[34] The viceroy had fulfilled the role the British envisioned, namely to pacify the country to facilitate the establishment of a secure station. The arguments used to persuade him to withdraw centred on the inadvisability of further antagonizing the tribes on the grounds that this could only lead to the ultimate defeat of Egyptian arms. Moreover, it was urged that the undertaking had already been too costly and could only bring poverty to Egypt in the long run. Campbell even had the audacity to urge the viceroy to induce the people of Yemen's interior to bring their goods to the ports of Yemen freely and to sell to and purchase merchandise from European merchants and to press him strongly that he should on no account conscript them or levy taxes on them. To Campbell, stability around the Red Sea, courtesy of Egyptian arms, was important because it would increase British India's commercial traffic with south Arabia.[35]

Ibrahim had already anticipated British strategy towards Aden and had warned his uncle (the viceroy) that, through the India government, Britain planned to control Aden for commercial as well as strategic reasons. This control, he argued, would divert trade away from Mocha, hitherto the principal port for the interior. It also meant a loss of important customs revenue, which Muḥammad 'Alī had counted on to offset the perennial negative balance of revenue of the Hijaz. The viceroy was equally upset that the British addressed the *faqīh* (jurist) of Aden by the title 'sultan', when in reality the authority signified by the title was vested legally by the Ottomans in the imam of Ṣan'ā'.[36]

Proceeding according to plan, the British government endorsed the Court of Directors' proposed appointment of the East India Company as packet agents to the ports of Suez, Jiddah, Cosseir and Mocha in anticipation of expanded trade. Campbell instructed these agents to provide provisional consular assistance to any British subject or vessel visiting these ports.[37] Captain Haines returned to Aden, this time to serve as the first political agent there. He was issued clear instructions to assert his presence by force if the 'Sultan' should not ratify the agreement. He was also ordered to avoid discussing commerce at this time with the neighbouring Arab tribes so as not to excite the jealous feelings of the viceroy of Egypt or, possibly, lead to embarrassing connections with or obligations to them.[38] Angered by these developments, Muḥammad ʻAlī put it bluntly to Campbell that in a *ferman*, by now in his possession for ten years, the sultan's government had authorized him to take possession of Aden and the rest of Yemen. The French consul general in Egypt, who alleged that the British intended to take Aden for the purposes of capturing Yemen's coffee trade and opening up Arabia for British manufacture, increased Muḥammad ʻAlī's anxieties. With the capture of Aden, the French argued, the British would eventually take Egypt as well.[39] The British, on the other hand, were no less suspicious of Egyptian motives in Yemen. They believed that upon conquering the country Muḥammad ʻAlī intended to monopolize that same coffee trade and use Yemen as an outlet for Egyptian manufacture.

The Foreign Office's political department was unconvinced that Ibrahim would succeed in subjugating the 'Sheikh Sherzebee [Sharʻab] territory, a rich coffee country called Houshereea [Ḥujarīyah], an area conveniently situated for trade with the port [Aden]'.[40] They were convinced that the *shaykh* wanted to enter into a treaty for trade and commerce with the British. Furthermore, the major tribes of the area, Dhu Muḥammad and Dhū Ḥusayn, were numerically strong and controlled the critical passes to Aden. British agents had been cultivating both. These factors had contributed to British intentions to shift their centre from Mocha to Aden. Moreover, Aden was closer to Ṣanʻā' by two days' journey.

Even if the British captured Ṣanʻā', London still maintained that the British could have better relations with the inhabitants of the interior, because 'the British name stands very high for good faith and justice'.[41] The British, however, were not relying on their good name alone to halt Egyptian advances in Yemen. Strategy called for continued friendly negotiations in an effort both to stop the Egyptians and to open up the area to friendly and free intercourse. The particular aim was to prevent Muḥammad ʻAlī from capturing Taʻizz, which would give him control over the whole country, whereby 'the entire commerce will be monopolized by Egypt and our India trade will be ruined'.[42]

Haines had reported to his superiors that he was able to enter into treaties of friendship and peace with 'nearly all the neighbouring states, and the roads from Aden into the interior are now open for supplies and commerce'.[43] It was all the more imperative now to apply pressure on Muḥammad ʻAlī to withdraw from Yemen. As Palmerston put it earlier in a dispatch to Campbell, 'Her Majesty's government were not aware that the occupation of that country by his [Muḥammad 'Alī's] troops, promoted any interest of Great Britain.'[44] From Aden, Haines sent a letter to Ibrahim informing him officially that as of 19 January 1839 Aden would be treated as a British dependency and requesting that he stay away.[45] The India government had been anxiously awaiting this development to ensure what it termed 'a fair competition with Mocha in commercial intercourse with the interior of Yemen'; otherwise, 'the cession of Aden would be of little value to the British in a commercial point of view.'[46]

With Muḥammad 'Alī claiming that his expedition to Yemen was with the Ottoman sultan's blessing, London instructed Ambassador Ponsonby at Istanbul to enquire from the Sublime Porte whether 'the conquest which Mehemet 'Ali had made in Arabia and on the shores of the Persian Gulf had been made in accordance with the wishes of the Sultan, and in pursuance of any authority or instructions given by the Sultan to Mehemet 'Ali'.[47]

Suspecting the viceroy's aims in the Gulf, Palmerston informed Campbell that he should tell Muḥammad 'Alī that, in view of rumours about his designs on Baghdad, 'the British Government could not permit him to establish his naval and military power on the shores of the Persian Gulf, and that, if he should persevere in such project, he must expect that a British force would dispossess him from any naval stations, at which he might attempt to place himself, on the Persian Gulf.'[48] Without waiting for confirmation from Istanbul, in September 1839 Palmerston instructed Campbell to inform Muḥammad 'Alī that the British government was officially requesting he withdraw his troops from Yemen. In a protocol concluded between Great Britain, Austria, Russia and Prussia (to form the Quadruple Alliance), the Ottoman government was supported in the request that Muḥammad 'Alī withdraw from Syria. Quite clearly the viceroy of Egypt, having fulfilled his unwitting role on behalf of Great Britain, now had to be confined to Egypt.

To underline his determination to keep Muḥammad 'Alī away from the area surrounding Aden in the first instance and to induce him to leave Yemen in the second, Palmerston notified the India Board not to be restrained in dealing with the tribal chiefs in the interior of Yemen, if they saw fit. In his stated view, quite emphatically put, the viceroy had 'no right whatever over the countries governed by those rulers'.[49] This rather blunt declaration reflected a hardening position in London. The British government had cause for alarm. In the course of 1838 the viceroy's armies finally succeeded in subduing rebellion against Ottoman authority everywhere, from the Ḥawrān in southern Syria to 'Asīr and the Tihāmah in south Arabia. His forces had reached the Gulf early in 1839, and Hurşid and Aḥmad were now in control of al-Ḥaṣā and Qaṭīf. Küçük Ibrahim had pacified and was in control of 'Asīr and Yemen. The Wahhābis of Nejd were neutralized for the moment. Muḥammad 'Alī, moreover, enjoyed strong sympathy in Baghdad, and it was feared that he might next move into that territory and reduce the port city of Basra at the head of the Gulf as well.[50] To top these triumphs, on 24 June 1839 the viceroy's brilliant commander and son Ibrahim Paşa succeeded in totally destroying the Ottoman forces sent against him in a battle near the little town of Nizip, near the northern border of Syria today.

From the point of view of Britain, which genuinely suspected France's motives in urging the viceroy on, all these moves, particularly those towards south Arabia and the Gulf, were deemed at best untimely and unwise, since they appeared to impact negatively on Britain's own interests and influence in that part of the world. They came at a time when the Russians were drawing closer to the Persian court and the shah's representative was in Cairo to work out closer relations between Persia and Egypt. The British were attempting to prevent the shah from capturing Herat, a strategic gateway to the Indian subcontinent, while they themselves were occupying the island of Karak in the Gulf.

Admiral Maitland was at this time ordered to prevent the Egyptian forces' occupation of Bahrain and, through Campbell, the India government sought to have instructions sent by Muḥammad 'Alī that Hurşid should stay away from Bahrain.[51]

In view of Palmerston's increasingly confrontational policies vis-à-vis Muḥammad 'Alī, Campbell's dream of an Anglo–Egyptian alliance to stabilize this significant part of the Ottoman Empire and to keep Britain's rivals away was now rapidly being shattered. Palmerston feared and mistrusted Muḥammad 'Alī and preferred to have the weak, ineffectual sultan as a substitute ally. Ostensibly to reassert Ottoman authority in Syria and Arabia, Palmerston was determined to confine the viceroy's armies to Egypt proper. He would allow him to make administrative improvements in the name of the sultan's government, but no more. The remarkable aspect of Palmerston's audacity was that it worked, to the chagrin of the Sublime Porte, many of whose ministers saw hope only in Muḥammad 'Alī being in control of areas where they themselves could not exercise effective authority.

France was in sympathy with the viceroy's plight, but the French king was not prepared to go to war against the Quadruple Alliance on 'Alī's behalf. Palmerston did not trust the French anyway and much preferred Britain to take the lead in imposing restraints on the viceroy of Egypt. Although Campbell had communicated Palmerston's official request for his withdrawal from Yemen to Muḥammad 'Alī, he himself was unhappy over the rapidly deteriorating relations between London and Cairo. He had laboured hard and long to promote links in the hope of reducing Egypt's ties with France and countering France's influence in Egyptian-dominated Syria.[52] But within months (in February 1840) Colonel Hodges had replaced Campbell as consul general in Egypt.

Unlike his predecessor, Hodges shared Palmerston's hostility towards the viceroy. Without proof or any reliable information to support his contention, Hodges reported to Palmerston that Muḥammad 'Alī had sent a secret mission to the imam of Ṣan'ā' urging him to drive the British out of Aden. He had allegedly promised in return to restore Ta'izz and the whole of Yemen's interior to the imam's administrative control. Should he not be prepared to respond, then the viceroy was prepared to administer the land in return for an annual subsidy from the imam, and his own forces would then take up the task of dislodging the British from Aden. Confronted with this 'intelligence', the viceroy contemptuously dismissed it as slanderous and untrue. He had no plans to dislodge the British from Aden, but rather to deliver Yemen from the incompetent rule of the imam, whose machinations and manifest weaknesses only served to encourage foreign elements to try to realize their ambitions at the expense of Yemen.[53]

However, the loss of Aden was not to be overlooked by the sons of the Sultan of Laḥj, who had signed the instrument of transfer, or by other tribes that were neighbours to Aden. They did not need any urging by Muḥammad 'Alī to carry on an armed struggle against the British there. Repeated attempts were made — in November 1839, May 1840 and July 1841 — under the leadership of the 'Abdali sultan to drive out the British, but to no avail: the British would not be dislodged.

Meanwhile, Muḥammad 'Alī decided to quit Yemen altogether. He was preparing for a major military and naval confrontation with the forces of both the Ottoman sultan and the Quadruple Alliance, the decision having been taken to force him out of Syria as well. His nephew, Küçük Ibrāhīm, returned with the Egyptian expedition from the Tihāmah after turning over the administration of the lowlands and the port cities of Mocha and Hodeida to Ḥusayn ibn 'Ali Ḥaydar, Sharīf of Abu 'Arīsh. The sharīf's brother, Abu Ṭālib, took charge of his fighting forces and responsibilities of defence. Thus ended Muḥammad 'Alī's adventures in south Arabia. He had come to restore the land to the rightful authority of the Ottoman sultan, only to find that he was being compelled to withdraw under the pressure of a carefully orchestrated policy of Palmerston in league with the sultan himself, who wanted Muḥammad 'Alī's own authority diminished.

In conclusion, one must note that while Muḥammad 'Alī succeeded in the mission that the Ottoman sultan had, by imperial decree, ordered him to undertake in 1828, the end result of his 12-year campaign was of dubious value. To be sure, the country was momentarily pacified, but the pacification had abetted British, not Ottoman, aims in that corner of Arabia. The British conveniently kept alive the question of Ottoman sovereignty for another decade, until their hold on Aden was cemented. In the end, as we shall see, the reaffirmation of imperial Ottoman sovereignty was to be achieved only with the conversion of Yemen into an Ottoman *vilayet*.

3. Renewal of Confrontation, 1840–49[1]

In Chapter 1 I covered the period from the beginnings of renewed Ottoman concern over Yemen to the Mocha incident of 1817. The British assault on Mocha that year aroused the suspicions of the sultan's government. The attack on what they saw as the back door to the holiest shrines of Islam was interpreted as part of a British design on Yemen as a whole, particularly after their political agent extracted a treaty from the imam of Ṣan'ā' that was seen as an attempt to legitimize their presence at Mocha without reference to Ottoman sovereign rights over the region.

During the next decade Britain sought to consolidate its hold on this corner of Arabia by stabilizing the Tihāmah and immediate hinterland. Unable to do so with their limited forces, they urged Muḥammad 'Alī, the viceroy of Egypt, to undertake a campaign of pacification in the 1830s, which, while not altogether successful, did gain a period of respite for the inhabitants and quieted tribal feuds and Wahhābi–'Asīri assaults on the Tihāmah's port towns. No sooner did the viceroy complete his costly campaign than Palmerston put pressure on him to withdraw from both Yemen and Syria, which was done in 1840 in exchange for his being granted hereditary rule over Egypt.

In this chapter I show how the absence of political stability and persisting insecurity induced the Ottoman government to take firm measures. These led to the re-establishment of direct rule over Yemen in an attempt to prevent the expansion of British influence and control out of the Aden enclave. For the Ottoman position, I relied on a dossier in the Ottoman archives called *Yemen meselesi* (*Problem of Yemen*). A detailed confidential report based on correspondence and memoranda shows how the British sought to justify their denial of Ottoman claims over the portions of Yemen in which they wanted to establish a permanent foothold, first at Mocha and, when that failed, at Aden.

Before withdrawing from the Tihāmah, Muḥammad 'Alī handed the administration of the district to Ḥusayn ibn 'Ali Ḥaydar, a *sharīf* from Abu 'Arīsh who had been a loyal supporter ever since he first entered the viceroy's service in 1836 as secretary to the Egyptian administrator for Mocha. Ibrahim Paşa, the viceroy's nephew and overall commander of the expedition, had appointed Ḥusayn over Hodeida, his brother Abu Ṭālib and commander of the contingents left behind. He recognized Ḥusayn as official *sharīf* of Abu 'Arīsh, thus granting him and members of the family almost full administrative control of the lowlands of Yemen. In exchange, Ḥusayn promised to pay an annual tribute of 90,000 German crowns to Muḥammad 'Alī who, after deducting expenses, was to relay the balance to the sultan's treasury in Istanbul.

From the start, Ḥusayn's two principal enemies, the *sharīf* and administrator of Mecca Muḥammad Ibn 'Awn and the imam of Ṣan'ā', challenged his control. They both coveted this pivotal region, but Muḥammad 'Alī trusted neither. He preferred Ḥusayn because he thought him more capable of standing up to the British than either the imam, whom he suspected of secretly favouring the British presence, or Ibn 'Awn, who was too far away to be effective. Ḥusayn had another challenger in the notorious chieftain Shaykh 'Ali Ḥamīdah of Bājil who also aspired to control the Tihāmah.

Ottoman accounts speak of Ḥusayn as a loyal administrator who strove to suppress the turbulent tribes, particularly the 'Asīris, and to enforce justice. They allege that it was his pursuit of justice and fulfilment of duty that led to resistance on the part of those the Ottomans dubbed *ḥasharāt*s (insects) in league with 'foreign elements', a reference to the British by agents at Aden and Mocha.

The British, on the other hand, alleged that this chief 'from the day of his appointment pursued a course of invariable hostility to British interests'.[2] Ḥusayn on his part did little to conceal his resentment of British intrusion and the manner in which they took hold of Aden. He was determined to make matters difficult for the vice-consul at Mocha and restrict his movements to the confines of the town itself. His other resolve was to prevent British contacts with tribes neighbouring Aden. It seems that he was successful for a while. In the words of Captain Haines, a political agent at Aden, 'overland communication may be considered at an end for the time being.'[3]

The *sharīf*'s conduct reflected to a large extent Ottoman resentment of the British authorities who had been manoeuvring to establish posts on the south Arabian coast by challenging Ottoman sovereign rights. It reflected also his frustrations over the seeming inability of the sultan's officials to suppress the tribes' feuds and marauding, which created instability and invited foreign powers to fish in troubled waters. Ḥusayn was determined in his tactless way to dislodge the British by whatever means possible. He hauled down the British flag at the port town of Mocha on the grounds that the Sublime Porte had not granted them formal consular rights, insulted Captain Gordon of the *Zenobia*, an East India Company vessel, who was then serving as vice-consul, and demanded that the Bombay government hand Aden over to him. Then in October 1840 a chief of al-Dunwah rebelled and occupied Ta'izz, proclaiming that he was charged with a sacred mission to throw the British out of Aden, but he was dispatched shortly afterwards by the imam's forces who saw in the British at Aden and Mocha possible allies in efforts to retrieve control of Yemen.

Indeed, shortly after Ibrahim Paşa handed Hodeida over to Ḥusayn, the imam sent his nephew to Aden to protest at this transfer and invited the agent to sign a treaty of friendship with him, but neither then nor on two subsequent occasions did Haines respond favourably. The government of Bombay wanted a neutral zone between Aden and the imam's possessions. It certainly did not wish to be drawn into the imam's feuds with rivals much more powerful at this time than himself, particularly when the legality of the British possession of Aden was in question.

Haines never trusted Ḥusayn from the day he first entered Egyptian service as scribe-secretary to Muḥammad Amīn Ağa, the viceroy's *mutasallim* of Mocha in 1836, nor did he underestimate the *sharīf*'s ability to make mischief.

When the viceroy agreed to evacuate Yemen, he surrendered control of Mocha to Ḥusayn on the pretext that the *sharīf* was the highest bidder and, besides, derived from a line of *sayyid*s of the Ashrafs. Ḥājj Yūsuf, a wealthy Hodeida merchant, personally pledged to secure the annual tribute Ḥusayn agreed to pay the central government. His other two rivals, the Imam of Ṣan'ā' and 'Ali Ḥamīdah of the Tihāmah were too poor to bid.

In recounting the events that precipitated the crisis of 1842–43, Haines alleged in a report to Bombay[4] that Ḥusayn felt strong enough to assert his independence, demanding the submission of the Imam of Ṣan'ā' and the placing of Aden under his control. Reportedly flushed with a new sense of power, he cut down the British flag at Mocha, issued an edict preventing Christians (mostly European traders) from riding in or near Mocha, and confined their entry and exit to one gate only. This he professedly did as an agent of the sultan's government, hence it was necessary to refer the matter to Istanbul for satisfaction.

The report of the *vali* of Hijaz (overseer of Yemen) from Jiddah treated British demands at Mocha as unreasonable and in contravention of Ottoman sovereign rights. He regarded them an insult to 'the Padishah [sultan] and Islam'. He attributed the incident to the illegal raising of the British flag at Mocha, implying extra-territorial privileges not formally granted by the sultan. He regretted the scuffle at the vice-consul's residence and the subsequent indignities suffered by his person. The *vali*, however, questioned the advisability of the India Board maintaining a formal post at Mocha.[5]

London forwarded the India Board's protests to Canning, who demanded satisfaction from the Porte, including the dismissal of Ḥusayn, even though Aberdeen had not instructed him to do so.[6] The foreign minister referred London's protests to the *Meclis-i Valâ-yi Ahkâm-i Adliye* (Supreme Council of Judicial Ordinances). He would not respond until he had investigated the situation at first hand.

The Mission of Aşraf Beg

The Sublime Porte obtained the sultan's approval to send Aşraf Beg[7] back to Yemen to investigate and implement a set of secret instructions. Aşraf was familiar with the land and the problems from his previous missions in the 1830s. Among his instructions, Aşraf was to stop in Egypt to consult the viceroy, whose experience in Yemen could prove useful. Accordingly, Aşraf visited Muḥammad 'Alī in March 1842.[8] Muḥammad 'Alī's subsequent letter to the sultan contains an index of the topics he discussed with Aşraf. While confessing to have been out of touch recently with Yemen, he counselled against either dismissing Ḥusayn or converting Yemen into an independent *vilayet* at that time, which was an option included in Aşraf's instructions. To depose Ḥusayn because he was a little zealous in the discharge of his duties would require a military-cum-naval operation beyond the capacity of the government to mount. Even if such an operation were possible, and successful, stability would not return to the area. The viceroy suggested that Aşraf consult further with the *vali* at Jiddah, the Sharīf of Mecca, and Ferik Ahmed Paşa, the military commander of the Hijaz.[9]

Aşraf was relieved to have the viceroy's views because they coincided with those of the ministers of the Porte. As a matter of fact, Aşraf carried secret instructions empowering him to bestow official recognition on Ḥusayn and extend his functions for another three years if he would agree to the conditions proposed by the Porte.

Upon reaching Jiddah, Aşraf discussed these terms with the *vali* and obtained his approval and endorsement. He reached Zabīd, the Ottoman governor's headquarters, in late September and avoided immediate contact with Consul Cruttenden. On 29 September he met Ḥusayn and discussed the government's terms, which fell under three headings:

- honouring commitments to the sultan's government;
- respecting that government's arrangements with the chief of 'Asīr, and
- accepting agreements reached with the British about Yemen.

He was to observe civility in dealing with their agent at Mocha, remit the tribute through the *vali* of Hijaz, and forward to the imperial kitchens the quantity of coffee beans previously levied on his district.

On neighbouring 'Asīr, Aşraf was empowered to confirm its chief in his post as official *mutasallim*, by a secret *ferman* from the *sadrazam*, if 'Ā'iḍ ibn Mur'i (the chief) accepted Ḥusayn's jurisdictional authority over 'Asīr. Another *ferman* would confer the governorship of Yemen on Ḥusayn for three years and render the Imam of Ṣan'ā' a *mutasallim* of Ḥusayn's district if the latter should accept the *vali* of Hijaz's administrative authority over Yemen.[10]

Ḥusayn agreed to all these conditions and stated so in an official communiqué to the government of the sultan and to 'Uthmān, *vali* of Hijaz.[11] The orders Aşraf carried made it clear that Yemen and 'Asīr would be administrative appendages of the Hijaz. Responsible authorities in Istanbul and the Hijaz felt this could be done only by conferring official recognition and strengthening thereby Ḥusayn's role despite some reservations.[12]

The 'Asīris had posed a constant threat to Mocha's inhabitants' security, disrupting trade and compelling many to abandon this important port town rather than put up with their marauding. In the interest of assuring Mocha some security the Porte insisted on Ḥusayn maintaining the annual tribute of 20,000 crowns to 'Ā'iḍ ibn Mur'i.[13]

While the Ottoman government was anxious to maintain friendly ties with Great Britain, such ties were not to have priority over important internal considerations, namely Ottoman sovereignty over the whole of Yemen. The resident vice-consul at Mocha first came to Mocha with a letter of acknowledgment from Muḥammad 'Alī, who was no longer the sultan's recognized agent in Yemen, and not from the Sublime Porte. Nevertheless, the sultan's government was now prepared to extend formal recognition provided the British accepted Ḥusayn as the *mutasallim* of Mocha.[14] The Porte's hesitancy in permitting the expansion of British trade stemmed from strong opposition from Arabian and Muslim traders, particularly those based in Jiddah. These merchants resented foreign merchants circumventing payment of duties by shipping goods via Massawa on the Eritrean coast, from India, and even from Yemen itself. Muslim traders were also avoiding paying customs duty and the treasury of the Hijaz was suffering a loss put at 3000 *kise akçe*s annually.[15] Meanwhile, the Sharīf of Mecca was pressing Istanbul for more funds to meet the expenses of policing the area.[16]

The Sublime Porte would have preferred the British to establish their consular post at Hodeida so as to put more distance between them and Ḥusayn. The ministers refused to accept British Ambassador Canning's demand that Ḥusayn be deposed. They recommended instead that the Ottoman foreign minister write a polite letter to smooth his ruffled feathers.[17] No flag raising would be allowed at Mocha until the British acceded to Ottoman terms.

British terms as Canning presented them revealed the lack of regard for Ottoman sovereignty. They reflected what Captain Cruttenden had demanded, briefly that Ḥusayn should levy only 2¼ per cent customs duty on goods carried by British vessels, be they of Hindu, British or even corsair origin, when native south Arabians paid the legal 3 per cent. He was to promise not to maltreat such traders even if their acts appeared to transcend provisions of applicable Islamic law. He was not to obstruct efforts of British subjects and protégés to obtain supplies from the ports of the Tihāmah under his jurisdiction. He was to conclude no treaties with the French or any other foreign power without prior agreement with the British Resident at Mocha. Full protection was to be accorded to all British subjects to move about freely in his domain and be maltreated neither by customs officials nor by Muḥammad 'Alī of Egypt's agents. Finally, Ḥusayn was to treat Britain's friends as his friends and her enemies as his enemies.[18]

To consider that the Sublime Porte would accede to such terms and expect someone of Ḥusayn's calibre to abide by them was neither logical nor reasonable. It is doubtful if the British themselves expected the sultan's government to accept them. Aden was already their choice as principal base in south Arabia; and if they could extract favourable terms for Mocha, so much the better. Otherwise they were prepared to withdraw from Mocha. Meanwhile, they could preoccupy Ḥusayn with Mocha and divert his attention away from Aden until such time as they might end his administration altogether.

As for Aşraf's mission, he got what he came for, namely Ḥusayn's submission to the government's, as well to 'Ā'iḍ ibn Mur'i's, terms. All that was needed now was some sort of formalization by the sultan's government.

Meanwhile, the India government was not sure it could accept Ḥusayn's administration for another three years. Haines reported to the secret committee on Aşraf's mission, termed by him 'an inquiry into the conduct of the Sheriff of Mocha'. He showed concern about Ḥusayn's confirmation in the post of administrator, fearing that it would lead next to an enquiry into Aden and the Indian trade with the Red Sea. Haines also noted that Aşraf avoided William Smith, consul at Mocha, lest by meeting him he might lend legality to his position, handing the *ferman* instead to Captain Haines. He did not wait for the flag to be hoisted at Aden, departing rather from Hodeida to Istanbul.[19]

The document handed to Haines included a request for particulars of the complaints about British trade and of the specific questions the Ottoman government had posed to the India government about Ottoman sovereign rights, namely:

- When did the Imam of Ṣan'ā' legally hold the port towns of the Tihāmah during the period when the British flag was reportedly allowed to be raised?
- For how long did Muḥammad 'Alī control this area by virtue of conquest? And
- what was the official date of the Ottoman recognition of Ḥusayn as administrator over the port towns?

In forwarding the document to India, Haines recommended that the India Board concern itself with the last point only and insist on the application of the 1838 Treaty of Commerce with the sultan's government in determining the amount of customs duty to be paid by British shipping. He objected to the absence of an apology in the Ottoman *ferman* for the insults the British flag and Resident suffered at Mocha, even though the *ferman* did authorize the raising of the flag and ordered that respect be shown to British merchants in future. No restitution was mentioned for plundered possessions. He was sceptical about Ḥusayn's ability to pay the annual tribute in addition to meeting local administrative and military expenses because Ottomans 'are weak in Arabia'.[20] He doubted moreover if either Ḥusayn or 'the aged ruler of Lahadj' would allow peaceful trade for long, even though for the moment between 200 and 500 camel loads were entering Aden daily. He was certain that both rulers would soon excite the tribes to annoy the British.

Haines's suspicions were confirmed by a letter from the 'Sultan [of] Bier Hamad [*sic*, Bīr Aḥmad] who resided only a few miles from Aden', in which it was alleged that Ḥusayn wrote to the Sultan of Laḥj who then proceeded to gather the tribes for a secret meeting. Fearing a possible attack, Haines recommended to the company that it should station the brig *Tigris* in Aden waters until the results of the 'secret conference' were known.[21]

Meanwhile, London was interested in resolving the legal status of Yemen to determine the amount of customs duty that could be levied on British shipping. The usual charge was 12 per cent on goods from Yemen, Abyssinia and adjoining areas brought into Jiddah, a clearly defined Ottoman port, thereby subjected to terms of the 1838 treaty.[22] Should it be determined that Yemen did indeed fall under Ottoman sovereignty, then the India Board would be confronted with the same rate of payment it hoped to circumvent by denying Ottoman sovereignty over the lowlands and the ports of the Tihāmah now formally administered by Ḥusayn for the sultan's government.[23]

The advocate general tendered his judgment in May 1844 and, as one might have expected, it favoured British policy objectives in the Red Sea. He ruled that Abyssinia was not part of the Ottoman Empire for commercial purposes. He conceded that between 1569 and 1630 Yemen was *de jure* under Ottoman sovereignty but that after 1663 (when Sultan Mehmed IV's forces were defeated) it passed under the control of *sayyid*s and since then under the control of the Imam of Ṣan'ā', thus depriving Yemen of a 'Turkish character'.

Regarding Mocha, the advocate ruled that Ḥusayn's rule was legitimate because he was appointed by a Sublime Porte agent (Muḥammad 'Alī) and confirmed in his post in 1842 in return for the payment of tribute, which he apparently had rendered on a regular basis. The sultan's government was ruled to possess at least *de facto* authority here and was thus responsible for its officers' actions. So it was legitimate to demand some satisfaction and compensation for Ḥusayn's mistreatment of British subjects. Aden, on the other hand, was conveniently treated as lying outside Ottoman *de jure* control. Thus, Ḥusayn's acquisition of a part of the coast bordering on it was regarded as illegal because the British advocate general deemed that his sovereign, the sultan, had no sovereign rights over it. He concluded that, with the exception of Mocha, no part of Yemen came under the provision of the 1838 treaty (sometimes referred to as a commercial convention).[24]

What was remarkable about the advocate's ruling is that in almost every instance it paralleled the suggestions put forth by the East India Board in replying to Lord Ripon's letter of enquiry[25] in which Aden was considered to have been ceded legally by the 'Sultan or Fakih of Aden', even if there was some question about his right to do so. It was held that Ottoman sovereignty had been interruptedly exercised over Yemen. The presence of Egyptian troops in this part of Arabia between 1833 and 1840 was treated as 'occupational', not an act buttressing Ottoman claims of sovereignty, let alone rights. Only the Hijaz was considered an undisputed Ottoman territory in Arabia.

What is interesting about this whole exercise in sovereignty determination is that it would not have taken place had it not been for the claims the East India Board, and specifically the Bombay government, made against Ḥusayn, 'the Emir of Mocha'.

The advocate general's report was forwarded to Canning with copies to India. The ambassador was instructed by Aberdeen, his superior in London, to use it as a guide in communicating with the sultan's government.[26] However much the British hoped for Ḥusayn's removal, they reluctantly conceded that he had been too firmly seated for Aşraf to unseat, even though the sultan's government had authorized the exercise of this option. Moreover, he enjoyed Muḥammad 'Alī of Egypt's support and the sultan could scarcely afford to alienate him further, given the strong influence the viceroy still wielded among conservative ministers in the Ottoman capital.

Instability in Nejd and Yemen

Radical changes were still in the offing. The sultan's government had not obtained its objectives, for both Nejd and Yemen appeared to resist stabilization. In September 1846 a joint report presented by the *vali* of the Hijaz and the Emir of Mecca alleged that Ḥusayn had defaulted on his payment of tribute and preoccupied himself with conquering not just the Tihāmah but the hinterland up to Ta'izz as well. His objective allegedly was to depose the Imam of Ṣan'ā' and replace him with Muḥammad Manṣūri, using up funds he should have remitted to the Jiddah treasury, as well as the 15,000 crowns owing to the chief of 'Asīr. Ahmed Beg, *miralay* of the Ottoman contingent in Yemen, was too weak to stop him. Vali 'Uthmān had made a number of trips to Yemen to investigate. Ḥusayn Efendi, the *divan*'s scribe, had also examined the situation at close range. All were concerned with the consequences of Ḥusayn being locked in battle with powerful enemies, namely Mur'ī al-Khāṭir and 'Ali Ḥamīdah, who had attacked an army depot and seized its arms and ammunition to make war on Ḥusayn. While the 'Asīr and Yām chiefs joined efforts to stop Ḥamīdah, they realized soon enough that this could be done only by force. Meanwhile, Ḥusayn's three-year appointment was due for renewal, and there was strong reluctance to recommend it because he had defaulted on tribute and on the supply of coffee beans owing to the imperial kitchens, and his policies threatened renewed conflict with the British.

Yet, despite all this, Ottoman officials in Jiddah and Mecca were prepared to recommend he be kept on for another term if he would leave 'Ali Ḥamīdah alone, deliver the annual tribute to Jiddah, pay the same to 'Asīr, and remain obedient to the sultan. If not, then they suggested the Sublime Porte assemble a land and sea force and prepare to attack him.[27]

The Emir of Mecca was investigating boundary disputes in 'Asīr when a marauding chief, Khafījah, invaded the Medina area inflicting heavy casualties on the defendants including notables, the *müdür* of Medina, the *shaykh* of the Ḥaram, the *nā'ib* of the Ḥaram, the servant of the *müdür*, the chief correspondence secretary and numerous other high-ranking citizens. The city itself was in distress and appealing for aid.[28] This took place only a few weeks after the *vali* had received a secret enquiry from the sultan's government concerning the strength of the two troublemakers of Arabia — Ḥusayn of Yemen and Fayṣal ibn Turki of Nejd.[29]

In a separate communiqué from the *vali*, Fayṣal is accused of precipitating disorder by killing the son of the chief of the 'Hamshirizades' (*sic*). To calm the situation, the *vali* urgently needed 2500 infantry and 1500 horses (cavalry), along with expenses totalling 2000 purses of *akçe*s.

The *vali* was convinced that no stability would return to 'Asīr without a measure of administrative autonomy and regular troops for policing it. He did not rule out a punitive strike against the tribal elements causing turmoil there. He favoured trapping and capturing 'Ali Ḥamīdah and holding him hostage to check his marauding followers. He mistrusted the British, whom he accused of conspiring with the Imam of Ṣan'ā' to eliminate Ḥusayn and thereby threaten the Hijaz. Thus, he favoured keeping Ḥusayn on for another three years provided he honoured his pledges to the sultan's government.

In the *vali*'s judgement, too many conditions needed appeasement to be redressed without the use of force. Under no circumstances would he tolerate an alliance between the British and the imam that could cost the sultan the Tihāmah, citing by way of example how the British gained final control of India. The consequences would be too disastrous to countenance when measured in the loss of trade and revenue, upon which both 'Asīr and the Hijaz were heavily dependent. He suggested that the *vali* of Egypt be instructed to prepare vessels to transport troops from Jiddah to Yemen, which would consist of two battalions of *nizamiye* (regular) troops and an additional two of *başıbozuk*s (irregulars) from Egypt (perhaps several regiments more) and 5000 purses of *akçe*s to meet expenses.[30]

The *vali*'s recommendations coincided with those of the *Meclis-i Valâ*, which were based on reports by 'Abd al-Muṭṭalib Efendi whose assessment of the situation they trusted.[31] 'Abd al-Muṭṭalib, a Hijazi notable, recognized the need to check both Fayṣal and Ḥusayn. But to lodge the latter would require substantial force, particularly if a successor were to be appointed. The Hijaz's income could be assured only if Yemen were stabilized, as when Muḥammad 'Alī briefly calmed both regions. He still considered entrusting Yemen's administration to an independent *vali*. Davud Paşa, custodian of the Prophet's *Ḥaram al-Sharīf* in Medina, was thought to have the makings of a good governor. He was seen to be capable and trustworthy, with administrative experience acquired first in Baghdad and then in the Hijaz. Moreover, Davud had maintained good relations with the bedouins and had first-hand knowledge of Yemen. He would make a good *vali*, wrote 'Abd al-Muṭṭalib, Sharīf of Mecca, to the sultan's government.

Aşraf's second mission

'Abd al-Muṭṭalib's recommendations reinforced Aşraf's view that the only practical solution would be to turn Yemen into an independent *vilayet*. When asked to return to Yemen, Aşraf was armed with a secret order empowering him to appoint Davud as *vali* should Ḥusayn prove uncooperative.

It was common knowledge that the administrators of the Hijaz mistrusted Ḥusayn and tended not to see his side of events in Yemen. The Sublime Porte was aware of the rift and, in the interest of impartiality, had authorized sending a reminder to the Emir of Mocha that stability and economic security were absolutely essential if revenues were to be secured and the tribute rendered as agreed. Ḥusayn, the scribe, made it clear to his namesake that a good portion of the expenses incurred in maintaining the two *haram*s (Mecca and Medina) depended on revenue from Yemen.

The emir was in full agreement and proclaimed from the mosque and *minbar* that he was a loyal and true servant of the sultan. His problem was how to avoid wasting funds on unnecessary campaigns when, as he put it, 'there are too many tribes and evil-doers in Yemen.' Many funds earmarked for tribute had been used for policing actions against marauders. He told the emissary from Mecca that he was indebted to the tune of 150,000 crowns, which was why he had been unable recently to pay tribute either to 'Asīr or Jiddah. If anyone doubted his veracity, 'then let him send ten investigators to assess the income and expenditure of Yemen and help himself to the surplus'.[32]

After studying the results of Ḥusayn's mission to Yemen, both Vali Raif and Emir Ibn 'Awn of Mecca decided to recommend reappointing Ḥusayn for another three years. Yemen had achieved some stability through Ḥusayn chastising 'Ali Ḥamīdah, so to have deposed him at this juncture could have encouraged him to conspire with the British at Aden against Ottoman interests in Yemen.[33] The *Meclis-i Valâ* in Istanbul had come to a similar conclusion. As for Fayṣal of Nejd, while conceding that he 'derived from a long line of malicious Wahhābis', it was considered prudent to keep him on until the end of the pilgrimage season, then deal with him firmly if he recanted his offer of loyalty. Then, either Khālid of the Sharq (Eastern Province) or 'Abdallah of Shammar[34] could replace him as administrator of Nejd.

Ḥusayn of Mocha was seen as the best of the unpleasant alternatives;

but again, if need be, he too could be dealt with forcefully after the pilgrimage. Troops would then be dispatched, even from Iraq, on British vessels if necessary, to chastise him. Under no circumstances would the *Meclis* countenance a situation in Yemen that might give the Imam of Ṣan'ā' any pretext to collaborate with the British and allow them to meddle further in the internal affairs of Yemen.[35]

As the ministers at Istanbul reasoned, should 'Ali Ḥamīdah, the prime mischief-maker, weaken Ḥusayn in battle, then he could entice the Yām and 'Asīr tribes to attempt to destroy him while Ḥamīdah got rid of the present Imam of Ṣan'ā' in favour of the relative Ḥusayn had deposed. The besieged imam could then invite the British to come to his rescue by virtue of a somewhat dubious treaty relationship concluded in December 1820. This would threaten the whole Hijaz and the Tihāmah with possible foreign occupation. It was therefore a matter of urgency to stabilize the situation. To that end Aşraf was instructed to return to Yemen for military mobilization to ensure the success of his mission.[36]

The Ottomans had learned to challenge Yemen's tribes and blamed their constant feuds, wars and marauding habits for the region's social, economic and political instability. They singled out the Dhu Muḥammad, Dhū Ḥusayn, Ḥāshid, Bājil and Yām tribes as causing much of the turmoil and referred to them as a bunch of *ruzalā* (mischief makers). The Tihāmah tribes wanted no traffic with these highlanders whom the Imam of Ṣan'ā' often instigated and manipulated. The only way the merchant colonies of the port towns could keep them at bay was by building and constantly reinforcing strong fortifications.[37]

Emir Ḥusayn's task was difficult; he had to contend with a lot to maintain stability and control. He knew he could win over the Porte's emissary if he could convince him that, with or without the British connivance allegedly aimed at ousting the Ottomans from Yemen, the Imam of Ṣan'ā' was behind much of the action against him and the lowlands.[38]

Fearing that Ḥusayn was too weak militarily to withstand a combined attack by the imam's supporters (and possibly the British) at Aden, the Sublime Porte authorized the dispatch of troops to Yemen. The loss of the ports and the revenue of their custom houses would have led to a major financial crisis for the administrators of the Hijaz.

Aşraf was instructed to consult the *müşür* of the Arabistan forces, who sometimes doubled as the *vali* of Sidon, even though the *müşür* had alerted Istanbul in advance that his troops in Syria were too depleted to spare any for Yemen. He was also asked to request assistance from Muḥammad ʻAlī of Egypt in mustering the required military force.[39]

The *emr-i âli* (imperial order) Aşraf carried clearly specified that should Ḥusayn fail to meet his obligations he would be deposed and replaced by a governor of the sultan's choosing. The order stipulated that Ḥusayn would then be allowed to return to his dwelling in Abu ʻArīsh where, if he caused no problems, he would receive a fixed income (amount unspecified).[40]

The order was neither delivered nor executed at this time because, as the Sublime Porte had instructed, on his way to Yemen Aşraf stopped in Egypt to consult the viceroy who, more than any other Ottoman *vali*, understood well the vicissitudes of Yemeni politics and difficulties in controlling this turbulent land. Muḥammad ʻAlī already had knowledge through his counterpart at Jiddah and the Emir of Mecca of Ḥusayn's entanglements with the imam (whom he replaced with another) and his ally ʻAlī Ḥamīdah. He received notice to prepare vessels for the transport of troops. But after weighing the risks and possible consequences, Muḥammad ʻAlī counselled him against the expedition to chastise Ḥusayn, let alone depose him.

Money was the key factor in the viceroy's consideration. It was in short supply in both Istanbul and Jiddah. He estimated it would cost 30,000 *kise* a year just to police Yemen with Ottoman troops. He was prepared to meet a part of the cost but expected Egypt's treasury to be reimbursed for it. Another consideration was the tribal situation, for there were too many tribes to keep in check. Tangling with chiefs like Ḥusayn and ʻAli Ḥamīdah could exhaust troops and bankrupt treasuries. Jiddah had only two battalions at its disposal and to ship them to Yemen would leave the Hijaz defenceless. To send more regular troops to Yemen would be wasting them because 'they will perish aimlessly' and Yemen's coffee crop would be destroyed. If that happened, American coffee would flood the market, forcing prices down and squeezing Yemen out of the competition, resulting in great losses of income. So, besides losing good fighting men, the Ottoman government would also lose badly needed revenues. The rule in the past, Muḥammad ʻAlī argued, was to encourage not destroy agricultural production in the Tihāmah. But if the ministers of the Porte still insisted on it, troops could be transported from Sidon on ships coming from Marseilles to Egypt, then overland to the Hijaz. To transport the Jiddah battalion would mean purchasing six or seven large transport vessels from India.[41]

Ibrahim Ağa, captain of the artillery unit at Jiddah, was summoned to Istanbul for consultation in November 1846. He told the government that to prepare for another expedition would require additional expenses for upkeep, pay, clothing (summer and winter), Korans for the troops and a monthly allowance for both irregular troops and cavalry units above the then present level.[42] Muḥammad Kâmil, *müşür* at Sidon, acknowledged the Sublime Porte's request but notified the ministers that he would defer sending the battalions requested until they had studied Muḥammad 'Alī's views and comments on the situation in Yemen.[43] Muḥammad 'Alī's response had arrived ten days earlier. He acknowledged Aşraf's official mission but recommended against the dispatch of troops at that time.[44]

On hearing the views submitted, the *sadrazam* cancelled its previous instructions to Aşraf and authorized the dispatch of one battalion of troops from Istanbul, instead of two from Sidon, together with 229 artillerymen and their equipment.[45] All correspondence on the subject was then referred to the *Meclis-i Valâ* for further deliberation. The *Meclis-i Hass* (Special Council) was also asked to study the matter.[46]

On 9 May Aşraf arrived in Jiddah, 18 days after leaving Suez by ship. He delivered 4000 purses to the treasury (funds allocated for troop expenses) and made it known that he would be guided by instructions the grand vizier had given him in March.[47] He met the *vali* on 15 May and delivered to him both 'oral and written messages' concerning the affairs of Yemen and 'Asīr. The wording of these messages was not fully disclosed, leaving one to speculate whether he carried additional secret instructions. Aşraf was unable to meet the Emir of Mecca, for he was away on a campaign in eastern Arabia to suppress uprisings in Ra's and Qaşīm and bring the eastern provinces under control.[48]

The Sublime Porte's instructions stressed the need for unanimity of opinion on the part of all concerned (the Viceroy of Egypt, the Vali of the Hijaz, the Emir of Mecca and Aşraf himself) over the solution best suited under the circumstances for Yemen's problem. The key issue to be considered was whether to depose Ḥusayn or keep him on for another three years in return for his strict adherence to commitments made. In their replies to Istanbul, the *vali* and *amir* had expressed readiness to abide by decisions arrived at in strict obedience to imperial orders.[49] The *emir* deferred further statements on whether to keep or replace Ḥusayn until he returned from the eastern provinces and the outcome of the pacification mission was known.[50]

On 13 July, Aşraf left Jiddah for Yemen accompanied by Hamdi Efendi who had replaced the deceased Ḥusayn as the *divan*'s scribe. Though the Emir of Mocha had failed to abide by assurances delivered through the previous scribe, Aşraf still met Ḥusayn and handed over to him the latest word from the imperial *divan* in Istanbul.[51]

News of the initial decision to dispatch fresh troops to the Hijaz under Maḥmūd Paşa's command reached British consul Charles Murray through the viceroy himself. He stated that the purpose of the proposed expedition was to check the troublesome mountain tribes of Yemen that were surrounding Aden, presumably to protect British lives and commerce in keeping with the provisions of the 1838 Treaty of Commerce between Great Britain and the Ottoman state. Muḥammad 'Alī seemed pessimistic about the proposed expedition's prospects of success given the difficult Yemeni terrain and the fact that Ottoman officials in the Hijaz were already engaged in a continuing campaign to pacify the defiant Wahhābi tribes of Nejd. Consul General Murray on the other hand chose to believe that Muḥammad 'Alī and the Sublime Porte were secretly in league to reoccupy Yemen. The viceroy responded by accusing the British of plotting with the Porte to send only a few men to accomplish an impossible task and thereby pave the way for their own intervention. Judging from his past experiences in Yemen, one can understand why the viceroy should have vowed never to get involved in that country again unless the Sublime Porte was prepared to forego Egypt's annual tribute of 60,000 purses (£300,000 sterling) to mobilize a needed force estimated at 10,000 men to pacify the tribes of Arabia.[52]

On learning that the *sadrazam* had advised against the expedition, Muḥammad 'Alī let Murray know that it was on his recommendation that it was done. Only one regiment was to be sent to the Hijaz, and this for the purpose of replenishing ranks and not for fighting tribes.

When Murray asked Palmerston about the viceroy's accusations of Anglo–Ottoman connivance[53] he was told that it was not his (Palmerston's) policy but that he would rather the viceroy believed it so that he could impress him with his, Palmerston's, own influence before the Porte. However, Palmerston agreed with the viceroy that to try and combat Yemeni and Hijazi rebels with limited forces would be a 'bad bargain for the Porte'.[54]

De facto vilayet for Yemen

By now the Sublime Porte was convinced that there could be no military solution to the Yemeni problem; it opted rather for a policy of appeasement and flattery to keep troublemakers in line. The two *meclis*es had studied the data the grand vizier turned over to them and reached the conclusion that it was more politic to appease than to fight Ḥusayn. Indeed, they were prepared to grant him hereditary rule over Yemen (as they had granted Muḥammad 'Alī in 1841 over Egypt) if it would give him the incentive to pacify the land, take firm control of it, and administer it on behalf of the sultan. As an encouragement they arranged for two gold-bejewelled medals (*nişan-i âli* or *nişan-i emaret*) to be given to Ḥusayn and his son, and another to appease the Emir of Mecca, for the Porte realized only too well that the emir did not miss an opportunity to discredit Ḥusayn and work towards ousting him. Fayṣal of Nejd was likewise appeased with the rank of *istabl* (imperial equerry) in return for a payment of the tribute to the amount of 10,000 crowns annually. 'Abd al-Muṭṭalib was likewise retained as emir.

If the policy of appeasing Ḥusayn failed then Aşraf was authorized to implement the *ferman* that approved his deposition and replacement. But that was unnecessary because, on 20 January 1848, the *Meclis-i Hass* recommended a rank of *mîr-i mirân* for Ḥusayn's eldest son with a salary of 100,000 *piastre*s, which put him in the same rank as a *paşa* who governed a province and made him equal to the *vali* of Hijaz. His youngest son was to receive the rank of *emir-i ümera* and a high-ranking *nişan*. All this was at the recommendation of Aşraf who felt that Ḥusayn was sincere in his loyalty to the sultan and that the problems confronting him were not all of his own making.

Since he was short of revenue, it was recommended that he offer a *bedel* (equivalent) in coffee and sugar. To appease merchants it was further decreed that no taxes be levied on goods shipped to the Hijaz from Yemen if it could be shown that customs duty had been collected on them at some Yemeni port; to charge such a duty would be tantamount to recognizing that Yemen lay outside Ottoman sovereignty. And, to retax goods shipped from one Ottoman possession to another would constitute an injustice.[55]

The sultan was relieved to receive the same recommendation from all three principal bodies — the *Valâ*, *Hass* and *Sadaret* — and in recognition of Aşrafi's work he authorized a high-ranking *nişan* for him encrusted with diamonds together with a green mantle edged with pearls, a scarlet mantle for the *vali* of the Hijaz, and a red one for the *emir* of Mecca to be dispatched with the *emir-i hac* (leader of the pilgrimage). Letters of appreciation were decreed and sent to the *vali*s of Egypt and the Hijaz, the Emir of Mecca, and the Emir of Yemen.[56] They also spelt out the conditions under which Ḥusayn would be reappointed and his authority strengthened by granting him the powers of a *de facto vali*. To maintain good relations with Yemeni tribes and the British at Aden, in a manner conforming to the empire's high standards, were among his responsibilities. He was to safeguard the line of communication with Yemen and keep records in a sort of *takvim-i vekâyi* (official almanac) for submission to and review by the Sublime Porte. He was not to withhold vital information from officials sent to Yemen to review its affairs.[57]

Lest jealousy overtake other ranking officials in the Hijaz, the Sublime Porte authorized *nişan*s to high-ranking aides of the *sharīf* and *emir* of Mecca, Tevfik Paşa (commander of troops) and treasurer Ahmed Ağa. And, for the first time, official government documents refer to Ḥusayn as '*vali* of Yemen'.[58]

But events unfolding in Yemen soon dashed government hopes. News of such happenings had not yet reached Istanbul when the sultan and his ministers uttered a sigh of relief.

The Imam of Ṣan'ā' rebels

Available documentary evidence fails to reveal how much time elapsed between the start of the next series of events and their being reported to Istanbul. One suspects strongly that Muḥammad Ibn 'Awn, the *emir* and *sharīf* of Mecca, was strongly implicated in them and there is circumstantial evidence to suggest that he encouraged the Imam of Ṣan'ā' to rise against Ḥusayn. The attack commenced late in 1847 but the earliest reference to it by the Sublime Porte was in May the following year.

Ottoman data show no action during the last six months of 1847 and this leaves one to wonder whether, given that Ibn 'Awn's own political ambitions extended from Mecca to Yemen, he deliberately suppressed news of events. That the imam chose to report to Ibn 'Awn on the course of his campaign leaves little doubt that he was given to understand he had the emir of Mecca's sympathy.

As noted earlier, Imam Muḥammad was appointed under the aegis of Ḥusayn himself. But apparently he chose to side with 'Ali Ḥamīdah to regain possession of the lowlands for the imamate, alleging that in the past they had always been part of the imam's holdings. Ḥusayn reminded him that the Sublime Porte had invested him with the administration of Yemen with a rank equivalent to a *vali*. The imam responded by declaring Ḥusayn a rebel, and when Ḥusayn resolved on taking possession of Ta'izz the imam sent his own men to capture this strategic town. By the time Ḥusayn arrived there with about 300 men, he found that the imam and 'Ali Ḥamīdah had set a trap for him at Wādi Burjah, seven hours away from Hodeida. The reinforcements led by his brother Yaḥya arrived too late from Abu 'Arīsh; consequently, Yaḥya was killed while the survivors were attempting to withdraw to Qaṭī' and Ḥusayn was wounded. Of the original 150 survivors fleeing from the battle, only 25 reached the fort. Dhū Muḥammad and Dhū Ḥusayn tribesmen, who had sided with the rebels and were pursuing them, besieged Ḥusayn at Qaṭī' and forced him to surrender 25 days later. By the terms of the surrender Ḥusayn agreed to surrender all the Tihāmah towns with the exception of Hodeida and Luḥayyah, the latter being left in the hands of Ḥusayn's brother to administer. In the meanwhile Aşraf, unaware of what was going on, had been waiting at Jiddah for transport to Suez on what had been decreed a successful mission.

One of Muḥammad 'Alī's ships returning from Massawa after having delivered the new *muḥāfiz*, Halil, brought news of the fighting to Suez. A Turkish letter dated 15 March was then rushed to the viceroy from Suez. Aşraf was worried about the explosive situation in Yemen, particularly when it was rumoured that the imam had asked the British for support. Hijaz officials led by the Ottoman commander at Mecca (Tevfik Paşa) were determined not to let the imam exercise authority over the Tihāmah. It was now revealed that the Sublime Porte and Viceroy of Egypt deliberately divided Yemen's administration between the Imam of Ṣan'ā' and the Emir of Mocha to prevent one powerful element dominating the region. Ḥusayn would act as a buffer between the imam at Ṣan'ā' and the British at Aden to ensure that the two were unable to strike up an effective alliance that would threaten Ottoman sovereignty over Yemen and disrupt the vital line of trade and communication with the Hijaz. The decision that reached Jiddah, in which Aşraf took part and which, as expected, Muḥammad 'Alī endorsed, was to chastise the imam, for all were of one mind that the imam was culpable.[59]

Yusuf Ağa, who had been the customs official at Hodeida since 1818, fled to Jiddah and reported that the uprising was the result of a joint conspiracy between the British and the imam to wrest control of Yemen from the Ottomans.[60] Aşraf expressed the same concern in relaying news of the event to Istanbul.[61]

On 29 January 1848 the imam wrote to the Sharīf of Mecca about his campaign against Ḥusayn, alleging that since the latter was spreading dissension in the land and causing much hardship he was compelled to take action against him. Besides, historically the Tihāmah belonged to Ṣan'ā' and he considered it his duty to recover it 'to enforce good and prevent the spread of evil'.[62] In another letter to the *sharīf* of the same date he promised to honour his request to 'be kind to our brother Yaḥya ibn Muḥammad Ḥamīd al-Dīn, who is fortunate to be one of yours [namely your supporters] and deserving of good grace.'[63] He alleged that by seizing Mocha, Zabīd and Bayt al-Faqīh he was only seeking to bring peace and security to the land.[64]

The assault on the port towns occasioned considerable hardship for their residents and merchants who, in a number of petitions to the Sublime Porte, complained of their trade being brutally disrupted and of the hardships visited upon their families, forcing a good number of traders to flee the land for as far north as Jiddah itself.[65]

The British were among the first to hear details of the events, which they forwarded to Alexandria and Istanbul. Ottoman accounts failed to reveal that Ḥusayn could obtain his release only by handing over 20,000 crowns to the Dhū Ḥusayn tribe holding him captive. The tribes appeared to vacillate between imam and Ḥusayn, depending on the fortunes of the battle. While all expected Ottoman troops to materialize in due course, the 'Asīr tribes wasted no time gathering and descending from their mountain strongholds to plunder the Tihāmah towns and sell back their loot to the highest bidder among its former owners. Ḥusayn clearly could exercise no authority outside what money might buy. These recent events showed him to possess no base for the exercise of power and authority. The money he needed was ordinarily obtained from customs revenue and compulsory levies on merchants, most of whom now had fled; also appeasement of the 'Asīr was by tribute payment, which now had been raised to 30,000 crowns per annum.[66]

As he himself was unable to report, it was left to his brother Ḥaydar 'Ali to write to 'Awn and present Ḥusayn's version of the facts, naturally laying the blame on the imam who reportedly goaded Ḥusayn into war in September 1847 by claiming the whole Yemen for himself as 'the land of his ancestors' and demanding that Ḥusayn get out of it. He begged the *sharīf* to send military assistance to punish the imam and secure the release of his brother, who in the meanwhile had been put up for sale.[67]

Needless to say, the consensus of official opinion in Arabia, Egypt and Istanbul favoured Ḥusayn's position. Indeed, a chronicler of events of the period referred to Ḥusayn as a good administrator, a *muḥiqq* (just person) who was only doing his duty when treacherously betrayed by the imam whom Ḥusayn had once favoured. He attributed Ḥusayn's military failure to the emir's inability to capture the key town of Bājil.[68]

The problem in retrospect

The best single assessment of the confused situation is in a petition drafted by Aşraf and top-ranking officials of the Hijaz dated 27 Rabīʿ al-Awwal 1264/4 March 1848. In reviewing Ottoman strategy for Yemen since Muḥammad ʿAlī had suppressed the Bilmez rebellion 15 years earlier, it stated that dividing Yemen between the imam and emir of Mocha was to ensure the stability of the *khatt* (line of communication) from the Hijaz. It was up to Ḥusayn to define clearly the area over which he held jurisdiction so as to avoid encroaching on that of the imam. However, given that he failed to do this, good government was to elude the land. The Sublime Porte in turn proceeded to appoint Ḥusayn without, as had been customary in the past, consulting the Imam of Ṣanʿā'; this was because the *vali* of the Hijaz wanted to end that custom. When Ṣanʿā' coveted Taʿizz for strategic reasons, Ḥusayn was obliged to prevent it. So the imam, who was referred to as the *mütevekkil* (deputy in charge) of Ṣanʿā', gathered a force of 7500 men and with ʿAli Ḥamīdah set out early in January 1848 to strip Ḥusayn of the lands he administered. When Ḥusayn attempted to surprise the imam's troops at Bājil, he himself was surprised. The mountain tribes in Ḥusayn's camp fled rather than fight for him. With a handful of his men Ḥusayn withdrew to Qaṭīʿ, only four hours away from Hodeida, where he held out for the next 28 days waiting for help that never arrived. Mediators arranged his surrender of the entire area between Bayt al-Faqīh and Mocha to the imam and his allies, but this area had been legally assigned to Ḥusayn to administer by provisions of an imperial decree and could not be reassigned without orders from the sultan.

Hence, the Emir of Mocha should still be considered the legal administrator of the Tihāmah. The petition praised Ḥusayn for not asking for help and expressed regret that neither the Yām tribes nor the ‘Asīris offered to rescue him. It was his nephew Ḥasan, Hodeida’s administrator, who sold the letters of credit on the customs of the port town to raise 10,000 crowns to pay for a fighting force that might rescue his uncle.

Rescuing Ḥusayn

Mahmud, *ferik* of the *nizamiye* contingent in the Hijaz, was determined that the imam should not be allowed to get away with his unprovoked attack on Ḥusayn and suggested dispatching a military expedition to punish him. The force would consist of two battalions (at the very least) each with 1000 regulars, 2000 irregulars, five artillery pieces, 1000 cavalry and 1000 *başıbozuk*s, plus all their equipment. The money would come from the treasury at Jiddah.

The division commander felt that time was of the essence if Ḥusayn was to be rescued and a possible rapprochement between the imam and himself, spelling doom for Ottoman sovereignty in Yemen, prevented. On the other hand, the imam might well succeed in exercising single-handed control over the entire land, holding Ḥusayn hostage and for ransom to the highest bidder who might attempt to resell him. All these nightmarish possibilities were contained in the information Yusuf Ağa supplied to officers of the Porte in the Hijaz.[69] The *vali*, the Emir of Mecca and his lieutenant Tevfik, with the endorsement of the sultan’s emissary Aşraf, recommended immediate action. The emir alleged that he had attempted a rescue mission via ‘Asīr, but that 15 days out of Medina a storm had blown away most of the supplies and ammunition, thus forcing him to retreat. Funds were limited, troops had not been paid for four months and morale was low. To make matters worse, they were being paid in *riyal*s at a rate of 23 *piastre*s each at a time when a *riyal* fetched up to 33 *piastre*s in the open market, so they were losing up to one-third in the value of their total pay. A petition submitted to Istanbul urged the government to send more money with Kapıcıbaşı Ibrahim Ağa, the Jiddah customs official who was then in Istanbul.

The *sadrazam* was seriously disturbed at the prospect of Yemen being lost to the Ottomans through one or other of the combatants calling on foreign help, namely the British. He also noted that there was an urgent need to bring Ottoman military contingents up to full strength in the Hijaz and to provide additional troops if an expedition were to be mounted. The Jiddah treasury, already under stress, could not meet the necessary expenses, let alone provide pay for the troops. Having consulted the *Meclis-i Hass* and *Serasker*, the *sadrazam* concluded in his *tezkere* to the sultan that responsibility for the situation in Yemen must now be shouldered in Istanbul. The documents received from the Hijaz accompanied the *sadr*'s request for permission to take up the matter with the *Meclis-i Valâ*.[70]

The *sadr* requested 4500 *kise akçe* and, once the troops were brought up to full strength, an annual expenditure of 18,000 *kise* for their pay and upkeep.[71] The sum was about 1500 *kise* lower than the amount the Hijaz had requested, but it was assumed that this was because the troops would have to go by sea to avoid being ambushed by 'Asīris on their way to the Tihāmah and the cost of sea transport would be higher.[72]

Review of Ottoman policy in Arabia

The *sadrazam* took advantage of the situation in Yemen to call for a review of Ottoman policy towards that part of the empire. The *Meclis-i Hass* endorsed an expedition to Yemen, but recommended that the Emir of Mecca lead it after being reinforced with the necessary troops and equipment. The *Meclis* also considered the situation in the Hadramawt, whose merchants, according to British complaints received in Istanbul, obeyed no rules of the sea, sailing into Red Sea ports at will. According to a report received from Isḥāq, the *naqīb* al-Ashrāf of Mecca who had been sent to investigate, the merchants of Hadramawt acted like a '*jumhūrīyah*' (*sic*) since they were only loosely governed, with the Banu Sādān (Ottoman word for *sayyids*) among them leading Ḥaḍramī traffic in trade with Red Sea ports. The al-Ḥaṣā and Qaṭīf 'ports of Najd' in the 'Bay of Basrah' (*sic*) should be placed under the *müdür* of Nejd's administration, namely Shaykh Fayṣal's, provided he behaves humanely. Good administration for 'Kuwait Bay' was considered a better alternative than having it fall into British hands.[73]

Before making a final recommendation, the *Meclis-i Valâ* wanted to deliberate further on the views of officials in the Hijaz that the ousting of Ḥusayn was proof of his lack of experience and finesse for the position to which he officially had been assigned. But his loyal services earned him good treatment and the imam's misbehaviour, chastisement.

His conduct had endangered Ottoman possessions and had risked losing the Tihāmah to the British. The *Meclis* recommended that a new map of Yemen be drawn with Aşraf and Tevfik overseeing the undertaking. Tevfik would head the expedition and the Emir of Mecca would act as supervisor. Albanian *başıbozuk*s, who were used to mountain fighting, would make up the core of the expedition and, to avoid unpredictable winds in the lower Red Sea, transport of the troops would be by steamer. If not enough steamers were available, the British consul at Alexandria could be asked to provide a few to supplement those at Jiddah. Some 5000 *akçe*s would be made available as an advance for financing the expedition and, since Ḥusayn had paid 15,000 crowns to the ʻAsīris, the region's finances would be examined with a view to making proper adjustments.

These recommendations came from a statement that Hijaz officials submitted to a meeting in Jiddah prior to Aşraf's departure. Muḥammad Ibn ʻAwn was chosen to supervise the expedition at that time because of his successful record in suppressing rebellion in Nejd. It was also decided at that meeting that someone should be put in charge of handling ʻAsīr's finances, police functions and tribal affairs; a new appointee to serve as 'Emir of Yemen' was likewise discussed. The Hijaz had fewer than 8000 troops and, for mountain fighting, Albanians (about 1000) would be best suited and they could also assist in repairing the forts of Yemen's *Hatt*. Muḥammad ʻAlī would be asked to provide troop transport since Jiddah's transport consisted of only two *şethiye*s (two- to three-mast boats of less than 100 feet).

Because the Imam of Ṣanʻā' had shed Muslim blood by attacking Ḥusayn, a secret *emirname* (royal decree) was to be issued to authorize a replacement for him as *müdür* of Ṣanʻā', with the choice being left to the commander of the expedition. On the other hand, if the imam and Ḥusayn could demonstrate they enjoyed a strong following and were willing to abide by their commitments to peace, then the commander might decide to confirm both in their respective posts. Meanwhile, engineers should be sent to establish a fort on one of the islands off Bāb al-Mandab to facilitate the transit of troops by sea. To head off problems in Hadramawt, Isḥāq Efendi would serve as emissary there. The affairs of Kuwait and neighbouring areas could be settled once those of Yemen were in order. More medals were authorized for the Emir of Mecca and his entourage by way of encouragement. The *sadr* approved these recommendations of the *Meclis* and the sultan issued the necessary decrees.[74] The only modification was a caveat stipulating that the 5000 purses authorized would come as a loan from the ministry of public works.

Tevfik Paşa, who was in the capital at the time, would carry back the decrees issued in Istanbul, with a bonus of 50,000 *piastre*s for the difficult task awaiting him. Ahmed Ağa, the treasurer of Jiddah who had escorted the *kiswah*, was awarded a personal gift of 20,000 *piastre*s.[75] The sultan also authorized a discussion with Muḥammad 'Alī about the passage of troops, clothing and equipment for them, and reimbursement of the Egyptian treasury for their cost.[76] Since it would be risky to entrust 5000 purses in gold for campaign expenses to the whims of transport, the sultan deemed it safer for a banker in Istanbul to issue a letter of credit for the amount to a correspondent in Alexandria, where the *defterdar* of Jiddah could take charge of it.[77] War tents were to be shipped to the emir and *vali*, and the third-class medal Tevfik had returned on receiving a higher one was assigned to Halim Efendi, the Emir of Mecca's scribe.[78]

While ministers of the Porte were taking measures to expedite the campaign, word reached the Emir of Mecca that Ḥusayn had been freed. His nephew Ḥasan had come to his rescue with a force of between 5000 and 8000, mostly Yām, tribesmen. When the imam was in Dhamār, two leagues away from Ṣan'ā', with 600 of his followers to negotiate a peace settlement, Ḥasan stormed the fort at Zabīd where the Dhū Ḥusayn contingent were holding his uncle and freed him. The imam immediately retreated to Ṣan'ā'.[79] His uncle Ḥasan and 'Ali ibn Mur'ī of 'Asīr converged on Mocha with 2000 men and recaptured it. Rumours reaching them suggested that the imam had also been there and that they had hoped to capture him too.

Having regained the Tihāmah and more, Ḥusayn asked the *vali* to reinstate him as governor, but the *vali* let him know that he would have to await further instructions.[80] He also wished to investigate the facts directly, so he went on by sea with 40 men to verify Ḥusayn's claim.[81]

The Sublime Porte learnt of Ḥusayn's deliverance while Tevfik was preparing to leave for Egypt to escort the *başıbozuk*s and the funds to Jiddah. An outbreak of pestilence in Alexandria had delayed their departure and he now wanted to know if it was still necessary to send an expedition to Yemen in view of Ḥusayn having regained control.[82]

The *sadrazam* waited to make a decision until he had received confirmation of the event.[83] Meanwhile, he sought advice from the *Meclis-i*

Hass, the *Meclis-i Valâ* and the *Meclis-i 'Ali Umumiye* who reviewed the reports sent by 'Abdallah (the Emir of Mecca's son who was left in charge when his father was on campaign) to Namik Paşa, *müdür* of Arabistan, and by Davud Paşa, the Shaykh of al-Ḥaram al-Nabawī (Medina). The decision reached was that since Ḥusayn and the imam could not cooperate, it was advisable to appoint an independent *vali* to govern Yemen, perhaps Davud himself. Money already delivered to Jiddah should have collateral (*bedel*). Arrangements should also be made to ensure delivery of the subsidy to 'Asīr, which Ḥusayn had cut off three years earlier.[84] The sultan concurred with their findings and recommendations.

They all agreed that Yemen was too valuable a possession to lose, mentioning every port and mountain town by name.[85] Granted, the Imam of Ṣan'ā' had once governed the whole region, but his defiance of Muḥammad 'Alī had led to the coastal towns being assigned to Sharīf Ḥusayn of Abu 'Arīsh to administer; the imam now undertook to recover these by force, which created instability and cost the treasury a great deal. İf governed properly, Yemen could yield an income of between 7000 and 8000 *kise akçe*s and the British would have no pretext for expanding their sphere of influence along the coast of Yemen. The Yemen's *qat* crop, it was suggested, could be used to pay members of the expedition.[86]

The British welcomed the decision not to appoint Ḥusayn. His hostility towards Europeans was widely known and they feared his ability to incite all tribes from south Arabia to northeast Africa against them. Appointing him ruler of Yemen under prevailing circumstances would only reinforce the notion that the sultan favoured him because of his opposition to the British and his tough stance against infidels. They would naturally have favoured the appointment of 'the lord' of Ṣan'ā' because of his vaunted title as *Sayyid al-Khilāfah* (lord of the successorship/caliphate) but they were not insisting on it. They too preferred the sultan to appoint a separate governor for Yemen.[87]

The decision to carry on with plans for the expedition was made at the urgings of the Hijaz officials. They felt a need to remind the British at Aden of Ottoman sovereignty over Yemen, particularly since Davud Paşa of Medina had stated in a communication to Istanbul that the imam had reached a secret agreement to sell Bandar 'Awn to them in return for their support. He argued that it was a known fact that they wanted Ḥusayn out. Besides, Davud was displeased about the French and British flying their flags at Jiddah, only hours away from the sacred *haram* of Islam.[88] Moreover, there was no guarantee against the British intervening should the Imam of Ṣan'ā' be defeated. It was imperative, therefore, to send Ottoman troops to assert the Ottoman presence and authority and restore confidence to the inhabitants who had endured great suffering.[89]

Tevfik agreed with the decision because, as he saw it, the imam and Ḥusayn both enjoyed equal military strength with neither being prepared to stop fighting until the other was eliminated. The inhabitants' suffering would aggravate the situation. In his opinion, the expedition should go on as planned until a suitable administrator for the whole of Yemen could be appointed.[90] Tevfik got his wish, plus 500 young *başıbozuks* to accompany him and replace older ones at Jiddah.[91]

The military expedition reached Yemen in 1849. Tevfik Kıbrıslı headed a force of 3000 men disembarking at Hodeida. Meanwhile, Ḥusayn was still exercising authority over the Tihāmah pending the announcement of new arrangements. Rumour had it that he was getting ready to expand his authority over the rest of Yemen and strengthen his hold by importing weapons and teachers from Europe. All this was despite the imam's opposition, the lack of unity among the tribes, the ambitions of dishonest relatives and mistrust of the British at Aden.[92]

Ḥusayn and his nephew Ḥasan, *kaymakam* of Hodeida, came to Hodeida to greet Tevfik and convince him that he, Ḥusayn, should be granted formal rule over Yemen through a renewed commitment to himself. But Tevfik simply read him the *emirname* that praised the family for loyal service to the sultan and ordered them back to their hometown of Abu 'Arīsh, granting them the income of the area stretching from Zuhra to Abu 'Arīsh to meet their expenses. An official directly appointed by the sultan would, he told them, govern the rest of the Tihāmah, but for the moment Tevfik would take charge of it.[93]

Meanwhile, the imam had written to Captain Haines at Aden asking for support, but got no commitment in return. So, rather than await orders from Tevfik, he decided to come to Hodeida just when Ibn 'Awn and Tevfik were issuing directives for him. The imam listened to the directives and invited Tevfik to accompany him back to Ṣan'ā' to proclaim the imperial decree defining the status of Yemen's administration. Tevfik at that time had only 2200 men at Hodeida and, while it was deemed risky for him to travel to Ṣan'ā' because the inhabitants could misconstrue it as a show of force to intimidate them, he still insisted they accompany him. In turn, 1000 warriors accompanied the imam. His strategy was to surprise the commander's troops during their first night in Ṣan'ā'. While the surprise attack inflicted casualties on the Ottoman troops and seriously wounded Tevfik, the imam's men were quickly defeated and scattered. Tevfik then formally deposed the imam and replaced him with 'Ali ibn Mahdi[94] as the official *mütevekkil* of Ṣan'ā'. Tevfik left Ṣan'ā' 25 days later after recovering some strength and returned to Hodeida exhausted with his troops.

Tevfik never recovered fully from his injuries. Ibn 'Awn returned to Mecca after replacing prevailing administrative ordinances with new ones, which, for all practical purposes, turned Yemen into a *vilayet*, thus enabling the imperial government to appoint an outsider to govern it without regard to the immediate wishes of the inhabitants.[95]

But to say that the new arrangements settled the Yemen problem is to belie events of subsequent years. The Ottomans might have brought stability to the Tihāmah, particularly after the Suez Canal was opened in 1869, which enabled them to move reinforcements all the way by sea, but in the highlands, feuds, disturbances and turmoil persisted, as evinced in the fact that nine *imams* struggled to govern the interior during the six years following Tevfik's death. It was not until the dispatch of Muhtâr Paşa in 1869 that Ottoman troops were able to assert effective control over the interior by establishing a permanent military garrison in nearly every key town and hamlet. Their mistrust of the British, however, did not diminish. Harassment through the tribes around Laḥj of the colony at Aden went on, but to no avail in the end.

In conclusion, we must question the wisdom of a policy based on Ottoman fear and suspicion of the British at Aden. Though the ensuing struggles proved costly and counter-productive, the Ottomans were in the end able to assert firmer control over Yemen by reintroducing direct rule. The British secured their grip by eliminating the menace Ḥusayn posed; and the Ottomans succeeded in preventing them from expanding their foothold. The natives for the moment lost control of their own administrative affairs and, for all practical purposes, Yemen remained a politically dishevelled entity given to feuds and rivalries with the major tribal configurations continuing their internecine struggles.

4. Ottoman Reconquest of the Tihāmah, 1849–72

Instability in Yemen and rivalries among tribal leaders and regional chiefs to assert dominion in the land obliged the Ottomans to take matters directly into their own hands. In this chapter I discuss these rivalries and their negative effect on the orderly process of governing, which impelled the Ottomans to return to the Tihāmah in 1849 after an absence of nearly two centuries. Their timing was propitious because these contending claims to the imamate had thrown the highlands into complete turmoil. A struggle had developed between Imam 'Ali ibn al-Mahdi in Ṣan'ā' and al-Manṣūr Aḥmad ibn Hāshim in Ṣa'dah, and between al-Mu'ayyad al-'Abbās ibn 'Abd al-Raḥmān, who succeeded al-Mahdi, and al-Manṣūr. The struggle was renewed, this time between Imam Aḥmad ibn Hāshim and al-Mutawakkil al-Muḥsin ibn Aḥmad who controlled al-Ahnum, generating tribal rivalries that tore apart the unity of the Yemenis and weakened their resistance to any internal force.[1] Added to this was the sectarian struggle that broke out between the Zaydis, Shāfi'is and Ismā'īlīs, which led to many disturbances and much divisiveness, with each party accusing the other of infidelity and the Zaydi imams benefiting from it to win over Yemeni tribes to their side on the grounds of defending the faith as they sought to strengthen their power base.[2]

Tiring of their own rivalries and the disturbances they generated, the claimants got together in al-Rawḍah north of Ṣan'ā' and decided to choose one of their ranks to lead. Ghālib ibn Muḥammad ibn Yaḥya, al-'Abbās ibn al-Mutawakkil Aḥmad and Aḥmad ibn 'Abdallah ibn Abu Ṭālib were among those assembled. They all agreed to support whoever was chosen. Ghālib was the one agreed upon and he took on the title of al-Hādi (Imam 1851–52). Then Aḥmad al-Ḥaymi, Imam Ghālib's vizier, manoeuvred to take control of Ṣan'ā' and this led to war between him and the imam. Even though Ghālib triumphed and the vizier agreed to submit, war was nevertheless renewed between both, which led al-Ḥaymi to call on the Ottomans, who were at this time in the Tihāmah, to help him overpower the imam. But then Ṣan'ā's inhabitants rose against al-Ḥaymi when he ordered the destruction of al-Tawāhi, one of Ṣan'ā's finest palaces, and he angered the commoners when he urged them to insult Aḥmad ibn Muḥammad al-Kibsi, one of the finest of Ṣan'ā's ulema. Forced to flee, al-Ḥaymi implored the Ottomans to come to his rescue but they did not respond to his appeal.[3]

This did not stabilize the highlands. Rivalries and disturbances continued among the Zaydi imams, between them and their deputies, with the ulema of Yemen, with the heads of tribes, as well as with those who belonged to other sects. Chaos induced the tribes to raid trade caravans, thus damaging trade, and the merchants of Yemen began to weigh the advantages of asking the Ottoman sultan to come to their rescue by stabilizing affairs and restoring order and tranquillity. They also knew that the return of the Ottomans would improve their trade, for the Ottomans would become their customers.[4]

Tired of the continuous raids and the fear they generated, the inhabitants of Ṣan'ā' yearned for security. All the imams and many ulema, notables and heads of tribes decided to call on the Ottoman sultan-caliph Abdülmecid (through the intercession of Sharīf Muḥammad Ibn 'Awn of Mecca) to come to their aid, for they knew that his troops in the Tihāmah had the means to enforce peace and security in the highlands.[5] With the country in a state of turmoil and the imams at war with each other, their unity and power broken, the Ottomans decided that the time was right to recover control of Yemen.

An expedition led by Tevfik Paşa reached Ṣan'ā' in July 1849 and was welcomed by Imam al-Mutawakkil outside the city, despite strong opposition from other members of the imam's family. Agitated by what appeared to be an act of betrayal, the inhabitants rose and killed about a hundred of the 1500 troops that had accompanied Tevfik, forcing the Ottomans to evacuate the highlands and fall back on the lowlands. 'Ali ibn al-Mahdi 'Abdallah, whom Tevfik had designated imam on 18 August 1849, led the attack, having now taken on the name of al-Hādi. Such intense family rivalry ensured that the dispute over the imamate would continue, jeopardizing peace and tranquillity.[6]

Al-Hādi soon faced considerable opposition from rival claimants to the imamate, with Ṣa'dah in the north now serving as the centre of opposition. He cruelly suppressed al-Mutwakkil ibn Muḥammad, confiscated his property and possessions on the grounds of treachery (cooperating with Ottoman authorities) and had his head cut off in prison on 11 December 1849.[7]

In the month ahead al-Hādi failed to suppress the vengeance seekers based in Ṣa'dah and the northern tribes who gathered, and in June 1850 selected another imam from the al-Qāsim house, 'Abbās ibn 'Abd al-Raḥmān, who officially called himself al-Mu'ayyad, and al-Hādi found himself deposed for the third time.[8] Turmoil did not abate and in February 1851 the inhabitants of Ṣan'ā' supported al-Hādi's return for the fourth time. Now he had to face a new rival, Ghālib ibn al-Mutawakkil Muḥammad ibn Yaḥya, whose father he had killed in prison.

So it went on until the inhabitants, exasperated by the parade of rivals, called on their elders to select a suitable leader. This they found in 1861 in Aḥmad al-Ḥaymi, whom they dubbed their *ḍaqīl*. But, as noted above, he was dismissed later for malfeasance, to be replaced by Muḥsin Mu'īd, who in 1872 came to the conclusion that it was in the highlanders' best interest to invite the Ottomans back to the highlands.

Administrative divisions

After returning to Yemen in 1849, the Ottomans reconstituted the country into a number of *sancak*s and *kaza*s headed by a native *kaymakam*, usually a *sharīf* of a leading family. They also decided to issue clear instructions to each in Arabic to avoid misunderstandings.[9] The *sancak*s figuring at this time in the administrative stabilization were Hodeida, Mocha, Luḥayyah, Abu 'Arīsh, and Ṣan'ā'. The *vilayet*'s administration was centred for the time being at Zabīd, since it was more accessible to the *vilayet* of Jiddah from where they kept abreast of developments in Yemen during the two centuries of their military absence. For the next 23 years after returning, the Ottoman *vali*s made no attempt to regain direct control of the highlands.[10]

Henceforth, the central government's policy was to pacify the country by calming tribal rivalries, suppressing resistance and marauding tribal renegades. Sadrazam Mehmed Reşid endorsed administrative measures that would reassure the chiefs and their followers, ensure stability, and enhance economic productivity to yield revenues sufficient to meet the local expenditures of administrators and the military stationed in Yemen.[11] Unfortunately, this objective was to prove difficult to attain. One of the biggest problems barring implementation of reform measures was the appointment of basically uninformed or incompetent officials to the top administrative positions. Accusations of corruption and extortion rarely died down and revolt of an exasperated Yemeni native leadership was inescapable.

Primary data taken primarily from Ottoman archival sources is used in this chapter to determine how much effort went into achieving what turned out to be the very difficult task of pacifying Yemen and improving its productivity following the return to direct Ottoman rule. It took a quarter of a century of continual effort in the face of numerous obstacles to reassert Ottoman sovereignty and effect just policies. It is necessary at this point to stress the danger of relying on unreliable data, thus wittingly or unwittingly distorting the facts about conditions and attitudes prevailing in the highlands.

English authors and travellers have put forward views based on unreliable data (perhaps from informants unfamiliar with the facts) to suggest that Ottoman misrule was at the core of the problem. In fact, instability caused by intense rivalry over the imamate had a lot more to do with the lack of administrative stability than wilful mismanagement through the officials' alleged greed.[12] More importantly, both in the Tihāmah and the highlands the Ottomans delegated authority to local chiefs who commanded some following and respect. If mismanagement ensued, it was due less to the wilful misconduct of Ottoman-appointed high functionaries than to the administrative misconduct of native administrators. The Ottomans' inability to marshal the large number of regular troops to police the mountainous regions and to check the encroachment of marauding tribesmen compounded the situation.

Imam Muḥammad ibn Yaḥya had signed an agreement with Tevfik in 1849 to acknowledge Ottoman sovereignty. He governed the highlands, received half the revenues and agreed to garrison 1000 Ottoman troops in Ṣan'ā'. Being unable to implant themselves firmly there, the Ottoman authorities in the lowlands (Tihāmah) tended to rely on the advice of Sharīf Ḥusayn of Abu 'Arīsh, whom the Ottomans had appointed governor *ad interim* of the Tihāmah following the departure of the Egyptians.

When Tevfik died from wounds shortly after his campaign in the highlands, the government appointed Mustafa Sabri Paşa as a replacement and the sultan issued him a *ferman* to that effect. Another imperial *ferman* designated 'Abdallah *sharīf* of Yemen with responsibility to safeguard the interests of the other *sharīf*s and tribes in his district, and to ensure their wellbeing in keeping with the imperial will.[13] He wrote to Sabri acknowledging his appointment as *vali* and assured him that his sole aim at present was to enforce justice and improve the lot of subjects as decreed by the *sharīḑah* and the lord of messengers (Prophet Muḥammad). He assured the *vali* that the Arabian tribes of Bakīl and Ḥāshid, east and west, those whose hearts were to be reconciled, those in need, and the *sayyid*s and *sharīf*s were dependent on the largess of his government.[14]

Valiship of Mustafa Sabri

Shortly after arriving in Hodeida to take up his *vali*ship, Mustafa Sabri ordered 'Abdallah ibn Sharaf, *kaymakam* of Mocha *sancak*, to meet him and the tribal chiefs of the *kaza* in Mocha. 'Abdallah at that time was engaged in putting down the rebellion of a number of tribal chiefs in his district. Three to five had been killed in a rising at the time. 'Abdallah was in Hodeida when the disturbance took place and he hastened back to Mocha to put down the rebellion, seizing about twenty leaders and imprisoning them. The cattle and sheep they had usurped were retrieved and matters quietened. A month and a half after arriving in Hodeida, which was to be Sabri's seat of administration, he issued directives to tribal chiefs to control disturbances in their districts and maintain order. Abkar Sharaf, the tribal chief of the mountainous area of Sānif, was well fortified and hard to dislodge even with troops organized for mountain combat; the fighting power available was not enough, and to take him dead or alive was not the answer. Sabri captured 100 rebels in the areas past Qanṭarat Shuhayr and brought them to Hodeida. He got another force ready and was heading for Bājil when he became ill because of bad weather and unsuitable clothing. He was bedridden for three to four days before passing away on Saturday 23 Ra 1267/26 January 1851. Tranquillity prevailed soon after and 'Abdallah suggested it would be useless to storm the mountain forts, recommending rather that both regular and irregular troops be used for policing purposes. After burying Sabri, 'Abdallah headed back to Mocha to ensure the collection of the *miri* taxes due to the state. The *sancak* of Mocha included the *kaza*s of Zabīd, Bayt al-Faqīh and Hays.[15]

Sabri realized from the start that he commanded insufficient troops to pacify both the lowlands and highlands of Yemen. He dispatched requests for an increase of his military force and its firing power. After consulting the relevant government departments, Sadrazam Mehmed Reşid Paşa endorsed the need for an additional battalion of regulars (*nizamiye*) organized from troops stationed in Iraq and Hijaz and 1500 irregulars (*başıbozuk*s) organized from local tribesmen. The imperial *tophane* (artillery depot) would provide 16 artillery pieces, including four mountain howitzers, shells, ordnance, draft animals to pull them, and all necessary supporting materials.[16] But after extensive enquiry, the government learned that the personnel available from Rumeli numbered only 600 *nizamiye* and the *tophane* was prepared to spare only four howitzers of the 16 artillery pieces requested, but no gunners, provided the treasury reimbursed it because its budget could not meet the demand. It was suggested that gunners for the howitzers be dispersed from the Arabistan army. Jiddah, as reported by its chief of ordnance, could spare neither gunners nor artillery, let alone combat troops. After a series of exchanges between the *serasker* and various ministers of the *maliye*, *tophane*, *dahiliye* and *sadaret*, the *Meclis-i Valâ* took note of Vali Sabri's request and of the government's endorsement of it, but made only contingent approval pending completion of recruitment for the army of Arabistan's 15 battalions of regulars and increasing *başıbozuk* enlistment. Only after this was done could the *vali*'s request be met. Meanwhile, only four mountain howitzers were deemed sufficient for his needs, which the *tophane* was ready to provide, but the gunners would have to be transferred out of the Arabistan army and its commander was to be so informed. Since the army was deemed to have greater need, the Jiddah *vali*'s military chief, Osman Ağa, was expected to provide the balance of the 600 *nizamiye* to fill a battalion and provide for 2000 *başıbozuk*s.[17]

Although prepared to answer force with force, Sabri decided it was prudent first to pursue a policy of conciliation towards obstinate chiefs. He recommended to the *sadaret* that allowances and gifts be authorized to them on the grounds of need or reconciliation, even though there was no precedent for it, and the *vali* of Jiddah endorsed his request. After consulting on how it was done in Jiddah, both the *maliye* (central treasury) and *Meclis-i Ahkâm-i Adliye* (council of justice) supported the recommendation to make gifts to the tribes and *shaykh*s as part of the effort to pacify them, and the *sadrazam* approved it with the proviso that the *defterdar* at Jiddah keep a record of the amounts expended.[18] The amount requested was 9826 *piastre*s for the fiscal year 1266/1849 and four military cloaks.

Qaşīm ibn Ḥasan was ordered to assemble the heads and chiefs of that *sancak* in Ta'izz; but he came instead accompanied by 20 to 30 *shaykh*s and *vaqīl*s (lawyers) and 200 Arab soldiers to a hospitality house in an area near Bayt al-Faqīh. Sabri was travelling via Bājil to meet Shaykh Qaşīm to discuss a subsistence allowance (*maaş*) with him and his men, but he died when he was still six hours from Bājil. *Başıbozuk*s who accompanied him stayed behind to police the area. Shaykh Qaşīm accompanied the body back to Hodeida for burial.[19]

Mehmed Sırrı's tenure

Mehmed Sırrı, who had been serving as *defterdar* (financial administrator) of Yemen, took charge and the notables accepted him pending fresh instructions from Istanbul. Sadrazam Mehmed Reşid recommended his appointment to the sultan and it was approved. The sultan also suggested that the *Meclis-i Valâ* should decide on his *maaş* and replacement as financial administrator. The *vali* and *sharīf* of Mecca were to work closely with Sırrı and provide him with proper guidance in fulfilling the mandate he inherited from Sabri.[20] The expedition to Ta'izz had for an aim detaining Qaşīm and holding him as surety (*rahīn*), but the troops involved, few in number, did not follow Sırrı's instructions.

Keeping Qaşīm in place was deemed wiser than holding him hostage. Besides, Qaşīm had demonstrated his sincerity when he wrote to 'Abdallah stressing his loyalty to the Ottoman state and declaring that if, as previously stated, his intention was to move to Ta'izz without risk of loss, this was the propitious time for it. He already had the assurance of support from a number of *shaykh*s who were all pleased with 'Abdallah as their functionary.

Qaşīm argued that it was safe to make the move, for a number of troublemaking *shaykh*s had been incarcerated and the Dhu Muḥammad had rallied their followers and were prepared to meet ibn al-Mahdi, who had left Ṣan'ā' for Yarīm with only eight days of supplies, to take on the son of Yaḥya 'Iyād and ibn Faḍl. 'The land is free ... opponents are in hand,' he argued, 'and those accompanying 'Ali ibn al-Mahdi al-Khawlāni have dispatched a letter of their *ḍuqqāl* to you and another to me after I had written to them when I left you, all affirming their satisfaction with you.'[21]

'Abdallah thought it inadvisable to make such a move until the sultan's government had met its financial commitments to the *shaykhs* loyal to their cause. He advised Sırrı to pay a living stipend to Qaşīm and his soldiers to sustain his loyalty and wait for new directives. The Ta'izz region, he argued, was mountainous, requiring a minimum of 1500 foot and 200 mounted *başıbozuk* and 4000 to 5000 *riyals* to keep them under control. 'If Qaşīm does not stay in place', warned 'Abdallah, 'the Imam of Ṣan'ā' will control Ta'izz through a *naqīb* [warden] and its defence towers would not be easy to destroy.'[22]

Both Sabri and Sırrı had submitted reports on prevailing conditions in the country with recommendations on how to improve them in accordance with imperial instructions to pacify Yemen and improve its productivity. In keeping with ancient customs, Sırrı suggested taking hostages from untrustworthy Bājil, Kuhaylah and 'Adwān tribes. He also recommended levying customary taxes like *zakah* on the various products the 'Ubūsi tribe had hitherto escaped paying for on the route to Jiddah.[23] The main item on the agenda of reform was to appease the tribes and their chiefs and provide for security by stationing troops in the towers in return for guarantees. Sabri went to Zabīd with some troops to investigate local arrangements for securing the Yemen line. Sabri was sceptical about Ṣa'dah's chief of chiefs Sayyid Aḥmad ibn Hāshim seizing Ṣan'ā' purportedly to restore the rule of law throughout the highlands in the name of Ottoman authorities and to safeguard the trade of its merchants, suspecting rather that he entertained ambitions of his own in doing so.[24]

In another report, Sabri had named the tribes in revolt and had specified which ones he believed could be won over. He admitted that since assuming responsibility for governing Yemen he had been unable to impose peace because of the defiance of the chiefs of the Bājil, Kuhaylah, 'Adwān and 'Ubūsi tribes whose tyrannical acts first had to be curbed. When he went to Hodeida to talk to these chiefs and ask them to desist, only three agreed to maintain peace and security and protect the inhabitants of their districts. In keeping with an old Arab custom, he asked them for hostages to ensure their obedience. He asked the 'Ubūsi chief, who had numerous followers and whose tribe controlled a mountainous area overlooking the strategic *Hatt-i Yemen*, to hand control of the towers over to the Ottoman troops. The *shaykh*, whom Sabri regarded as no more than a highwayman, refused on three different occasions, so he was left with no alternative but to use force against him. However, between cavalry and *başıbozuks*, he had only

1500 men. He hoped to recruit 1000 Arab fighters and, with two artillery pieces, dispatch his *kethüda*, Mehmed Naci Efendi, to defiant villages and tribes to give them one last chance to surrender hostages and stop marauding.

Sabri, on the other hand, was at a loss to respond to requests from 'Udayn and Shar'ab chiefs to provide a policing force. Similar requests came from Ṣan'ā' and Ta'izz. With authorization from the *serasker*, Sabri put a force together, appointed Mustafa Paşa *kaymakam ad interim* of Hodeida then, in keeping with his instructions, set out to dissuade the defiant *shaykh*s to pacify the tribes by peaceful means and gain their loyalty without recourse to force and intimidation.[25]

A battalion of *nizamiye* led by Sabri Paşa and accompanied by *başıbozuk*s and recruits from Yām set out from Hodeida to Zabīd and the Raymah mountain area to talk to Arab chiefs and give them assurances. The holdout at al-Luḥayyah was ended and the rebels on the island of Kamarān were subdued; taxes of 5000–6000 *riyal*s were to be levied on new production. Given that the populace had proffered its obedience, it was deemed better policy to govern through the chiefs than directly, both in the Tihāmah and the highlands. That there was confidence in this policy working can be determined from the number of troops the Ottomans planned to station there.[26]

Mehmed Reşid Paşa, the *sadrazam*, approved recommendations for enforcing stability and security as Sabri proposed.[27] Not all chiefs, however, had submitted and force was sent to subdue the Matāwifah who resided in the area of Jabal Maqṣa', not far from Zabīd, and were plundering travellers and merchants by their command of the roads from their fortified mountaintop.[28]

While on his way with *nizamiye* to Zabīd and Bayt al-Faqīh on 25 M 1267/30 November 1850, Mehmed Sırrı affirmed that he would enforce imperial directives to quiet the tribes by appeasement to ensure better administration, thus abiding by the instructions that Mustafa Sabri had received.[29]

Sırrı's list for administrative improvements

In his petition to the *sadaret,* Sırrı asked for more troops and funds to meet the crisis the tribal activities posed.[30] The *sadrazam* forwarded the *vali*'s recommendations for improving Yemen's administration to the sultan for consideration.[31] The sultan authorized the *kapudan paşa* (his brother-in-law Halil) to send his *yavur kaymakam* (aid deputy) Ismet Beg to Mocha with the requested instructions. These reaffirmed those that his predecessor had issued, namely first to control the tribes, which he substantially did, and next to secure the country's stability so that its productivity and industry could develop and expand. Other desiderata included controlling production, expanding trade and ensuring the flow of information on progress being made by keeping good records. At the first hint of trouble, it would be advisable, he suggested, to bring in the tribal chiefs to reassure them that their positions and abodes were secure. All necessary, fair and acceptable steps were to be taken to head off discontent, or to contain it.

Having delivered these instructions, Ismet was to cross the Red Sea from Mocha to Massawa to ask Mirliva Mehmed Paşa to explain why the Ethiopian coast and isles were being badly administered, to examine prevailing conditions and enquire about the general health and morale of the troops and their commanders, and to establish the status of the forts and castles, emphasizing steps to improve them as needed.[32]

The first of two matters brought to the imperial government's attention at this time related to the discovery of good quality coal at Ḥaddādīn, on the Ta'izz–Aden road, which Sabri had recommended be mined by authorizing the Ta'izz administration under Qaşīm ibn Ḥasan, *kaymakam* of the *sancak*, to extract it.[33] The second was a more delicate one because it involved expenditures from an already strained budget.

When Sinan Paşa launched the second expedition to recover Yemen from its rebellious imams in 1569–70,[34] he had made promises to loyal chiefs whose support or neutralization he badly needed. He forgave Sayyid Ḥasan ibn Muḥammad 'Aṭṭār for failing to pay the *vergi rüsumet* (taxes, charges, customs) of his district. Now, almost 300 years later, one of his descendants, Sayyid Sulayman Quraysh, produced the *senet* (note) and asked for it to be renewed, which the sultan's government agreed to do.[35]

To keep Ḥasan and 'Ali in check it was now important to reinforce Ḥaydar's authority. Ḥaydar had been appeased with a robe of honour, but he now wanted administrative control of the fort at Jāzān, which the imperial government had abandoned and which overlooked the sea outlet of Abu 'Arīsh. He would keep a record of expenses and tighten his administrative control if he could have the fort, 20 soldiers to man it, two artillery experts and one customs official, a secretary and sufficient supplies to maintain it.[36] Boosting the morale of military commanders by acknowledging their services was endorsed by the imperial government acting on the recommendations of Sırrı, who obtained the rank of *sarsevari* (head of cavalry) for both Behram Ağa and Süleiman Ağa with a fourth degree imperial *hocalik* (master) medal.[37]

Safeguarding the ports

Maintaining the ports for quick access to the sea was a cause for concern. That of Qaşīm Paşa was in a serious state of disrepair and reconstruction of its dock was deemed urgent.[38] Another problem Sırrı faced was untoward activity at the port of Zayla‘ in Yemen. The British, the *vali* reported, had unloaded 10,000 muskets and 15 artillery pieces with large quantities of ammunition, which they claimed were destined for Ethiopia. With the situation in the Ottoman Empire's Ethiopian holdings far from stable and suspicious of their motives, the Sublime Porte ordered an enquiry into the matter. A lengthy report from Massawa's leading notables and merchants spoke of misadministration and insecurity on all sides. The former *naip* (deputy) Ḥasan ibn Idris had plundered the inhabitants and stripped them of their wealth. Complaints to the Mirliva Paşa of the *bandar* (Massawa) or *muḥāfiz* of the province about the *naip* confiscating more than 700 of their cattle and slaughtering them for his entourage and troops went unheeded, as did complaints about the inhabitants and merchants being deprived of their goods through highway robberies.[39]

The *kaymakam* of Zayla‘ reported that the port was far from Ethiopia, thus intensifying Ottoman suspicions and, given that there were many wild tribes in between, official alarm. The *vali* reported further that in the days of Izzet Paşa's governorship over Massawa, a British ship had unloaded 16 cases of muskets, artillery and a variety of assault weapons and that they and the French had proceeded next to set up quarters on an island off Massawa, the seat of the Ottoman administration of the region. Complaints to the *vali* of Jiddah were forwarded to Istanbul and an investigating official was sent out, but no further action was taken.[40]

The *sadaret* was unable to produce a record of Kaymakam Ibrahim of Massawa's alarming report to the *vali* of Jiddah. The latter had in turn forwarded it to the *vali* of Yemen and now demanded to know what had happened to it. The unloading of war materials at Zayla‘ was condemned and the slowness in dispatching supplies and ammunition to the army in Yemen was equally condemned.

Meeting financial obligations

How to handle financial commitments was equally worrying. The treasury had allocated 1000 *riyal*s a month to the *shaykh mashāyikh* (chief of chiefs) of Bājil for administering the area and for his loyal and good service, but the *gümrük* (customs duty) on *qat* was unaccounted for; the salt mine had been neglected when it needed to generate revenue; other financial matters were still unsettled yet no commitment was to be made before a full accounting was in the imperial government's hands. The *shaykh* of Bājil was to receive compensation as promised and the welfare of the troops was not to be neglected by order of the *sadrazam*, who also once again was ready to overlook the sins of Sharīf Ḥasan and to authorize him *aman* (safety).[41] With respect to the military, the *sadrazam* wanted the *seraskeriyet* (central military headquarters in Istanbul) to act on the request of Sa'dallah Beg, the *kaymakam* of the imperial troops in Yemen, to increase their numbers.[42]

Supplies and pay for troops, however, were hard to come by and *Vali* Sırrı was at a loss to meet the needs of his *vilayet.* Some 20,000 *erdeb*[43] of grain had been allocated from Egypt for the year 1268 but did not arrive. He was willing to take half in kind and half in *bedel.*[44]

The wise steps taken by Mocha's *kaymakam*, 'Abdallah ibn Sharaf, who without enough troops was still able to stabilize the *Hatt-i Yemen* for the time being with his underpaid *başıbozuk*s and to ensure stability and productivity, temporarily smoothed matters over.[45] The *shaykh mashāyikh* of Ta'izz *sancak*, Qaşīm ibn Ḥasan[46] wanted 1200 troops, an artillery piece, some *akçe*[47] and a *hilat* (robe of honour) in return for pacifying his district without war or cost. Sırrı believed the demands were reasonable and would endorse them if the sultan's government judged them in the Ottoman interest. Sırrı saw the logic of meeting this request given that he had only a handful of cavalry and foot to spare, acknowledging the letters of Khawlān chiefs in support of Qaşīm who, if reinforced, would better ensure security in the Ta'izz *sancak.*[48]

Turbulence in 'Asīr

Bad administration was not only Yemen's misfortune. Reports from the *vali* of Jiddah indicated that 'Asīris too had been unaccustomed to good government. The rugged land they inhabited did not induce them to obey administrative directives. They had been attacking Hijazi villages, pilgrims and Qunfidhah itself for two years. Kaymakam 'Ā'iḍ sought to assuage the *vali* by claiming that only a handful of chiefs was involved in the raids, which took place only after Sharīf Ḥusayn had been dismissed and his *maaş*, as well as the subsidy of 5000 to 6000 *riyal*s paid annually to the 'Asīris, had been stopped.[49] Abdülaziz Ağah, *vali* of Jiddah, told the Ottoman government that much expenditure and more troops than were available would be required to suppress them.[50] Both the *sadrazam* and sultan responded positively to his asserted need, but the fulfilment was slow in coming because they preferred the *vali* first to undertake a policy of gaining their loyalty by peaceful means.[51]

Bitter feelings had lingered since the oppression imposed by Sharīf Ḥasan (of Abu 'Arīsh) after Sharif Ḥaydar replaced his brother Ḥusayn, who lacked the military means to impose order, as *kaymakam* of Abu 'Arīsh.[52] The *vali*'s report was forwarded to the *Meclis-i Valâ* for authorization to take action on a list of requests submitted by Mustafa Paşa who, on completing his investigation, concluded that more troops and war materials were needed.[53] Arab tribes were not easily intimidated, he argued, suggesting that a battalion of regulars would be needed at Hodeida to ensure trade, to protect sea traffic and to assure the inhabitants. He recommended the same for Mocha, as well as rebuilding its fort, towers and police facility to encourage merchants and the inhabitants to return. With their return he aimed to ensure the collection of customs duties and other revenues to prevent the port of Ṣan'ā'–Ta'izz–'Udayn being lost to the British at Aden for interior trade. Inhabitants needed to be assured and merchants protected, he argued, hence the need to station a battalion at Mocha.[54]

Rivalries in Abu 'Arīsh and Sırrı's mishandling of them

The situation in the Tihāmah was far from stable. Ḥusayn ibn Muḥammad was fighting with his paternal cousin al-Ḥasan ibn al-Ḥusayn for control of Abu 'Arīsh and this split the inhabitants of that city, which served as the capital of the Mikhlāf al-Sulaymāni, into two rival camps. Al-Ḥasan barricaded himself in the palace of Najrān and began to fire cannon shots at his rival who was barricaded in the al-Shāmikh palace. The shots often landed in the city and killed many innocent people. Ḥusayn managed in the end to have his rival and cousin assassinated, and he alone now ruled the Mikhlāf while the Ottomans were busy strengthening their influence in the Tihāmah.

With Ḥusayn's rule no better than that of his predecessor, peace and stability disappeared. The inhabitants called on the Ottomans to rescue them from Ḥusayn's brutal rule, but nobody wanted to confront him; they knew they would lose.[55] His brutality continued and matters got worse, obliging the head of the city, Ḥasan al-Ḥamzi, to invite Muḥammad ibn 'Ā'id, the emir of 'Asīr, to come to their aid after promising him the support of its inhabitants. The invitation pleased the emir because he entertained ambitions both to dominate the Mikhlāf and expel the Ottomans.

The emir succeeded in ridding Abu 'Arīsh of the troublesome Ḥusayn who had to flee for his life in 1863. The 'Asīris' victory in the Mikhlāf seemed to encourage a rising against the Ottomans in the Tihāmah. Pressures mounted until the *mutasarrif* of Hodeida, 'Ali Yavur Paşa, was forced to seek the aid of Izzet Hakkı Paşa, the then governor of Hijaz. The arrival of fresh Ottoman forces from Jiddah obliged the 'Asīris to withdraw from Hodeida and to fortify themselves in their mountain strongholds.

It became evident soon after he took charge following Sabri's untimely death that Sırrı was not up to handling delicate administrative matters with tact and fairness. He made decisions that worked against what the sultan's government hoped to accomplish in pacifying some tribes and leaders. Before he died while on his way to Abu 'Arīsh with 500 Yām recruits, Sabri had appointed Ḥasan to replace Ḥusayn as *kaymakam*, but Sırrı deposed him and appointed Sharīf Ḥaydar in his place. He also spent funds allocated to Ḥasan and used foul language on him and his followers at a time when the *Hatt-i Yemen* appeared quiet.[56] 'Abdallah of Mocha further reported that, on Sabri's death, Sırrı had deposed the *kaza müdürü* (district administrator), *gümrükcü* (customs official) and other officials, including the administrator of Mocha whom Sabri had appointed, and replaced them with his own men. His conduct was unbecoming a high official charged with implementing sound administrative policies when the country was badly in need of stabilization.[57] 'Abdallah deemed it necessary to report such conduct to Abdülaziz Ağah, *vali* of Jiddah.

Meanwhile, Sırrı was locked in battle with Sharīf Ḥasan who, with his brother 'Ali and 7000 Yām followers, had again attacked and temporarily occupied the fort at al-Luḥayyah. A battalion and company of regulars supported by *başıbozuk*s and artillery, with Cretan Ḥasan Ağa (chief of the foot) and Yusuf Ağa (chief of the mounted force), beat the assailants at Zaydīyah and inflicted on the Yām one of their worst defeats in more than 150 years. Some 380 Christians of Najrān, who were in the fort, helped chase and cut down the Yām rascals.[58] Mustafa Beg, *kaymakam* of al-Luḥayyah, reported details of the decisive defeat inflicted on Sharīf Ḥasan and his followers to Abdülaziz Ağah, *vali* of Jiddah, with an account of the booty gained in ammunition, supplies and other material, together with a list of possessions confiscated from Ḥasan for the benefit of the imperial army. He was confident now that the *Hatt-i Yemen* was secure at last. The *vali* in turn reported the news to the *sadaret* with an assurance that he had dispatched 150 tons of wheat, barley and other supplies to Yemen.[59]

Sharīf Ḥasan was determined, by force if necessary, to recover the administration of Abu 'Arīsh over which Sabri had appointed him *ad interim kaymakam*. Sırrı had deposed him and made Ḥaydar *kaymakam* instead. Indeed, Sharīf Ḥasan and his brother 'Ali had at no time ceased to plot with the 'Asīris, even after being pardoned and allowed to settle down in Abu 'Arīsh to recover administrative control of the Tihāmah. The plot involved seizing the Tihāmah in a joint undertaking after the 'Īd al-Aḍḥa. Sırrı sent an urgent message to the *vali* of Jiddah to dispatch two companies of regulars and one of the six imperial battalions stationed at Mecca for a total of six *nizamiye* companies together with all necessary supplies. Meanwhile, Sharīf Ḥasan was imprisoned in the fort.[60] With the sultan's approval, the imperial government authorized Jiddah's *vali* to dispatch the military units and supplies requested.[61]

Ḥasan and his brother 'Ali put together a force of Yām tribesmen and began to plunder the neighbouring areas' cattle, camels and possessions, ignoring all letters and appeals from officials to desist. Exiled Ḥusayn's son Muḥammad came by sea to the *kaymakam* of Luḥayyah, Mustafa Beg, for help. The problem was further aggravated by Sırrı not honouring a *buyrultu* (official order) his predecessor had issued to the Yām committing them to pay a subsistence allowance of 10,000 *riyal*s, half of which would have derived from money committed to Abu 'Arīsh and the other half from income allocated to Luḥayyah. The military expedition against the rebels ended in decisive defeat, with 70 Yām fighters killed, most of their equipment and supplies captured and Ḥasan fleeing to the hills above Abu 'Arīsh.[62] Sırrı appreciated more than ever the need to pay a subsistence allowance to loyal Yām fighters in Ottoman service and, with the support of Jiddah's Ağah Paşa, recommended this to Istanbul for approval, which was especially necessary given the shortage of regular troops to put in Yemen's service. Jabal al-Nishim's Yām *shaykh* based his argument on the fact that they had previously received such *maaş* from Tihāmah's revenues, which the *sharīfs* of Abu 'Arīsh delivered and that policy was continued during the brief tenure of Muḥammad Ibn 'Awn, as well as by the *valis*.

Sabri had started discussing his and his follower's *maaş* with the *shaykh*, but talks were suspended when he died and Ḥaydar took over. They could not afford to wait until Sharīf Ḥusayn was, if ever, reinstated, so Ḥaydar, his replacement, urged an immediate response.[63] Sırrı warned Istanbul that the *shaykh* was well placed to stir up trouble for Ottomans, both openly and secretly, unless his *maaş* were paid.[64]

This was not his only problem. His attempts to diffuse the situation at Abu 'Arīsh were not a complete success because he still could not count on Sharīf Ḥasan to desist, despite his having given him and his brother 'Ali a written pledge of security. Sırrı reported that Ḥasan and 10,000 warriors had threatened Ḥaydar the year before. He pitted the Yām against him and 1600 died in their failed attack. Next, as revenge, he threatened to call in 10,000 'Asīri warriors under Shaykh 'Ā'id, but Ottoman troops responded and they were forced to retreat. Having been foiled twice, Ḥasan returned to Abu 'Arīsh to seek *aman* (shelter).

On the *Valâ*'s recommendation, the *maliye naziri* (supervisor of finance) sent a report to the sultan about the urgent need for forts in Yemen and for imperial troops (a company of *nizamiye* artillerymen) to man and safeguard them. The troops were to be supplied with summer and winter uniforms and given subsistence allowances amounting in all to 5192 *piastres* and seven *paras*. The imperial treasury was requested to compensate the *nizamiye*'s treasury for paying it out.[65]

The *Meclis-i Valâ* had been deliberating for months over how to boost troops and revenue to meet local expenses. Qaşīm of Ta'izz had been tactless in dealing with his district; security on the Aden to Mocha route needed reinforcing because, as matters stood, merchants were often in danger. They asked for two additional *nizamiye* companies, one from Egypt and one from Jiddah, with a transfer of their salaries and allowances. They also asked for 600 *kises* of funds to be transferred from Jiddah's to Yemen's treasury, as a loan to be repaid when its revenues improved and with the imperial treasury meeting the difference. A number of camels, one per five to ten soldiers, were also to be procured from Egypt. In addition, both Jiddah and Egypt were to supply 1450 *erdeb* of grain, with Egypt supplying an additional 500 *erdeb* of fava beans during the 1270 fiscal year.[66] The urgent request for action had been dispatched with Kaymakam Şemsi Efendi, and the *Meclis-i Husūsî* of the *sadaret* forwarded it on to the *Valâ* for determination.[67]

The Vali of Egypt's involvement

The rebels, however, did not give up. They remained fortified in a number of spots along the coast, so could interfere with commercial ships passing by the 'Asīri coastline. This in turn compelled Izzet Hakkı, the *vali*, and Sharīf 'Abdallah, the ruler of Mecca, to launch an expedition to stop their piracy. But the two could not cooperate and friction between them enabled the rebels to continue their actions unchecked. Indeed, it was rumoured that 'Abdallah was secretly instigating the 'Asīris to end Ottoman rule in their region. The Sublime Porte called on Egypt for help and Khedive Ismā'īl saw a chance to better his position, as a quid pro quo, by having the sultan authorize the succession to rule in Egypt in Ismā'īl's own immediate descendants. An expedition of 5444 foot and *başıbozuk* cavalry was organized and left Suez for Yemen on 3 June 1864. The khedive had to honour an 1841 agreement between his grandfather and the Ottomans that decreed that the Egyptian army was, if called upon, to cooperate with the Ottomans. The khedive, however, was not eager to do battle, remembering only too well how his grandfather, Muḥammad 'Alī, had done the Ottomans' bidding in Arabia against the Wahhābis in the earlier decade of the century only to gain nothing in the end. Ismā'īl now preferred to use diplomacy to reconcile the two sides without the need to shed blood to end the 'Asīri intervention in the Tihāmah.

Meanwhile, Sharīf 'Abdallah mobilized a force of 2500 foot and *başıbozuk* cavalry and left the Hijaz on 12 August 1864 for Yemen by land. The combined Meccan, Egyptian and Ottoman forces the *sharīf* and his brother led totalled 8500, while the Egyptian unit Ismail Sadik Beg led totalled 4200. The 'Asīri rebels faced this combined force with 20,000 fighting men and 40 cannons, against their opponents' eight and were, besides, well fortified in their mountain strongholds. So the *sharīf* decided not to engage them. Ismail had also informed his commander not to engage the 'Asīris if the danger was too great and prospects of losses high.[68] The Sublime Porte insisted that the Egyptian force remain at the port of Qunfidhah until the situation stabilized even though the emir of 'Asīr had indicated his readiness for peace. This did not go down well with the khedive, for expenses to date had exceeded 40,000 *kise* (200,000 Egyptian pounds).[69] After two years of not engaging the emir of 'Asīr in battle, the regular and irregular Egyptian forces were withdrawn from the Hijaz and north Yemen in January 1866.

The Sublime Porte, khedive and *sharīf* exchanged thank you notes and congratulations for ending the confrontation with Muḥammad Ibn 'Ā'id.[70] The khedive thanked Muḥammad for his cooperation and sent him gifts — an Egyptian-made golden rifle, a large fully-equipped tent and a pair of handguns. The khedive was eager to foster good relations with all men of influence in the Hijaz and Yemen.[71] A year later, however, he had to warn the emir against launching attacks on the *vilayet* of Hijaz and the Tihāmah, as he had been contemplating doing once again. He informed his *kapukehya*, representative before the Sublime Porte, that he intended to contribute to the stability of that region in the best interests of both Egypt and the Ottomans. But this did not last long, for in 1871, during Abdülaziz's sultanate, he once again invaded the Mikhlāf al-Sulaymāni and the Tihāmah with the intention of subjecting that region to his rule and chasing the Ottomans out. His forces reached Zabīd and Mocha in the south, forcing the evacuation of Ottoman troops by sea to Hodeida. The Ottoman commander, 'Ali Paşa al-Ḥalabi, engaged his forces and he suffered devastating losses, especially at al-Zaydīyah as they were withdrawing to 'Asīr.[72]

Ottoman reinforcements end 'Asīri invasion

When the sultan's government learned of the 'Asīri invasion, a decision was taken to end once and for all Muḥammad's marauding activities. Mehmed Redif Paşa was put in charge of a large force of more than 6000 soldiers, which, equipped with cannons suitable for mountain bombardment, landed at Qunfidhah in late 1871. Egypt responded by sending 500 tons of rice, 50 tons of cooking butter, 25 tons of sugar and other foodstuffs to the Ottoman expeditionary force. Half was to be shipped to Hodeida and the rest to wherever Redif Paşa ordered it.[73]

Ottoman forces attacked the emir's strongholds. With Redif leading a unit from the west and Ahmed Muhtâr Paşa a force from the east, they caught him in a vice and, after laying siege to his very own place of refuge, obliged him to surrender after an intense five-day battle during which tribal followers like Rijāl al-Ma' and al-Mafraḥ had given up. Muhtâr Paşa gave them assurances of safety in return for submission and cessation of all hostile acts against the Ottomans.[74] Muḥammad Ibn ʻAwn, whom the Ottomans had appointed Sharīf of Mecca in 1856, allowed the emir of ʻAsīr to keep his possessions, forts and horses and receive a living stipend for himself and his family from the Ottomans as well as appointments to high official positions for deserving chiefs. In return, the sultan insisted the emir turn over to the Ottoman commander in Yemen what he had usurped from that *vilayet*. He agreed to the terms of the *ferman* and surrendered to Muhtâr Paşa, who had laid siege to his palace, what was demanded of him.[75] When he and his chiefs had surrendered, Redif violated the *ferman*'s terms by executing the emir and 35 of his chiefs from the tribes that supported him in April 1872. When word of this violation reached Istanbul, the angered sultan had Redif stripped of his command, which was then handed to Muhtâr Paşa.[76]

The Ottomans attached the Mikhlāf al-Sulaymāni and ʻAsīr to the area under their control and confiscated all the emir's horses, weapons, money, cannons and precious stones.[77] This quietened the land for a while, though the peace did not last as long as the one the Egyptians managed to achieve in the 1840s during Muḥammad ʻAlī's reign. The inhabitants were simply awaiting an opportunity to renew their efforts to end Ottoman domination in the lowlands; but in the meantime, the pacification and stabilization of the Tihāmah paved the way for the Ottomans to regain control of the highlands of Yemen, which they achieved in 1872.

On the positive side, Sırrı argued that Sabri had agreed to pay the chief of the Yām *maaş* in return for supplying fighting men as needed. ʻAsīri tribes, he argued, were in turmoil and the Yām, who had been loyal to Sharīf Ḥasan, were their neighbours. Their service was needed to pursue the peace the central government enjoined. 'We need also', he continued, 'support from the Dhu Muḥammad, Banu Ḥāshid, and Dhū Ḥusayn, because if an uprising takes place, we would not be able to put it down with the troops at our disposal.'[78] The sultan's government was not prepared to incur the expense of dispatching 1000 troops without ensuring that they could be met from the 1267 revenues (of Yemen).[79]

Reporting on the true revenues and expenses as per instructions from Istanbul and records kept by Kapıcı Süleiman Beg, who served as Sabri's treasurer, and Hakkı Beg, who served a few years later as *mal müdürü* (financial administrator) of both Hodeida and Mocha, and whose integrity was never questioned, Ağah Pasha of Jiddah put the net figure at 4000 *kise*,[80] after 100,000 *piastre*s had been paid out to the poor and needy. Süleiman alleged that Sabri was unaware of the cruelty and extortionist policy of Sharīf ʻAbdallah, *kaymakam* of the Mocha–Luḥayyah area, which created a shortage in the *maaş* of officials.[81] He stated that when Sharīf Ḥusayn was in charge, taxes were fixed at a certain level with the stipulation that there would be no increases because the inhabitants could not meet them.

At the *seraskeriyet*'s recommendation, the 1200 men he requested were to be recruited from Egypt and the Sudan because the Rumeli and Arabistan armies could not spare them and neither could Jiddah. Sırrı did not believe that such troops would acclimatize to Yemeni altitudes, given how badly they had fared when Muḥammad ʻAlī had used them to subdue the Wahhābi resistance in Arabia and Yemen.[82] Sadrazam Reşid Paşa would authorize such substitutes for *nizamiye* troops only as a last resort.[83] Sırrı in the meanwhile was attempting to continue the late Sabri's policy of winning over the tribes with kindness and sympathy to ensure good administration and productivity, as the sultan had ordered; but the rowdiness of certain elements of the Yām, who had been raiding al-Luḥayyah at the instigation of Ḥasan, Sharīf Ḥusayn's nephew, first had to be controlled. This was feasible only by force and stationing regular troops at strategic points to suppress their marauding and reassure the inhabitants, but the *vali* of Jiddah still had not dispatched the battalion of regulars and necessary supplies.[84]

Mahmud replaces Sırrı

It was evident that Sırrı was not up to the task he inherited, so he was to be replaced. Dr Paolo Etvino,[85] who had accompanied the body of the deceased Sabri a few months earlier, brought two documents to the *sadaret* — one from the Imam of Ṣanʻā' to *Sharīf* ʻAwn and the other to the *Vali* of Jiddah. Imam Ghālib sought a monthly allowance of 4000 *riyal*s to keep order in the highlands. Mahmud, the new *vali*, and *Sharīf* ʻAbd al-Muṭṭalib Efendi of Mecca both considered the request reasonable.[86] The *sadaret* and sultan approved and authorized the minister of health to find a suitable medical supervisory position for Paolo. The *vali* of Yemen had dispatched a request to the imperial medical department, approved by the *Meclis-i Valâ* and the sultan himself, for three doctors and surgeons, three pharmacists, medical and surgical instruments and medicines.[87] The imperial treasury was to meet the total cost of 136,520 *piastre*s because Yemen's treasury was deficient. The *maliye* would have the authority to adjust the expenditure later by deducting it from Yemen's treasury.[88]

The *vilayet*'s finances posed a critical problem, serious enough for the *defterdar*, Emin Lütfü Efendi, to recommend he resign and return to the capital to save his salary for the treasury and to turn over his duties to ʻAli Efendi, the *mal katipi* (financial recorder) of the *vilayet*.[89] *Vali* Sayyid Mahmud reluctantly endorsed this gesture of a good man and his replacement.

Emin reported the *vilayet*'s financial expenditure at 997,340 *piastre*s and 8 *para*s or the equivalent of 1994 *kise*, 340 *piastre*s and 8 *para*s, a sum against which no revenues were listed.[90] *Vali* Sayyid Mahmud reported a surplus of 4800 *kise* for the year and the *Meclis-i Valâ* asked the *maliye* how to dispose of it. The *maliye*'s analysis revealed that officials in Yemen were drawing 175,000 *piastre*s in *maaş* when the sum should have been 136,000; 1344 of the difference was given out as salaries for attendants of the mosques. It was calculated that the treasury could benefit by 40,000, from which adjustments taken would leave 12,000 for *maaş*: 7315 as before and 5000 to Hodeida for the *kaymakam* and *muḥāfiz*, both residing in Hodeida, the seat of the *vilayet*. The *vali* considered the request as just and proper for maintaining order in the ranks and for stabilizing both income and expenditure.[91]

Conditions in the highlands

Ghālib had been forced out of Ṣanʻā'. He and Emir Muḥammad ibn Sharaf al-Dīn of Kawkabān, both loyal to the Ottoman state, undertook a military expedition to recover control from the usurper and his helpers among defiant Yāms, and to bring peace to half a million inhabitants of the region with the help of local Arab troops whose loyalties were constantly shifting. In his letter to Sırrı enticing him to come with his troops either to Raymah or Taʻizz where he would join them with his own fighting men, Muḥammad stressed his loyalty to the sultan and reminded him that his father had been killed in the service of the Ottomans. He also explained how he had recovered Ṣanʻā' from troublemakers supporting ʻAbbās ibn al-Mutawakkil and drove them out of the city, scattering them and punishing those captured. Both stated that this would be the appropriate time to assert Ottoman authority in the highlands and avail the sultan of its many revenues and to reinforce stability by sending regular forces to be stationed there.[92]

Ghālib stressed the need to station imperial troops at the appropriate places from Ta'izz to Ṣan'ā' to ensure imperial control. Furthermore, he stated that he had addressed the same request to Sharīf 'Abdallah, son of Imam Muḥammad ibn Yaḥya. He concluded by asking that the allowance of 4000 *riyal*s a month, which Ibn 'Awn had promised him when Imam al-Mutwakkil called on him in Hodeida, and which both the *sadrazam* and the sultan had approved, be paid up. He also urged that troops be stationed at regular posts in the highlands to ensure Ottoman sovereignty. Of particular interest was Ghālib's statement that Ṣan'ā' and its environs did not need an Ottoman presence, but that given his father's loyal service he wished to continue in the same vein.[93] What perhaps rendered the request for troops urgent was that powerful rivals were laying claim to and constantly challenging his possession of the imamate, which, according to Muḥammad ibn Sharaf al-Dīn, threw the whole region from Ṣa'dah in the extreme north to 'Adan in the extreme south into turmoil and desperation over prevailing lawlessness and lack of security, necessitating firm action on the part of the authorities.[94]

The need for stability was understandable given that there had been three different imams in three years. Under the circumstances, Sırrı deemed it necessary to station a core of regular Ottoman troops in the highlands on whom the imam could rely to maintain order. This in turn meant allocating them a *maaş* or *bedel*. Also, two broken brass artillery pieces at the Ṣan'ā' fort would have to be recast or replaced. Ghālib had asked the *Vali* of Jiddah, who had already requested 1000 regulars from Istanbul, for artillery and regular troops. Sersuvari (head cavalryman) Behram Ağa was dispatched to Ghālib to enquire into recruiting loyal Arabs in the hope that the Yām might be appeased short of combat.[95] Altogether the *Hatt-i Yemen* had only 4000 troops, far from sufficient to maintain stability and peace; moreover, the Arab tribes of the Ṣan'ā' region were accused of oppressing the inhabitants. Given the arduous task facing the imam and his loyalty to the sultan, Mustafa suggested he be granted a robe of honour in recognition of his services to date.[96]

The *vilayet*'s financial status did not permit recruitment on the scale needed. Moreover, Imam Ghālib's *maaş* had not been paid for some time. In lengthy and eloquent addresses separately to Muḥammad Ibn 'Awn and the sultan, Ghālib recounted the services of his late father, Imam al-Mutawakkil Muḥammad ibn Yaḥya, to the Ottoman state. He told of his surrender of Ṣan'ā' to the authority of Sharif 'Awn upon his arrival in Jiddah and the stationing of Ottoman troops at the well-known

Qaṣr Ghamdān in Ṣan'ā', which led to his being treacherously killed and Ottoman troops attacked. When Ghālib took over after replacing al-Mutawakkil, he expected the central imperial government to help and to authorize his vengeance. He recovered control of Ṣan'ā' and the rest of its *sancak* in August 1851 and sent emissaries to the *vali* at Hodeida with an offer to secure Ṣan'ā' and its revenues for the Ottoman state. However, they were intercepted and killed *en route* by al-Makrami, who had usurped Ḥarāz, which compelled Ghālib to take action against him and to seize Manākhah in the process.

More than a year passed and the allowance was still not forthcoming, so Ghālib came to Hodeida and met Sırrı's successor, Vali Mahmud, who treated him respectfully and kindly. He once again stressed his family's loyal services to the imperial state and lay before him his predicament, namely that since the assassination of his father and his assumption of the imamate he had received no monetary compensation or allowance from the government. Moreover, he was responsible for the livelihood of more than 50 members, all of whom could survive only with subsidies from the sultan, to whom they remained loyal, and upon whom they were now dependent for subsistence. Ghālib urged the *vali* to support their request and relay it to the sultan.[97] *Sharīf* 'Abd al-Muṭṭalib and *Vali* Sayyid Mahmud endorsed his petition and forwarded it to the *sadaret*, which passed it on to the *Meclis-i Valâ* for review and approval. The *Valâ* supported the *vali*'s recommendation, which was to grant Ghālib 1000 *riyal*s from the treasury, shawls and swords, a handsome robe of honour and two battalions of *nizamiye* troops in recognition of his fine and loyal service to the state and his pacification of the Ta'izz to Ṣan'ā' region. A *maaş* was authorized but the amount was left to the *maliye* to determine.[98]

A quarter century of rivalry, conflict and instability thus allowed the Ottomans to return to the highlands at the invitation of Ghālib ibn Muḥammad, who followed in his father's footsteps. They did not have to fight their way back this time because the inhabitants had lost faith and trust in their imams and sought relief at the hands of the Turks.

The main reason to regain effective control of Yemen was to prevent foreign powers, especially Great Britain and Italy, penetrating this significant corner of the Ottoman Empire. Direct control was the only possible deterrent because the rivalries among Yemeni leaders and tribes created enough instability to encourage foreign intervention. When Egypt under the rule of Muḥammad 'Alī was able to pacify and stabilize the land until the middle of the nineteenth century, the Ottomans felt no urgent need to exercise direct control once more to protect the holy sites and ensure their sovereignty over Arabia, which was now being encroached upon from the south by the British. The task was facilitated by the opening of the Suez Canal in 1869, which enabled them to transport troops more effectively by sea than by land, as hitherto had been the case.

In conclusion, we might observe that the ongoing instability in the lowlands due to assaults on legitimate authority by ambitious chieftains coupled with constant ʻAsīri encroachments preoccupied the Ottomans who had insufficient money and personnel to meet the challenges. Looming immediately on the horizon was the growing instability in the highlands and the inability of their designated governor, Imam Ghālib, to counter the challenges of his relatives who sought to replace him. The Ottomans were now left with no alternative for stabilizing the highlands short of taking charge directly of its administration.

5. Ottoman Return to the Highlands, 1872–82

By 1872 the Ottomans had for the time being completed the pacification of both the Tihāmah and ʻAsīr regions. A constant thorn in their side, Muḥammad ibn ʻĀ'id, had been reduced to submission.[1] The sultan's government now deemed the time propitious to respond to the appeals of the imam and his ally Sharaf al-Dīn at Kawkabān and move its forces up to the highlands, where Zaydi tribesmen were in a state of turmoil because the current imam's relatives were challenging his legitimacy. In this chapter I show that it was far from easy to occupy and stabilize the highlands. The Ottoman commanders encountered untold attacks and almost constant resistance.

In reoccupying the highlands after an absence of more than two centuries, besides pacifying the region, the Ottomans wanted to counter the spread of British influence among the tribes of the south and southeast and to reassert their sovereign rights in the face of the British challenge. A new phase in Anglo–Ottoman confrontation was about to begin. This conflicting situation was to last into the early twentieth century when boundaries were finally defined.[2]

On 4 March 1872, Mirliva Veli Paşa and Miralay Musa Beg, leading five battalions drawn from the second, third and fifth regiments and accompanied by Reşid[3] and some auxiliary units composed of loyal Yām tribesmen, left Hodeida for Ṣanʻā' expecting a peaceful transition through Ḥarāz, whose chief, Dāʻī Ḥasan ibn Ismāʻīl had sent a friendly message assuring his loyalty to Ahmed Muhtâr Paşa, who commanded Ottoman forces when he was in the process of subduing ʻAsīr.[4]

Reducing Jabal Ḥarāz's resistance

Dāʻī Ḥasan ibn Ismāʻīl's friendly message to Muhtâr was merely a ruse designed to stall an Ottoman occupation of his region. Reaching the highlands necessitated control of this strategic region astride the main route to Ṣan‘ā’. The Ottomans doubted his loyalty, given his past good relations with the ‘Asīri chief against whom they had struggled hard to reimpose their control over his region. The commandant sent him gifts in advance in the hope of pacifying him, while still reckoning on the need to dispatch a division of troops from Hodeida to ensure his submission should he decide to oppose their ascent. It was not an easy task at best given the ruggedness of the terrain, the difficulty of traversing this mountainous region and the strong fortification of the Dā‘ī at ‘Aṭṭārah, perched, as it was, on top of Jabal Ḥarāz.[5]

Leading a contingent of troops, Fezli Beg reached ‘Aṭṭārah in Wādi Ḥār a day later. Kaymakam Riza Beg, who was attached to the war command in Istanbul, administered it at this time. The *dā‘ī*, along with his family and relatives, were ensconced meanwhile in the naturally fortified fort of ‘Aṭṭārah. A number of scouts in advance of the troops were fired upon. Seeking to avoid a confrontation, the commandant sent word to the *dā‘ī* that the troops were not being dispatched against him, but were simply passing through on their way to Ṣan‘ā’. In his reply, the *dā‘ī* insisted that no one had the right to enter his domains through which he claimed the road to Ṣan‘ā’ did not pass.[6]

An early skirmish ended in defeat for the Ismā‘īlīs and enabled the Ottomans to position a couple of battalions with artillery around the fortified area of ‘Aṭṭārah. The fort fell after a siege of nine days and the *dā‘ī* surrendered.[7] His family consisted of 20 children and 50 women who had taken refuge there convinced that the fort was impenetrable, yet it took only a few artillery shots to compel its surrender. The key areas of the mountain were Shibām, Matwaḥ, Masār and Kâmil. Three battalions were dispatched under the command of Kul Ağası Mustafa Efendi towards Masār and Matwaḥ to reduce their forts. Captain Abdülrahman Ağa led a company from the fifth regiment's first battalion towards Shibām's fort, and Miralay Musa Beg and Kul Ağası Ismail Efendi of the Imperial Military Command set out to Kâmil's fort and Manākhah's *kasaba* at the head of the first battalion of the third regiment. Overawed by the force mobilized against them, the defenders of all the forts, mostly Yām tribesmen inimical to the Ottomans, fled without their weapons and without engaging the Ottoman troops. Shaykh Ḥusayn al-‘Amrī and his brother ‘Ali al-‘Amrī of Ḥajrah, a major town near Manākhah, as well as Shaykh ‘Abdallah of Kâmil, had offered their friendship to the Ottomans and were rewarded with a *kaput* (military cloak) and *shal* (cashmere shawl).[8] Müşür Muhtâr insisted that the *dā'ī* and his family leave the fort of 'Aṭṭārah. They were allowed to take all their belongings with them.

Before leaving 'Aṭṭārah for Manākhah, he ordered the fort completely torn down.[9] Not trusting to leave the *dā'ī* anywhere in Yemen, he had him escorted to Hodeida for transport to Istanbul.[10] With such a show of Ottoman force and resolve, the chiefs of the region all offered loyalty and received assurances of security. The road to Ṣanfūr, a strategic town along the road to Ṣan'ā' was now secure, and Muhtâr was able to order the transport of supplies and munitions from Hodeida (and from storage in Bājil) to the main staging area, which he intended for the highlands at Ṣanfūr.[11]

The capture of Jabal Ḥarāz and its forts, defended principally by the *dā'ī*'s son Aḥmad, was to serve as a lesson to other recalcitrant chiefs, who quickly took advantage of the security offered them in return for obedience. Appeasing the opposition with gifts and official appointments was the Ottomans' general policy in Yemen when confronting difficult situations. Fortunately for them, most of the inhabitants of the Ḥarāz region had submitted peacefully.[12]

With Jabal Ḥarāz securely in Ottoman hands, Müşür Ahmed Muhtâr departed from Hodeida, having left Defterdar Edip Efendi behind as *kaymakam*, and headed for 'Aṭṭārah accompanied by Colonel Fezli Beg,[13] a mortar, and two mountain guns, passing through Bājil on their way. Brigadier Musa Paşa replaced Fezli as the commander at Hodeida.

A Ṣan'ā' welcome for the Ottomans

Emissaries from Ṣan'ā' sought assurances that Tevfik Paşa's offer in 1849 to allow them to practise their Zaydi faith in peace, would be honoured. Muhtâr received emissaries *Shaykh* Muḥsin Mu'īd and *Sharīf* Ḥusayn Ja'mān graciously and gave them the assurances they sought. Muhtâr appointed Sağkul Ağası Mustafa Efendi *kaymakam* of Jabal Ḥarāz and left a battalion of troops to police Matwaḥ, Shibām, Masār, Kâmil and Manākhah's *kasaba*. He appointed Râmiz Efendi to command and deposited supplies for the troops and ammunition for 20 days, then, at dawn on 10 April, left Manākhah for Ṣan'ā' at the head of five-and-a-half battalions and an artillery unit. All his high ranking officers accompanied him: Mirliva Veli Paşa, Miralay Fezli, Musa Beg, Kaymakam Yusuf Riza Beg of the War Command, Piyade Kaymakam

Reşid Beg, the rest of the military officials, as well as the emissaries who had come from Ṣan'ā'. Following some secret scouting to ensure their safety, the force entered the city on 12 April, now assured of a peaceful welcome.[14] Indeed, more than 200 leading personalities — Imam Ghālib, his sons, the *shaykh*s, ulema, other notables and grandees — went out to greet him shouting 'victory to the sultan'.[15] After a military display accompanied by a military band, the troops headed to the fort southeast of the city at the bottom of Jabal Nuqum.

The ousted imam had alienated a good segment of the inhabitants. Muḥsin Mū'īd played a major role in deposing him and elevating Ghālib to the imamate. Now, together with Ghālib, he was honoured and decorated with medals.[16] Muḥsin Mu'īd had enjoyed much prestige after deposing Muḥsin Shahārī. He was looked upon as the '*shaykh* of the country' before he placed Ghālib in the imamate.[17] The *müdür* received both men with great ceremony in the fort's palace — which had been decorated in advance — with the crowds shouting 'long live the sultan'. As an expression of gratitude for his loyalty and support, Muḥsin was granted a lifetime subsidy and appointed to the *meclis* of the *vilayet*.[18]

Colonel Fezli Beg, hitherto in charge of the *karakol* (sentry post), was appointed *mutasarrıf* of Ṣan'ā' to look after the inhabitants' welfare and grant security to the tribes. To ensure the safety of several hundred women and children, who often assembled in the *maydān* (open courtyard) south of the city, the troops decided to build a new barracks for troops there. All efforts were made to calm the inhabitants and protect them against the attacks of rebels who had resisted the imamate of Ghālib long before the Ottomans came to his defence.[19]

Reducing resistance in the Ṣan'ā' region

But Muḥsin Shahārī, locating himself south of Ṣan'ā' in Ḥaddah after being ousted from the imamate he had usurped, conspired against Ghālib and the Ottomans. He rallied supporters and, accompanied by three mountain artillery pieces, laid siege to 'Abdallah Daf'ī's towers and within two hours reduced them to rubble. Two regiments chased the fleeing culprits, stormed their strongholds, killed a good many and captured 23, suffering only a handful of fatalities. To the north of Ṣan'ā', outside Bāb al-Shu'ūb, dwelt the Ḥārith tribe. They commanded a number of fortified places from which they beleaguered the inhabitants. 'Abdallah Daf'ī had captured one of the forts sometime earlier.

Believing the combined rebel forces could defeat Ottoman troops, Muḥsin Shahārī gathered armed followers and came to the defence of Daf'ī, who was under siege by Ottoman troops. To deny Shahārī control of the Dhu Marmar fort, seven hours' journey to the northeast of Ṣan'ā', the *müşür* sent a unit to reassure the inhabitants of Wādi Sirr and to tear down the structures on top of the natural protrusion, which rose 400 metres from the base to the top. The third battalion of the first regiment was dispatched to Maḥfaq to protect the communication route between Hodeida and Ṣan'ā'. Major Hussein Evni Efendi was dispatched with two companies of the same battalion to set up command at Matnah and Masājid after tearing down their fort for security reasons. While *en route* to Ḥarāz, the *müşür* instructed Kul Ağası Selim Ağa to construct depots for supplies at Ṣanfūr with the aid of four companies of the second regiment.[20] From these depots came much-needed military supplies to dislodge the rebels led by Daf'ī, whose force was now enlarged by Salḥashūr, Banu Sar'ab and Arḥab tribesmen led by 'Amīr ibn 'Alwān al-'Udhrī's son and Muḥsin Shahārī.

To distract the Ottomans, they urged Dhu Muḥammad tribesmen to attack Ṣan'ā', ostensibly to avenge themselves on the imperial troops, then sack and plunder the city as a reward. To head off their attacks and punish them for such boldness, Mirliva Veli Paşa and Reşid Beg led two battalions and two mountain guns and artillery pieces and fell upon the village of the *shaykh* of the Dughīsh tribes, which bordered Yarīm, where the rebels had assembled and barricaded themselves behind towering walls that enclosed over 40 dwellings, as well as the 'Udhrī *shaykh*'s shelter. The enclosure extended 2000 metres in a straight line, over which rose nine large towers. The rebels were well fortified in the 'Jewish quarter', which too had protecting towers and trenches, but were surprised and terrified by the sudden appearance of a sizeable Ottoman force on 29 April.

Led by Major Ahmed Feyzi Beg, the troops boldly stormed the walls past the trenches, which caused most of the rebels to flee. Those who could not escape surrendered when the Ottoman troops pounded them with artillery and daring assaults. More than 200 were killed or injured whereas only ten Ottomans were killed or wounded.[21] Fortifications and towers were torn down. After intense bombardment heard as far away as Ṣan'ā', the Arḥabs' resistance collapsed within a few days. They sought quarters *en masse*, as did the *shaykh* of the 'Udhrīs and of other defiant sub-tribes. The Ottomans granted it 'in the name of Islam', and the Ottoman commanders returned with their troops to Ṣan'ā' after taking possession of Dhu Marmar fort.[22]

The *sadaret* and sultan both dispatched telegrams via Aden on 25 April 1872 congratulating the troops and their commanders for taking control of Ṣan'ā' and its environs.[23] In accordance with previous instructions, the *müşür* was to introduce administrative reforms at this point. But before he could do so he found himself compelled to eliminate a number of pockets of resistance in Kawkabān, Jabal Raymah and the environs of 'Amrān.

Reducing resistance in the Kawkabān region

After securing their base near Ṣan'ā' and making the necessary arrangements, Ottoman troops fanned out — encountering only feeble resistance and sustaining minimal casualties — until they reached the naturally fortified regions of Kawkabān, Thulā, al-Maḥwīt and much of the Ḥāshids' territory.[24] Kawkabān and Raymah posed the greatest threat to enforcing the Ottoman presence. The military strategy was to eliminate pockets of rebellion and resistance in both Kawkabān and Jabal Raymah and to tear down towers and forts that could threaten the security of the troops after the subjugation of Raymah. Miralay Hacci Reşid (author of the military account) was sent to Kawkabān, where it became obvious that it would take a long siege to bring down the fort, having defied also Sinan Paşa's military attempts to reduce it in 1569.[25]

The Emir of Kawkabān, Aḥmad ibn Muḥammad ibn Sharaf al-Dīn, had shown loyalty to the Ottomans by supporting Imam Ghālib. They now suspected that his loyalty came more from convenience than conviction. To ensure that he remained in the fold, a show of force was deemed prudent. Ottomans hoped this would enable them to take charge of the fort of Kawkabān given its strategic location and the need to convince rebels in the neighbourhood not to disrupt Ottoman control.[26] Lying astride the route within striking distance was the fort of Bayt al-'Izz, which the Ottomans were fortunate to be able to control because of the loyalty of *Shaykh* Ṣāliḥ of the Ḥamdān tribe who administered it and which they now used as a base to move troops towards Kawkabān.

A number of head-on assaults and artillery barrages during a six-month siege failed to force open the main gate of Kawkabān, which could only be reached by crossing a narrow bridge.[27] Aḥmad decided to spare himself and followers in the fort further aggravating attacks by seeking security from the Ottoman commander. Once granted, Ottoman troops were allowed to station contingents there to safeguard the area. Aḥmad offered his obedience and was allowed to stay on with Miralay Musa Beg serving as commandant. Control of Bayt al-'Izz fort allowed the Ottomans to stop 1500 Ḥāshid and Banu Dawāj rebels coming to relieve the besieged at Kawkabān and to entice the *shaykh*s of the region to resist. The fall of Kawkabān had a sobering impact on other rebels in the region. A military contingent under Major Hussein Evni tore down the fort of al-'Arūs, which is within sight of Kawkabān.

On 3 June Mirliva Veli Paşa learned of their conspiracy. He sent Kul Ağası Yunus Efendi with a battalion of troops to interdict them. Yunus surprised them at Bayt Ṣan'ā' in the neighbourhood of the village of Bughur, where they had assembled at a two-and-a-half hour march northwest of Kawkabān. He fell upon them suddenly and killed or wounded 200, captured 23 and scattered the rest. *Shaykh* Ṣāliḥ ibn Haydar al-Ma'marī of the Ḥāshid tribe was among the killed. A number of Ḥāshid leaders were taken alive, including Nāshir ibn 'Alī Aḥmar. In both encounters the Ottomans suffered two killed and 58 wounded. The next day Yusuf Riza Beg, a deputy of the war command (*kaymakam erkan harp*) led prisoners and war equipment to Ṣan'ā'. They entered the city to the tunes of a military band and a display of military triumph designed to impress the inhabitants and to deter those who might entertain rebellion.[28]

When the Ottoman forces were laying siege to Kawkabān, Muḥsin Shahārī, 'Ali ibn Ḥasan Makrami and 'Ali ibn Shawīt of the Yām united to attack them and to entice the inhabitants in the 'Amrān area to join them. Word reached Fezli Paşa of the plot at 'Amrān from Ṣan'ā'. He ordered ten companies of troops from the first and second regiment and artillery against them with Hilmi Beg in command of the force. The expedition was mobilized on 28 November and was ordered to 'Amrān, eight hours away. Fezli also learned that the rebels were assembled at Raydat al-Yamān, four hours from 'Amrān. Up to 5000 were awaiting the Ottomans at al-Ghawlah. Hilmi fell upon them on 29 November and in a battle lasting from nine at night to one in the morning defeated and scattered them without any losses to his men.[29]

Another pocket of resistance near 'Amrān was eliminated when Fezli Paşa, Riza Beg of the general staff, Major Rağip Efendi, three companies of imperial troops, an artillery piece and 20 mounted police set out on 29 May to subdue 1500 rebels fortified at Ḥajjah and Bayt al-

'Izz. Their aim was to interdict reinforcements from Ṣan'ā' for the Kawkabān siege by preventing them from traversing the pass. Rağip fell upon them, killing a few hundred and capturing 80. The rest fled with Ottoman troops in pursuit.[30] Muḥsin Shahārī and the rest of the Makramis behind the conspiracy and rebellion were scattered.

Pacification continued in the 'Amrān district where, after military operations five hours away at Sarārah, the rebels were defeated and the inhabitants offered obedience at a cost of one Ottoman soldier killed. At the fort of Kahlān, eight hours northwest of 'Amrān, where three other forts were located, the inhabitants also offered submission and obedience. A number of *zaptiye* (police) were assigned to each. Fezli Paşa had returned to Ṣan'ā' by mid-December after reorganizing the administration of 'Amrān, setting it up as a *kaza* and assigning to it a contingent of troops to check the assaults of the Ḥāshids and Yāms. Meanwhile, having himself completed his task of settling matters in Kawkabān, Miralay 'Ali Beg headed back to Ṣan'ā'.

At al-Ṭawīlah, a six-hour march west of Kawkabān, Shaykh Yaḥya ibn Ḥasan, confident in the nearly impenetrable three forts perched on top of three peaks very close to each other, was prepared to resist. The *müşür* sent Major Ḥusayn Efendi of the first regiment's third battalion from Kawkabān with three companies and a Vituret artillery piece. The force left Kawkabān at midnight and confronted the rebels in their stronghold at dawn. The rebels decided not to resist; they sought and received quarters in return. The forts remained temporarily under the patrol of the police force already in place. Major Ḥusayn Efendi of the first regiment's third battalion was transferred from Masājid to the command of Kawkabān. The fort at Thulā, which the Ottomans had never been able to reduce militarily in the past, had submitted more readily by the middle of June.

At al-Maḥwīt, *Shaykh* Ṣarm, a close friend of Sayyid Aḥmad of Kawkabān and the manager of his affairs, was also prepared to resist. So, on 4 September, Fezli dispatched Yunus Efendi to Maṣna'ah's fort with four companies of imperial troops. The fort submitted without resisting. *Shaykh* Ṣarm had been captured earlier and sent under security guard to Ṣan'ā', where the *müşür* ordered his imprisonment on account of his intrigues in arousing the tribes. Leaving two companies behind to man the fort, Yunus then returned to Kawkabān.[31]

No sooner did the Ottomans try to put the final touch on the *müdürlüks* of Silfīyah and environs after taking charge of Kawkabān than the tribes around Ja'farīyah and Kusmah decided to resist. Ahmed Feyzi Beg, the *kaymakam* of foot soldiers with headquarters at al-Jabīy, the seat of the *kaza*, led two columns of troops to chastise the rebels; another seven companies were led out of al-Jabīy, three from Ṣanfūr to the pass of Zaghal in the heart of al-Salfīyah, where the rebels had assembled. A company was dispatched to Sūq al-Rubū', at the entrance to the pass, where Banu Wāḥid and Banu al-Qarḏ tribesmen fired on them. Troops arriving from Ṣanfūr with artillery pieces trapped the rebels in the middle of the pass. The inhabitants of the village fled. The next morning the troops moved towards the pass of al-Jamrān where the Banu al-Qarḍ had assembled to resist. The troops attacked and captured their stronghold. Inhabitants raised white flags and sought forgiveness and security, granted only after they agreed to honour all conditions. Next came the turn of Kusmah and al-Ja'farīyah. Close by, near the town of Dhahbūd, was the fort of Ḍali'. It was ordered to be torn down.

Within 20 days, the reforms introduced encompassed the *kaza* of 'Ans. Officials of the *nahiye* were appointed. After the surrender of Dhahbūd, eight disturbers of the peace were captured and sent to Ṣan'ā'. A battalion of troops was stationed at Dhahbūd with two months of provisions and munitions. Feyzi then moved on to 'Utmah. At Shaḥr and Qaṭī', nine hours away, a band of criminals had been oppressing the inhabitants after fortifying themselves in towers, which they controlled. The inhabitants were ordered to tear down all 14 of them.[32]

One of the two contingents of troops stationed at Shahārah was dispatched two days later to 'Adan.[33] It was a steep ascent requiring three hours of climbing to reach and the muleteers had to lighten the transport animals' loads. Five companies of soldiers and supplies were required to capture the fort of 'Amār in the neighbourhood of 'Adan, which once was under Ḥāshid jurisdiction, and a centre of the imam. A company of soldiers was left to guard it.[34]

Reducing resistance in Jabal Raymah

After securing the regions of Ṣan'ā' and Kawkabān, the *müşür* assigned Reşid Paşa[35] the difficult task of bringing Jabal Raymah under control. Some 130 sub-tribes inhabited this region, in which there were more than 900 villages and 15,000 dwellings. To prepare for the assault on the rebels fortified in Jabal Raymah, Reşid was sent to Ṣanfūr on the

Hodeida–Ṣan'ā' route to arrange for and supervise the transport of supplies from Bājil to Ṣanfūr. Süleiman Beg, who served in the *kaymakamlık* of Hodeida, was appointed *kaymakam* of Jabal Ḥarāz with authorization to obtain 150 camels, later increased by a further 100. Muhtâr Paşa had already designated Ṣanfūr the main depot for providing supplies and war materials during the siege of Kawkabān. Sayyid 'Abdallah Yaḥya al-Ḍil'i was the overall *shaykh* of Raymah and he and his allies among the *shaykh*s of the area refused to come to the Ottoman camp and accept a written offer of security in exchange for submission and obedience to authority.[36] Still, to avoid bloodshed and destruction, the Ottomans delegated the respected Muḥammad 'Abd al-Bārī to plead with the defiant leaders, but to no avail. Reşid had no alternative but to use force against them. After all supplies and equipment had been brought up to Ṣanfūr, he moved against them with the third battalion of the fifth regiment reserve, accompanied by 19 'weak-kneed' muleteers.

Raymah was not only naturally fortified but also strategically located to bar traffic and threaten the line of communication between Hodeida and Ṣan'ā' if not secured militarily. This was clearly demonstrated in 1858 when, with two battalions, Süleimanlı Ahmed Paşa tried to pacify the region. He sent his men up through the valley of Rabāṭ and Dārī only to be met by Badaj, Banu Ḥadad and Ḥawr tribesmen who surrounded the expedition, trapped the advancing force in the pass, cut off the road and access to a water supply, and inflicted heavy losses on the Ottoman army, which was forced to retreat after running out of munitions. Lack of mobility and incompetence in executing plans were blamed for the defeat and the army's forced withdrawal. Nine years later Ottoman forces brought the mountain areas of Ḥufāsh and Milḥān under control. By 1864 the 'Abs and Banu Aslam tribes had accepted the Ottomans' administration, which enabled them to expand the revenue-yielding region around Hodeida and to meet the expenses of 3000 soldiers, with surplus *miri* taxes sent to the treasury at Jiddah.[37]

Given Jabal Raymah's significance for revenue yielding purposes and seeking to avoid the fate of Süleimanlıyeli's expedition 18 years earlier, Reşid tried to win over the recalcitrant chiefs by peaceful means. He sent letters to Sayyid 'Abdallah, leader of the region's rebel chiefs, whose older brother Sayyid 'Ali had led the resistance to Ottoman advance, calling on all to accept an offer of 500 *riyal*s in exchange for their submission and loyalty. Gifts were also offered if they agreed to pay the *'ushr* taxes previously levied on them. But the *shaykh*s rejected Reşid's offer and he now had little choice but to mobilize troops against them. The rebels controlled al-Jabīy, strategically located near a narrow pass, protected by towers and administered by Aḥmad ibn Aḥmad. To get to the heart of rebel country, the Ottomans had to defeat the rebels defending the pass and towers dominating it.[38] Reinforcements arrived from Ṣan'ā' under the command of Major Haydar Beg, who defeated and scattered the defenders.

Reşid had already secured the loyalty of the inhabitants around Ṣanfūr, so was assured of not being attacked while heading into the heart of Raymah with his troops. On hearing that troops were heading in his direction, Aḥmad came out to make enquiries and stall them as 'Abdallah prepared for battle. Ottoman troops positioned themselves on the northwest side opposite the mesa where two valleys converged. The mountain above the pass was about 1500 metres long and at some point 100 and at another 50 metres wide. A number of dwellings and storage facilities, a village, an administrative building with three large cisterns, a small mosque, next to which war materials could be stored, were at the top of the mesa, which was well defended from every side. Earlier, Süleiman had secured the cooperation of the tribes and camel leaders in Wādi Ḥār to move the supplies quickly.[39] A battalion and a half of troops had already been stationed at Ṣanfūr to safeguard this critical route and keep the lines of supply open to troops stationed at Ṣan'ā'. Some rebels pretended to offer their submission, but reacted with hostility instead. In the fighting that ensued two companies stormed the rebels' strongholds, killed a good many, scattered the rest, and destroyed their strongholds. Two soldiers were 'martyred' and a handful wounded.[40] The troops gained control of the mesa, but resistance continued under the leadership of Muḥammad Zayd Hadmī and a few other recalcitrant *shaykh*s near Bāb Thulth, a short distance away from al-Jabīy, who terrorized villages that had submitted to the Ottomans. With more troops and supplies brought up from Bājil and Ṣanfūr, the rebels, numbering no more than 700, yielded after three to four days of fighting. Sayyid Yaḥya, who meanwhile was barricaded at Ja'farīyah, sought the intercession of Sayyid Muḥammad 'Abd al-Bārī of Ṣan'ā' with the *müşür* to obtain a pardon for them, which he agreed to grant on condition they submitted to Ottoman authority. The defiant *shaykh*s and other village chiefs quickly appeared to offer regrets and seek pardon.[41] With the rebels defeated or in flight and in keeping with the *müşür*'s previous instructions, Reşid treated the tribes inhabiting Jabal Raymah and its environs kindly and wisely after tearing down the towers and forts that could threaten the Ottoman troops' safety in that region. The inhabitants could now return to their ploughing and trading.[42] Until it was decided whether Raymah would be administered as a *vekalet* or *kaymakamlık*, the *müsür* instructed Reşid to appoint Ahmed Feyzi, a major in command of the fourth reserve regiment's second battalion, as provisional *kaymakam* of Jabal Raymah.[43] With three companies of the fifth regiment's first battalion accompanying him, Feyzi took up residence at al-Jabīy and Reşid returned to Ṣan'ā' with the rest of the troops. He stopped at Ṣanfūr in Ḥarāz for a day to deposit a battalion of troops under the command of Major Ibrahim Efendi to police the area.[44]

Securing the Ta'izz region

Pacification and reconciliation of the tribes in the Ta'izz region were also indicated as a prelude to administrative reorganization and reform in the south. Shaykh Amīn, who earlier had offered loyalty to the authorities in Ṣan'ā', was at present administering the port of Mocha. Mirliva Musa Paşa was dispatched from Istanbul to secure the southern half of Yemen. He arrived in Mocha via Hodeida and, after making necessary administrative arrangements and preparations for travel, proceeded to Ta'izz on 4 September, reaching it in the late afternoon two days later. Two battalions of imperial troops, Colonel Hüsrev Beg, Shaykh Amīn and other notables loyal to the Ottomans accompanied him. Notables and inhabitants generally welcomed Musa and his party outside the town where they had awaited his arrival.

After taking possession of the imposing Qāhirīyah fort and other defence towers in the area, Hüsrev was appointed administrator of the town of Ta'izz and given four companies of troops for policing purposes. The Qāhirīyah fort served both as official residence and headquarters. Tribal chiefs and notables of the Ta'izz region were called upon to proffer their loyalty and submit to Ottoman authority. Most of the inhabitants did, but some powerful chiefs refused and, to force their submission, the Ottomans were compelled to mobilize troops against those who intended to continue to resist.[45]

Major Ibrahim Ağa, along with Amīn of the Arab *zaptiye* and four companies of troops of the third army's third regiment's third battalion, was dispatched to Jabal Jaysh (southwest) and Jabal Ṣabūr (southeast) with a mountain division to bring the rebels under control and enforce the payment of taxes. Other units reduced resistance at 20 to 30 forts under 'Abdallah Ba'dān and Ḥasan Sharīf, in a region that was well fortified from earlier Ottoman days. After a few skirmishes and moderate casualties sustained by rebels, Ottoman troops stormed the two forts where the two chiefs were ensconced with battle-axes and shovels opening the way. The rebels in the end suffered more than 100 casualties with five killed and an equal number of Ottoman troops were wounded. The two surrendered and the inhabitants in the surrounding area quickly offered submission. The triumphant troops then returned to Ta'izz.[46]

Another area of resistance was in the *kaza* of 'Udayn, where some inaccessible forts were located and where one Aḥmad ibn Murshid, who claimed descent from the Prophet's family, hatched intrigues with some of the Dhu Muḥammad, urging them not to submit to Ottoman authority. Hüsrev mobilized a battalion of troops armed with a mountain artillery piece, picks, axes and flame throwers to storm the great fort, with its 15 entrances and towers, of the powerful Dhu Muḥammad and Dhū Ḥusayn rebels. The troops attacked and, after exploding one of the rebels' munitions depots, captured the fort's towers, forced the surrender of the rebels, who lost 60 or more lives, and took Muḥammad Nājī and ten of his aides prisoner. Ottoman troops suffered 15 killed and 13 wounded. The rebels yielded, the inhabitants offered their submission and the troops returned to Ta'izz. In the *kaza* of 'Ans, dependencies such as Jahrān and 'Utmah submitted and agreed to pay the taxes levied previously.[47]

Defiance was encountered also in the *nahiye*s of lower and upper Wuṣāb. The towering impenetrable mountains of the region emboldened the rebels to confront the Ottoman soldiers. As the Ottoman troops approached, a summons went out to the *'uqqāl* and *shaykh*s to submit and, with the exception of the Banu Maslam and Banu Naqadh, most responded. Necip Efendi was dispatched with four companies and an artillery piece to subjugate the Maslam tribes fortified in the mountains; eight of the *shaykh*s were captured, one fled. Their fort was destroyed and the rest of the inhabitants sought quarters. To prevent further rebellion in the region, 600 *zaptiye* were assigned to patrol the area and ensure the collection of taxes from which their *maaş* was to be paid. This necessitated first fixing the levy of *vergi* and *miri* taxes to be collected. Towers and forts were rehabilitated to house the *zaptiye*.

Mirliva Feyzi led two battalions into the Khaḍā tribe's country to punish its *shaykhs* for defiance. They too were well fortified in massive buildings and forts. But the imperial troops stormed them and bravely engaged the rebels, inflicting many deaths and compelling ten *shaykhs* to surrender after much destruction. For their defiance, the tribe was heavily punished and its towers thoroughly destroyed; Feyzi's and the other leaders' contingents then returned to Ṣan'ā'.

Other troops were dispatched to the Radā', Dhamār and 'Ans areas to suppress brigands who had pounced on farmers and destroyed their crops and cattle. Yunus led six companies to tear down the towers used by those who refused to obey, and burnt a number of dwellings to set an example and deter those who had been defiant in villages near Ma'bar.

After granting accommodation to the *shaykhs* of Jalīlah, Ḥujarīyah, Ibb, 'Udayn, Mocha, 'Amārah and Qa'ṭabah in the *sancak* of Ta'izz, the Ottoman commanders kept some of the towers for policing purposes and destroyed the rest.

The Ta'izz region was now sufficiently pacified and in submission to enable Ottoman authorities to put its administration in order. Süleiman Beg, the *kaymakam* of Jabal Ḥarāz, was appointed *mutasarrıf* of the Ta'izz *sancak* and its appendages. He arrived from Ṣan'ā' with officials appointed over the *nahiyes*. With 4600 square kilometres, the Ottomans treated Laḥj as a part of Ta'izz *sancak*. The British, on the other hand, treated it as an integral part of the nine semi-autonomous districts administered by the *shaykhs* whom they subsidized. The Ottomans challenged the British assertion, which remained a point of contention between both until resolved in 1909, when borders defining the British sphere of influence were finally established. Its inhabitants at this time exceeded 130,000 and the Ottomans insisted that they alone had the right to govern this area, in keeping with the sultan's sovereign rights.[48]

Meanwhile, Ministry of War aide-de-camp Kulağası Yusuf Efendi came from Istanbul to congratulate officers and troops for recovering Ṣan'ā' and to deliver the sultan's imperial instructions for Yemen's administrative reorganization. Two days later Miralay Reşid Beg escorted the fourth regiment of reserves' second battalion back to Istanbul on board the ship that brought the *müşür* to Yemen, reaching it 18 days later.[49]

Pacification completed

It took Ottoman forces a year (1872–73) during Ahmed Muhtâr Paşa's tenure to reduce the rebellion of defiant tribes, to overcome Sharaf al-

Dīn of Kawkabān's resistance and take control of his region (which extended to the Tihāmah), to suppress the al-Ḥaḍā tribe's revolt and to kill its chief. His successor, Ahmed Eyüp Paşa, ended the revolt of the Khawlān tribes and the resistance of Tihāmah tribesmen who had been under the spell of one who claimed magical works. In 1876, during his successor Mustafa Asim's tenure, after intense battles and losses on both sides they managed to quell the uprising of the Ḥāshid and Arḥab tribes, whom the *vali* appeased with gifts and other largess.[50] Then the tribes of Jabal al-Bukhārī in the land of Makhādir south of Ṣan'ā' rose in revolt; this necessitated dispatching an expedition against them. It was led by the *kaymakam* of Ibb and Jiblah supported by loyal Dhu Muḥammad tribesmen, who succeeded in putting down the revolt, in killing many of the rebels and in plundering their possessions.[51]

Believing that the *ulema* of Yemen were behind much of the incentive to rise, the Ottomans decided to crack down on those they suspected of calling for the rebellion. Mustafa Asim had appointed 'Abdallah al-Ṣabbāgh al-Ṭrābulsī as deputy of the *sharī'ah* court in Ṣan'ā'. It is alleged that this deputy involved himself in the sects' disputes and thereby caused animosity between them and the *vali* of Yemen, who reacted by imprisoning and exiling some of the *ulema* to end their resistance. He prepared a list and ordered them to appear, but then had troops surround them as they left the government building. About 40 *ulema* were arrested and sent to Hodeida to prison where they dwelt for two years. Muḥammad Ḥamīd al-Dīn, father of the future Imam Yaḥya and Aḥmad ibn Muḥammad al-Kibsi, head of the *ulema*, were among them and some of them died either in prison or in exile.[52]

In 1878, when Ismail Hakkı became *vali*, they were freed on the recommendation of Muḥammad 'Ārif al-Mardīnī, a judge in Hodeida known for his sympathy to ulema. This bridged the gap between the inhabitants and their new governor who seemed to bode well for future relations between Yemenis and Ottomans. Peace reigned and the *vali* set up Rüşdiye schools in which to educate the children. He was also the first to establish a police force from among the inhabitants, known also as *Hamidiye* units, to maintain order and fulfil administrative functions in the interior. An historian of Yemen alleged that this *rapprochement* with the Yemenis and the building up of a native force would lead to his dispensing with Ottoman units and might end up with his detaching himself from the Ottoman state, which led to his dismissal from office.[53]

Izzet's conciliatory efforts did not, however, win over all Yemenis, especially those of the northern part of the country, which remained under the administration of Imam al-Mutawakkil Muḥsin ibn Aḥmad, referred to in Ottoman chronicles as Shahārī,[54] until his death in 1878 when al-Hādī Sharaf al-Dīn assumed the *da'wah* and the title of 'imam' for himself in Jabal al-Ahnum six months later. His tenure coincided with the *vali*ship of Mehmed Izzet who assumed the post in 1882 when his predecessor had been dismissed. Izzet worked hard to gain the Yemenis' confidence and loyalty, but the spread of deceit, connivance and bribery among Turkish officials had the opposite effect, thus widening the gap between Ottomans and Yemenis and leading to renewed uprisings. They centred this time on Khawlān and Ḥajjah, obliging the *vali* to intervene with troops to quell them after a number of severe military encounters.

Setting the administration in order

Measures were introduced to reorganize 'Asīr after its military pacification in 1870/1. When the Ottomans reached Ṣan'ā' in 1872 and took over the administration and records from Imam 'Ali ibn al-Mahdi, they at least guaranteed his freedom and arranged a monthly stipend for him. The *müşür*'s first order of business now was to appoint deputy *mutasarrıf*s for both the Ṣan'ā' and Ta'izz *sancak*s. Commencing in 1872, after the Ṣan'ā' region was firmly under control, Ahmed Muhtâr Paşa set about restructuring the administration of the Yemen *vilayet*, dividing it into four *liva*s or *sancak*s, with Ṣan'ā' city serving as capital of the *vilayet*. The three other *sancak*s besides Ṣan'ā' were 'Asīr, Hodeida and Ta'izz, each headed by a *mutasarrıf*.[55] To the *sancak* of Ṣan'ā' were attached the *kaza*s of 'Ans, Dhamār, Yarīm and Ḥajjah, whose administrative status until then had been undefined. After reorganizing the *kaza*s of Yemen, the *vali* appointed deputies as follows:

Sancak of Ṣan'ā'	Ḥasan al-Akwa' Efendi
Jabal Ḥarāz	'Ali ibn Ḥusayn al-Ḥarāzi Efendi
'Amrān	Muḥammad al-'Imrānī Efendi
'Ans	Ḥusayn al-Ghashm Efendi
Dhamār	'Ali ibn Ḥusayn al-Maghribi Efendi
Perim	Muḥammad ibn Yaḥya al-Shawkāni
Kawkabān	'Ali ibn Muḥammad al-Kharāshi

After granting accommodation to Jabal Raymah's inhabitants and following instructions from the *vilayet*'s headquarters (Ṣan'ā'), the Jabal was attached to the *sancak* of Hodeida with al-Jabīy serving as the centre of the *kaymakamlık*. Its surroundings were erected into separate *nahiye*s, namely those of Mawstah, Ja'farīyah and al-Salfīyah. Kusmah served as the *müdürlük* of Mawstah with Aḥmad ibn Yūsuf Maḥjar as *müdür*; Sayyid Yaḥya was appointed *müdür* of Ja'farīyah and Muḥammad ibn 'Ali Muntaṣir *müdür* of al-Salfīyah with Sūq al-Sabt as headquarters. Deputies and other officials were appointed, together with *zaptiye*, for the *müdüriyet*. The elders, *shaykh*s and *kethüda*s of the salvaged villages in the *nahiye*s were brought together and informed of the divisions instituted, and those to whom they should report. *Defter*s were delivered to each *kaza* for the purpose of levying and recording the personal *vergi* to be collected according to instructions from *vilayet* headquarters.[56] The central government authorized subventions, medals and gifts to the *shaykh*s and emirs to celebrate the conquest of Ṣan'ā'.[57] Mecca's citizens and *sharīf*s congratulated the sultan on the 'conquest' of Ṣan'ā'.[58] The capital was likewise in a celebratory mood on this occasion.[59] The sultan reviewed with satisfaction details of the repossession of Yemen as forwarded from Yemen to the various ministries.[60] The *vali* was commended for the victories in Yemen and given instructions for the discharge of his responsibilities.[61] Artillery officer Mehmed Ağa was praised for his work, promoted to major and appointed to the imperial *Tophane* in Istanbul.[62]

Hilmi Paşa, the *mutasarrıf* of the Hodeida *sancak* resigned on account of ill health and was replaced by Miralay 'Ali Beg from the military general staff. Physical facilities were repaired and bridges rebuilt in the capital. He also delivered to Müşür Ahmed Muhtâr a high jewel-encrusted first-class Ottoman *mecidiye* medal from the sultan in recognition of his successful work.[63] The imam henceforth was to play a subordinate role in the administration of the country, serving as a subsidiary official of the Ottoman governor general.[64]

The reorganization of the *vilayet* of Yemen, as instructed by Istanbul, took 14 months to complete (from March 1872 to April 1873).[65] By then all officials assigned to the areas under control in Yemen were in place; their financial needs for administering authorized;[66] and their names entered in the *salname*.[67] Former emirs of Maswar in the *kaza* of Kawkabān, an appendage of the *sancak* of Ṣan'ā', were to be given a pension, presumably for faithful service in the past and loyalty to the

Ottoman state.[68] The Ministry of the Interior asked for a *mektupçu* to be appointed to Ṣan‘ā’[69] and Ismail Efendi was chosen for the post.[70]

To maintain order in the capital, three companies of soldiers were stationed inside the Ṣan‘ā’ fort at the Sitr gate. To support their stay, the Ottomans built working and living quarters, an ammunition depot and a number of storage facilities. A hospital with 300 beds and all medical facilities was built in Mutawakkil's *bustān*, outside the old ‘palace’ area of the fort, to serve the seventh army[71] and another military hospital was authorized for Hodeida.[72] Other facilities constructed included barracks for troops, housing for staff officers and a large *konak* opposite the imam's residence from the Bakrīyah mosque. They built a road from Ṣan‘ā’ to Hodeida via Ṣanfūr and Manākhah to be used for transport by animals and movement of troops. In addition, they rehabilitated the ports. Permission was given to extend a telegraph line to Ṣan‘ā’ when the cost of it was ascertained.[73]

On 27 Ra 1290/25 May 1873 Commandant Ahmed Muhtâr Paşa was appointed minister of public works. On 12 September 1874 he left on board the Austrian Lloyd Company's steamer *Oreste*, which had come to Hodeida to transport him back to Istanbul, and he took up his new appointment immediately on arrival there.[74] Ahmed Eyüp Paşa, commandant of the seventh army with the title of both vizier and *müşür*, replaced him. He was appointed *vali* of Yemen on 23 May 1873 and granted all travel expenses.[75] Ferik Izzet Paşa was made chief of staff; Mirliva Hafiz Ismail Hakkı Paşa and Tevfik Paşa were appointed to the general military staff; Kutri ‘Ali Paşa was appointed *mutasarrıf* of Ṣan‘ā’, Petro Paşa *mutasarrıf* of Hodeida and Mehmed Paşa *mutasarrıf* of Ta‘izz. All other military and civil officials were now in place.[76]

The next step was to organize the *vilayet*'s finances. The treasury was particularly keen to collect customs fees and levies on tobacco, which hitherto had eluded it. *Defterdar* Edip Efendi was commissioned to sort out the *vilayet*'s finances and ensure the flow of revenue to the treasury.[77] After completing his mission he entrusted the task of overseeing tax collection to assistants who had come with him and left Ṣan‘ā’ for Istanbul on 12 September as instructed.[78] Osman Efendi, the accountant at Medina, was assigned temporary financial responsibilities pending the arrival of Halil Muhtâr Efendi, who never made it because he fell ill while crossing the Suez Canal, returned to Istanbul from Ismā‘īlīyah and died. The *defterdarlık* was then entrusted to Osman Efendi, who until then had served as *muhasıpçı* (controller of accounts) of Medina, but he too died while awaiting official appointment from Istanbul. Rüşdi Efendi was then appointed.[79] Hilmi Paşa, *mutasarrıf* of Hodeida, also became ill; he resigned and the office was turned over to Miralay 'Ali Beg, who was dispatched to Yemen to take charge.

In mid-April 1872, the division of military reserves operating in Yemen was disbanded and ordered back to Istanbul, together with its officers and commanders. Its brigadiers and generals remained behind to take command of the newly organized seventh army out of the units that still remained in Yemen, namely battalions of the third and fifth army. A number of regiments from other armies were assigned from Istanbul to join the seventh in Yemen. Ahmed Eyüp Paşa, who had headed the first army, was appointed commander of the newly organized seventh army and given at the same time the *vali*ship of Yemen. Battalions of the fifth army were transferred to the first from their location in Hodeida; another battalion was exchanged for the one stationed at Jabal Raymah. Battalions sent from Istanbul replaced the reserves, with each having its own financial accountant.[80] Reserve units not returned to Istanbul were assigned to maintain the peace in other areas of Yemen where trouble could be expected.[81] General Veli Paşa was appointed commandant of military headquarters in Ta'izz.

In the three years between 1869 and 1872, the Ottomans believed they had completed military operations to pacify and stabilize the country. During this period more than 22,000 troops had seen service in Yemen. In their campaigns against rebels, about 4000 were killed and about 1800 confined to hospitals for a variety of illnesses; with housing facilities inadequate, many had to be housed in tents under trying physical conditions.

Commissions were appointed to regulate the salaries and expenses of troops and officials, and the sums to be paid authorized by respective Ottoman ministries.[82] All other civil and military officials were in place, including the head of the *Divan-i Temyiz*,[83] by the time Ahmed Muhtâr left Yemen by ship from Hodeida.[84]

Renewal of rebellion

'Abdallah Daf'i and his Arḥab followers destroyed a large fort north of the capital. The head of the tribe, 'Amīr ibn 'Alwān al-'Udhrī, was stirring up other tribes. He would not be appeased or dissuaded, so in mid-December 1872 the *kaymakam* marched his troops, battalions of the first and third regiment, into Arḥab country, four hours out of Ṣan'ā' where 4000 rebels had assembled. The Ottoman troops stormed their forts killing about 400 and capturing 30. They then tore down the forts and, according to the *kaymakam*'s report, only nine of their men were injured.[85] Rebels in Kawkabān were besieged for six months and their bridges destroyed before they surrendered seeking surety. In Ta'izz they were barricaded in 13 fortresses, where they were overrun and destroyed. In 'Asīr someone claiming to be the *mahdi* preached public order and calm, which was a bonus for its Ottoman administrator.[86]

East of Ṣan'ā' in the district of Khawlān, Shukrī Kuhāyil, a Jew aspiring to Messianic prophecy managed to stir up the Banu Bahlūl tribes against the administration. More than 2000 began to raid 'Ataqah and to confiscate money and grain. The commandant mobilized three battalions and four cannons against them and bombarded them with shrapnel, killing about 150 and injuring a like number. The rest fled and were scattered. The Jews of Yemen were treated like anybody else; they rode mounts, built three-storey houses and carried weapons; had they been deprived of rights then one could understand why Kuhāyil would incite to rebellion. So the Ottoman commander surmised that he was simply a charlatan, hating the Ottomans and out for personal gain.[87]

Previously, the policy had been to forgive rebels once they agreed to obey 'those in charge over them' (in the words of the Qur'ān), but this time a new policy was to be followed. It came about when an element of the Ḥāshid teamed up with Muḥsin Shahārī and also started to agitate the Arḥab tribesmen. Miralay Mustafa Rifki mobilized six battalions out of Ṣan'ā' and, with six artillery pieces, headed for 'Amrān. It would appear that a spy reported the coming of the troops because when they reached Raydah, east of 'Amrān, the rebels fell upon them. In the ensuing battle, which lasted two-and-a-half hours, the rebels were defeated and the troops continued on to a place called Ghawlat al-'Ujayb, where they erected the 'tents of triumph'.

'Amrān was a staging place for supplies and ammunition for the Ottomans. Here they awaited the replenishment of both before moving on to confront Muḥsin Shahārī. Their next destination was Khamir, where the inhabitants were extraordinarily cautious and alert to all sorts of untoward movements, understandably so since they eagerly protected the agricultural and trade pursuits that brought them prosperity and comfort. It would appear that some, spying for the rebels, reported the advent of the troops to the rebels, who surprised them and slaughtered

60 soldiers one evening in the heart of Khamrah, injuring many more. They also captured 200 pieces of weaponry and a catapult. Miralay Mustafa Beg, who led the force, appeared to have been insufficiently vigilant to avert the surprise attack when there was a *karakol* in the area responsible for being on the alert. Mustafa was held responsible for the losses they suffered. Atif believed that a higher-ranking officer might have been able to bring more experience to bear on averting military tactical errors.[88]

With the weapons and ammunition they captured, the rebels contemplated another attack on the Ottoman force, but Muḥsin Shahārī was thinking about moving against Ṣan'ā' itself. Meanwhile, Ahmed Eyüp Paşa had resigned and was replaced by the *vali* and commandant of Crete, Müşür Raûf Paşa, who had been exiled to Crete after the 'Asīr debacle. The 200 troops stationed there petitioned the sultan's government to pardon him, which they did. He was ordered to Istanbul, was assigned a staff and was dispatched to Jiddah by a special ship. He visited the *sharīf* at Mecca to seek his advice. Moved to tears by the *sharīf*'s words, he returned to Jiddah and awaited sea transport to Hodeida. But before he could embark for Hodeida, he was appointed minister of the navy and returned to Istanbul.

Attempts to take Ṣa'dah

Complying with instructions from Istanbul, Mustafa Asim Paşa planned next to take over Ṣa'dah and its environs, where claims to the imamate were still being made. Ismail Hakkı Paşa, who was in charge of the expedition, left the *merkez* at the head of ten battalions of foot soldiers and a battery of portable and mountain cannons with all the equipment and supplies necessary to take on the Ḥāshid. No sooner did they reach Shahārah than some chiefs appeared with offers to help transport troops. But, on reaching the pass of Shahārah, 1500 tribesmen, headed by imam claimant Muḥsin Shahārī, surprised them and surrounded them from the front, rear and above. The rebels were determined to prevent the troops reaching Ṣa'dah and to force Ismail to return to Ṣan'ā'. To create a diversion, he ordered followers east of Ṣan'ā' to stage an attack on the defence towers Ottoman guards manned in that region. Word reached Ismail about the plan. He secretly ordered a battalion to move out quickly by night and, come morning, they surprised the rebels, killing and injuring more than 200 and capturing their supplies, camels and standards. Only one Ottoman soldier lost his life. The Yām took a beating and each fled to his hiding place for safety after plundering the defeated Ḥāshids' arms, supplies and other provisions. Inhabitants of Manhīyah, centre of the Makrami chief, attacked his residence and plundered his money and belongings. The Ottomans tacitly encouraged them to do so as a punishment for his defiance.

Word of the disaster reached Muḥsin Shahārī and 'Ali ibn Ḥasan al-Makramī, who were spreading sedition at Khamir. It shattered their resolve and they decided to flee. The Ḥāshid tribes opted for submission, and their chief, 'Ali ibn 'Ā'id Shawīt sought safety from the *müşür*; in return for his submission and offer of loyalty, he was appointed *müdür* over all the Ḥāshid tribes.[89]

Mount Maswar was as towering and impenetrable as Kawkabān and its fort was equally difficult to conquer. Major Hussein Evni Efendi led a contingent of troops to it and, with careful preparations and stealth, managed to capture it and assign policing units to it.[90] In 1874, Mustafa Asim Paşa arrived in Ṣan'ā' as commandant and *vali*. He soon had to confront the savage uprising of the Arḥab, 'Iyāl Yazīd and Ḥāshid tribesmen who, heartened by the Ottoman defeat at Khamir, continued their defiance. To avenge the previous defeat and recover weapons and artillery lost, chief of staff Ismail Hakkı commanded eight battalions and a battery of cannons to chastise and compel obedience from Ḥāshid and Banu 'Abd rebels. After a brief encounter, the rebels were totally defeated and sought pardon and safety. The commandant would grant this only if their chiefs came forth and surrendered the weapons captured and provided hostages as guarantee.

After chastising Ḥāshid rebel leaders and introducing some reforms, Ismail returned to Ṣan'ā' to concentrate on reform and development. He built a Rüşdiye school, refurbished the Bakrīyah mosque, completed a bath opposite it, and regulated the *vergi* and other *'ushr* taxes.

To placate the Ḥāshids and Arḥabs, the *müşür* appointed *zaptiye* and bandsmen from their ranks. He also appointed their chiefs to local posts as administrators. On the other hand, as a precaution against further outbreaks he decided to exile 15 of the more difficult chiefs and *sayyid*s, shipping them out via Hodeida. Among those exiled were former Imam Ḥamīd al-Dīn, who had deceived Ferik Hafiz Ismail Paşa by pretending to work for peace after he and other rebellious *shaykh*s had been pardoned and were expected to maintain order in their districts. Asim Paşa was considered an upright and capable person in the discharge of his civil and military duties. He served well during the five years of his appointment, working for peace, stability and progress. To construct roads and bridges he brought in a French engineer and, as the year 1876 approached, there was ample evidence of Yemeni development and progress. Two years later he was replaced and the country entered on another painful path.

Ferik Ismail Hakkı Paşa, former chief of staff of the seventh army, arrived in Ṣan'ā' as Asim's replacement in 1878. With the approval of the government, which was eager to enlarge the regular force by enlisting native Yemenis, Hakkı proceeded to organize *Hamidiye* battalions from the local inhabitants and to concentrate on reforms.[91] Yemenis expressed much interest in joining such units, according to reports reaching Istanbul.[92] Before long, the tribes around Khawlān refused to pay outstanding *miri* taxes and rebelled, and the *paşa* led the newly organized troops against them to collect the taxes due with which to pay the expenses of these newly constituted *Hamidiye* units.

In 1880, Ferik Ismail was removed from his post and replaced by Ferik Izzet Paşa, the chief of staff of the sixth imperial army, who arrived in Hodeida by ship from Basra. By the time he reached Ṣan'ā' he had learnt that he had been elevated to the rank of vizier and *müşür*, and had been awarded the Ottoman medal of distinction that accompanies such rank.

Meanwhile, the ever-troublesome Muḥsin Shahārī died and Sharaf al-Dīn replaced him as imam claimant. In keeping with his pledge to his supporters, he immediately declared his rebelliousness, took charge of Ḥajjah's *kaza* and extended his control to Ẓafīr. To recover both, Izzet dispatched Miralay Refik Beg with a contingent of troops. But Ẓafīr was well fortified and its roads inaccessible. After a number of attacks, the troops incurred heavy losses in killed and wounded and were unable to recapture Ẓafīr. A seven-month siege ensued and the troops ran out of ammunition and supplies. Fortunately for them, the rebels decided to give up resistance and to flee by night, thus enabling the troops to reoccupy it. The Ottoman government kept on exploring ways to get rid of him for a number of years.[93]

Securing and pacifying these areas was only part of the battle. Local officials — *müdürs*, *mutasarrıfs* and *kaymakams*, often appointed from the tribes — found every opportunity to extort funds (15 to 20 per cent more than legal levies) from the local inhabitants, secure in the knowledge that the *merkez* government was too far away to catch up with them. Unable to raise enough money to pay the newly organized *Hamidiye* units, whose salaries had fallen in arrears, orders arrived to disband them and to retrieve the weapons they had been issued.

The *Hamidiye* battalions were well trained and disciplined, and many were recruited from the families of Ṣan'ā' itself. Deprived of a decent livelihood, the disbanded units had to fend for themselves. It appeared there would be some reprieve when a shepherd in the Ṣan'ā' region reported he had discovered a pile of gold. Upon further scrutiny it turned out to be a mineral not gold.[94] Some sought to avenge themselves on the tribes who defaulted or withheld the legally due taxes while remaining loyal to the government; others joined Sharaf al-Dīn, and still others took to banditry. The security so painstakingly cultivated now vanished and the inhabitants were disillusioned by the Ottoman authorities' helplessness in redressing the inhabitants' accumulating grievances. Those with means emigrated to Istanbul and elsewhere.

Thus Yemen, 'Asīr included, entered a new period of turmoil and rebelliousness. Measures to promote the *vilayet*'s welfare were not enacted. Yet, a remarkable amount of construction, rehabilitation and the building of new public buildings took place during this period when funds were still available.[95] Courts of adjudication, medical facilities, roads and bridges were neglected and soon fell into disrepair. In desperation, Istanbul sent inspector after inspector to investigate the problems and recommend solutions. These required immediate implementation, but distance and time worked against them. It took several months for proposals to reach the capital and be debated before decisions could reach Ṣan'ā'. Meanwhile, the situation was declining rapidly and the blame fell on local officials who, in turn, blamed the deterioration on the selfishness of the imam and *shaykh*s who acted without conscience.

In 1884, Eduard Glaser, the Austrian explorer of Sabaean inscriptions, stopped in Istanbul for a few days after having spent two years in Yemen. He reported that Ottoman forces scored brilliant victories over rebels after the formation of the seventh army corps. When he arrived in Ṣan'ā' in October 1882, he had found Ottoman control limited to a line from al-Luḥayyah tọ Ḥajjah, encompassing 'Amrān, Ṣan'ā', Dhamār, Radā', Qa'ṭabah and the region between Ta'izz and Mocha. The Ḥāshid and Bakīl *mutasarriflik* and land east and north of Ṣan'ā' remained hostile to the government. The 'fanatic Sharaf al-Dīn's Zaydī *dā'ī* of the Yām of Najrān' led the latter. He alleged that the whole area northeast of Ṣa'dah to the Persian Gulf was also hostile to the Ottoman government. On the other hand, the appointment as commander in chief of Izzet Paşa, who had served in Yemen and Baghdad before returning, impressed him. Izzet, he claimed, took on Sharaf al-Dīn, wrested control of al-Sūdah from him, and chased him from Shahārah, the key to Ṣa'dah. Glaser had accompanied the troops on various expeditions; he praised them for their valorous daring sorties against numbers superior to theirs, which gained them the cities and the submission of their inhabitants to Ṣan'ā's authority. Their success was attributed also to the loyal support of 'Abdallah al-Ḍil'ī. Izzet checked the powerful Yām, Ḥāshid and Bakīl by employing a policy of divide and rule against them. The *dā'ī* of the Yām sent his son to Ṣan'ā' to offer submission, and Glaser took the opportunity to lecture him on the virtue of submission to the sultan (Abdülhamid II), reminding him that the sultan was the 'true caliph and shadow of God on earth'. Glaser, who had an inflated opinion of his diplomatic prowess, claimed that the Ottomans could now count on these Ismā'īlī descendants of the Carmathians, as well as on the Bakīl and Khawlān to submit. Otherwise, it would have taken 10,000 men to control them.[96]

The progress achieved in pacifying the tribes, promoting education and economic projects, constructing public works and solving administrative problems eventually came to naught. The inhabitants' main priority was security and protection from extortion, which did not last. The importance of this strategic part of Arabia to the protector of the holy sites (the sultan caliph) was not lost on Istanbul and attempts were still being made to find solutions. But the treasuries, central and local, could not muster the necessary funds.

These unfortunate developments occurred during the tenure of Izzet Paşa, when the administrative and military machinery had ground to a halt and funds were depleted. His death in April 1882 saved him further torment. His family buried him in the Bakrīyah mosque's cemetery. He was replaced by Ferik Ahmed Feyzi Paşa, the commandant and *mutasarrıf* of 'Asīr, who left for Ṣan'ā' to take up his post as *müşür* and *vali* on 14 April of the same year. Under his tenure, Ṣan'ā' and 'Asīr entered a new era of accomplishments, both positive and negative.

In all fairness to the Ottomans, one must conclude that in the ten years since their return to the highlands they expended every sincere effort to pacify the land, appease its tribes by forgiving their rebellious chiefs even to the extent of appointing them to administrative posts, and introducing reforms to enhance the country's economic welfare, but with little immediate success. The diversity of Yemen's tribal configurations and the impossibility of appeasing one without alienating the other, or of preventing the positions among them shifting vis-à-vis the central administration at Ṣan'ā', militated against stability. Therefore, if I were to take the official record of Ottoman involvement into consideration, I would have to blame the tribes' lawlessness and their chieftains' greed, not to mention the feud over the imamate, more than any misadministration on the part of the Ottomans. They had reasserted control over the highlands, but that proved of temporary duration.

6. Administrative Abuses and Rebellion

With Yemen's administrative and financial degeneration, by 1883 it was obvious that some adjustments had to be made. The *vali* notified the sultan's government of the need for detailed and clear instructions to regain the *vilayet*'s wellbeing. He suggested that explicit instructions be communicated directly and orally to specified individuals who would bring them back.[1] Attempts were made during the following year to readjust the configuration of local administrative districts and to appoint competent administrators at the provincial level throughout the *vilayet* in Yemen. This was to bring in fresh blood and achieve a more responsive government in the hope of improving procedures and achieving better results in upgrading the country's economic status. It was based on the assumption that the tribes would cease their agitation and intertribal strife. Vali Izzet also suggested that, given the need for more troops for local policing, they might, with the sultan's approval and if sufficient funds and provisions were made available, recruit locals through their own *shaykh*s for army service, but not necessarily in Yemen.[2] Ferik Ahmed Feyzi, a seventh army commandant, was taking precautions but was short of recruits, while Sharaf al-Dīn had been assembling an army of up to 2000 among the Ḥāshids and from the coastal area from his new headquarters at Ṣa'dah, which augured badly for tranquillity in Yemen.[3]

Readjusting administrative units

The central government was made aware of the need for administrative, military and financial reform in Yemen and had received two lists to that effect from both the *vali* and the commandant of the army who were awaiting results. Consultations with the *seraskeriyet* had taken place and Mirliva Ömer Lütfü of the general staff had suggested an inspection of the military administration in Yemen. A *tezkeré seniyé* from the *sadaret* to the *seraskeriyet* authorized it.[4]

In the readjustments that ensued, the *kaza* of al-Luḥayyah was attached to the *sancak* of Hodeida. Kamarān island, with 200 houses and 1200 inhabitants, was attached to al-Luḥayyah. The strategic village of Sānif, an hour-and-a-half away on the main coast, was considered sufficiently important for the imperial government to appoint it a *müdür*, former police supervisor Salih Beg, at the recommendation of the *Şura-yi Devlet* (Consultative Council of State), with a monthly salary of 750 *piastres*.[5] Jāzān districts attached to the *kaza* of Abu ‘Arīsh, an appendage of Hodeida, were reorganized.[6] What remained to be done was to integrate the *kaymakamlık* of Bilād al Rūs and the Banu Bahlūl *nahiye* with the *sancak* of Ṣan‘ā’, and of the Khawlān *nahiye* together with the list stipulating amounts of taxes to be levied.[7] The Jabal 'Iyāl Sarīḥ tribe was attached to the *kaza* of ‘Amrān and constituted a separate *nahiye* within it.[8]

Security concerns in the southern border area led to discussions in the *Meclis-i Vükelâ* and a decision to tighten control over the *nahiye* of Qa‘ṭabah, al-Maqāṭarah and Jabal Ḥubaysh to check the encroachment of the British. They agreed to construct a *karakol* at Jalīlah on the border and station a battalion of troops there with a cannon, and another *karakol* in the *kaza* of Qa‘ṭabah at Janbiyān, in addition to stationing 40 *zaptiye* in the Mikhlāf of Shu‘ayb, if their numbers permitted, and giving them salaries and expenses in keeping with the recommendations from Yemen's administration.[9]

Appointments, dismissals and transfers

The central government sent instructions to install new *kaymakams* for most of Yemen's districts, specifically for Ḥarāz, ‘Ans, Dhamār, Jabal Raymah, Abu ‘Arīsh, Ḥajūr, Ḥujarīyah, Qunfidhah, Ghāmid, Mahāyil in ‘Asīr, Zabīd, Sirt, Ahmed Arif of the *Şura-yı Devlet qalami* for Mocha, ‘Abd al-Salām for ‘Udayn, and Osman Fehmi for Perim. Zabīd's *kaymakam* was promoted to third rank.[10] A policy of appeasement was introduced in areas where tribes were difficult to control, as in Ṣa‘dah and its environs. The military command in Istanbul suggested that the units stationed there meet the tribal chiefs and use kindness and wise exhortation to gain their loyalty. Ottoman officers were told to mediate tribal differences and help settle disputes.[11]

Halil Şihab, former *kaymakam* of the *kaza* of Kawkabān, was appointed to the *divan* of the *kaymakamlık* after a vacancy of two years, then elevated to the *kaymakamlık* four days later.[12] Three days later Şâkir Efendi was appointed *kaymakam* of the *kaza* of Qa'ṭabah.[13] Mehmed Fihmi Efendi was reappointed to the *kaymakamlık* of the *kaza* of Dhamār.[14] 'Ali Âkif Efendi was appointed *kaymakam* over the *kaza* of Radā', which an imperial *iradé seniyé* of 17 September 1886 had attached to the *sancak* of Ṣan'ā'.[15] Another *iradé seniyé* of 10 July 1886 confirmed Ziya Beg as *kaymakam* of Luḥayyah; he was already a member of the *kaymakamlık*'s administration.[16] Four days earlier an imperial order assigned Mustafa Efendi, former *kaymakam* of Mocha, to the same post in the *kaza* of Bayt al-Faqīh.[17] A *buyrultu âli* of 1 August 1886 authorized the extension of the telegraph line to the *kasaba* of Mocha once the cost had been established.[18]

Other appointments were authorized. Rizvan was reconfirmed to the *kaymakamlık* of Bājil (27 February 1886); Tevfik Beg, the *kaymakam* of Ḥarāz, was transferred to the *kaymakamlık* of Qunfidhah with second rank. This was after the dismissal of its and the *kaymakam* of 'Ans's Mustafa Efendi (14 April 1886), who two years later was accorded the rank of *mîr-i mirân*, usually granted to the governor of a province or *paşa* (16 June 1888).[19]

The constant shuffle of appointees in the top posts of administrative districts is thought to have been due to a lack of confidence in the ability of officials to discharge their responsibilities adequately, either through a lack of enthusiasm on their part to administer the districts to which they had been assigned or because of disenchantment over the pay cuts occasioned by the dire financial stringency of a central government that had declared bankruptcy. The duration of service often did not last two years. Dismissals were occasioned as much by illicit gains from embezzlement or bribery as by laxness in the collection of taxes.

Numerous assignments, reassignments and salary adjustments were made during the period 1887–89, including the top posts in Yemen. Osman Paşa, former *vali* of Aleppo, was appointed in 1877 as commandant of the seventh army and *vali* of Yemen.[20] The sultan approved a *dahiliye* petition to have Shams al-Dīn Efendi, *kaymakam* of the *kaza* of 'Amrān, and Walīy al-Dīn, *kaymakam* of Bājil, exchange posts with each other.[21] Kazim Efendi was appointed *kaymakam* of Mahāyil.[22] Shaykh Yaḥya Nāshir *müdür* of the *nahiye* in the *kaza* of Sūdah in the north and his deputy, Sayyid ‘Ali ibn Yaḥya al-Murtaḍa Efendi, were reconfirmed to its *müdürlük* and kept on (10 July 1888).[23] The Banu Marwān tribe in the *kaza* of Abu ‘Arīsh was granted the status of an administrative *nahiye* to be called ‘Asimat with its *müdür*'s salary set at 750 *piastre*s and its secretary's at 200.[24] Mehmed Emin Beg, former *kaymakam* of Zabīd was elevated to the rank of *mîr-i mirân* and made *mutasarrıf* of Hodeida (5 August 1888).[25]

The *mutasarrıf* of the *sancak* of Ta‘izz was dismissed[26] and replaced by Yaḥya Nüzhet, who had been separated from the *mutasarrıflık* of Fezan.[27] Having delayed his journey to take up his post as *mutasarrıf* of Ta‘izz, the *Şura-yı Devlet* issued a *mazbata* demanding that Yahya Nüzhet return half the 4650 *piastre*s he had received in advance.[28] Granting half a salary did not go down well with the *vali* and higher officials who argued that halving their salaries on whatever pretext would not guarantee them a living, so they petitioned Istanbul for full payment.[29] The sultan's government had to authorize severance pay for dismissed officials, including former Mutassarıf Reşid of Hodeida and Cemil Paşa of the *merkez* (Ṣan‘ā'), who each received 1500 *piastre*s.[30] Aziz Paşa, former *vali* of Yemen, asked the government for 7500 *piastres* in severance pay.[31]

Former *mektupçu* of Baghdad, Mustafa Beg, was appointed to the *mutasarrıflık* of Hodeida by an order of the *dahiliye*.[32] Salih Paşa, former *mutasarrıf* of Tripolitania's *merkez* was appointed *mutasarrıf* of Ta‘izz. Hussein Faiz, former chief of correspondence in Tripoli (Syria) was appointed *mektupçu* of Yemen.[33] Izzet Beg was dismissed as *kaymakam* of ‘Ans and replaced by Ziya Beg, the *kaymakam* of Luḥayyah, who in turn was replaced by Hodeida's *müdür* of *âşàr*.[34] Mehmed Emin Beg Tevfik Beg, former *kaymakam* of Kawkabān, was appointed *kaymakam* of Ḥarāz.[35] Rifat Efendi, former first-rank *kaymakam* of Maṭrāṭah, was made *kaymakam* of the *kaza* of Kawkabān.[36] Reşid Paşa, former *defterdar* Tevfik Efendi, *müdür* of *âşàr* Mehmed, and assistant manager of supplies, Halil Efendi, were all detained on suspicion of irregular conduct and embezzlement and remanded to the courts to prove their innocence, while Cemil Paşa, former *mutasarrıf* of Hodeida, and other officials were to be subjected to trial by a *mazbata* of the *Şura-yı Devlet* and the imperial order sustaining it.[37]

Mirliva Ömer Paşa, commandant and *mutasarrıf* of ‘Asīr was dismissed and replaced by Ferik Ömer Paşa, commandant of the Hijaz military division, according to a *tezkeré* received from the imperial military command in Istanbul.[38] The central government would not approve his dismissal and replacement until investigations in the *vilayet* were completed and the results communicated to Istanbul. Meanwhile, authorization was given for a deputy to serve as a temporary appointment pending the final outcome.[39] Mahmud Beg, assistant to the *vali* of Yemen, was dismissed for questionable conduct and, by order of the sultan, deemed unsuitable for any further service in the country. No replacement was named.[40] Mahmud, however, was still seeking another appointment after being replaced by ʻAli Efendi, who was promoted from first to second rank.[41]

Tightening control of finances

The financial situation in Yemen required attention. A report from the bureau of accounting to the *dahiliye* recommended tightening control over and providing more accurate accounting from Yemen, where the current management of finances was failing to yield the revenues expected let alone those needed to meet administrative expenses there.[42] Amounts to be levied and collected annually from Khawlān had not yet been determined and the government would receive authorization to do so after the ministry of the interior had made its determination.[43]

The situation was not conducive to the orderly levying and collection of taxes. Officials were insensitive to the inhabitants' predicaments and sent troops to collect the *miri* by force when the inhabitants balked at paying. When Şükrü served as secretary in Yemen he noted that Hodeida would yield 30,000 *riyal*s net per month after allowances for administrative expenses were deducted. The same, he stated, could be obtained from Taʻizz if officials would cultivate good relations with the inhabitants. When he had served in Yemen, of the 300 troops stationed in Hodeida 200 had to be supplied with grain and rice imported from Istanbul and Basra, at a minimum cost to the central treasury of 50,000 *lira*s. Moreover, the authorities could not send enough troops to collect all the required taxes. When Izzet Paşa was *vali*, he noted, each battalion consisted of only 600 soldiers and most of the seventh army officers sent to Yemen were either lieutenants or captains, not the type to get involved in unpleasant dealings to collect taxes from resentful Yemenis. Given the present upheavals in Yemen and ʻAsīr, it would take 30 to 40 battalions to pacify the land. Revenues could not flow again until the country calmed down, he concluded.[44]

Regulating the judiciary

The *Meclis-i Mahsus* in Istanbul had decreed that appeal courts be re-established and judges appointed in the *vilayet*s of Yemen, Tripolitania, Basra and Baghdad. Baghdad had a court of justice and an appeal court. Its *vali* supported Basra's former *vali*'s request to establish an appeal court in Basra. Given the distance between the cities, both *vilayet*s under this arrangement would keep their courts of justice.[45] The central treasury would meet the salaries and expenses of the courts of first instance in criminal cases, besides those authorized generally.[46] The *meclis* stated that, where appropriate, army courts in Yemen should be regulated and a deputy judge appointed to head the *sharī'ah* court in the *sancak* of Ṣan'ā', an appeal court, and a court of first instance council. It also decreed that judges supervise criminal and civil cases and head councils of the courts of first instance for Hodeida, 'Asīr and the other *sancak*s.[47] The inhabitants favoured *nizamiye* courts and would under no circumstances support their abolition, according to the *vali*'s reports.[48] *Sharīḍah* courts were reinforced in both Yemen and 'Asīr and their territorial boundaries redefined for each district at a later date.[49]

Orders were issued to organize the finances of the commercial court in Hodeida. The head of the court was authorized a monthly salary of 1500 *piastre*s; the head scribe 750; the second secretary 400 and the third 200; each of the two court members 700; the two court ushers 400; the janitor 5 and the same amount for stationery.[50] Orders were also given to regulate tobacco processing in accordance with the *Şura-yi Devlet*'s recommendations.[51]

Increased foreign pressure

Ever since implanting themselves at Aden in 1840, the English had been pressing northwards. When the Ottomans returned to the highlands they pushed southwards to exercise their rightful authority over Yemen. The border area around Qa'ṭabah was in turmoil. Tribes there took advantage of the situation not only to pounce on traders but also to charge for goods passing through their territory. Some decided to accept Queen Victoria's protection through her agents in south Yemen. The Sultan of Laḥj's territory was crucial for trade transit and every type of pressure was brought to have him secure his territory. The Italians in turn wanted to establish themselves at Mocha from where they could conduct their trade with the interior.[52]

Trade, however, consisted of illicit gunrunning to the tribes in revolt against the Ottoman authority. The *mutasarrif* of Ta'izz informed Ahmed Feyzi, the commander of forces for the whole of Yemen, that some Englishmen were sending large amounts of arms, ammunition and even artillery across the unmarked line of demarcation at Ṣabīḥah to the emirs of al-Ḍāli', Ḥawāshib and Bīr Aḥmad. Consequently, people were fleeing to the mountain and to Ḥujarīyah for safety. Feyzi cabled the *sadrazam* with this disturbing report and he, in turn, passed it on to the imperial *divan*, stating that the Ottoman embassy in London had protested against such activity before and had been assured that the British government would order illicit and provocative activity in that corner of Arabia stopped.[53] Defining the demarcation line more precisely would reduce transgressions. The general staff of the war ministry assigned Ibrahim Seyfi and Mustafa Remzi Beg, armed with an authorization from the *serasker*, to cooperate with English agents to resolve the problem.[54] A related problem of possible incursion came in a report from Münir Paşa, Ottoman ambassador to Paris and Brussels, who said that France was renewing its request for Shaykh Sa'īd, which, with British expansionism in the neighbourhood as well as in the Gulf of Basra, would only pose a greater threat to Ottoman sovereignty. Troops were ordered to the area to ensure that no landings by the French could take place at this strategic corner of Bāb al-Mandab.[55]

Noting references to the British and Italians passing on arms secretly and inciting tribes to rebellion, a commission formed at the palace to discuss what improvements to introduce in Yemen's administration recommended that appropriate measures be authorized to put an end to such traffic.[56] An Ottoman naval vessel arrested the captain of a *sunbūq* off Midi and, despite the Italian consul's protests, held him prisoner in Hodeida for 35 days. The Italian embassy reacted by sending its chief dragoman to the Ottoman foreign ministry to inform it that it intended to dispatch a naval war vessel to the Yemeni coast to force the release of its captain.[57] The Ottomans were facing the same problem at Massawa where the Italians wanted them to allow one Italian vessel to patrol off Hodeida, but were refused. The embassy in Rome sought instructions on how to deal with such persistence on the part of the Italian government.[58]

With England pressing for a concession to build coal depots in the port of Hodeida, the Ottomans' main concern was to ensure that granting them permission did not legitimate foreigners' demands to acquire property rights there. The administrator was instructed to be careful and to make it clear that the property would only be leased at a predetermined fee and for a set period of time.[59]

The Ottomans were worried about the whole length of the coastal area. Not only had piracy to be contained but also unpredictable weather and severe winds posed a problem for docking steam vessels, especially in the straits of Kamarān island. To alleviate the problem, the council of ministers authorized the navy ministry, at the central treasury's expense, to send out and chain four floats and a pair of anchors to the area.[60] Also at the central treasury's cost, two steamboats would patrol the southern coast to stop smugglers out of Aden and, on the tobacco administration's recommendation, fortify the passage between Yemen and Aden.[61] The *Meclis-i Vükelâ* agreed to protect the coast, especially the stretch from Midi to Jāzān, by building barracks at Midi to protect the entry to the port[62] and a port at the Hodeida landing.[63] Customs headquarters, hitherto located at Ḥalīy, were to be relocated in the *nahiye* of Wasīm.[64] The *sadaret* considered farming out the task of stopping illicit traffic in tobacco and weapons to the director of a tobacco company, Vicomte Georges de Zograb, and authorized the initiation of discussions with him.[65]

Given rebellion and intertribal strife, plus the smuggling of arms into the region and archaeological treasures out of the *sancak* of 'Asīr, constant surveillance along the coast became necessary.[66] The *Bahriye Nezareti* (navy ministry) was instructed to detail three gunboats to reinforce the five already allotted to the Red Sea with two specifically consigned to the Yemeni coast.[67] Trouble was brewing across the Red Sea. A secret memorandum from an informer in Sawākin described the disturbed situation in Sudan and Ethiopia, with special reference to the Italians' activities in the Red Sea.[68] Sudan's trade was being funnelled through Massawa. The Italians had set up a post at Ayliye in its neighbourhood. A conflict was expected between them and natives using Sumara as their staging place for the Ethiopian trade.[69] Given the seriousness of the situation in the Massawa and Sawākin areas, the navy forwarded the secret report to its gun ships in the Red Sea with orders to be on the alert in case of outbreaks.[70] The *Journal de Débat* in Paris, which Ottoman observers in Egypt followed closely, pointed to foreign intrigues in the region of 'Asīr and along the Yemeni coast.[71]

Events at Sawākin and Massawa plus the possibility of open conflict induced the Sublime Porte to take precautionary measures by increasing the size of the Hijaz military division.[72] Given their growing ties with Germany, the Ottomans agreed to the establishment of a coal depot on one of the islands. A son and a nephew of Abu 'l-Huda, a confidant of the sultan,[73] facilitated the deal. The British objected to the whole affair and, according to their account, the *Marie* unloaded 53 tons of coal on the island of Kamarān, which it had hauled from Lisbon. Its captain was allegedly grounded there, but he did not receive directives to take it back on board, as the British had demanded. When a complaint was lodged with Istanbul, the Ottoman government allowed another 5000 tons to be stored on Kunh island, six miles from Farasān, where the Ottoman flag was flying. A small gunboat was kept there, but German warships feared that the British might attempt to use the coal depot, which could be expanded to handle double the amount.

According to the agreement reached between the two countries, the Ottomans were to construct the storage facilities and the Germans to provide the coal. An article in the *Levant Herald*, quoting the Turkish *Sabah*, said the facility would be international, the British already having had a cargo of coal stored there, hence no special advantage would allegedly accrue to Germany from the agreement.[74]

Appointment of Ahmed Feyzi as Vali of Yemen

The Ottoman presence in Yemen was strengthened by appointing Ahmed Feyzi, former *mutasarrif* of 'Asīr, *vali* and commandant of Yemen by an imperial order dated 8 Ca 1302/14 February 1885.[75] He became responsible for weeding out corruption, bribery and embezzlement, especially in levying and collecting the *üşriye* and *zakah* taxes. He soon received instructions to bring to account and trial major and minor officials accused of embezzlement during the *vali*ship of the late Izzet Paşa. They included Cemil, former *mutasarrif* of Hodeida; Reşid Paşa, *mutasarrif* of Ṣan'ā'; Defterdar Tevfik Efendi; Treasurer Mehmed 'Ali Efendi, Ta'izz's deputy collector of *üşriye* revenue; 'Ali Riza Efendi, the *merkez*'s director of tribal affairs; Mehmed Efendi and a few others. All were to be sent to the *vilayet* of Hijaz for investigation and trial.[76] 'Abd al-Ḥay Efendi, a court official in the *sancak* of Hodeida, was chained in the fort of Hodeida pending his investigation and trial.[77]

The *Meclis-i Mahsus* also ordered the chief of police to arrest and remand for trial a number of *shaykh*s who had been collecting *üşriye* and *vergi* taxes and were now accused of embezzlement.[78] The *Meclis-i*

Vükelâ had authorized these collections in return for a *bedel* at the rate of one collector for each 15 villages in the *nahiye* and to deliver them to the treasury of the *kaza*.[79] The inevitability of irregularities such as extortion and embezzlement was the most damaging effect of having to rely on local officials, perhaps through lack of choice given the number of collectors required to do the collection in the whole country. Indeed, even the deceased former *vali* of Yemen Izzet Paşa had been accused of irregularities and, to stop rumours over the issue, the *dahiliye* had ordered investigative reports to be sent to Istanbul quickly for verification.[80] More than 200,000 *kuruş* of his estate had been forwarded to the treasury and there was pressure for it to be paid out to administrative officials of the Hijaz, but no authorization was to be made before the investigation into irregularities during Izzet's tenure had been completed and the final court decision made.[80]

7. Confrontation in South Yemen

The previous chapter covered the intensification of the rebellion, the sultan's failure to acquire an accurate account of its causes and, despite various commissions sent out to investigate, the inhabitants' grievances. These, coupled with the challenge to Ottoman authority of Britain cultivating the southern tribes, posed an ongoing problem to the exercise of Ottoman sovereign rights in the whole of Yemen. In this chapter I focus on the nature of this challenge and its long-term impact on both sides.

The conflict between the British and the Ottomans in south Yemen began in 1821 when Captain Haines of the Indian navy extracted, through intimidation and threats of bombardment, an agreement from the 'Sultan' of Laḥj who exercised jurisdiction over Aden. The sultan was illiterate and did not know what he had endorsed. His more literate family members were infuriated by his unwitting giveaway and declared the agreement null and void. Haines would not countenance this action and the tactics he pursued to browbeat further the ignorant Laḥjis into accepting what had been endorsed led to a series of confrontations and internal turmoil in the Laḥj district. The sultan in the meanwhile was in a quandary. To ward off his rebellious nephews and brothers, he became increasingly dependent on the unwelcome British agent at Aden for support. Thus began a tug of war that lasted three-quarters of a century. This was not only between the British Resident and his neighbours but also with the Ottomans, who had returned to the *sancak* of Ta'izz in 1872 and sought to protect those who resisted the British intrusion as well as those dependent on the Resident agent for support. In a desperate effort to justify their occupation of Aden by international law, the India government, to whom the Resident was accountable, undertook to question and challenge the Ottoman right of sovereignty over the areas into which they had intruded, a confrontation that was eventually to reach the highest legal authorities in Britain for resolution.

The historical record

When the Ottomans were expelled from Yemen in 1630, the chiefs of Aden, Qa'ṭabah and Yāfi' in the *sancak* of Ta'izz reverted to their old tribal methods of rule, like (according to the Aden Resident's report) in the highlands of west Scotland. The head of a group of families became the acknowledged chief of a tribe and the office became hereditary, 'but his authority was akin to that of a president of a republic rather than that of a prince'. He could exercise authority only on the basis of customs and the traditional laws of the tribe. Should he defy them, he would lose respect and loyalty; in short, he ruled by consultation. The only capital punishment allowed was for apostasy from Islam. The guilty in other cases of murder were usually done away with by stealth. The *sayyid*s, whose influence permeated the tribes and districts because of their alleged descent from the Prophet Muḥammad and their superior knowledge of Islam and the 'affected sanctity' acquired from it, shared the power. Few matters of importance were resolved without their intervention or sanction.

Between 1730 and 1740, the Sunni population of Aden expelled the Zaydī *dawlah*, the Imam of Ṣan'ā's representative, and the chiefs of the region gained instant independence, taking on different titles 'as their vanity decreed', the most common being 'sultan'. The 'Abdalis acquired control of Aden, Bīr Aḥmad, Laḥj and other villages to the north. They consisted of two principal clans: Sallami and 'Uzaybis. Their first chief, 'Abd al-Karīm Faḍl, took the title of 'sultan' and erected a fort at Bīr Aḥmad, which he put in the care of *Shaykh* Mahdi ibn 'Ali of the 'Aqrabis, a sub-tribe of the 'Abdalis. About 15 years later Mahdi joined 'Abd al-Rāḥ, a general of the Imam of Ṣan'ā' who had espoused his master's cause against the sultan and defeated him after a three-month siege of Aden. Laḥj was meanwhile in the hands of 'Abd al-Rāḥ, whose departure was purchased with a large sum of money. Bīr Aḥmad and the small fort behind 'little Aden' were ceded to *Shaykh* Mahdi, the recognized chief of the newly independent 'Aqrabi tribe. He agreed to pay the sultan 330 dollars a year in return for foregoing all claims to the port's revenue and respecting the sultan's authority.

The British capture of Aden

According to published accounts, the British were looking for a coal depot to service their steamers *en route* to India. It took 700 tons of coal for a round-trip from Suez to Bombay. A number of possible sites had been explored and abandoned as unsuitable.[1] East India Company officials decided on Aden. It occupied three square miles; its bay was crescent shaped, facing east with a sea wall front and mountains behind and it had only 600 inhabitants. Its capture in 1839 was for more than a coal depot. It was for promoting British commerce — access to the coffee of the highlands and trading possibilities — as well as for military and political reasons.[2] Arab authors claim that for '20 years the British circled the area like a bird of prey waiting to pounce on its wounded victim, seeking a pretext to seize it'. It is alleged that Ottoman Sultan Abdülmecid granted a *ferman* to that effect shortly after he ascended the throne in 1839, yet the same Arab authors assert that only Arabs, and no one else, had the right to dispense with their own lands.[3]

An incident played into British hands when, while passing Aden for trading purposes, one of their sailing ships sank and Arab tribesmen boarded it and plundered its contents. The Bombay government dispatched a warship with 300 soldiers under the command of Captain Haines to demand compensation. He went ashore in Aden and negotiated with the Sultan of Laḥj, who happened to be in Aden at the time. The sultan refused to yield to British demands on the grounds that pirates were not the responsibility of governing authorities on land. When Haines brandished the Ottoman sultan's *ferman*, the Sultan of Laḥj retorted, 'Who is this Ottoman sultan and what right has he to give away the land of others?'[4]

Having failed to convince the sultan, Haines bombarded Aden from his warship on 19 January 1839. The ruler of Laḥj ordered his guards to defend the port, but they failed in the face of overwhelming military and naval power. The British now occupied Aden and agreed to compensate the sultan with an annual payment of 6000 *riyal*s. They occupied an Aden port called al-Tawāhi in the name of the India Company. Its 600 inhabitants lived in huts and engaged mainly in fishing.

To firm up their control over Aden, the British sought to evict the sultan from it. This led to another showdown and another military defeat for the sultan, who now abandoned his residence in Aden. The British forced him to agree to the following conditions:

- acknowledge English dominance and accept their 'protection';
- complete independence for the interior of the country;
- encounters between Arabs and the sultan were to be direct without English interference;
- the sultan had the right to issue laws as required by his country;
- he could not conclude agreements with foreigners (non-Arabs);
- he was to have his own flag and soldiers, and had the right to grant title and rank;
- the Bāb 'Adan would serve as the dividing line, with lands on the other side, including Shaykh 'Uthmān, being the possession of the sultanate of Laḥj, and
- no foreigner was to own property in Laḥj.

Until now Arabia had been spared foreign occupation. The British were the first to penetrate it.[5]

Aden at this time belonged to *Shaykh* Muḥsin ibn Faḍl, chief of the 'Abdali tribe who, following the occupation of the town, retired with his family to Laḥj. Angered by the occupation, the Arabs of the region sought to evict the British by force, but to no avail. In November 1839, 5000 Arab tribesmen tried to retake the town but were repulsed and 200 were killed. Another equally large attack followed in May 1840 with similar results. The Faḍli tribe on this occasion assisted the 'Abdalis and between them they sustained 300 casualties. To punish the Faḍlis for joining the fray, Captain Haines blockaded their coast, cut off their supplies from Aden and bombarded Shuqarah on the coast. This policy was enforced until the Faḍlis sued for peace. Repeated requests led in early 1843 to the conclusion of peace with the 'Abdalis in return for the payment of a stipend of 541 dollars.

Negotiations and intimidation to further political and commercial interests eventually resulted in a number of agreements being drawn up with tribes in the areas around Aden.[6] The Bombay government recognized that Aden's peace and prosperity, and its garrison depended at all times on the state of their relations with the neighbouring tribes, which required that they rest on a firm and satisfactory basis. This was particularly important in the event of the British having to engage an unfriendly European power.[7] The tribes around Aden were divided into numerous sub-tribes and families who submitted to titular chiefs or engaged in offensive and defensive operations only when it suited them. The 'Abdalis were divided into about 30 different groups and one of their sub-tribes, the 'Aqrabis, inhabited Bīr Aḥmad and was hostile to the 'sultan'.

The 'Abdalis were the wealthiest and least warlike of the tribes. They were able to maintain their acquired territory and independence; but, while bound to the British, by and large they were still unable to protect the roads leading to Aden, as was expected of them. They increased in wealth, importance and general prosperity and became the paramount native power in the district. The sale of Aden gave them an immense advantage. With the stipend from the British government, the chief was able to maintain a standing army of about 400 foreign black mercenaries, superior to that of any of the surrounding chiefs. The greatly increased demand in Aden for the produce the 'Abdalis raised, as well as the extra merchandise passing through their territory, on which a treaty with England enabled the chief to levy 2 per cent *ad valorem* duty, made him far more affluent than his neighbours and secure against a coalition of needy and adverse tribes eager to appropriate his property and prosperity. Their friendship with the English, however, earned them the enmity of the Faḍli and 'Aqrabi tribes, and the distrust of the others who accused the sultan of becoming an infidel, thus providing them with an excuse to quarrel with him.

The 'Abdalis' chief town was Laḥj, 30 miles north of Aden, and great caravans bearing the country's produce passed through it from Ṣan'ā'. The Sultan of Laḥj, the English and even the Ottomans at Massawa across the Red Sea paid the inland tribes through whose territory their trade commodities passed certain sums to ensure their transit. The India government ratified a treaty on 7 May 1849 with the Sultan of Laḥj to allow subjects of Aden–Laḥj and the English to visit Laḥj, or any part of the territory, either for commerce or pleasure and to ensure their protection. He was paid a stipend of MT$ 22.5[8] a month to keep the roads through his territory safe. He had 2000 fighting men under his command and easy access to a further 3000 from his allies. While his heavy military equipment consisted of only one brass cannon, supplied by Captain Haines, his men were well equipped with armed matchlocks, swords, spears and daggers, which they used with skill.

Other neighbours of the English in Aden included the 'Aqrabis, who had separated from the 'Abdalis and become independent under the leadership of Mahdi, whose son Ḥaydar took up where his father left off and set up residence in the strong castle of Bīr Aḥmad. Their patrimony extended over only a few hundred acres of land in the immediate vicinity of the castle, which yielded a little *jawāri* and other pulses. They also owned the small harbour behind 'little Aden', giving Bīr Aḥmad the advantage of a seaport and the dues levied on goods passing through it, which provided the tribe and its chief with most of its revenue until the British closed it down for the part the 'Aqrabis played in attacking the *Auckland*. They also derived some income through a little trade with the Ṣubayḥis and their caravans passing through Bīr Aḥmad to Aden. They were generally poor and addicted to drunkenness on account of all the toddy they extracted from their palm trees. Though the whole tribe could muster no more than 200 fighting men, their turbulence and restlessness, helped by the immunity their fortress gave them, buoyed them up.

Their growing hostility towards the English was said to have derived from two acts, the abolition of all customs dues at Aden, which diverted trade from their port (*bandar*) to Aden, and the appropriation by the Sultan of Laḥj of the *huswa*,[9] or water wells, which the 'Aqrabis claimed as their own, to supply water to Indian navy ships at a rate of 2.5 *rupee*s per 100 gallons. They had entered into an 'engagement of friendship and peace' with the English on 31 January 1839, but were envious of their neighbours, the 'Abdalis', increasing prosperity and the countenance and support the latter received from the British.

The Ṣubayḥis, who inhabited the region between Mocha and Aden up to the straits of Bāb al-Mandab, were powerful. Divided into numerous clans led by different *shaykh*s, their numbers were estimated at 12,000. They were defined as a wild race and the more settled adjacent tribes regarded them as bedouin. Some cultivated land, raising a little grain and a few vegetables to bring to market in Aden, mainly through Bīr Aḥmad, but for the most part they were nomads living in tents and notoriously addicted to plunder. No other tribe could count on their allegiance in war. Though valuable caravans (*qāfilah*s) passed through their country to Aden and many were described as industrious and useful members of society, they were still considered to be the 'gypsies' of Yemen. In 1839, five of their chiefs entered into an agreement with Captain Haines that there should be peace between them and the English. What profit they gained was from the caravans passing through Bīr Aḥmad. They could defy the English despite their limited fighting force of 200 because of their impenetrable fort.

Another neighbouring tribe, inhabiting the area northwest of the 'Abdalis, were the Ḥawshabis, a powerful division of the Yāfi'is, who took no part in the hostilities against the English. With their fertile land producing grain, coffee, madder, aloes, honey, ghee and senna, they were described as very industrious agriculturists. They supplied Aden's markets with flour and grain. They were well-disposed towards the English, taking no part with the 'Abdalis or Faḍlis in hostile action towards them.

The Sharjabis were neighbours of the Ḥawshabis. Their country was as rich as the Ḥawshabis' and produced both good-quality grapes in the neighbourhood of Ta'izz and *qat*. The Yemenis considered the leaves of the *qat* tree, which were chewed for the slightly exhilarating effect they produced, an indispensable luxury.

The 'Awlaqis were described as poor but brave and powerful. They were divided into an upper section inhabiting the inland mountains and a lower section inhabiting the area touching the sea east of the Faḍlis. Their sultan Munaṣṣar and his cousin 'Ali ibn Bakir, his chief counsellor and general, could bring 7000 men to a battlefield. The English felt it expedient to provide support and money to the lower 'Awlaqis who were in contact with them, so they could check the Faḍlis. Their district was considered rich in grain, but little of it reached Aden except in times of scarcity. They exported most of it from the port of Ashwār, about 50 miles east of Shuqarah. In the 'bond' with the English of 16 June 1839, Sultan Muḥsin promised to keep the roads to Aden open and to hold responsible anyone who interfered with the flow of merchandise and the transit of individuals to Faḍlis or any part of the territory either for commerce or pleasure. The commitment was renewed on 20 February 1844 excluding Article 3, which held the *shaykh* responsible for acts committed in his domain, thus forfeiting all salaries.

The territory of the Faḍlis, who were regarded as more powerful than the 'Aqrabis, lay immediately east of Aden. Beside the chief town of 'Asala, it consisted of the roadstead of Shuqarah and about 12 other villages, some of which were defended by small forts or towers. The British treated them as deadly enemies who murdered English subjects, insulted them, sheltered murderers, excited other tribes against them and cut supplies to Aden. They inhabited the area northeast of Aden, possessing the entire seacoast up to the border of 'Awlaqi country and inland as far as the high range of hills that formed the boundary with the Yāfi'is. Their land produced a few vegetables, barely enough grain for their own subsistence, but mostly reeds and *jawli* used in the construction of temporary housing at Aden. The *bandar* of Shuqarah provided the Faḍlis with their principal source of revenue before Aden was declared a free port, leading to the decline of the principal source of revenue for the tribe and its chief. This no doubt served to increase their hostility to the British.

The English described the Faḍlis as poor, fanatical, rapacious, cruel, and without fear of reprisal. They subsisted by war and plunder, with nothing to lose but their cattle, which they would drive to the mountains on the first approach of an enemy. The Faḍlis' warlike character was reflected in their chief, Sultan Aḥmad ibn 'Abdallah, who claimed descent from the Banu Umayyah of the Hijaz. Regarding himself as the 'pillar of Islam', he commanded influence and respect from the Kuhāl tribes inhabiting the hilly country to the north of the Faḍlis', whose 3000 bedouin fighters supplemented his own 600. He too had his stipend of MT$ 364.5 suspended within six months of the English occupation for breaking his promise to keep the road to Aden open, which led to the bombardment of Shuqarah by ships and the Indian navy. The next encounter took place in 1843 when a coalition of 1000 Arabs, led by the Faḍlis, sought to dislodge the English from Aden. Fresh agreements were of no use in restraining attacks by some Faḍlis on English trade routes through their domain. Relations between the British and the Faḍlis were at this low par in 1850 when a seaman from the *Auckland* was murdered, resulting in more intense confrontations.

The Yāfi'is occupied a large tract of country to the north of the Faḍlis, allegedly as far north as Ṣan'ā'. English observers described them as the most powerful tribe in Yemen, for seven chiefs who could each muster over 2000 fighting men led them. Coffee was the chief produce of their country, followed by madder, grain, matchlock and wine. They were held to be a brave race of men, generally at enmity with the Faḍlis who prudently avoided entanglement with them.

The return of Ottoman military forces to south Yemen and the pacification of the region inevitably increased friction with the Laḥj area, for the British had sought to bend the will of its rulers through bribery and intimidation. The Ottomans regarded British interference as an infringement of their sovereign rights, which the government of Bombay did its utmost to challenge, unsuccessfully.

Laḥj was ruled by Shaykh Faḍl of the Arḥab tribe whose grandfather had been appointed troop commander by Imam al-Manṣūr ibn Qaṣīm two centuries earlier when he governed most of Yemen. The grandfather had seized control of Laḥj and had got its *shaykh*s to recognize his descendants as lords of the area. When the Ottomans sought to bring him back into the fold, he made contact via Aden with the British authorities appointed by the India government. They extended him the protection he sought, recognizing him as 'Sultan of Lahaj'. Ḥawāshib, which was an appendage of Ta'izz, also drifted out of its administrative control when Faḍl appointed a *müdür*, *zaptiye* and other officials over it. The British ambassador in Istanbul suggested his government seek the approval of the sultan's government to 'grant autonomy to the Laḥaj and Ḥawāshib countries', but the Foreign Office denied the request on the grounds that it would recognize Ottoman rights of sovereignty over them and thus treat British involvement as revoking such rights.[10]

British involvement from the beginning was anything but a stabilizing factor because the ruler was more interested in promoting his own and his family's ambitions than serving British interests. This was well attested after 1851 by the number of incidents arousing British ire. The sultan desired at first that his brother Fuḍayl be recognized as his successor, but the Bombay governor in council notified Captain S. B. Haines, British political agent at Aden, not to accede to the sultan's request. The British would interfere only if their interests required it, leaving it to the people of Laḥj to decide the succession in accordance with their own laws and customs.[11]

Aggravating incidents

A number of incidents involving the murder of British officers and attendants aggravated relations between the Resident at Aden and his neighbours to the north during this long period of interaction.[12] When Captain Milne of the Aden agency was killed while on a hunting expedition close to Laḥj country in March 1851, Haines sought permission to retaliate by destroying the village in which the incident took place. The secretary to the government of India, who was convinced that the sultan was innocent, overruled him on the grounds that it is 'better that they think we are weak than to perpetuate injustice on an innocent village'.[13] The government feared that the sultan might retaliate by blocking the road on which they depended for the delivery of supplies to Aden. The secret committee in India agreed to Captain Haines's suggestion that the stipend be cut. But other than to bring in troops from India to force the culprit's surrender, the only alternative was to depend on the sultan's goodwill. The agency reported to Bombay that the sultan promised to apprehend the culprits, and Secretary Goldsmid expressed his government's satisfaction.

This, however, was not the only incident reflecting disaffection with the British presence. There were reports also of Arabs firing on British commercial ships and of the killing of sailors and officers in 1851.[14] Protests from Aden elicited a promise from the Sultan of Laḥj to protect traffic on the road to Aden. The Resident hoped that the sultan would be strong enough to head off the Fuḍayli chief, whose subsidy the government of British India had cut off earlier. They also promised to restore the stipend to the chief of Laḥj when he punished the culprits named in a letter from Haines.[15] The Faḍlis stood their ground, and the Resident realized that relations could not be cut off much longer. Hence, the governor general of India authorized resumption in February 1854, and a year later they resumed paying the stipend to the Faḍlis and reopened the port of Bīr Aḥmad.

Haines, on the other hand, was still bent on punishing them. He decided to use the ‘Awlaqis against the Faḍlis and to use horses to protect Aden. He encouraged the ‘Awlaqi chief to occupy ‘Magatayn’ (*sic*), confident the garrison at Aden was sufficient to seize Bīr Aḥmad if need be. It was indispensable for the security of trade, which could not be attained by existing defensive works. Vast fortifications could not defend roads beyond gunshot, hence the need for cavalry. An occasional sloop could defend the seaside, but guns were no guarantee because many who knew their locations could come by night and destroy their cities at the harbour and threaten the bay front. Batteries at the point were sufficient, but the garrison was not, which is why Haines argued for more troops and barracks at the point, where the main defensive outlook was only the tower at Ra's Marbūt.[16]

The case of al-Baghli

While the inhabitants of this region questioned their sultan's dependence on a British subsidy and protection, they themselves did not consider it necessary to honour such a commitment. Friction at the popular level led to British sailors and officers being murdered and to the sultan refusing to hand over the murderers for execution. Exasperated British officials complained of the ‘defiance of these Arabs and the Afghans’ compared with the docility of Indian Muslims. The sultan's refusal was based on Islamic law, which precluded the surrender of Muslims to infidels. Captain Haines faced a similar situation on 13 June 1850 when the sultan refused to surrender al-Baghli, the murderer of a seaman from the *Auckland* who had fled to the Fuḍaylis for refuge. Fears of retaliation led the sultan of the Baghlis to ally himself with the chief of Bīr Aḥmad and to block the road to Aden. Bīr Aḥmad was well suited for his forays and retreat to safety. The British were in a quandary; they had cut off the subsidy of 364.5 German crowns per annum and the chief threatened to retrieve this by attacking the caravans heading south towards Aden.

Colonel James Outram, who replaced Haines as political Resident at Aden, blamed the deteriorating relationship with their avowed protégés on Captain Haines's stubborn and arrogant ways. Haines had asked the sultan to depose the chief of Bīr Aḥmad in 1850 when he had no jurisdiction over him. Haines could not get the chief to surrender al-Baghli, even after laying siege to Bīr Aḥmad. His insistence had caused much loss of life, but nevertheless Haines continued to ignore the Bīr Aḥmad chief's independence. On 2 September 1851, 16 months later, Haines got a letter from the chief accusing him of falsely blaming him and saying that he was forwarding the letter to the Sultan of Laḥj. In forcing Haines to negotiate with him over delivering the culprit, the chief was manoeuvring to have the British recognize his independence by default. No delivery ensued and the Fuḍayli chief resided instead with his Bīr Aḥmad colleague.

According to Outram's report, in his eagerness to exact retribution for the atrocities perpetrated, Haines had been insensible to the fact that 'he means by which it was intimated to him the object should be affected, were deliberate assassination, and secret poisoning'. Instead, in the Arabic letter Haines submitted to India (different in crucial details from the English translation), he had ordered 'killing under any circumstance', which gave a false impression of the British government's intentions. The victim was to be a Sayyid Salih bin Somli (*sic*), allegedly one of the murderers. He was to be put to death by poison, but the sultan and Bīr Aḥmad people wanted al-Baghli either to kill himself or be enticed to the hills where the sultan could do it. Even the 'Aqrabi chiefs promised to have him done in before the end of October 1851. They also insisted that the Ottomans give up interfering with tribes under treaty ties to Great Britain.[17]

Another impertinent British demand was to prevent the Ottomans stationing troops on the coast of Arabia because it would interfere with their efforts to suppress the slave trade in which Arab maritime tribes engaged. In another argument they sought an Ottoman concession to draw a border around their area of Aden to ward off Ottoman troop encroachments.[18] This once again opened up the debate about Ottoman sovereignty rights in the southwest corner of Arabia and about Egyptian ones at the opposite end of Bāb al-Mandab on the African side.

Debate on sovereignty

Hertslet of the Foreign Office compiled a 64-page report on 5 March 1874 entitled 'Memorandum on the Turkish Claim to Sovereignty over the Eastern Shores of the Red Sea and the whole of the Western Shore of the same Sea, including the African Coast from Suez to Guardafu' in which he dismissed the issue of the legality of Aden's cession and treated the Egyptian presence (1833–38) as an 'occupation'.[19] After claiming the Aden dependency of Yemen, Muḥammad 'Alī, viceroy of Egypt and the Ottoman sultan's agent in Arabia at the time, was compelled, following his forced exit from Syria and Arabia by the Quadruple Alliance (Great Britain, Austria, Russia and Prussia) in 1840, to vacate the Tihāmah of Yemen as well.

By mid-September, Haines still believed that Sultan 'Ali Muḥammad Ḥasan of Laḥj would take al-Baghli's life. The British wanted the murderers of both Milne and the sailor either publicly executed or delivered to them to show that justice had been done. In January 1852, the sultan claimed that the *sayyid* implicated in Milne's death had died, poisoned by a woman of the entourage. But there was no evidence that al-Baghli had been killed as alleged; indeed, the evidence pointed to both murderers still being alive and free. The British government was upset by the lack of public retribution according to the laws of the land. Poisoning the *sayyid* was deemed a political sham designed to spare the sultan further embarrassing demands on his account. Meanwhile, the whole of Aden was convinced that the *sayyid* was still alive. Outram's investigation led to the conclusion that vacillating British policy and a lack of vigour were to blame.

When Brigadier Clarke replaced Haines the following year it was hoped that he would negotiate a way out of the quandary with the chief, but Clarke refused to resolve the matter by negotiation and coercion appeared the only solution. Compelling the sultan to purchase peace from time to time was the only way to prevent him plundering caravans and ruining trade with Aden. Firing long shots from a Mahi schooner and Elphinstone's boats had no effect on stopping the raids. Indeed, the Fuḍaylis not only refused to accept conciliatory offers, but, in the eyes of the British, they were seen as insulting in tone, defiant and humiliating. The Fuḍayli chief's alliance with the 'Aqrabis in 1852 allowed him to pass through Laḥj territory to Bīr Aḥmad, from where he could harass the sultan and interrupt supplies to Aden.

Obstructing the delivery of supplies reached new heights in 1853 when for ten days Aden could not count on any. The only way to lift the blockade was to create a diversionary attack. The sultan manoeuvred an enemy into conducting a foray into the Fuḍayli chief's territory. It yielded a temporary truce. The wily chief then lined up a number of the sultan's hitherto neutral enemies against him. Clarke's policy reinforced the chief's notion that the English were *kāfir*s (infidels) and blustering bullies whom one need not fear. There was a danger now that the coalition could crush the sultan and isolate Aden.[20]

Impact of Ottoman return to south Yemen

The return of Ottoman forces to the south of Yemen and the reclaiming of sovereignty rights presented the British authorities with a new set of problems. The tribal chiefs who could not be counted on to observe their accommodation arrangements with the India government were now in a position to play off the Ottomans against the British stationed in Aden.

Sir Elliot, the British ambassador in Istanbul, lodged a protest with the Sublime Porte in which he accused the Ottoman administrators in south Yemen of intimidating British protégés. The Porte, it was alleged, promised that their governor would be told to withdraw Ottoman troops from Laḥj and Ḥawshabi country.[21] As reported later, Ambassador Elliot called on Reşid Paşa, the Ottoman minister of foreign affairs, to inform him that Britain had treaty arrangements with the tribes and wanted no Ottoman interference with them. He claimed that he got 'the run around from Reshid' and was ignored when he asked to speak to the grand vizier. Reşid replied that Kâmil Paşa, then governor of Jerusalem, would be sent on a fact-finding mission to Yemen. He allegedly promised that orders would be sent to the governor general (*vali* of Yemen) not to molest any tribes that claimed British protection. Such a promise was not the first of its kind, according to Elliot, and in his view, it held no value. He blamed Reşid's 'acting in bad faith' on the Ottoman minister of war, 'who at this moment is strong enough to act independently of other ministers'.[22]

Another reason for British protest was that allegedly in 1840 the Ottomans had held the son of the 'Alawi Shaykh of Qa'ṭabah hostage, ordering him not to give in to the British demand to yield Aden. The British then took the position that it was up to the Sublime Porte to prove that it held *de jure* rights over Yemen. Until then, the memorandum stated that the Ottomans could claim Jiddah and Mocha as their possessions, and British Aden as theirs. Queen Victoria's advocate's report admitted that the whole of Yemen had been both *de facto* and *de jure* part of the Ottoman Empire up to the year 1663, when the Ottoman sultan's forces there were defeated and, consequently, the dominion of Yemen passed to its *sayyid*s, headed by the Imam of Ṣan'ā', who acted independently of his Ottoman sovereign.

When in 1849 Tevfik Paşa, entrusted to reassert Ottoman control over the whole country, led Ottoman forces back to the Yemeni lowlands, he allowed the imam to continue administering Yemen, but under the Ottoman sultan's sovereignty. Half the revenue collected was to be remitted to the imperial treasury and the other half allocated to benefit the country and meet its administrative costs. To maintain order and enforce the obedience of unruly tribesmen, 1000 soldiers were to be stationed in the fortresses of Yemen. The imam would receive 3700 German crowns a month from the revenue before the central treasury's deduction was made, but the wily imam parlayed the amount into 25,000 crowns, 1700 of which were levied on merchants travelling from Mocha to Hodeida to be repaid to them in their customs account.

The Aden Resident was of the opinion that the Turks would not benefit from trying to assert control over the coastal areas. He proceeded to recount events to prove how they had failed to reassert their sovereign rights. In March 1866, British troops launched a military operation against Shuqarah's port under Fuḍayli control, 60 miles east of Aden, destroying the town and its environs and compelling the tribe to submit to the Aden government.

In May the following year the emir of the Azens (*sic*) drove the Ottomans out of the same territory from which they had driven him. In December 1872, Ottoman troops landed at Hodeida on their way to take control of Ṣan'ā', which they did on 24 April 1873, followed by overtures to the chiefs around Aden.[23]

In January 1869, for MT$ 80,000 two Frenchmen (Mass and Poilex) bought a place from the *shaykh* of the Haqrani tribe called Bandar of Shaykh Sa'īd, commonly known as Sheikh Said, with a view to establishing a factory there directly opposite the island of Perim. The cession included the cape of Bāb al-Mandab. The Porte was furious and took its *shaykh*, 'Ali Thābit, to task, but he retorted in astonishment that no one but his family ever governed that territory and the French government denied any knowledge of the transaction. In May 1870, the Ottoman foreign minister declared that his government would send a warship there to ensure against such encroachments. In December that year the French announced that they would withdraw from Shaykh Sa'īd.

Ottoman legal rights in Arabia

In a note to the British government dated 28 January 1874, Musurus, the Ottoman ambassador to London, asserted that the sultan held sovereignty over the whole of Arabia, including Yemen and Laḥj, 'as successor of the Prophet and the chief of the universal Caliphat'. The British, on the other hand, denied this title to the interior, either by occupation or priority of discovery, or even by statement; they denied also the caliphal claim since it would entitle the sultan to sovereignty over half the world and the pope to the other half.

It was not the first time claims to sovereignty via caliphal authority were injected in purely political matters. In July 1848 the British had denied Sharīf Ḥusayn ibn Ḥaydar's right over Yemen by such authority on the grounds that he was unsuitable for governing. They countered by stating that 'if the Porte has in reality any just claim to the country, then surely the vice-regent, who even yet retains the title of the "sword of the Khalifat", is the Imaum of Senna [Ṣan'ā']'.

The Earl of Granville passed on a compromise proposal to the Duke of Argyll for consideration that 'the Sultan as Khaliph should grant an autonomy to the Lahaej and Howshebee countries'. Musurus's proposal elicited an emphatic negative from the India Office on 12 January 1874, for it would imply recognizing Ottoman sovereignty over the country.[24]

Having consulted the sultan's government, on 26 January 1874 Musurus relayed to the Duke of Granville the contents of a telegram from Reşid Paşa, Ottoman foreign minister, stating that 'our imperial government does not compromise sovereignty over Laḥj but won't interfere with treaty obligations transacted between the *shaykh*s and others; the presence of our imperial army in Yemen is by right; Arabia is the cradle of Islam; the Sultan is the Prophet's *khalīfah*; he has rights and obligations *vis-à-vis* the Holy Cities.'[25]

British encroachments on Ottoman possessions in the Arabian Peninsula consisted of numerous forced 'treaty' arrangements with hapless native chiefs.[26] They occasioned two important documents, both dated 6 August 1879 and both from Faḍl ibn 'Alawi, a *sayyid* of Hadramawt, to the Ottaman sultan. They summed up the attitude of the Arabian chiefs, whom the British considered their stipendiary, thus entitling them to rights not justified by international law. Given the importance of the documents, I reproduce them *verbatim* in English from the Arabic original.[27]

British manoeuvres in the south, which Arab historians link to the 1892 rebellion, gave the Ottomans another problem[28] because, for no apparent gain, they were stirring up and smuggling rifles to the tribes. The Ottomans had assiduously cultivated good ties with the tribes bordering the British enclave at Qabṭīyah, Laḥj, al-Ḍāli' and the Ḥawshabis' lands and their government had provided monthly stipends to the chiefs of this region to keep them loyal, matching what the British were doing to pacify them and thus secure the safety of trade caravans out of Aden to the interior of Yemen.[29] Rumours reached Istanbul by cipher dispatches from the *kaymakam* of Ta'izz that the British planned to build a railroad into the nine districts under their influence, which would have meant constructing posts and stationing police along the route. In many ways the Ottoman presence aided the British in that it curbed the excesses of tribes that otherwise might have pounced on the caravan trade of those under their protective umbrella in the south, but they never conceded anything that would challenge their sovereignty over the region and, if the rumour were true, the plan would violate agreements reached with the British at Aden.[30]

Fifteen years earlier, Lord Granville had insisted that the boundary of the chief of Ḍali''s territory, now under British jurisdiction, should be defined and Musurus, the Ottoman ambassador in London, had forwarded his request to Istanbul with a promise that the matter would be investigated. Though the Sublime Porte conceded jurisdiction over the chief to the British, it was not prepared to alienate its sovereignty over it and the matter remained in limbo. When *Vali* Izzet Paşa sought advice from the sultan's government on 5 September 1882, the reply did not endorse Granville's request other than to agree to define the boundaries without yielding jurisdiction.[31]

Ottoman and British exchanges over the Laḥj crisis

The crisis started when the Sultan of Laḥj, Shaykh Faḍl ibn Muḥsin al-'Abdali, called on Brigadier-General Schneider[32] at Aden on 24 October 1872 to present him with a letter that Faḍl had received from Müşür Ahmed Muhtâr Paşa of Yemen, dated 8 B 1289/11 September 1872, inviting him to declare his allegiance to the Ottoman sultan. Schneider advised Faḍl to tell the *müşür* that he must first consult the British government, which paid him a stipend and with whom he had a treaty. When Pisani, Ambassador Elliot's dragoman, called on Halil Paşa in Istanbul to relay Granville's request, he was told that Laḥj was a closed topic of discussion; it belonged to the sultan. An irate Granville fired off a dispatch on 30 January 1873 to Elliot stating: 'I directed you to state that for 200 years Yemen had been independent of Turkish rule and Great Britain has the right to enter into treaty relations with the tribes.' His ire was no less intense when he learned that the Ottoman official in Aden received instructions from the governor of Ta'izz stating that the *müşür* at Ṣan'ā' appointed the chief of the Ḥawshabis head of his district with a monthly salary of MT$ 50 and had ordered a detachment of troops to be sent into this district. On 12 May 1873 Brigadier-General Schneider reported that three days earlier 'Ali ibn Muqbil 'Abd al-Hādi, the young chief of the al-Ḍāli' tribe, had informed him that he had responded to a letter from the Ottoman authorities received some months before by going to Qa'ṭabah and making his submission. This led to the appointment of a *muḥāfız* over his country, who took up residence at the palace. The officer levied a tax of 8 per cent on all goods arriving from Aden that remained for sale at al-Ḍāli', and 2.5 per cent on those proceeding to Aden. He pledged to pay MT$ 800 a year from his revenue to the Ottoman treasury in exchange for a salary of $40 a month. As a token of good behaviour, 'Ali gave him a hostage who resided in Ta'izz. Schneider claimed to have told the emir that the India government was responsible for those granted stipends and with whom it had treaty commitments, stating that the presence of Ottoman troops around Aden did not appear to conform with the Porte's authorization. He stopped short of recommending that the emir throw out the Ottoman *muḥāfız*.

Granville sent a telegram to Elliot on 5 June 1873 stating that in his view the Sublime Porte had not authorized troops in the vicinity of Aden, for it was inconsistent with successive assurances from the Ottoman government and they should be recalled immediately. But, according to a dispatch from Schneider to the Duke of Argyll on 27 May, Turkish troops and 200 irregulars had arrived from Qa'ṭabah at Rāhdah, the capital of the Ḥawshabi district. There were already 500 troops at Marṣad in Ṣubayḥi country. Troops stationed in both places were to meet at Zayda. Schneider could only speculate that the *müşür* at Ṣan'ā' had not yet received instructions to withdraw them. A communiqué from Reşid Paşa to Elliot of 15 July 1873 assured the British envoy that the Ottoman sultan's government had no wish to stir up trouble between the British and their stipendiaries, that the house of the Ḥawshabi sultan would be evacuated without compromise to the flag, that Turkish vessels would continue to trade with Hadramawt and that he foresaw good neighbourly relations with them in Yemen. These assurances were repeated on 5 August with a promise that the governor-general of Yemen, Ahmed Eyüp Paşa, would receive orders to withdraw the troops; but they were still there in October.

The reason for this can be traced to a response from Eyüp to the grand vizier of 6 August 1873, in which he refuted the British embassy's word. Having conducted his own enquiries, the Ottoman governor-general learned that the Ṣubayḥi district adjoining Mocha was a *kaza* dependency of it and that its inhabitants, by their own inclination, considered themselves subjects of the Ottomans under the governing authority of the *kaymakam* of Ḥujarīyah; since both districts were peaceful, there was no need to send troops there. The inhabitants of the small *nahiye* of the Ḥawshabis also considered themselves subjects of the Porte by their own desire, being governed, as before, by their own *müşür*, 'Ali Māni Efendi. They had been obedient and quiet until Faḍl Muḥsin, the Shaykh of Laḥj, became their enemy, persecuting them and encroaching upon their lands. He was warned, but did not desist; indeed, he had interfered 'vexatiously' (*sic*) with the whole district of the Ḥawshabis, usurping the rights of inhabitants near Zayda, including the property of the *müşür*, 'Ali Māni. The British embassy had no right to complain, argued Eyüp, stating 'we take all necessary measures to curb those activities as per imperial command.'

The case of 'Abdallah

Ahmed Eyüp had reported in his dispatch that 'Abdallah, the Sultan of Laḥj's brother, had been involved in a fight in the bazaar in which a number were killed; 25 Ottoman soldiers were called in to occupy 'Abdallah's fortified house where he, with his sons, had yielded to the Ottoman sultan's authority. Schneider then decided to send troops to help the sultan. When the sultan visited Schneider in October, he blamed his brother's followers for starting the fight, claiming that when he went to capture him, 'Abdallah had called in the 25 *zaptiye* stationed at Shuqarah, who insisted the sultan release the nephews Faḍl and Muḥsin (sons of 'Abdallah) whom he had held hostage. The commander denied British allegations that he was interfering where he was not needed by stating that 'Abdallah and his family were Ottoman subjects and that they had come to protect him. The sultan also alleged that their commander had asked to have his men placed in his small fort, but refused on the grounds that it was already crowded on account of the month of Ramaḍān. On learning of the incident, the grand vizier sent a telegram to the governor-general of Yemen on 3 November 1873 stating that he had no business sending *zaptiye* outside the district at the request of some *shaykh*s and ordered they be withdrawn and he be informed when it was done. But, according to the British Resident, by the middle of November they still had not withdrawn.[33]

In a telegram of 9 December 1873 Granville informed Elliot that he had received a message from the Resident at Aden informing him that the Ottomans had withdrawn their soldiers from Laḥj and that the whole area between Laḥj and Ta'izz had been cleared of Ottoman troops, so he need not send reinforcements. On the same date, the sultan's two hostile brothers surrendered to the Resident and were sent to Aden as state prisoners. British troops captured and were to destroy their forts. The Resident promised to deal with the Ḥawshabi chief at an early date and sanctions were anticipated. On 7 December, Resident Schneider chided 'Abdallah for rising against a brother the *shaykh*s of Laḥj had duly elected as sultan, for calling in the Turks, and for dealing with his brother's enemy, 'Ali Māni of the Ḥawshabis. Captain Hunter and his soldiers took him prisoner and the forts he surrendered were demolished that same day, 7 December.

Turkish troops occupied Laḥj and Ḥawshabi country in 1873 and the British immediately insisted they withdraw. Apparently, the sultan and his brother 'Abdallah were quarrelling. 'Abdallah called on the Ottomans to help settle the dispute with his brother, the sultan. The Ottoman governor at Ta'izz, the capital of the *sancak* technically administering the territory into which the British had encroached, responded that

'Abdallah was a Turkish subject. The sultan, on the other hand, insisted that Ottoman intervention was not needed. He called on the Resident instead to stop the hostilities, which brought into focus the rights of sovereignty and British interference with them.[34]

It would appear that 'Abdallah ended up as a state prisoner living in comfort at Aden and the Resident was instructed to release him on condition he did not return to Yemen, but to keep his brother and son hostages. 'Abdallah's family resided in the sultan's palace, which was apparently why he was being kept in poor health.[35]

If firmness, as Schneider called it, was to teach the Arabs a lesson, it had little lasting effect. Emir 'Ali Muqbil wrote Schneider a letter, which he received on 28 April 1874, saying that soon after he had written to him the *kaymakam* had come for help, accompanied by 22 Turks and 700 *zaptiye*, which, with supporting Arabs, increased their numbers to 2200 men. They fired on his followers because of their dealings with Schneider, which resulted in bloodshed and death. Muqbil wrote:

> We proceed to Dhali al-Ḍāli" to collect more men, while the Turkish troops increased by another 120 and, together with the Arabs, are bent on coming after me. I sent you a letter for help, but you did not reply. Do you intend to keep your promise under the arrangement and help me before we are ruined? Don't blame me for the roads because of your indifference. They collect transit dues from my subjects while we spend money for keeping the roads safe!

After learning that Schneider had occupied 'Abdallah's forts by force, Reşid sent a telegram to Musurus on 12 January 1874 stating that the spirit of conciliation had not resolved the Laḥj affair. 'We have no intention of abandoning the possession of the territory to the British', declared Reşid. 'Abdallah was entitled to seek help from the Ottoman authorities next door. The British attack on and capture of 'Abdallah and his brother, who enjoyed imperial protection, was another violation. They did not seem to want to understand the Ottomans' special position in Arabia, the cradle of Islam, and the status of the sultan (Ottoman) as successor to the Prophet and head of the universal caliphate, protector of the holy sites.

The British could make up for their painful act by sending 'Abdallah to Istanbul. 'Abdallah, his brother and their families ended up incarcerated in Aden, and Bombay wanted the Resident, Colonel Schneider, to find out whether the Sultan of Laḥj was willing to pay for their maintenance once freed and permitted to stay in Aden.[36]

In a dispatch dated 10 February 1874, the secretary of the India government's political and secret department advised the under-secretary of state for foreign affairs in London to ignore the Ottoman government's remonstrance on the grounds that 'the Sultan has no rights in this part of the world such as to entitle him to interfere in the internal affairs of various chiefs around Aden.'

Ambassador Elliot was convinced that the Ottoman government had no real idea about what was going on in south Yemen because of muddled language and did not realize that al-Ḍāli' belonged to a stipendiary chief. The grand vizier issued instructions to the governor general to withdraw 200 Ottoman troops from the house of 'Ali ibn Muqbil. Nuri Süleiman, the *mutasarrıf* of Ta'izz, had issued a *buyrultu* on 15 February 1873 to 'Ali ibn Muqbil after he offered to submit to Ottoman authority, appointing him *müşür* of Laḥj under the immediate supervision of Hayrallah Ağa, the *kaymakam*.

A year after his submission to Ottoman authority and reverting to British dependency, 'Ali found himself once again under the Ottoman gun. Writing to Schneider on 9 December 1874, he once again blamed him for not coming to his help when the Turks brought their big cannons to Qa'ṭabah, 'causing fear to the men of 'Ali, while all you can say is be patient; your friendship only gets us in trouble!'

A dispatch of 11 August 1874 from the Foreign Office to Elliot announcing the withdrawal of troops from al-Ḍāli', stated that one of the emir's chiefs had signed a document denying that 'Ali ibn Muqbil had any right to rule the country, and appointed 'Abdallah ibn Ma'ūd to the emirship. The Resident also believed that the *mutasarrıf*'s agents were still plotting with 'Ali ibn Ma'ūd, *shaykh* of the Ḥawshabis.

Judging from their testimony and reports, by the end of 1874 the British had been unable to effect a solid working relationship with the chiefs of tribes around Aden. The fear of what they termed 'Turkish interference in the affairs of Lahaj and Aden' had induced the secret government of India to authorize its political residents to negotiate treaty arrangements with the chiefs of the 'Abdalis, Faḍlis, 'Aqrabis and Ḥawshabis because of the instability caused by the rebellions against the Sultan of Laḥj by his brother and nephews. They urged the withdrawal of Ottoman troops from Laḥj, but to no avail.[37] The Ottomans still held the upper hand over the region, and the tribal chiefs the British Resident had wooed were more apt to slink away than stand with him under demonstrable pressure from Ottoman governing officials in the region. The case of Laḥj clearly illustrates this dilemma of the India government, which barred it from extending its influence into the interior of south Yemen at this time.[38]

Negotiations between the Ottoman sultan's government and London lasted for 40 days and ended with the Ottomans conceding the title of sultan to the Laḥj chief and appointing the *shaykh* of the Ḥawshabis their official administrator under the nominal administration of the *kaymakam* of Ta'izz, while for all practical purposes his territory remained outside its *sancak*.[39] At no time during this period, however, did the sultan's government compromise what it claimed to be its sovereign rights in the whole of Arabia or concede any portion of its territory officially to the British. Nor did it at a later date permit them to purchase land from the *shaykh* of al-Ḍali' *kaza* of the Ta'izz *sancak*, whom they had taken under their protection. The *sadaret* instructed its ambassador to make it clear to Lord Granville that no such infringement of Ottoman territorial rights would be permitted, and asked him to order his officials in Aden to desist from such manoeuvres.[40]

Stabilizing the border

The boundary between territories enjoying British protection and the Ottomans immediately to the north, with Ta'izz adjoining them, had not yet been clearly defined, which made the British at Aden particularly eager to acquire the *shaykhs*' protection and to enjoy their largesse. In 1904 the Ottoman government undertook to review the proposed boundary setting as recorded prior to dispatching troops to engage rebels in the south.[41] The British embassy had requested clarification and the government sought to accommodate.[42] They were eager to have the dividing boundary more clearly defined as al-Ḍāli' lines were in question.[43] This provided its *shaykh* with the excuse to collect 100 *liras* from the Ottomans for his alleged administrative service.[44] Ottoman authorities at Ta'izz also sought exemption from paying customs fees on coal landed there by British companies.[45]

With all their family feuds and shifting allegiances it was not always easy for the British at Aden to control the tribes under their protection.

This of course created instability at a time when turmoil in the north tended to affect attitudes in the south. The emir of al-Ḍali', Shāyif ibn Sayf ibn 'Abd al-Hādi ibn Ḥasan, is a case in point. He visited Aden and sought protection for his territory. However, Resident H. M. Mason had reservations about him, as he reported to the Bombay government, but nonetheless had to acknowledge that both his people and the British recognized his legitimacy. The British agreed to extend him the recognition he sought provided he mended his ways with the subordinate chiefs, did not enter into treaty agreements with others, did not cede or mortgage his domain to any power other than the British, kept the roads to and from Aden open and secure, adhered strictly to the boundary drawn up by the joint British–Turkish Commission, stopped his tribesmen creating disturbances and maintained a minimum of 50 men in a state of efficiency and to the satisfaction of the British Resident at Aden. In return, he was to receive MT$ 100 a month, plus an additional $100 for his men.[46] The British advisers on the scene considered it inadvisable to grant such money because they had no faith in the emir, whose integrity they questioned and whose conduct since the initial treaty of 1888 had been less than trustworthy.[47]

In view of the imam's uprising and to maintain the status quo in the nine cantons, neither the Ottomans nor the British were to send troops to them. A note from the Ottoman ambassador in London about border delimitation induced the government to instruct its commissioners to proceed with the delimitation of the Ṣubayḥi border by a line running from Quddam outside Bāb al-Mandab to the sea of Aden littoral, on condition the villages and wells of al-Turbah and its territory, bordered by a line terminating at Shaykh Murād, remained in the *vilayet* of Yemen. There was no mention of delimiting the boundary northeast of the desert, but a promise was given that the territory in question would not be ceded to a third power.[48] The British, however, were not prepared to promise they would keep their troops outside the delimited zones, which the Ottoman Ambassador Musurus in London found unacceptable, and a disturbance of the status quo.[49]

Controlling the border area was not always without incident between the Ottomans and British. In 1906, part of the Ṣubayḥis' Barhami tribe raided Ottoman territory and looted 85 camels from the Ḥakami, Ḥātimah and Qawāsimah tribes in the vicinity of Mawza'. The British ordered their immediate return.[50]

The Bombay government discouraged Major Jacob, the political

Resident at al-Ḍāli', from having a connection with Turkish officials on the other side of the frontier. On the Ṣubayḥi border near Mafālis, the Manṣūri *shaykh* was informed that persons residing on the Turkish side of the recently demarcated border were Turkish subjects and liable to the jurisdiction and revenue demands of the Turkish authority, while those on the British-protected side were relieved of any further liability to the Ottoman authority, a solution Major Jacob found acceptable as a way of eliminating friction.[51]

A tribe astride the border could not avoid such friction. For instance, the Shujayfah resided on both sides, though most were within the Manṣūri limits. The Ottoman government *müşür* was only interested in collecting certain rightful dues for that portion of the Shujayfah who resided within Turkish limits. The British told their protégé that there was no reason for alarm, instructing him to withdraw the armed men he had dispatched to the area and send them home. He was to inform the Resident of any wrongful claims.[52]

Wrangling over sovereignty and British insistence at Aden on controlling the southern Yemeni tribes, despite strong resistance from relatives of the 'sultans' who signed protection agreements with them, intensified rather than resolved disputes when the Ottomans sought to reassert their rights by supporting the dissidents.

8. Suggested Plans of Reform

We noted in the previous chapters that a thorny problem the Ottomans confronted was the unwelcome intrusion of the British in south Yemen. Their manoeuvring to expand their influence with tribes south of Ta'izz impelled the Ottomans to move troops south to contain British plans and strengthen tribal leaders trying to combat British expansionist policies. The net result of such manoeuvrings was to delay for a quarter of a century final agreement on an official demarcation of the border between British stipendiary tribes and directly-administered Ottoman territories to the north where rebellion had intensified and the need for visible reform had become urgent if the Ottoman sultan's administration in Yemen was to last.

Within a decade of implanting themselves at Aden, ostensibly to acquire a coal depot to service their ships to and from India, the British began to think of acquiring a trade route to the north to expand their commercial activities. This in turn aroused resistance not only from unsympathetic tribal chiefs, but from Ottoman authorities as well, which encouraged them to side with those tribes nominally under their authority. This engendered a struggle between the British and the Ottomans that lasted until 1900, when a process set in to define spheres of authority between the contending powers.

The defeat of Ottoman forces in and following the siege of Ṣan'ā' during the Zaydi uprising of 1905 coincided with the rise of disaffection with Ottoman administrative policies in the Arab provinces generally. The imperial powers' press trumpeted the victories of the imam's forces as the harbinger of an Arab nationalism and of an Arab-Islamic caliphate to replace the Ottoman. In the triumph of Arab nationalism it saw also the rise to predominance of British influence throughout the Arab world, the abrupt eclipse of the German influence, and the *reductio ad nihilum* of the Ottoman influence in international circles.

First, let me provide a brief survey of Ottoman policy in Yemen. The Ottomans officially regained administrative control of the highlands in 1849, but their physical presence was only enforceable in 1872; a year later, they turned the whole land (except the southern part which Britain controlled) into a *vilayet* of four prefectures (*mutasarrifiyes*),[1] each subdivided further into counties (*kazas*) and districts (*nahiyes*).[2] The opening of the Suez Canal in 1869 made the Ottomans more aware of Yemen's strategic and commercial importance. It also made it possible to move troops directly by sea in an attempt to suppress the ongoing revolts by the Zaydi imam and his allies among the Ismā'īlī tribes.[3]

As Ottoman investigators came to realize, not all Yemen's problems stemmed from misadministration. The country's agriculture had long been neglected and the potential productivity and tax revenue from it sharply reduced to the point of being insufficient to meet the expenses of the local administration let alone provide salaries for policing units.

The absence of customs posts in key areas along the coast encouraged large-scale smuggling. Revenue, as a consequence, was far below realizable levels. To make matters worse, the intensification of imperial rivalries in the lower Red Sea (British in Aden versus Italians in Eritrea and French in Djibouti) began to spill over into Yemen. Both the British from Aden and the Italians from Eritrea were accused of encouraging the imam's rebellion in the interests of promoting their economic ventures in the highlands.

Such detractions, coupled with incompetent administrators, made it practically impossible for the sultan's government to implement the radical changes necessary to stabilize the country and secure a hold over it. Expenditures in lives and money failed to suppress the forces of rebellion. Yemen had become a burdensome liability, but the Ottomans were not about to abandon this southern gateway to the holiest sites of Islam and thereby jeopardize the sultan's prestige in a newly aroused Muslim world.

As one foreign traveller noted, Yemen's history from 1872 to 1911 (when an agreement was reached at last with the imam) is replete with wars intensified by massacres, vengeance and hunger.[4] The protracted siege of Ṣan'ā' and its aftermath, which cost more than 10,000 Ottoman lives, followed by catastrophic losses at Shahārah, where Ottoman troops were caught in a narrow pass and were nearly annihilated, induced the Sublime Porte once again to appoint Ahmed Feyzi, the veteran of 30 years of campaigning in the Arab provinces, commander of an Ottoman task force and governor *ad interim* of Yemen; but he too met with little success. Ottoman troops were shaken by heavy losses and demoralized by lack of pay. Syrian units refused to stay on when their term of service had expired; they demanded they be sent home and eventually were allowed to leave.

Mission of Hussein Hilmi

In 1894, Hussein Hilmi of the Egyptian khedival family came to Yemen with specific instructions to recommend policy changes that would pacify and stabilize the country, relieve pressure on an already overburdened treasury, and reduce opportunities for foreigners to meddle in the internal affairs of the land. The problems confronting a sound administration policy lay, as he put it, in:

- unwise action by Ottoman army officers and officials who did not comply with instructions, thus angering the tribes;
- the absence of effective means to contain the reaction of the tribes when aroused; and
- the ambitions of both Imam al-Manṣūr and afterwards his son Yaḥya to acquire autonomy for the Zaydis and their allies in the highlands, with Ṣa'dah, when not Ṣan'ā', serving as the base of their operations against Ottoman authority.[5]

As governor (1898–1902), Hilmi introduced administrative changes that appealed to the inhabitants, but became the target of an assassination attempt by army officers loyal to Müşür Aptullah, who wanted to recruit Yemenis for military service and send those held within to prison outside the country. Hilmi's tenure as *vali* coincided with the Reform Commission's recommendations summarizing four years of investigation (1898–1902). The cost of fighting rebellion during this period averaged between 15,000 and 20,000 *liras* a month, a considerable drain on the treasury when, as the *maliye naziri* reported, the per annum revenue of Yemen was only 450,000 *liras*.[6] Even under Abdülhamid, when the sultanate for a while controlled the whole country from 'Asīr to the outer limits of Aden, Yemen generated insufficient revenue to provide for all administrative expenditures.

In 1901 the sultan's government sent a commission to make a truce with the imam, but the Sublime Porte ministers rejected the conditions he laid down. The military party resolved on firm action. Müşür Aptullah replaced Hilmi as *vali ad interim.* He had been serving as commander of Ottoman forces stationed in Arabia, which included the seventh army corps. Aptullah was not only arrogant but he was also incompetent as an administrator and did little to ameliorate the worsening conditions caused by high prices and insecure travel. Zarānīq tribesmen of the Tihāmah were preying on trade routes, both on land and at sea.[7] Moreover, some tribal chiefs accused Aptullah of being oblivious to British encroachments in the south and of neglecting 'the boundary' with Aden, thereby allowing the British to extend their control over the district (*nahiye*) of al-Ḍāli' in 1902.[8]

The lack of demarcations separating tribes the British controlled or influenced from those technically under Ottoman sovereignty aggravated the problem in the south. Besides, in the absence of any customs or policing posts, smuggling went on unabated across undefined tribal zones. The piracy in the Red Sea by Zarānīq and Banu Marwān tribesmen had created a crisis for Aptullah with the Italians, whose shipping they had been raiding for some time and the Italian admiral was threatening to bombard the coastal area from north of Midi to Hodeida.[9] Aptullah's problems lay not only in stopping piracy in the Red Sea, but also in devising ways of preventing the Italians smuggling arms to the imam through intermediaries.[10]

While Aptullah was distracted from other policing action in the highlands, revolt soon broke out in Abhā of 'Asīr and spread southward to Ibb and Jiblah in the Ta'izz prefecture. Another commission was sent out. It too reported that outbreaks were the result of unusually harsh suppressive measures adopted by army officers.[11]

The Ottoman government saw a real need to define the border in the south and strengthen its naval forces in the Red Sea to prevent smuggling and retrieve revenue lost by uncontrolled imports. A report by Mahmud Nedim, then minister of the interior, called attention to the fact that the lines of communication with Yemen, both by land and sea, had been insecure for a number of years, thus facilitating the smuggling of arms and rendering impossible the task of pacification.[12] Nedim urged the Sublime Porte to take all necessary steps to end illicit trafficking, especially in contraband, even disarming the inhabitants if need be. The problem, as he well noted, lay in the 400-mile Yemeni coastline along which mostly shallow waters (four to five feet deep) prevailed, making it possible for larger vessels to anchor only within a two- to three-mile distance from the shore. Lighter vessels (*sunbūqs*), on the other hand, could slip right past them and anchor offshore with their smuggled goods and weapons. To end such trafficking, Nedim recommended deploying a battalion of troops along the coast armed with a number of light artillery pieces, assisted offshore by eight armed steamships. To contain smuggling by land in the south, he recommended establishing four customs posts stretching from Qa'ṭabah northeastward through Laḥj with a major military post at Ḥujarīyah to prohibit arms traffic to Ta'izz.[13]

Italian and British activities off the coast and in the highlands

To the alarm of both Ottomans and British, Italian activity off the coast of Yemen intensified after 1881. By 1898 their warships were intimidating the authorities in Hodeida at the slightest pretext. They bombarded Midi north of al-Luḥayyah in October 1902 because the Ottomans were too slow to indemnify them for losses they and their protégés had sustained off Massawa on the Eritrean coast during the Banu Marwān raids. In September 1907, they sent a gunboat to Hodeida (where only six Italian citizens resided) following some disturbances there, and by the end of that year the Florida-Rubattino shipping line had inaugurated a passenger and cargo service between Genoa and Aden with stops both ways. Their consulate at Hodeida had been in existence since April 1903.[14]

When the Ottomans resumed control of the highlands in 1872, the British had been accustomed to viewing this territory as two districts by a boundary not yet delimited but 'apparent to the tribes'. They established a *de facto* protectorate over a large part of the hinterland, far beyond their base at Aden, despite the objections even of Gladstone, who feared that such an expansion involved 'the most indefinite obligations. It binds us to support those over whose conduct to others we have no control.'[15]

In 1900, negotiations failed to dislodge a Yemeni chief's occupation of a fort at al-Shurayjah in Ḥawshabi territory, which the British claimed to be under their influence. They sent in a force of 500 to dislodge him and succeeded only after engaging Ottoman troops who had supported the chief.[16] The incident showed that the race on both sides to enlist tribes in their respective camps would lead to more incidents. An agreement was reached in 1902 to define the boundary, though no formal treaty ensued from the negotiations that went on for a number of years. The imam criticized Ottoman efforts to establish any borderline on the grounds that his own jurisdiction extended over the whole of Yemen, both north and south.

Eduard Glaser's mission

The sultan now resolved more than ever to settle the matter peacefully, but from his underlings he got only confusing reports and recommendations on how to do so. Himself a product of German training and with much faith in German expertise, he recommended sending Dr Eduard Glaser (1855–1908)[17] on an investigative mission. So in 1907, on behalf of Sultan Abdülhamid, the Sublime Porte commissioned Glaser, an expert on Yemen who spoke Arabic and had been on friendly terms with Ottoman officers when he had worked in the country as an ethnographer two decades earlier, to study the situation at close range. The sultan was genuinely interested in introducing reforms that would stabilize the country and increase its economic prosperity. A number of commissions had been sent out before, but their recommendations for reform did not usually prove viable and remained largely unimplemented.[18]

Glaser submitted his report and an accompanying map to Istanbul. It focused on conditions in the *vilayet*, especially in the eastern region. It was translated into Ottoman and reviewed in a session of the Council of Ministers in January 1907, then passed to the minister of the interior.[19]

From the contents of a report Glaser submitted in February 1907, it seems that he was asked to devise a strategy that would (1) win over or isolate Imam Yaḥya and (2) prevent a possible British link with him from territories they controlled or influenced in the southern region of Yemen.[20]

Rather than risk further embroilment with the Ottomans and border tribes, after 1907 the British resolved to confine their efforts strictly to the Aden territory and to offer no fresh treaties or protectorates to tribes beyond. Their activities in the interior were, however, a major reason for Eduard Glaser's mission, which might indirectly have contributed to their decision to withdraw from it. The British Resident at Aden, however, stated that 'the Turks had no valid ground to fear our advance for self aggrandizement.'[21] Smuggling, he alleged, was the work of

Ṣubayḥi 'chevalier-brigands' (*sic*) and not of the Sultan of Laḥj, whom the Ottomans suspected. It was also not done on behalf of the imam, but rather on behalf of the Sultan of Lahj, who sought arms for self-defence against miscreants. Political Resident Jacob alleged that it was the French from Djibouti, not British agents, who were pushing a lot of arms into Arabia. Their Le Gras carbine was highly sought after as a weapon because Arabs were able to refill cartridge cases for them at home. He also stated that since 1883 the government of India had banned the entry into Aden of arms and precision rifles, replacing the Le Gras with the Martini-Henry rifle, supposedly to check the flow of ammunition to the tribes.[22]

The defeat of Ottoman arms in Yemen caught the attention of the Arab nationalist and anti-Ottoman press in Europe, which saw it as a triumph for Arab nationalism and British strategy, which sought to dominate or influence Arabia by helping either the imam or some other Arabian chieftain gain the coveted title of caliph.[23] The French press was almost hysterical over such a possibility. The triumph of Britain would signal the demise of what was left of the Ottoman presence and, with it, the crumbling of the German dream to expand the kaiser's economic ventures into Arabia and the Gulf with the building of the railroad.[24] This was seen as a distinct possibility after the British entered into a treaty relationship in 1899 with Shaykh Mubārak al-Ṣabāḥ of Kuwait, the proposed terminus of the Baghdad Bahn.[25]

The role of Herman Burckhardt

Dismissed by the British press as a 'farrago of nonsense', such allegations were still believed in Istanbul. In February 1907, a young German 'ethnographer' with a good knowledge of Arabic and Turkish, Herman Burckhardt, got a quick *iradé* from the Sublime Porte (when no other foreigner could) to travel to Yemen, purportedly to conduct archaeological fieldwork 'in a region full of insurrection'. A correspondent from Istanbul wrote to *Les Pyramides* (*al-Ahrām*), which represented Cairo's French press, broadly insinuating that Burckhardt's journey was for other than its declared purpose.[26] When questioned by his chargé in Cairo, Chancellor von Bülow denied that there were any political aims to Burckhardt's mission.[27] His going to Yemen was allegedly the result of efforts by the well-known Italian merchant, Giuseppe Caprotti of Magenta, an importer–exporter, representative of the Turkish Tobacco

Regie and resident of Yemen for 20 years with whom the young scholar had been in contact since he had first met him in Berlin.[28]

Within a month of arriving in the highlands via Aden, Burckhardt submitted a detailed political report on the situation in Yemen to Dr Moritz, the German director of the khedival library in Cairo. He left little doubt that Ahmed Feyzi, the iron man of Ottoman arms in Arabia, was not about to put down the imam's rebellion. One of his recommendations, echoed later by Glaser, was to circle Arabia with a railway, urging quick steps to be taken to construct the much-rumoured line from Hodeida to Ṣan'ā' to 'Amrān north of the city, to facilitate the movement of troops and maintain close communications through a series of posts, thus assuring Ottoman authority in Yemen.[29]

It is interesting to note in this regard that a French engineer called Zabrowski had previously submitted a plan to build just such a line to a group of French bankers, which, as Chargé Grünau surmised in Cairo, might explain why Burckhardt's mission created such a fuss. More interestingly, it was rumoured that should a line be authorized, the Italians from across the Red Sea stood an excellent chance of getting the bid because of their good relations with the imam.[30]

Unlike Burckhardt, who met his death in Yemen a few years later,[31] Glaser was no novice in Yemeni affairs, having been in the country in 1883/4 accompanying Ottoman troops on their forays against rebels and later providing expert advice on the country's affairs.[32] Nor was he the first to be charged with an investigative mission by the Sublime Porte.

Namik Beg came out in 1892 and listened to an outpouring of Yemeni complaints, mostly about the harsh measures Ottoman officials were adopting and about Ahmed Feyzi's refusal to recognize Imam al-Manṣūr as a legitimate spokesman of Yemenis, let alone grant him the authority he sought over the Zaydis. Feyzi attempted in vain to convince highland chiefs that the sultan's government was genuinely interested in safeguarding Yemeni welfare and defending the land against foreign encroachments, one of their important concerns.[33]

But the Ottomans were not persuaded. As the Glaser report shows, they remained convinced that the imam's forces were receiving military supplies through British-controlled access ways. To counter the flow, Glaser proposed establishing a *cordon sanitaire*, what he termed 'the Shāfi'i line of defence',[34] to bar access to the imam's forces and supporters. The British, moreover, would have to be persuaded, preferably by diplomatic means, to establish military posts on their side of the cordon to halt the illicit traffic in ammunition and goods. The cordon would extend northeast from Qa'ṭabah to Ma'rib and would include the salt mines of al-Ayādīm in the desert east of Bayḥān and Ḥarīb. Exploiting these mines, moreover, would provide a pretext for entering into negotiations with the British for mutual restraint. The mines were seen as an important source of income for the tribes and their chiefs, as well as for the 'sultans', emirs and *sharīf*s of the Ma'rib area. Establishing a military post there, he argued, would facilitate the surveillance of routes from Hadramawt into Yemen, so curbing threats and menaces from the south. Ma'rib thus held critical military and strategic importance for Ottoman politics even if the proposed cordon reached only as far as Ḥarīb–Bayḥān, or even just to al-Ayādīm.[35]

At this time Ma'rib was a mere village of 600 inhabitants, the last of al-Jawf's predominantly Shāfi'i outposts. Some Zaydis lived there, but a Sharifian family, headed by 'Abd al-Raḥmān, ruled it. The British had courted al-Raḥmān off and on and in recent years had issued several invitations to his son Ḥusayn to come to Aden to conclude a treaty with them. Though no friend of the Ottomans, the emir did not, however, succumb to the temptation. He preferred to remain neutral and independent. Glaser had befriended Ḥusayn on previous visits and through him was persuaded to remain loyal to the Ottoman side.

In 1884, Izzet Paşa (*vali* and *müşür*) invited Glaser to explore the Ma'rib region with him to help win over its emir in case fighting broke out with the imam and his supporters. Izzet argued that if the emir did not at least remain neutral in such an eventuality, then loyal Yām tribesmen of the Najrān valley could be used to check him.

In 1888–90, al-Qu'ayṭi' of Hadramawt, the British *jamadār*, once again attempted to lure the *sharīf* into liaising with the Aden administration, but again he resisted. The British or their agents were constantly courting Ḥusayn's father, 'Abd al-Raḥmān. Should they succeed, argued Glaser, they would become the Imam of Ṣan'ā's political neighbours, thus extending their influence from Bāb al-Mandab and Qa'ṭabah northeastwards to Radā' and the Khawlān of Banu Jabr, to al-Jawf, Niḥim, Arḥab, Jabal 'Iyāl Yazīd and ultimately to 'Asīr. In such an extension of influence, Glaser argued, the British would come to dominate not only the Red Sea with their formidable fleet but also, through their ties with tribal chiefs, Yemen's whole line of communication (*khatt*), thus rendering Ottoman control of the country untenable.[36]

Glaser deemed it crucial that the Sublime Porte retained control of

Ma'rib–Bayḥān. Control could be assured by one of two ways, he argued: (1) military occupation or (2) reconstruction of the dam at Ma'rib. He ruled out the first option as strategically unsuitable for the area; besides, it could drive the emir into the arms of the British at Aden. An Ottoman initiative to reconstruct the dam would assure the friendship and loyalty of the emir and inhabitants of the region.[37] The reconstruction, moreover, would not be costly because 'half of it still stands as from the time before Christ'.[38]

Glaser could not stress enough the benefits of the dam. Not only would it increase greatly the land already under cultivation but also it could service between 100,000 and 150,000 new inhabitants. Many of the marauding tribes could be settled and allowed to engage in agriculture rather than vent their hostility towards Ottoman rule. More importantly, it would become much easier to defend the region.

Building a railroad from Ṣan'ā' to Ma'rib and extending it from Ṣan'ā' to Hodeida would make possible the movement of troops should they be required. A military outpost at Ṣāyir, extended to Qa'ṭabah by rail from Ma'rib, would tighten the proposed cordon. In this manner, he argued, 'we can hermetically seal Yemen to English influence from Aden, isolate the Imam and cut off his supply of ammunition and gunpowder from the Red Sea side with the help of Ottoman ships and military posts on the coast'.[39]

Glaser recommended that negotiations with the *sharīf*'s family of Mecca be kept secret so as not to alert the imam. He also suggested redeveloping al-Jawf, a fertile region in ancient times on account of the irrigation canals that watered it (as in the plain of Ma'rib).

With the realization of such schemes, Glaser was convinced that 'we will then be in a position to dictate the conditions to the Imam and reattach him to Ottoman influence.' This would become a definite probability once the imam saw revenue flowing in from the cultivation of vast new lands in an agriculturally rich region. He would have a share in the revenue if he permitted the construction of a railroad to 'Asīr across territory he controlled, even if he had to be granted a subvention to gain such approval. He would also have to allow small military forts to be built along the proposed line to police the area. In this manner, it was hoped that his confidence and loyalty might be regained.[40]

Glaser also recommended paying attention to 'the great Yām tribe of Wādi Najrān', strategically situated northeast of the imam's territory and east of 'Asīr. He personally knew the *dā'ī* of this Ismā'īlī tribe, al-

Fakhrī 'Abdallah ibn Aḥmad al-Makramī, and knew that their Bāṭini (esoteric) faith distinguished them markedly from both the Zaydis and Shāfi'is with whom they shared Yemen. They were closer to the Druzes of Ḥawrān in south Syria and to their coreligionists in Ahmadabad and Hyderabad in India. The Indian connection, he argued, rendered them both important and dangerous: it was therefore urgent that they be reattached to Ottoman influence and brought in line with the established authority in Yemen. Izzet Paşa, he continued, had tried to win them over in 1883, but there was no measurable success because his successors neither persisted nor reinforced Izzet's commitment to the Yām. If not their friendship, at least their neutrality would greatly aid efforts to control the lands they inhabited. Again, good communications, he argued, were needed, including a rail line.

The stress on rail communications as a way of consolidating control was evident throughout Glaser's report. Rail in the interior of Yemen, he argued, does what war and commercial ships do for the coastal area: it is the 'iron voice'.[41] The central government already appreciated its value for the Hijaz and the speed at which it was constructed aroused the admiration of the entire civilized world. 'How much greater it would be', he added, 'if it could be extended from Ṭa'if to Ta'izz.'[42]

The only potential threat to the whole scheme would come from the imam, which could be dealt with by military action or pacification. Again he ruled out military force and suggested relying on peaceful means. Military force would fail because the imam owned a few thousand modern rifles, knew the country well and was better acclimatized than any foreigner could aspire to be. Imperial troops could not better him in such rugged terrain, as Glaser himself found out when he accompanied four Ottoman battalions to al-Sūdah in 1883, with their manoeuvrability highly restricted by narrow defiles, extended supply lines and limited drinking water. Resort to force had to be the last recourse. However renowned Ottoman fighting men might be, 'perhaps the best and bravest in the world', coping with almost subhuman conditions on an ongoing basis invariably threatened discipline and created disorder in the ranks.

Glaser favoured winning over the imam with clever persuasion and money. To save time, for it could have been a drawn-out process, Glaser suggested commencing immediately with the construction of the rail line from Ṭa'if in the Hijaz. From Abhā a spur would extend to the Red Sea coast. Even if it did not reach Ṣan'ā', the Ottomans could still move more troops by sea within striking distance of potential targets in the imam's territory. Moreover, the railroad would keep its value because it could be used to develop commerce and agriculture, thus imparting new energy to the country and augmenting its revenue base.[43] Implicit in his emphasis on a railroad as a means of consolidating interior communications for military and possibly commercial purposes were the potential financial benefits for German enterprises already engaged in constructing rail lines inside the Ottoman Empire.

Glaser was equally mindful of the foreign influence in Yemen, a country he compared with Ethiopia, in which France, England and Italy conspired to carve the land between them to the exclusion of such European states as Germany and Austro-Hungary. With the British already ensconced in Aden, the Italians now sought to become firmly established in Hodeida and Ṣan'ā'. All the Ottoman government could do at this stage was maintain close surveillance over the activities of the agents of both powers, perhaps through quietly subsidized merchants.[44]

Other suspect foreign activities Glaser mentioned but failed to identify were those of a Swedish 'Arabic linguist' he had encountered on an earlier visit to Yemen who was now operating out of Aden. The 'linguist' was luring scholars and other important personalities to the imam's side. 'I suspect strongly the "linguistic" work of this scholar,' wrote Glaser. 'He is aggravating the situation in Yemen through his work, one time in favour of the English, another in favour of the Italians at Massawa. It is quite conceivable, although I cannot prove it, that he is presently aiding the Italians for the second time.'[45] He cautioned the Sublime Porte against providing the Italians with any pretext to meddle in the internal affairs of the *vilayet* or antagonizing them in any way because in his opinion they were well positioned strategically (at Massawa across the Red Sea) to damage Ottoman prestige and administration in Yemen.[46]

Another development militating against Ottoman authority in Yemen, as elsewhere in the Arab provinces at this time, was the rise of what he described as the 'Arab nationalist party'. Even though its aims were to unite all the Arabs of the Ottoman Empire and form one Arabic kingdom, and to develop close ties with the Zaydi imam, Glaser did not counsel the Sublime Porte to pay close attention to it because for the moment he did not see the party posing any serious threat to Ottoman interests in Yemen.[47] He reasoned that because France and Britain 'protected' some of these Arab lands, they had equally to fear the nationalist party and consequently would refuse to allow it to make much progress.[48]

Quite clearly, as indicated in this chapter, the Ottomans' concern impelled the sultan himself to take charge and to dispatch missions by members of his own *mabeyn* (entourage) or by an outsider whom he trusted to study the situation and make recommendations that could be implemented. Yemen was more immediately threatened during this interval when Imam al-Manṣūr and his son Yaḥya, who succeeded him, embarked on new rebellions, which, as we shall see, ended in forcing Abdülhamid and his Young Turk successors to face up to realities and come to terms with Yemenis, as we shall see in subsequent chapters.

9. Imam al-Manṣūr's Rebellion, 1883–1904

As we saw earlier, alongside the urgent need for radical reform of the administration and local government structures, there was an awareness that Yemeni society contained fundamental cultural and social differences. The Zaydi imam and the Ismāʻīlī *dāʻī* led the main contending parties. While disagreeing over details of sectarian observance and over the basic philosophy of the tenets of their commonly shared Shi'i sect, they nevertheless agreed that each should be free to practise their beliefs and customs unimpeded by legislation emanating from the Sunni centre or the sultanate. When the Tanzimat became established in the mid-nineteenth century, new legislation based on prevailing European models, which the Yemenis generally and the Zaydis in particular distrusted and termed heretical, was seen to contradict the tenets and provisions of the Islamic Sharīʻah. On religious and political grounds both sects opposed the legislation Tanzimat ministers introduced.[1] Opposition was more often expressed in a rebellion on the battlefield than through negotiations, which often went unheeded. The resumption of resistance was this time more intense and with broader support from tribes whose loyalty to the Ottomans had hitherto been more on principle than by conviction. The focus in this chapter is on the steps taken, often unsuccessfully, to redress the deteriorating situation and improve administrative practices in an attempt to introduce a measure of stability to Ottoman Yemen. But first let us look at the imam's own advisers who served as the custodians of Zaydi legal customs.

The role of Zaydi ulema

Zaydi ulema served as an imam's respected and honoured principal advisers and formed the basis of his power. Not only did they interpret the law but they also pronounced on public morality and on Yemeni society's educated elite. 'They had the authority to legitimize the rulers' authority and policies, to act as mediators in their disputes, and to serve administrators in their rudimentary bureaucracy.' In return for their services, ulema expected financial compensation and the heeding of their advice 'to accept their intercession, to preserve and defend Islamic norms', to respect the requirements for the imamate as Zaydi jurists laid down and to maintain public order. A major requirement was for the imam to be a learned scholar, but this was not always observed.[2]

With the degeneration of the administrative and financial situation in Yemen, by 1883 it had become obvious that radical changes had to be made. The *vali* notified the sultan's government of the need for detailed and clear instructions if the wellbeing of the *vilayet* was to be regained. He suggested that explicit instructions be communicated directly and orally to specified individuals who would bring them back.[3] Attempts were made during the following year to readjust the configuration of local administrative districts and to appoint competent administrators at the provincial level throughout the *vilayet* in Yemen. They hoped that with fresh blood and a more responsive government they would be able to improve procedures and achieve better results in upgrading the economic status of the country. This was based on the assumption that the tribes would cease their agitation and intertribal strife. Given the need for more troops for local policing, *Vali* Izzet also suggested that they might, with the sultan's approval and if sufficient funds and provisions were made available, recruit locals through their own *shaykh*s for army service and not necessarily in Yemen.[4]

Events at Sawākin and Massawa and the possibility of open conflict induced the Sublime Porte to take precautionary measures by increasing the numbers of the Hijaz military division.[5]

The *Meclis-i Mahsus* also ordered the chief of police to arrest and remand for trial a number of *mashāyikh* (elders, chiefs), who had served as collectors of *üşriye* and *vergi* taxes and who were now accused of embezzlement.[6] The *Meclis-i Vükelâ* authorized one collector for each 15 villages in the *nahiye*, who was to deliver the taxes to the treasury of the *kaza* in return for a *bedel*.[7] The most damaging effect of relying on local officials was that irregularities such as extortion and embezzlement became inevitable, but perhaps there was no choice given the number of collectors needed to cover the country as a whole.

Indeed, even the deceased Izzet Paşa, former *vali* of Yemen, had been accused of irregularities and, to end rumours over the issue, the *dahiliye* hurriedly sent to Istanbul for verification and ordered investigative reports.[8] More than 200,000 *kuruş* of his estate had been forwarded to the treasury and there was pressure for it to be paid out to administrative officials in the Hijaz, but no authorization was to be given before completion of the investigation into the irregularities during Izzet's tenure and the final court decision had been made.[9]

Ferik Ahmed Feyzi, commandant of the seventh army, was taking precautions but was short of recruits, while Sharaf al-Dīn, one of the opponents, had been assembling an army of up to 2000 from the Ḥāshids and the coastal tribes from his new headquarters at Ṣa'dah, which did not augur well for tranquillity in Yemen.[10]

The Ottomans were concerned about goods being moved from port to port to avoid paying customs fees. Smuggling was responsible for much of this evasion, so the Ottomans decided to curb it by strengthening the defences of Kamarān island and the coast opposite it, which meant building barracks and other service facilities for the troops stationed there.[11] The Ottoman Council of Ministers decided to tie Massawa's customs fees to those of Egypt. This made the Italians liable for fees on the goods they unloaded there and they were not to be allowed to evade paying them as in the immediate past.[12]

The foreign ministry was instructed to send an enciphered telegram to its chargé d'affaires in Rome to lodge a formal protest with the Italian government about the illegal activities of its subjects in the Red Sea.[13] To strengthen patrolling units there, the Ottoman navy ordered 15 steam torpedo boats (five had been delivered already) from Germany, with whom they had a meeting of minds.[14] To protect themselves from sabotage by hostile tribes engaged in smuggling, communications were strengthened by laying a cable line to Perim via Mocha to connect with Hodeida and Hijaz. It was to be laid under water from Perim to Sawākin–Shaykh Sa'īd onwards.[15]

Renewal of tribal revolts and conflicts

In 1888, sustained revolts broke out almost everywhere in Yemen that had been considered pacified, taxing to the limit Ottoman military units and resources to combat them. Intertribal conflicts were creating turbulence in the Ṣan'ā' and Hodeida districts, while al-Manṣūr was busy stirring up ill feeling against the Ottomans among the Ḥāshid and Bakīl tribes. His aim was to consolidate his leadership at the expense of his rivals and then confront the Ottomans by rallying the major tribes to his side. The *vali*, as he notified the *seraskeriyet* in Istanbul, sought to end the conflict by dispatching two companies against them.[16] In Bayt al-Faqīh in the Hodeida district, the Zarānīqs' defiance and intra-family and tribal conflicts obliged the commandant of Hodeida, Ahmed Paşa, to mobilize two companies of imperial troops to chastise the tribe and straighten out their thinking should they fail to rectify their ways and cease their disturbance.[17]

In the area southeast of Ṣan'ā', Murād and other tribesmen assembled about 2000 troublemakers, of whom 900 were stealthily sent off to seize leather and other supplies from 900 soldiers and 427 elderly and sick people under the jurisdiction of a special commission in the 'Ubūd area. Authorization was received to compensate those soldiers who lost leather and clothing from the *miri* income of the *vilayet*.[18]

Orders were given to reinforce policing in the Ḥujarīyah district and to confirm administrative arrangements for localities in it such as Mahal, Qubṭīyah, Nasātarah and others. A *karakol* was to be built at Jiblah and 40 policemen stationed there. With the spread of tribal uprisings against the Ottomans, the Zaydi imams decided to take advantage of such defiance to rally the tribes under their leadership and make it into a national resistance. This became clear when al-Manṣūr bil-Lāh Muḥammad ibn Yaḥya Muḥammad ibn Ismā'īl Ḥamīd al-Dīn inherited the mantle of resistance from Imam Sharaf al-Dīn by consensus of the ulema in July 1890, after they were unable to find a more suitable replacement.[19] Vali Asim had detained him along with those ulema who had associated with Imam Muḥsin Shahārī[20] earlier. All now were determined to combat what they called oppression at the hands of the 'Ajam, namely the Turks.[21]

Al-Mansūr was urged to leave San'ā' for his personal safety. He went to Ṣa'dah and, from there, to the impenetrable Jabal al-Ahnum from where he began to address appeals to all the tribes of Yemen to join in a common uprising against the Ottomans. He had access to his brother-in-law Sharaf al-Dīn's treasury with which to finance the uprising. His appeal was successful judging from how quickly the tribes moved to lay siege to San'ā' in 1891, after capturing the forts of al-Zafir, Ḥajjah, Maswar wa al-Sharaf, Yarīm, Dhamār, Ḥufāsh, Milhan, al-Rawdaḥ and others in the region surrounding San'ā'.[22]

According to al-Wāsi'i, there was not a corner of Yemen where al-

Mansūr and his allies did not engage the Ottomans in skirmish or battle: he besieged San'ā' twice and captured Turkish soldiers often. They chased him to his station known as Qaflat al-'Adhar in Ḥāshid country twice in large numbers and with military equipment that struck awe in the eyes of beholders.[23] Before besieging San'ā', he engaged the Ottoman troops in battle in the Sharafayn mountains of the Ḥajūr region in 1890 where he defeated them and killed the commander, Mehmed Arif. The defeat had a strong negative impact on the Ottomans.[24]

The tribes of Ḥamdān revolted in 1891 under the leadership of Shaykh Yaḥya ibn Yaḥya Dawrah. Accompanied by al-Sayyid Muḥammad ibn 'Ali al-Shuwayyi', *shaykh* of the tribes of Ḍila', Ottoman commander 'Ali Paşa headed towards Qā' al-Manqabah where the tribes of Ḥamdān had gathered. They were led by al-Sayyid Aḥmad ibn Muḥammad al-Shar'i al-Ḥasani who also led a large contingent of Yemeni tribes. Shortly before Vali Ismail Hakkı's death in 1891, an intense battle ensued with indecisive results. After his death more tribal uprisings followed in most of Yemen, especially in the country of al-Bustān, a large *mikhlāf* west of the city of Ṣan'ā' in the neighbourhood of 'Ans, al-Ḥaymah, Ḥamdān and Sanḥān, where tribesmen uprooted telegraph posts and plundered the mail coming from Istanbul to Ṣan'ā'. This followed in the shadow of the siege of that city.

Threats to the military from rebellious tribes necessitated an appeal for 40,000 *lira*s to pay for new recruits, their provisions, firearms and uniforms (two sets for each) and for their quick dispatch; also, according to a report by Izzet Paşa to the *seraskeriyet*, for a civil assistant to the *vali*.[25] Authorization was given to help the administrative task and punish the tribes for their defiance. Funds were to be sent (15,000 *lira*s at a time), not for administration but because there were some questions concerning the *vali*.[26] Ferik Ismail Hakkı reported having insufficient troops available to him to quell widespread disorder, hence his urgent request for more. Altogether there were only 8000 troops in Yemen.[27] The 4000 available plus the 2000 stationed in 'Asīr made up only one-quarter of the force assigned. Transfers without replacements had accounted for such depletions. He urged the *seraskeriyet* in Istanbul quickly to dispatch at least six battalions if he wished to contain the rebellion.[28]

In another encoded telegram to Istanbul, the commandant stated that Ḥamīd al-Dīn had 800 Martini rifles and concealed rifles. Rebels in the Hodeida region had attacked Qaflah, the capital of the *kaza* of Ḥajūr, where only one battalion was stationed. Hodeida rushed another battalion to its defence, and another one-and-a-half from Ḥajjah under Arif Beg. They engaged the rebels (killing 60 and wounding 80 against three martyred and five wounded Ottoman soldiers). They then fled to a village near Shāhil and were regrouping. The commandant reported that another battalion would be needed to engage them again.[29]

All attempts to contain the rebellion in the *kaza* of Ḥajūr al-Shām in the *sancak* of Hodeida in mountain areas 2000 metres above sea level met with reversal. The 80,000 inhabitants of the 20 villages in the region remained defiant. On 12 August 1890, the commandant at Hodeida sent Miralay Mustafa Beg of the 49th regiment to storm the region, which he did with some success and to the shouts of 'long live the *padişah*' by his troops. Meanwhile, two regiments arrived from Hijaz encompassing 16 battalions, of which two were sent to defend Ḥajwar and the rest directed to Ṣan'ā'.[30] Mirliva (Major General) 'Ali Paşa was in command there. He attacked the east side of the mountain and, in a battle lasting from morning to evening, succeeded in dislodging the rebels from their strongholds and wounding their leader, thus wiping out his influence over his tribe. According to a 16 August 1890 telegram from Feyzi Paşa, who had replaced Ismail as commandant of the seventh army, in five to ten days the area would be quiet and reform measures would have been introduced.[31] To help finance the measures needed to chastise the rebels, the *Meclis-i Vükelâ* instructed the *Maliye Nezareti* to authorize the use of Hodeida's customs duties and other state income designated to meet the needs of the hungry, as well as the debt owing to the Hijaz.[32]

Osman Paşa's valiship

Osman Paşa assumed the *vali*ship of Yemen in 1888. He was a reconciler and was able to obtain from the sultan's government a monthly subsistence allowance of 1000 *riyal*s for Muḥammad, the son of the late Imam al-Mutawakkil Muḥsin (Shahārī) and his brothers in return for his declaration of loyalty and residing in Ṣan'ā'. Head of the ulema Aḥmad ibn Muḥammad al-Kibsi and *mufti* of the *vilayet* Ḥasan al-Akwa' succeeded in doing so through their intercession with Osman.[33]

Pacifying potential troublemakers was one accomplishment. The *vilayet* had not counted on natural disasters, on the earthquakes, lack of rain and locust invasions that brought drought, hunger and severe hardship. Risings against the Ottomans and campaigns to suppress them by whatever means simply caused planting to be neglected and agriculture destroyed, which merely increased hunger and led to high prices.

The drought and famine were especially bad during the *vali*ship of Feyzi Paşa, who was accused of treating his subjects harshly by sending his troops to such far off localities as Ḥamdān, Sanḥān and al-Bustān to confiscate grain from the inhabitants' homes. He earned the hatred of most Yemenis when he openly humiliated Muḥammad al-Shuwayyi', the magistrate of Ḍila', by dragging him by the hand in the government square before the view of a large crowd.

Effect of maladministration

A number of military leaders complained to the Sublime Porte about the inhabitants treating them badly because of the drought and famine that had spread throughout the country, particularly around Arḥab. They blamed it all on the *vali*'s bad judgement, unwise practices, brutality and abusiveness in storming the homes of natives and confiscating their crops and possessions without respecting any sanctity.

Conditions became so intolerable that Feyzi's own officers filed complaints against him to the sultan, who summoned him to Istanbul and allegedly rebuked him so strongly that he fainted. He then transferred him after only one year's service in Yemen to the command of the Mecca army division. That numerous complaints forwarded to the respective ministries in Istanbul were never brought before the *sadrazam* or sultan for fear of incurring their anger compounded the problem.[34]

The seventh army was short of food and other supplies, according to reports reaching the *seraskeriyet* in successive telegrams and petitions. On hearing this, the *dahiliye* authorized the transport of food and other military supplies to Yemen and notified the military command and the administrative *meclis* of the *vilayet* accordingly. The *maliye* was to allocate a certain number of *akçe*s, sell 50,000 kilograms of corn and instruct the navy to authorize transport by steamer to Yemen.[35] To alleviate shortages, the *vali* was authorized to purchase flour, barley, corn, wheat, rice and other grains from elsewhere. Prices were to be negotiated and the provisions sent by sea and land with customs dues temporarily suspended, according to *Meclis-i Vükelâ* instructions.[36]

Aziz Paşa, who arrived in 1886, was one of the more faithful *vali*s assigned to Yemen. He discharged his responsibility with concern for Ottoman subjects and did much to end arbitrary administrative practices. He forbade the soldiers to collect grain and other foodstuff from the inhabitants. He put an end to bribery and placed a limit on the use of authority and its abuse by Turkish officials who had become accustomed to such practices.[37] Abdülhamid had little trust in his advisers, which would explain why on his accession to rule he separated the civil from the military in administering the *vilayet*s. He took a personal interest in the affairs of the provinces and became directly involved in ensuring that one could checkmate the other and hold each other in line.[38] But this did not always work according to plan. Sometimes an administrative unit would endeavour to discredit another and accuse it of betraying the imperial interest, which only made matters worse. This happened in Yemen when the military wrote to the Sublime Porte to instruct the *vali* to authorize an attack on the districts that had submitted to the imam's rule only to prove the incompetence of the *vali* should he hesitate to execute an order. The military informed the sultan that if they did not attack first, the imam would attack the districts under the jurisdiction of the Ottomans and throw them out of Yemen.[39]

Not to be shown in a negative light, Vali Aziz Paşa directed an Ottoman force under Hussein Hayri to subdue the Zaydi imam in north Yemen. A major battle took place in the 'Iyal Yazid mountain, which ended in an Ottoman defeat and forcible retreat to 'Amrān after suffering major losses. The military attributed its defeat to improper advice from Shaykh 'Abdallah ibn Aḥmad al-Ḍil'i who had been granted the title of *paşa* and was serving on the central administrative council. The military allegedly wanted to drive a wedge between the *vali* and his Yemeni counsellor and to discredit his relationship with the Yemeni general after he had done much to reconcile them to him and vice versa. They even succeeded in doing the same with his replacement Osman Paşa when, in 1888, to get al-Ḍil'i further out of the way, they asked the sultan's government to exile him, which it did, to Acre in Palestine without the benefit of a trial or opportunity to prove his innocence. A contingent of troops held him prior to his exile and another, under Ahmed Rüşdü, seized his possessions from his hometown east of 'Amrān.[40] Yemeni authors recounting this period of decline in Ottoman rule attribute much of the ailment to the prevalence of bribery at the highest levels of government as well as in the provinces, a practice that only intensified the Yemenis' resentment towards their government, no less than the arbitrary and humiliating manner in which officials treated them. The disease had become widespread and officials coming to Yemen enriched themselves by this process, using all sorts of deviant methods to squeeze the natives.

When Osman Nuri Paşa became *vali* in 1888, subordinate officials duped him into issuing summonses to all the *mashāyikh* from Ta'izz to 'Asīr, Hodeida and other *kaza*s to appear in Ṣan'ā'. At the same time they spread a rumour that the *vali* intended to exile them for disturbing the peace. Frightened by such a prospect, they offered their *kaymakam*s and *mutasarrif*s sums of money to remit to the *vali* to intercede on their behalf with the sultan. This, according to al-Wāsi'i, was one of the tricks they employed to squeeze the wealth from the *mashāyikh*.

Al-Qāḍi Yaḥya al-Mujāhid, the *mufti* of Ta'izz renowned for his honest service and loyalty to the Ottomans, did not fall for such tricks and was persecuted. He ignored the threats of the *mutasarrif*, recently arrived in Ta'izz, and was seized by Turkish soldiers in his home. They confiscated his wealth and tossed him in gaol without regard for his service to them in the past and the great respect he enjoyed among his people. He remained in prison until the *merkez* at Ṣan'ā' realized why he was being held and released him. He sent a telegram to the sultan explaining what had been done to him and an *iradé seniyé* was issued to dismiss the *mutasarrif* of Ta'izz. However, the *vali* feared that Yaḥya might also turn the sultan against him. Given that the *mutasarrif* had promised to return what he had confiscated from him, some notables urged Yaḥya to forgive him for his foul deed, but Yaḥya refused, insisting the sultan put him on trial.[41] Afraid of the consequences, the *vali* summoned the military commanders and got them to write a memorandum to the sultan, which he had the council endorse. It asked for Yaḥya's removal from Yemen and alleged that his claim against the *mutasarrif* of Ta'izz was unfounded. On his arrival in Istanbul, the sultan allocated him an allowance for three years while awaiting the trial he had requested but that never took place. He asked for permission to return to Yemen but the sultan allegedly denied it. He remained in Istanbul until he died of grief, away from his homeland and family.[42]

Very few high officials sought to govern honestly and forbid bribery. They usually did not last because their subordinates, who indulged in the practice, would resort to any devious method to engineer their removal. Such was the case of Osman Nuri, who replaced Osman as *vali* in 1890. Things calmed down during his tenure and the country yielded good crops and incomes. However, when he put pressure on his officials not to resort to bribery, they turned against him and conspired to have him removed from office. They sent a memorandum to the Sublime Porte alleging that he was unfit to govern and demanded his removal from office, which they did in a telegram, despite his good service and the intervention of the commandant of Hodeida, who went to Istanbul to prove his innocence and expose the doings of the lesser officials. To avoid clashes, the sultan did not reassign Osman Nuri to Yemen, but appointed him rather *vali* of Hijaz.

His dismissal angered the Yemenis, who asserted that in terms of good conduct and fine administration, he was the best *vali* ever to have come to Yemen. While other *vali*s openly flaunted the importance of their office by having cavalry and guards proceed alongside their carriage as they travelled to work, Osman Nuri[43] usually walked to work, or on rare occasions rode a female mule from his home in Bi'r al-'Azab accompanied only by his *yaver* (aide-de-camp). Also, he gave much of his salary to charity (*sadaqah*).[44]

In an attempt to counter the *vali*'s arbitrariness and his officials' corruption, and to remand the guilty for punishment, in 1890 the sultan reappointed Ismail Hakkı Paşa as *vali* (he first served as *vali* of Yemen in 1878). He was returned to the post because of his experience and familiarity with the country's administrative affairs. His reappointment probably gained the Ottomans a say in the Aden *sancak* from which petitions under seal by Şeyhülmeşayihi 'Ali 'Abdullah and Shaykh Du'āz had appealed for Ottoman support.[45] Shortly afterwards, Imam al-Hādi Sharaf al-Dīn died in Ṣa'dah and was succeeded by al-Manṣūr Muḥammad ibn Yaḥya Ḥamīd al-Dīn, father of Imam Yaḥya, during whose tenure the Ottomans made their final exit from Yemen. Ismail remained until his death and burial near the Bakrīyah mosque.[46]

Causes of rebellion

Al-Wāsi'i alleged that the Yemeni rising was the direct result of severe persecution of the inhabitants, rendering the forbidden legal, abandoning the injunctions of the faith, committing the illicit and abominations like debauchery and licentiousness, as well as engaging in prostitution and wine drinking. The imams took advantage of this to arouse the Yemenis' moral sensibilities and solidify the leadership among them. But other factors were also paramount, namely when the *kaymakam* set out to collect the *âşâr* (tithes) on agricultural products levied on the settled population, he would exceed the levied amount and pocket it without issuing a receipt, then inform the government that they did not pay any. The government would then issue orders to burn and plunder their homes.

Because local chiefs assigned to collect taxes were unreliable and often dishonest, to ensure the proper inflow of revenue the local administration sent soldiers with the collectors. If they encountered resistance, the soldiers would attack the village and often violate its women without regard to the negative consequences to the Ottoman government. Most officials did not believe they were obliged to perform a patriotic deed to enhance the Ottoman image. Their main concern was to become rich as quickly as possible and let the devil take the hindmost.[47] The tribes of Yemen sought at this juncture the freedom to conduct their own internal affairs and not be saddled with administrators appointed by the *merkez* in Ṣan'ā' who exploited them and had little regard for their welfare.

The situation in Yemen deteriorated rapidly and disorder soon turned to open rebellion. With al-Manṣūr ibn Muḥammad Ḥamīd al-Dīn being blamed for the renewal of the uprising, the central government, at the military command's request, took action to reinforce men and supplies in Yemen.[48] The Ottomans could not afford to allow the situation to get out of hand because it would jeopardize their position in the Hijaz and further threaten their administration in south Yemen. Despite his generous subsidies to them, the sultan distrusted the *ashrāf* of Mecca; he feared they might decide to appoint a caliph from a descendant of the Prophet, and that the tribesmen of Hijaz and 'Asīr might support such a move. The Ottomans had difficulty controlling the land, first in the highland peaks and impenetrable valleys where defiant tribes could hold back their military assaults, and next in the lowlands where the heat and lack of sufficient water made it impossible to station the large numbers of troops dispatched from Anatolia who were accustomed to more moderate and colder climates.[49]

Increased defiance called for preventive measures. In April 1890 the Sublime Porte authorized the dispatch of 2990 troops to check the potential spread of disorder.[50]

The siege of Ṣan'ā'

The sustained siege of Ṣan'ā' began in autumn 1892 when Ottoman troops had lost skirmishes with rebels on the outskirts of the city and had retreated to within its walls at Qā' al-Yahūd (Jewish Quarter) in the western part to await reinforcements. The battle took place at al-Jardā', a village the Ottoman troops wrongly believed had been evacuated after heavy bombardment. When the Ottomans, led by 'Ali Paşa and accompanied by Yemeni *shaykh*s loyal to them,[51] entered the village they found themselves surrounded by rebels led by Aḥmad, son of Imam al-Mutawakkil Muḥsin. A frightful massacre ensued with the Yemenis using all weapons from *janbiyāh*s to rifles against the soldiers. Only a few escaped and worked their way to Ṣan'ā'.[52] News of the Ottoman defeat encouraged other tribesmen to join the rebel force, which now converged on Ṣan'ā' from all parts of Yemen. Shortly afterwards, another intense battle occurred at Jabal Nuqum, south of the city near the cemetery. Some attempted to break out north of the city, but were defeated and forced back into it. It is said that 70,000 Yemenis from all tribes besieged the city.[53] The Yemenis' old short-range rifles, with which they were armed, did little damage to the Turks fortified within the official residence and around the perimeter of the wall of Ṣan'ā' who fired back with superior rifles at the besieging Yemenis.

The sustained siege cast fear in the hearts of the inhabitants and led to food shortages and higher prices. The besiegers used long ladders made of hardened walnut wood to climb the walls when the condition of the besieged had severely deteriorated through lack of food, adequate clothing, illness and disease, for they dwelt in unhealthy residences, while those greedy to overwhelm and plunder the city intensified their efforts to seize it.[54] The inhabitants suffered no less than the Turks, for they prayed day and night to God for deliverance. They were forced to sell their possessions to obtain scarce food. The rebels fell upon anybody who ventured out to escape the intolerable conditions, robbing them and violating their women. This disobeyed Imam al-Manṣūr's orders that they secure the roads, give aid to the poor and weak, and rescue those suffering unusual weakness and hardship.[55]

Other concentrations of Ottoman troops, as in Dhamār, Ta'izz, Ibb, Yarīm, 'Amrān, Ḥajjah and al-Ṭawīlah, came under attack at the same time. A wall surrounding 'Amrān was stormed, as was Manākhah after a feeble resistance. All were seized; high-rank Ottoman soldiers who surrendered were sent to the imam after giving up their arms and were well received and treated. In many instances, the tribesmen offered food and clothing to fleeing Turkish soldiers and gave them money to reach Aden and/or escape their life of soldiering by other means. Some even joined the tribes in rebellion.[56] Thus, the imam gained control of most of the Turkish strongholds and the rebellion spread like wildfire. In many parts, high officials surrendered and were sent captive to the Zaydi imam. The siege of Ṣan'ā' intensified as the Ottomans lost prestige and respect. Reports reaching Europe claimed that the city had fallen to the rebels and the *sadrazam* was hard pressed to deny them, as his diplomats had been instructed to do.[57]

News of the catastrophe cast gloom over the central government and impressed on the *sadaret* the urgency to dispatch more troops to lift the siege of Ṣan'ā' and relieve the besieged Ottoman forces.[58] All the main interior towns, with the exception of 'Amrān, Ẓafīr and Ṣan'ā', had fallen to the rebels. Hodeida and other coastal cities were secure against attack, though the coastal inhabitants, kept at bay by periodic appearances of Ottoman troops in would-be trouble areas, were no less hostile. Merchants and inhabitants generally kept in with Ottoman officials and were able to benefit from them, like escaping paying taxes on certain goods, thus remaining aloof of the popular resistance elsewhere.[59]

The government responded by appointing Ahmed Feyzi, commandant of the seventeenth detachment and former governor of Hijaz, to the command of the seventh army and the *vali*ship of Yemen with a view to suppressing the rebellion and re-establishing order. An urgent telegram from Yemen reported the capture of the Ta'izz commandant by the Ḥāshids, with whom he had been engaged in battle as they attacked the *kaza* of 'Ans.[60] He learned of the seriousness of the situation on reaching Hodeida and decided as a first step to regain Manākhah before waiting to secure logistical support for the expedition.

After seizing Manākhah, Ahmed Feyzi left behind a contingent to protect it and safeguard the main route as he and his force headed off for Ṣan'ā'. At a narrow pass 30 miles along the way, rebellious tribes took up positions and engaged Feyzi's troops in a battle that lasted for 12 days before the rebels were scattered and Feyzi's force could continue on its journey. Another battle took place at Sūq al-Khamīs, a day's march from the city, which ended in another Ottoman triumph. Then, as the Ottoman troops approached the city, the imam's rebel force, which had been besieging Ṣan'ā' from Jabal Nuqum, decided to flee south to the mountains. Feyzi entered the city to the joy and relief of its inhabitants[61] and the rebels began to retreat.

Soon after taking control of the city, Feyzi decided to reorganize the *vilayet*'s administration. The first measure he announced was to pardon all who had rebelled against the state so they could return peacefully to their homes and resume their normal lives. Tribes in the neighbourhood of Ṣan'ā' welcomed this gesture and declared their loyalty and obedience to the new *vali*, with the exception of Jarbān's two villages at a two-hour march northwest of Ṣan'ā'. A contingent of troops accompanied by 'Ali al-Bilbalī (later accorded the title of *paşa*) then subdued, plundered and burnt the two villages. Harsh as the measure was, the two villages had been notoriously defiant of imams even in the days before the Ottomans and this time had been the first to rise against them.[62]

A particularly nasty incident involving the Turkish governor of Dhamār, Mehmed Rüşdü Paşa, demanding taxes from the *shaykh* of a tribe settled nearby, revealed just how much hatred misadministration at a local level had aroused and the determination of the parties concerned to meet force with force. The governor threatened the *shaykh* who, having sworn to wreak vengeance on the governor, was obliged to flee for his life. Then, while the governor was away on an official call, the *shaykh*'s tribe attacked his residence, killing all 11 members of his family and his servants.[63] When he learnt what had happened to his family and household, Rüşdü returned quickly to Dhamār and, with a contingent of troops, wiped out the entire tribe that had violated his household. He later led 400 troops to collect taxes by force from the Banu Marwān who dwelt east of Luḥayyah, but failed when a Yemeni tribal force took them by surprise before they could reach safety and Rüşdü was among the killed. Being pressured to collect taxes only aroused the resistance of tribes from 'Asīr to the farthest parts of Yemen and strengthened the Yemenis' resolve to achieve independence.[64]

Lack of sensitivity to the Zaydi faith, which the Sunni Turks regarded as an unenlightened heretical sect, compounded by a failure to respect the injunctions of Islam, refraining from praying and from other obligations the Zaydis took seriously, aggravated the problem. The enmity also had a political dimension. Zaydis were now acting as a political party to resist the Ottomans by force and the sultan's government was taking counter measures to put down the imam-led resistance. A French observer in the capital alleged that the sultan's government was receiving inaccurate information about the military's and war ministry's roles in precipitating a general uprising in Yemen.[65] According to the *seraskeriyet*, based on reports from Yemen, it was unwise to keep and use irregular troops and they should be returned to Istanbul, half in August and the other half in September (1892). If the uprisings in the country were to be put down, the commandant reported, they needed 32 battalions of regulars with six months' pay in advance and to bring the men serving in the fifth army up to normal levels. The *seraskeriyet* requested 5000 *lira*s for transport.[66]

In the light of the sieges and military defeats, the government rushed through reinforcements, including eight battalions of *redif* (irregulars), to be recruited quickly, equipped with all the necessary supplies and dispatched to areas of rebellion so that they could suppress the uprisings before they intensified.[67] The *maliye* and *seraskeriyet* were both asked to submit a list of costs for shipping eight battalions of troops, two mountain cannon batteries and supplies for four months so that arrangements could be made with utmost haste.[68] The *sadâret* also authorized the dispatch of officials to investigate the seriousness of the situation.[69]

Deliberations at the sultan's palace by his staff included the idea of changing Yemen into a viceroyalty along the lines of Egypt, with three *vilayet*s under one governor general and a commanding military officer subordinated to him. The staff recommended recalling Aptullah Paşa on account of the excessive cruelties of the troops serving under him. Another item of discussion was the recruitment of 61 squadrons on the model of the Hamidiyah units with the higher officers being Turks. A new tax base would produce about six million Turkish *lira*s. The Arab party at the palace headed by Abu 'l-Huda al-Ṣayyādi was unanimous in recommending the change, with the basic plan enjoying the Islamic party's endorsement. The London *Standard* posited that should this occur then the Eastern Question might take a new turn.[70]

Meanwhile, the *sadâret* demanded the *seraskeriyet* explain why Yemen's tranquillity was so radically disturbed and the order was forwarded to the general command in Yemen for an answer.[71] The reply received by telegram alluded to the repression of the inhabitants of Shāhil and Sharafayn[72] as the cause of the general uprising.[73] The central government had dismissed Hasan Edip Paşa from his post in Yemen and imprisoned him; now he was to be transferred to a house of detention. At the request of the Commission of Military Inspection, the supervisor of taxes, Mehmed Şükrü Efendi, was remanded in custody pending trial.[74]

According to a *mazbata* sent to Yemen's military command and to a military commission's report, the sultan also set up a commission of inquiry, including Major 'Ali, Lieutenant Ahmet and Shaykh 'Abdallah, to investigate closely the causes of rebellion and its spread.[75] As the rebellion intensified, troops sent earlier to bring the rascal Hamiduddin to heel did not suffice. An urgent telegram for more troops was sent to the *seraskeriyet* in Istanbul and forwarded to the *sadrazam* and sultan for immediate action.[76] In retaliation for the imam's activities and in the hope of discouraging further ones, Feyzi arrested his father-in-law and two brothers-in-law for spying, ordered the detention of their property managers and confiscated their goods. He then sought advice from the *sadâret* about whether he should execute the imam's in-laws for sedition, to that end asking permission to set up a court martial in Yemen to try all those inciting to rebellion.[77]

Feyzi received authorization to organize a mobile squadron that could move swiftly to quell any uprising, especially when he learnt that fighting men loyal to Ḥamīd al-Dīn were assembling near 'Amrān.[78] Ferik Süleiman Paşa of the *bahriye*, Mirliva Hasan Riza of the *erkân-i harbiye* (or Ferid Rifât Paşa) and Mirliva Ahmed Hilmi Beg were authorized to travel as a commission of reform to investigate the civil, financial and military administrations and report their findings to the sultan's government.[79] One immediate response was to appoint Hamdi Paşa of the *bahriye* and Hasan Riza Paşa, the latter as the next *vali*.[80]

Feyzi instructed Ismail Paşa to take control of Dhamār and Yarīm after he had instituted *'urfi* decrees, which were tantamount to abolishing all the laws of the *vilayet*, and granted a prize to all those who could bring him the head of a rebel. He authorized his troops to raid and plunder any villages that staged new rebellions. Ismail took Dhamār without resistance, leaving a contingent to police it, then Ibb, Jiblah, and Ta'izz followed.[81] Mirliva Ahmed Paşa, commandant at Hodeida, reported rebellious stirrings in 'Asīr and the need to reinforce his troops to the military general staff in Istanbul and to Serasker Riza Paşa, who passed the request on to the *sadâret* on 20 October 1891.[82]

The English traveller Harris was highly impressed by the Ottomans' ability to suppress uprisings without foreigners being able to detect their methods, which enabled Feyzi swiftly to turn the tables on the rebels. When Harris suddenly rushed to Ṣan'ā' as Feyzi was busy lifting the siege of the city, the commandant became convinced that he was spying on the Ottomans.[83] With all his retinue, he was arrested and escorted under guard to Hodeida from where he was shipped out. The failure of the uprisings was attributed to the negative stance of the Zaydi imam who stirred up the tribes. Imam al-Manṣūr remained detached, while the Yemeni rebels carried on and failed.

Quelling the rebellion in 1892 involved 4000 Ottoman troops having to fight battles in nearly inaccessible mountain areas against well-armed fortified villages. The immunity provided by nature emboldened them to defy taxpayers sent to collect what was due to the government. On the other hand, victory on the battlefields proved costly in that the income now realized fell to one-tenth of what had been received in the past. Moreover, the cost of maintaining a large contingent of troops was prohibitive and to increase tax levies would inevitably have led to additional rebellions.

The imams' weaknesses and rivalries created an atmosphere of disorder in which caravans passing through their territories became vulnerable to plunder. The sharp increase in customs duties on imports and exports at Hodeida and other Yemeni ports adversely affected Ottoman revenue on trade and caused much of it to be diverted to Aden, which was a free port at that time. Some Arab chieftains told Harris that much of the support for the Yemeni rebellion came from the British at Aden, with adventurers and traders smuggling in many of the weapons from the French port at Abwak (Obouc) opposite the Yemeni coast.[84]

In August 1896, the marine minister issued an order to bar the smuggling of arms to rebels. To implement it, the shipyards in Istanbul and Izmir needed to build 24 vessels, including gunboats. The minister of finance claimed it was impossible to fill such an order because at least half a million *lira*s would be required to equip the boats and there were no funds available at that time. In a report a year earlier, the minister had expressed the need for 100,000 *lira*s annually to complete construction. The shipyard at Karadağ needed 800,000 *lira*s to construct some of the vessels, but had received nothing to date.

A *tezkeré âliye* of 15 June 1898 stated that the Yemeni coast was completely devoid of security and that local *shaykh*s were freely smuggling arms. To stop them was the key question, which the *Meclis-i Mahsus* answered by allocating only 120,000 *lira*s with the sultan's endorsement; the *bahriye* had not yet received a *para*, but required a minimum of 100,000 just to complete the vessels already under construction. The only answer the *bahriye* could come up with was to divert vessels of the fleet in service elsewhere to the Yemeni coast.[85]

The situation along the coast was becoming tense. Italian war vessels were intimidating Mocha, demanding the return of *sunbūq*s confiscated because of lack of proper documentation but used by smugglers flying the Italian flag. The *vali* would not respond until he received directions from the imperial government and a formal complaint was lodged with the Italian embassy about its naval officers encouraging smuggling in the Red Sea.[86] Italian warships threatened Hodeida, Luḥayyah and Midi, and the Italian consul demanded the return of goods plundered by Abu 'Arīsh tribesmen. The government told the governor to enforce the applicable laws and to dispatch warships to those parts of the Red Sea in question, along with two companies of mounted troops by land to capture the rascals and confiscate their loot and boats.[87] The Ottoman navy, however, was stretched to the limit. It had to patrol shores all the way from Basra to Jiddah and try to determine how to come up with funds to increase ships and personnel for the purpose.[88]

As the sultan had directed, Nüsret Paşa, the governor of Hodeida, attempted to stem the tide of smuggling and prevent losses to the treasury by establishing a customs house at Midi, in the Banu Marwān region where, according to a report in the *Yemen News* (of Ṣan'ā'), arms and tobacco had for some time past been smuggled to the interior.[89] The warship *Devar Deria*, commanded by Hamdi Beg, with six other vessels under his command, transported the governor to Midi, from where he led 100 cavalry up the coast towards Luḥayyah. A customs house was established at Midi and a defence post was considered for Kamarān. On the way to Jāzān, however, the cavalry clashed with a party of 'Asīris when the *Nurül-Bahr* and three other ships of the fleet patrolling the 'Asīri coast in the neighbourhood of al-Wasīm shelled one of the villages involved in the attack, causing casualties and forcing the inhabitants to flee towards the interior.[90]

Meanwhile, it was rumoured that 35 regiments, each averaging 400 men, were about to leave Istanbul for the upper Yāfi'i region's western frontier, presumably to reinforce defences against British encroachments from the south.[91] *Vali* Hussein Hilmi had told the sultan's *mabeyn* that for some time the British government had been interfering in the administration of the nine districts. He repeated the allegations of Ta'izz's *mutasarrif* that they planned to build a railroad into that area, which would affect adversely the trade of the region for the Ottomans. Even if these were just rumours, it was prudent for the Ottomans to take the necessary precautions to safeguard their interests there.[92]

A journal submitted by Ahmed Efendi, a lieutenant in the gendarme of Ta'izz, stated that, with the *shaykh* of Laḥj's knowledge, structures were being erected in the port of 'Ārā in Ṣubayḥī country at the instigation of the British, who were contemplating building in other parts of the nine-district region as well.[93] A disturbing piece of news reaching Istanbul reported the British advancing on Shaykh 'Uthmān with 900 troops and five artillery pieces. A protest was lodged with the British ambassador in Istanbul. The *sadaret* then instructed the commandant of the seventh army to take whatever steps were necessary to prevent any crossing of the border agreed upon by both. Tribal chiefs in the area were to be instructed to observe border demarcations strictly. The sultan told his ministers to insist on Ottoman territory being respected and to throw the British back by force should they violate the agreement setting the boundary.[94] Some 20 English and Indian soldiers crossed into the Ḥawshabis' Darājah to establish a post to defend the road. They were forced to withdraw when the Ottoman commander at Ta'izz, acting on the sultan's orders of 27 July 1901 to the commandant of the seventh army, threatened military action. He reported assigning a few aids to keep an eye on Darājah.[95]

Sultan Abdülhamid's attempts at appeasement

When Sultan Abdülhamid took office and was confronted with major military engagements in his European possessions, he decided to deplete his forces in the Arab provinces; indeed, he even sought to recruit soldiers there. So, with a policy of appeasement clearly indicated, he sought to reconcile the Yemenis. When Muhtâr Paşa's period as governor ended, the sultan appointed Asim with instructions to implement fair administrative measures. Asim displayed great enthusiasm, even winning over Ḥāshid and Arḥab tribesmen by appointing them to the police force. He employed a French engineer on a 50-*lira* salary to design new roads, allocating 600,000 *lira*s to that end. But his policy of reconciliation did not last. Cracks soon appeared in Osman Paşa's administration when the tax collections organized by local chiefs led to irregularities and discontent.[96]

Imam al-Manṣūr bil-Lāh Muḥammad ibn Yaḥya (1889–1904),[97] in seeking to eliminate his rivals, consolidate his leadership and launch a liberation movement against the Ottomans, appealed to powerful *shaykh*s like 'Abdallah ibn Yaḥya al-Wāsi'i[98] to join him.[99] On learning of the uprising, the sultan opted to use diplomacy to find an acceptable solution to the Yemeni crisis. He wrote to the imam urging him to stop shedding blood and warned him against taking on the more powerful Ottoman troops who were not only highly courageous but also had modern armaments. He even offered him a monthly stipend and a high rank among the men of the Ottoman state.[100] The imam allegedly replied that the rising was not to realize political power or leadership, but rather to enforce the laws of the Sharī'ah, namely to promote good and prevent evil, to protect subjects from the exploitation of officials, and to forbid wine drinking, prostitution and all illicit acts as decreed by God. The point of the uprising was to set limits, relieve the oppressed and enforce justice. He drafted a petition signed by the *mashāyikh* and notables of Ṣan'ā' detailing the excesses of Turkish officials and their acts against the rules of Islam.[101]

In conclusion, all military efforts to prevent the intensification and widening of rebellion had failed, especially when the most tested of Ottoman leaders in the field like Ahmed Feyzi found themselves resorting to harsher and more brutal methods that only enabled Imam al-Manṣūr to rally more Yemenis behind his leadership. Again, the sultan's attempts to appease the rebels came to naught as the imam resented the application of laws deemed un-Islamic and officials sent out to govern, especially those of the lower echelons, lacked the will and honesty to govern without further exploiting the Yemenis. As we shall see in subsequent chapters, the point of no return had been reached and the rebellion continued until successfully concluded by the imam's son Yaḥya.

10. Spread of Rebellion, 1883–1904

With intense rivalry over the imamate, the principals could now quit squabbling and unite to resist the unpopular Tanzimat measures that were considered contradictory to — and that had often supplanted — the Sharī'ah decrees. Imam al-Manṣūr was able to rally heads of tribes in what now had become a common struggle to lift the oppressive hand of the unpopular and exploitative Turkish officials in the name of upholding the decrees of Islam.[1] Vali Hussein Hilmi, concerned about the deteriorating situation, requested specific guidelines on how to reorder the *Hatt-i Yemen* to comply with the sultan's earlier instructions.[2]

While the sultan's response surprised the imam, it was nevertheless a first step towards direct communication between the two of them. Meanwhile, guerrilla-type warfare continued with communication lines being cut, supplies plundered and Turkish soldiers ambushed. Four hours east of Manākhah, at Ḥujrat ibn al-Mahdi, the inhabitants of al-Ḥaymah set upon a caravan of 200 camels carrying quantities of rice, flour, weapons, military uniforms and other necessary supplies from Hodeida to Ṣan'ā', plundering it and the post, and cutting off telegraphic lines. On learning of what had happened, a military contingent was sent against them, killing many, and destroying and burning 11 villages in the process.[3] Commandant Feyzi noticed that most of the resistance came from the land of the Ḥāshids, north of Ṣan'ā', so he decided to subdue the area once and for all. After making the necessary preparations he set out to win over its notables. He sent money and presents to the *shaykh*s and heads, ensuring that each received what was suitable for his rank. But the Banu 'Abd tribe would not submit and were defeated after intense fighting. To conform with the methods both sides employed, Feyzi plundered their belongings, destroyed their homes and kept on engaging the recalcitrant party in battle until he reached Qaflat al-'Adhar, Imam al-Manṣūr's headquarters in the land of the Ḥāshids. In the meanwhile, the imam had taken off with arms and equipment to defensive posts at the tops of mountains and Feyzi was unable to reach him. He returned to Ṣan'ā' after suffering heavy losses in men, equipment and materials.

The same kind of resistance erupted in the *kaza* of 'Ans, a two-day journey southwest of Ṣan'ā', led by Shaykh 'Ali al-Miqdād, who had previously been a loyal supporter of the Ottomans. It is alleged that he changed sides because a corrupt officer, wishing to conceal his exploitative ways, had decided to alienate him. He summoned Shaykh 'Ali and had him tortured by tying him to the wheel of a cannon, breaking his hand and causing him to faint from the pain. At this point the *shaykh* vouched to carry on the battle against the Ottomans until his country was freed of Turkish domination. On learning of his pledge, the authorities retaliated by burning down his house.[4]

With a party of loyal followers known for their courage and sacrifice, Shaykh 'Ali launched a guerrilla-type war against Ottoman troops, raiding their centres and chasing their officials in the *kaza* of 'Ans and its dependencies, in the eastern mountain region, in the lands of Banu Khālid and Banu Qushayb in Ḥawrān and in Jabal Ānis. Years passed and the Turkish authorities were unable to stop his raids. In desperation they destroyed, plundered and burnt more than 300 villages he had entered, some of which had excelled in the study of religious sciences.[5]

'Ali al-Balīli led the expedition against him. In the battle that ensued in the dependency of Qushayb, east of Sūq al-Jum'ah, a bullet hit 'Ali in the head. The rebels cut off his head and sent it to the imam because he was considered a traitor to the cause of the imamate. Both Yemenis and Turks lamented his death, for he was highly respected for his love of scholarship and as head of the municipality of Ṣan'ā'. He was replaced by his brother who took charge of customs and properties of the state, thereby amassing a huge fortune of which he spent a good deal to promote the welfare of the inhabitants.

On returning to the *merkez*, Feyzi was deeply saddened by news of 'Ali's death and insisted that nearby mountain tops be fortified to defend the city against the rebels' attacks, which continued to confound Yemen's Ottoman administration. Feyzi retaliated again in 1892 by arresting a party of ulema and *shaykh*s whom he accused of being in contact with the imam. They included Yaḥya al-Kibsi, Muḥammad ibn Hasan al-Dallāl, Sa'd al-Dīn al-Zubayrī, members of the al-'Iryānī and al-Ḥarāzi families, noted for their learning and scholarship, as well as other tribal leaders and notables, numbering 55 men, who were exiled to Rhodes island for no other crime than having ties with the imam.[6]

News of such arbitrary behaviour induced Sultan Abdülhamid to send another investigative team headed by Namik Beg to Yemen in 1892 to ascertain the causes of the revolt. Namik spent some time in Ṣan'ā' interviewing leaders who invariably complained about the cruel and exploitative behaviour of Turkish officials, which they believed was the main cause of the revolt. These complaints, however, served no purpose other than to increase Feyzi's pressure on the Yemenis once Namik had returned to Istanbul.[7] Another commission of inquiry, this time numbering 14 men, was sent out the same year. They arrived in Yemen at a time of drought and famine in and around Ṣan'ā', brought on by the intense fighting and highly oppressive *iltizām* system.[8] The investigators reported complaints to the capital, but again without any immediate action being taken.

Waqf (mortmain) affairs were neglected because the tribes refused to hand over their produce. This situation prevailed until Al-Sayyid al-Jamāli ibn 'Ali al-Muṭā' became supervisor of the *awqāf*.[9] He was a friend of Muḥammad Hāshim, aide-de-camp of the *vali* Ahmed Feyzi. This benefited the new supervisor and enabled him to regulate *waqf* affairs, imprison the defiant and warn the *'ummāl*[10] to present accurate accounts of what they had collected. He also rebuilt and fitted out many mosques, including the great mosque of Ṣan'ā'.

Attempts by Ottoman officials to give Yemenis a Turkish colouring were another contributory factor in the uprisings. In 1895, Feyzi ordered all officials to wear Turkish dress uniform with a fez instead of the traditional Yemeni *'amāmah* (headgear). This was in addition to his demand that the Yemenis assist him to the tune of 24,000 *riyal*s, with an additional 70,000 slated in for the following year. This may be seen not necessarily as undue extortion, but rather as proof of the sorrowful state of Yemeni financial affairs at the time and the desperate need for funds to meet the cost of the Ottoman presence in the country after much waste in the ongoing rebellions and the struggle to quell them.

The conduct of one official called Mirzāḥ who arrested, insulted, tortured and imprisoned leaders and ordinary Yemenis alike without evidence or trial, aggravated matters further and induced the Yemenis to create a secret resistance that blew up Turkish official buildings and residences in all parts of the capital. This secret resistance caused fear and anxiety among the Turks, especially when an explosion took place in the courthouse while the judge, court officials and all parties to a trial were present. It scared the *vali* even more, for the court building was adjacent to his and his aides' official residences. Feyzi ordered the arrest and imprisonment of everyone in the courthouse except the judge, who was Turkish. They remained in prison for eight months, but this did not deter the resistance, which continued to blow up official administrative buildings, including the post and telegraph office.[11]

Unable to control the situation, in 1892 Ahmed Feyzi sent an emissary, a member of the ulema named ʻAbdallah al-Ḥuḍwarī, to Imam al-Manṣūr to propose a truce. He swore that the sultan's intentions towards the Yemenis were honourable and that all he wanted was to defend the land and prevent it from falling into European hands.[12] The imam, however, rejected the proposal and insisted the *vali* first abandon the present administrative ordinances, resulting as they had from Tanzimat reforms, and reinstate those ordained by the Islamic Sharīʻah. Quite clearly, the application of Tanzimat decrees to Yemen, as in other Islamic Arab provinces, augured badly for the perpetuation of Ottoman rule because the Yemenis deemed them injurious to Islam and its Sharīʻah.

Meanwhile, sporadic fighting was reported in Jabal al-Sharq's *nahiye* between some rebels and Ottoman troops in which a captain, his lieutenant and a number of regular soldiers were wounded. They were quickly reinforced by Miralay Aptullah Bey and Binbaşi Şükrü Beg who undertook to wipe them out, according to a report sent to Istanbul.[13] Feyzi also sought to erect a series of defence towers and, from the fifth army, requisitioned salt, stone gunpowder, mines, fuses, cannons, cartridges, swords and other military equipment.[14]

In 1896 the sultan sent al-Sayyid Muḥammad al-Rifāʻi Ḥasani to the imam with a letter urging him to conclude a truce. The letter has not survived, but according to al-Wāsiʻi the imam objected to its contents and repeated his complaints about the oppressive behaviour of Ottoman officials, whom he accused of failing to abide by the ordinances of God in Islam as enunciated by His Prophet, of committing the forbidden and of oppressing the weak, insisting that the Sharīʻah be implemented. He begged the sultan to solve the Yemeni crisis by withdrawing Ottoman forces from Yemen and opposing the party of infidels, not the party of the Prophet. He concluded by stating that the Ottoman state had withdrawn from many of its European possessions and should do the same by withdrawing from Yemen and permit the Zaydi imams, the Prophet's descendants, who at the hands of the infidel administrators had been reduced to the level of infidels, to administer their own affairs.[15]

Whether moved by the imam's reply or not, in 1896 the sultan decided to send another commission of inquiry to Yemen. It consisted of Ferik Ağah, already attached to the seventh army, Mirliva Ahmed Paşa, Hüsnü Beg, president of the army's general staff, Niyâzi, *defterdar* of the *vilayet*, and Sami Efendi, director of posts and telegraphs, who held talks with Feyzi, commandant and *vali* of Yemen. They found they disagreed with Feyzi's position and recommended to the *seraskeriyet* that he be transferred to another post.[16] The *serasker* forwarded the commission's reports condemning Feyzi's handling of the situation and of humiliating Ferik Ağah of his own staff, together with Feyzi's reply, explaining his stance and his dealings with the *ferik* after the latter had beaten up his own attendant. Feyzi had already recommended that the *ferik*, with Mirliva Ahmed, be transferred to the fourth army stationed at Harput.[17]

With the military fortunes of the Ottomans on the decline, Aptullah Paşa, who at the time commanded the fifth army at Damascus, replaced Feyzi Paşa. Forces in Yemen were increased to 54 battalions of infantry, nine batteries of artillery and two squadrons.

Hilmi Paşa's valiship

In 1897 the sultan's government removed Feyzi from his post as *vali* and replaced him with Hussein Hilmi Paşa. This pleased the Yemenis because he promised to establish justice and preserve the peace and security of the land, and he did indeed institute a number of reforms. He donated 24,000 *riyal*s to the poor of Ṣan'ā', as he did to a number of other Yemeni cities. He received more than 500 complaints against Muḥammad Hāshim, the former *vali*'s aide-de-camp, so the new *vali* had him imprisoned along with other officials who had abused their authority and oppressed the inhabitants.

Hilmi was noted for his love of knowledge and support of the ulema. He set up an administration for education, established a number of Koranic schools, a hostel for teachers, vocational and elementary schools, and made education obligatory for all Yemenis, relying always on ulema and *fuqahā'* to support his enterprises.[18] The imams discontinued these initiatives when they took full charge of the country after independence. By order of the sultan, he also recruited and dispatched to Istanbul 83 young tribal men to be distributed to different imperial military preparatory schools for musical service.[19]

Hilmi was fair minded in administering the country, relying on the advice of learned men, ulema and those experienced in politics. Hüsnü Beg, who headed this informal consultative group, gathered a valuable library of manuscripts and had many that were unavailable for purchase copied, despite the high cost. In the policies he pursued, Hilmi can be regarded as having planted the rudiments of a democratic process, which again was not pursued after independence in 1918.

To placate the Yemenis further, Hilmi persuaded the Sublime Porte to instruct all officials to revert to wearing traditional Yemeni headgear in lieu of the fez his predecessor had ordered.[20] He showed admirable lack of fear in facing the anger of Turkish officials who were unaccustomed to wearing the Yemeni headgear. He had issued an order in 1898 forbidding his officials to receive bribes, and he punished anyone who did. Indeed, he was obliged to dismiss a number of Turkish officials from their posts who defied his orders, among them a *kaymakam* who later tried to shoot him, but only succeeded in wounding the *vali* while his attendants quickly managed to dispatch the assailant.

Hilmi faced a formidable opponent in Müşür Aptullah Paşa, who disagreed with his policies and sought to have him ousted so that he could replace him.[21] To antagonize the *vali*, Aptullah assembled 400 men for dispatch to Tripolitania to strengthen the Ottoman contingent there. He also sought to exile Yemeni prisoners, but the *vali* objected. The sultan supported Aptullah's position, even though Hilmi had written to advise him that such a move would weaken the military's position in Yemen unless the threat of rebellion were contained, which the exile of Yemenis was bound to prevent.[22]

In October 1898, 36 Ottoman battalions found themselves in a battle with 40,000 Yemenis near Shāhil. The Turks lost heavily and were obliged to retreat to al-Qifal. In June the following year, when the weather had improved, Aptullah attacked the Shāhil strongholds and, after sustaining 2000 fatalities, captured the rebels. A month earlier Aptullah had seized Khamir from the rebels. The British military attaché, who reported on the campaigns, knew neither how they were conducted nor how medical arrangements had been made.[23]

This soon became apparent in the region of al-Sharafayn in the *sancak* of Hodeida where, buoyed by the strength of his following, Imam al-Manṣūr mounted new attacks on the Ottoman forces, which had been reduced to 8000 for the whole of Yemen, with about 4000 stationed in the region. The commandant ordered five battalions under Râşid Paşa to storm Ḥajūr, but he did not carry out the order literally. Though the rebels allegedly sustained 1000 casualties, they kept up their resistance and continued to storm an Ottoman *karakol* there for two months, eventually overpowering it and capturing or killing 28 defenders.[24]

Hadi Paşa was told to attack al-Faṣīḥ with two battalions. While approaching the village through a mountain pass 200 rebels unexpectedly opened fire on them and, after sustaining many casualties, they were forced to withdraw. Aptullah Paşa, who had succeeded Feyzi as commandant, ordered his lieutenants to seize al-Sharafayn where 1300 rebels had been ensconced in the mountains. After defeating the imperial troops in an earlier battle, the rebels captured 327 of their Martini rifles. This precipitated an appeal by high-ranking officers in the field for more firepower and both the *serasker* and sultan quickly approved their request for Maxim Nordenfeld machine guns.[25]

Aptullah Paşa's valiship

Given the relative calm during Hilmi's tenure, the central government decided to send another negotiating party in an attempt once again to reach a truce with Imam al-Manṣūr. However, the sultan did not approve the conditions laid down, so Hilmi was dismissed and replaced as *vali* by his antagonist Aptullah Paşa, who now simultaneously occupied both posts, of governor and commandant, after the two had been separated in the interests of checks and balance.

The Yemenis lamented Hilmi's departure because he was one of the few governors who worked to improve the situation in the country, while his replacement was more interested in magnifying himself and taking to extravagant outward displays of his personal importance as well as that of the Ottoman state. He erected a huge post topped by a golden crescent, symbol of the state, outside the gate of Bāb al-Yaman, which lasted only ten years before being brought down.[26] He was given also to entertainment, song and luxury, despite his advanced age.

On the positive side, to provide better military control over conditions in the country, he extended telegraph lines southwards from the capital to Ta'izz and to a number of other important Yemeni cities. Nonetheless, there was very little tranquillity during his tenure because once again Yemen became the victim of drought, inflation, oppression and corruption. Also, the Zarānīq of the Tihāmah, who were renowned for their bravery and daring, were among the tribes to renew their uprisings against the Ottomans. They cut telegraph lines, plundered commercial caravans and engaged in intense battles with Ottoman troops unable to reach them because they did not live in fixed abodes but rather in easy to replace straw huts.

On 26 July 1899, a native informant reported to the British from Ṣan'ā' that the *vali* was removing and replacing *shaykh*s in Dhamār, Qa'ṭabah, Yarīm, 'Udayn and elsewhere for the benefit of those regions and was sending the 60 deposed *shaykh*s to the *merkez* for detention. Shaykh 'Ali Bā 'Abdallah of 'Udayn refused to respond to the summons unless 800 men (instead of the 50 authorized) accompanied him. In the north the imam was rousing the Ashrāf and chiefs of al-Qiblah. From his headquarters in Ṣa'dah he set out to capture the districts of Qifal al-Shamr and Bilād al-Sharq. Troops were sent against them and to Khawlān to the east to suppress the revolt of the al-Ashrāf who had captured 70 Turkish soldiers. Other contingents engaged the Bani Maṭar who too had rebelled. Fighting also erupted in the south between Ottoman soldiers and the Banu Nahāri (a branch of Ashrāf and Dhu Muḥammad tribesmen) in which 25 were killed and 50 wounded among the Turks and 16 wounded among the tribesmen, who abandoned their fort, which the Turks destroyed before returning to Ta'izz. The people of 'Udayn, who were coffee producers, were unhappy about taxes being imposed on the product to prevent it being shipped to Aden. Moreover, they had accurate weapons and were not afraid to register their defiance.[27] They would repair their forts destroyed by the Turks, while the latter were strengthening their own fortifications and erecting new ones in the capital and elsewhere. The Turks also engaged 'Ali ibn Murshid al-Muḥammadi's tribesmen in battle at 'Uzlat al-'Adan, losing one man and destroying the little fort the tribesmen who took to the mountains had abandoned. When Ramaḍān was over, the Turks sent two regiments to scout possible movements among the tribes of al-Ḥujarīyah and to collect the taxes they had withheld. They stabbed an officer who came back to collect more taxes and thus brought upon the head of the defiant town troops that threatened to tear it down unless the culprit was surrendered to them.[28] On the positive side, the Ottomans built a large hospital for military and civilian use with all expenses paid by the government.[29]

On instructions from Istanbul and at the government's expense, the *vali* was to build a European-style boys' school of art and science at Ṣan'ā'. The city authorities purchased cloth, yarn and skins of all kinds, hired local workmen such as blacksmiths, carpenters and weavers, and paid them wages to teach Yemeni boys how to make the various things soldiers needed that would otherwise have to be hauled in from Istanbul. Given the general insecurity in the city, a curfew was imposed, shops were ordered to close after dark and the *vali*, who had just been promoted to the rank of vizier on 13 December 1899, undertook to summon and interrogate the *shaykh*s, with instructions to ship the untrustworthy ones to Istanbul. Some fled to Ḥamīd al-Dīn, others like Shaykh Shahrī of Ibb refused to pay the land tax and when three Turkish soldiers were found murdered on the road to Ḥajjah a force of 400 was sent against him. However, in an ambush from hiding, 14 of his followers managed to kill an equal number of troops.[30]

The Ottomans assigned 400 troops to al-Zandāni and Ashwār near Qa'ṭabah to guard the roads and places, and an equal number to collect taxes. They appointed Yaḥya ibn Qaṣīm as *müdür* of the customs house at Mafālis on a salary of $400 plus $200 extra to spend on securing the roads. Ḥimar's *shaykh mashāyikh* was appointed *müdür* of Māwiyah, a vast district between Ta'izz and Aden, on a salary of $150 plus $400 to secure the roads.[31]

Attempts were made to mediate between the Ottomans and the imam, with the Ottomans proposing that the imam be assigned the area north of Ḥajjah up to Ṣa'dah as a *mutasarrif* on a salary of $1000 a month provided he did not retain the title of imam.

Confrontation with the British in the south

A confrontation with the British political residency at Aden arose from disputes over jurisdiction in the tribal areas bordering Aden where British-subsidized *shaykh*s were threatening the southern districts of the Ta'izz *sancak.*

To check encroachments, the Ottomans wanted to wean British-protected tribes away from the Aden residency and to defend tribal boundaries. They built (and assigned a garrison to) a small fort near al-Dārijah in Ḥawshabi territory, though by the terms of an agreement of 6 August 1895 Ḥawshabi territory was under British protection, as was al-Dārijah, only eight miles from the sultan's residence. The Ottomans were concerned because they had heard that Shāyif ibn Sayf, the emir of al-Ḍāli', had approached the British for a protection treaty. In 1873 the British had notified the Ottoman government that they considered the emir independent of their jurisdiction and claimed to have maintained good relations with him over the years. They were adamant about not letting the Turks absorb this territory, for it would allow them to restrict trade with Aden by giving them control of the route to Ṣan'ā' over Ḥardaba and put them in control of the route from al-Ḥusayn to al-Qāra in Yāfi'i country, along with a considerable amount of trade. Moreover, the healthy climate in the hills of Waliy Ḥasan, with the road to it running through the friendly country of 'Abdalis, Ḥawshabis and 'Alawis who had protection treaties with the British, made it suitable for a sanatorium. Besides, the emir was *de facto* in Britain's sphere of influence and he hated Turks.[32] A report in late 1899 accused the Turks of moving troops towards al-Ḍāli' in Amīri country. When, in 1887, the British concluded protection agreements with some of the tribes in the south, the then Resident suggested they ease up their diplomatic pressure on the Ottomans and allow them to absorb certain tribes in exchange for clearly-defined borders. But the Bombay government refused to go along with its Resident's recommendation on the grounds that, although the Ottomans had rights over some of their villages, the Amīris inhabited a well-watered country on the road to Ṣan'ā' about 40 miles from Ta'izz. By agreement with the British, the chief had been receiving a subsidy to keep the roads safe since 1880. The Residency was worried about the impact of Ottomans establishing themselves in the country without frontiers being defined, for it would allow them to encroach on neighbouring tribes and perhaps threaten the peace of Aden's hinterland. It was recommended that the Istanbul embassy put pressure on the Ottomans to stop the advance of their troops.[33]

The British Resident urged his superiors to insist that Ottoman troops be withdrawn from the area.[34] The Resident sent out an Englishman to survey the border areas. He discovered Ottoman forts in Ḥawshabi territory despite the *seraskeriyet* having denied they were there. A local Ottoman official, Shaykh Muḥammad Nāṣir Muqbil of Ḥumar, apparently built and occupied the fort at al-Dārijah and told his Ḥawshabi followers to say they were Ottoman subjects. The Resident claimed that the forts constituted an encroachment and should be demolished.[35] The *vali* of Yemen denied there were military forts or Ottoman troops in the area and that, apart from a *cordon sanitaire* on the frontier, no measures had been taken and no aggression made on Ḥawshabi territory.

A subsequent report to the British embassy alleged that the sultan had instructed the Ottoman foreign minister to cable the *vali* in Yemen to make Muqbil leave the fort.[36] The government of India had warned many times that if this did not happen, Britain's Hawshabi allies would be encouraged to expel the intruder.[37] The Resident cabled Lansdowne that 400 infantry and six mountain guns had been sent on 14 July 1901 to al-Dārijah to destroy the fort and expel the *shaykh*'s followers even if the Turks were present in large numbers.[38] In a conversation with the Ottoman government on 29 July, Tevfik Paşa promised Ambassador O'Conor that the Ottomans would help get Shaykh Muḥammad Nāṣir out of al-Dārijah. He told Lansdowne that the Porte and the sultan were most conciliatory and that he suspected the *vali* in Yemen had acted on his own in sending the troops.[39] Tevfik told O'Conor that Yemen's *vali* had sent him a telegram stating that several tribes had assembled at Ta'izz and on the Ḥawshabi frontier to prepare to avenge the expulsion of Shaykh Muqbil from al-Dārijah's fort, which he claimed was his by right. Lansdowne was still convinced that Muqbil had acted on the *vali*'s instructions and with his help in seizing and reinforcing the fort and maintained that a protest to the sultan's government was in order.[40]

O'Conor reported to Salisbury that he had met Foreign Minister Tevfik Paşa on 21 May and was told that, according to the *vali* of Yemen and the commandant there, the forts in existence were old, none had been built recently, and were probably in the desert area of the boundary. Tevfik saw no reason to delimit boundaries.[41] The Foreign Office instructed Sanduson of the India Office to encourage the sultan to take possession of the fort and said that the British government would then relay the intelligence to the Porte.[42] The *mutasarrif* of Ta'izz had told Foreign Minister Tevfik Paşa that the Ḥawshabi *shaykh* and 1000 bandits armed with a cannon obtained from the sultan of Laḥj had crossed the frontier and had murdered and pillaged the inhabitants of al-Qumāra'h (not far from Ta'izz). The *shaykh* of the district was told to obtain the assistance of other tribes near the frontier to repel the invaders and protect lives. Tevfik advised the British to instruct their Resident in Aden to take all necessary measures to prevent such outrages in the future.[43]

The *sadaret* reported to the sultan that disputes between the Ottoman government and the British over areas in the *sancak* of Ta'izz stemmed from a British foreign ministry proposal to establish a railroad through these territories, as reported to the Ottoman government. His Imperial

Majesty the Sultan was to decide whether to permit this to take place given its implications for Ottoman sovereignty and security.[44]

India Office reports claimed that the Ottomans were encroaching on al-Ḍāli's territory. This, according to the *vali*'s report, was apparently what the *shaykh* of that region wanted the British Resident to believe, but the Resident could find no truth in his allegation.[45] Undefined tribal border lines had led to disputes and the India Office suggested asking the Ottoman government to agree on a joint commission to examine Captain Wahab's tracing of 1891 and get the political officer at Aden to inspect Amīri country lying in the British protectorate. The Ottoman ambassador had made this proposal to the British government and it was agreed on in principle.[46] Indeed, they commissioned a map draft of the disputed boundaries and authorized setting the boundary of the nine districts in dispute.[47] The boundary situation was not easily resolved because the British had no treaty with the upper 'Awlaqis and Yāfi'is and it was deemed advisable to incorporate them since they bordered the desert. With respect to Wahab's tracings, neither the Ottomans, nor the British government, nor the Amīris apparently admitted to them.[48] The Viceroy of India commended Major Davies, first assistant Resident at Aden, for his services in seeking to define the borders.[49]

The Ottomans had no illusions about British intentions, especially since they had been arming and providing ammunition to the tribes under their protection. In January 1900 the political Resident of Aden requested permission to issue ammunition to Arab chiefs. The governor in council of Bombay approved the request on the grounds that the trade in arms from the French settlement at Djibouti was growing. He stated that if the chiefs could not afford to buy ammunition the British should allow each 100 rounds a year, which might encourage the chiefs to levy a contribution on any party passing through their territory. They were not to purchase any more ammunition than required for legitimate purposes, but the Resident should be able to make presents of up to 1500 rounds a year to each chief, limited to 300 complementary rounds over what he could purchase. The Resident was to submit monthly statements of all sales and gifts of ammunition with full reasons given in every case in which a chief was allowed to purchase more than 1500 rounds or was given more than 300 rounds a year.[50]

In a telegram to the viceroy, Hamilton of the India Office asked the Bombay government for facts on this matter.[51] Meanwhile, the *vali* of Yemen notified the Sublime Porte that the *shaykh*s of Laḥj and

Ḥawshab were attacking villages in the dependency of Ta'izz with the assistance of 300 soldiers sent by the Aden Resident and 2000 tribesmen armed with nine cannons and two more being dispatched from Aden. The Ottoman ambassador relayed the contents of the *vali*'s telegram to the British government of 3 December 1900 protesting strongly against such actions and demanding they cease.[52] The Foreign Office in turn ordered an investigation by the India Office and a report. The governor of Bombay reported back that there was no truth at all to the *vali*'s allegations, claiming that no operation had been directed against Ta'izz dependencies, only in Ṣubayḥī and 'Abdali country.[53]

In an interview with the tobacco company inspector, the sultan of Laḥj alleged that the Ottoman government was doing badly in Yemen because the British were instigating rebellion and using him to liaise, which he denied, claiming also that it was untrue that the British were allowing arms through his country from the coast. The *mutasarrif* of Ta'izz suggested he station an officer at the customs house in Laḥj (on the frontier of Shaykh 'Uthmān) to recover dues on tobacco because the British had a monopoly on the trade and had lost a lot through smuggling. He promised to pay the sultan 1000 dollars a month from recovered income, but he refused on the grounds that his agreement with the Resident at Aden did not permit trafficking with foreigners without their advice.[54]

Aptullah was able neither to suppress them nor to defend the border with Aden, for in 1902 the British had expanded their territorial influence northwards to the *nahiye* of al-Dāli'. In failing to object to the British expansion, Aptullah had angered the central government, which decided to dismiss him and replace him as *vali* with Tevfik Paşa.[55] It also raised concern over the unsettled boundary of the nine districts and the need to define the dividing line.

Outbreak of new disturbances

When all seemed settled, the Ottomans recalled some regular troops and sent two brigades of irregulars from Acre and Adana to replace the ill and infirm regulars. The rebellion seemed to be over, though discord appeared permanent. However, the troops spent barely a year there before being scheduled to return. As the British military attaché Colonel Ponsonby reported to O'Conor in Istanbul, and he in turn to Salisbury in London, the Turks were up against 600,000 Wahhābis and two million Shi'ites (*sic*) who objected to their presence and to their role in helping Turkish officials enrich themselves. Moreover, they did not recognize the sultan's caliphate.

As Ponsonby put it, 'unless the Turks can raise an army of natives suitable for combat in the highlands and model it on the English system, they should withdraw from Yemen.' He praised Hilmi for his honesty and capability but 'too much was expected of him by way of instituting reforms and being sensitive to Yemen viewpoints'. At the first sign of revolt in May 1898, the Turkish battalion was mauled and the telegraph wire to Hodeida cut. Newspapers in Istanbul announced victory in August at a loss of 2500 rebels for only eight Turks, and the minister of war proclaimed the war at an end. Reports shortly thereafter had the country in disturbance again while the government insisted it was tranquil except for a small area around Ṣa'dah.[56]

Because his campaigns against the Ottomans were failing, the imam reportedly approached the British at Aden (through the sultan of Laḥj) to conclude a protectorate agreement with him, but the Resident at Aden repeated, as he had done before (through the India Office in a letter of 28 April 1899) that England was on friendly terms with the Ottoman state and would not entertain his request. In a report to the government of Bombay from the Aden Residency, on 5 December 1899 Brigadier General Creagh said he had met the sultan of Laḥj at Shaykh 'Uthmān and that he had shown him a letter from the imam of Ṣan'ā' asking the sultan to convey to the Resident his wish for British protection.[57] In 1900 new disturbances broke out in the principal cities of Ṣan'ā' and Ta'izz. Encoded messages from the *merkez* requested the appointments of a chief commissioner of police and 15 additional ones, each to be paid 750 *piastre*s a month, for the six now serving could hardly control the deteriorating situation.[58] Rebels in the Ānis region were inciting the inhabitants to rise. In resisting, the battalion stationed there inflicted three deaths, a few injuries and the capture of one rifle.[59] Rebels in the *kaza*s of Ibb and 'Udayn of the *sancak* of Ta'izz refused to desist and, under orders of the imperial command, troops stationed in the area compelled them to surrender. Five rifles were surrendered at the hands of Shaykh Sa'īd al-Jirāfi of the *kaza* of Ḥarār.[60]

Under imperial instructions, Lieutenant Ziya Efendi of the police force was escorting 70 rebels to Tripolitania who had been captured in encounters elsewhere.[61] Other rebels at Rawḍah outside Ṣan'ā' were inciting Arḥab tribesmen to rebel with promises to pay 150 *riyal*s to each and to provide them with ammunition and provisions. The commandant requested another battalion to head this off. He also needed medical men because he had at hand only one doctor serving seven battalions. He asked for the quick dispatch of medical supplies and clothing as fast as possible.[62]

Word from Hodeida came that Kaymakam Aptullah Buni Paşa of Bājil had sent a major with a battalion of troops on 3 November 1900 to Dāhi (*sic*) to collect taxes. Five headmen had set out to collect $4000 owed to the government but the tribal chiefs refused to pay up. Government troops attacked, only to suffer 107 casualties, most of which were deaths. The *vali* sent 4000 more troops to occupy the combatants' villages; they left 24 days later with a fine of $40,000 levied on the rebellious tribes and paid in sheep, goats and camels. They took 40 prisoners, including two *shaykh*s. The total cost to the Ottomans was 250 Turks and an unspecified number of Arabs in their ranks.[63]

The British reported from Yemen that disturbances were erupting anew and that the government had dispersed 15,000 troops under the command of Aptullah Paşa to quell them, but with little success. The British military attaché Lieutenant Colonel Maunsell said that the tribes supporting the imam had inflicted 400 losses. Losses in the Ta'izz area were reportedly played down. Sultan Abdülhamid was sufficiently concerned to send a commission of inquiry on 4 May led by General of Division Mustafa Paşa and including Hasan Bey, son of Abu l-Huda, his well-known confidential adviser in religious matters, to talk the tribes back to loyalty.[64]

An estimated 10,000 rebels assaulted Manākhah and blocked the road from Manākhah to Ṣan'ā'. The commandant at Hodeida reported to the *seraskeriyet* that not only Manākhah, but also Ḥajjah and Ḥajūr were surrounded and contacts with Ṣan'ā' were cut off, that the rebels harboured no fear of the caliph-sultan (Abdülhamid) and only with sizeable reinforcements could Ottoman forces measure up to the increasing strength of the insurgents.[65]

Another report stated that the rebels had surrounded Ibb and raided the post office at Ta'izz. According to the *mutasarrif* of Ta'izz's report to the *seraskeriyet*, preparations to defend the *kaza* of Ibb and repel rebels assembled there would require five companies of troops. Miralay Sa'd Beg stationed in Ta'izz needed ample additional supplies and ammunition for the troops. Miralay Riza in Hodeida reported that the rebels around Manākhah, joined by bedouins, were planning to march on Hodeida.[66] The *vali* urgently requested 15,000 more troops to counter attacks from all sides. The Zarānīq cut off the road south of Hodeida and plundered 60,000 *riyal*s as the shipment passed by Bayt al-Faqīh on its way to Zabīd.[67]

The sultan's government was in a bind: not enough troops could be made available even after depleting the second, third and fourth armies of their personnel and arms. At most, even after recruiting by lot, they might muster between 8000 and 10,000. On 7 May 1901 only 1300 recruits left for Yemen from Izmir and about 2000 from Adana, enough only to replace troops wasted to disease.[68] Horses were in short supply. The shipment of personnel, equipment, supplies and horses for the cavalry by land and sea would entail great cost with money also being in short supply.[69]

With the steady stream of bad news reaching the capital, recruits were balking at boarding transport ships to Yemen. The British vice consul at Adana reported that 5000 troops, 2500 of which were recruits at Mersin, passed through on their way to Yemen, with some having to be chained and carried on board. So gloomy were reports of heavy losses in Yemen that the inhabitants were convinced that not a person sent there would return, for an increasing number of stories of starvation, sickness and burial arrived, and the terrible ferocity of the enemy dampened any will to fight.[70]

The government allegedly mobilized an army of 30,000 and sent it to Hodeida. It was quickly dispatched to Ṣan'ā' on arrival. Transport for troops could be obtained only by requisition and demand for food supplies was a common cause of disturbance. Turkish troops were ambushed as they struggled on their march to collect supplies.

The military situation in Yemen was deteriorating rapidly. According to the *Hodeida News* dispatched from Aden on 3 May 1901, the brother of the *shaykh* of the Zarānīq, who controlled the territory between Hodeida and Zabīd, had killed a Turkish officer and two soldiers and looted about MT$ 20,000 of Turkish government revenue. He had 2000 well-trained men among his followers who were armed with modern rifles. Rather than arrest his own brother, the *shaykh* of the tribe recovered $14,000, of which $4000 came from his own pocket. No inland trade was carried on between Hodeida and Zabīd, only by sea.

The Zarānīq, who paid tax through a highly respected *shaykh* whom they considered a holy man, had resisted Turkish authority for many years. They complained of Turks raiding their *shaykh*'s godown on suspicion it was filled with smuggled tobacco and arms when a careful search yielded only coffee berries and other legal goods.[71] An English official of the public debt who had just returned from Yemen confirmed that the Ottomans controlled only those parts of the country where they had troops. The *sayyid* of Marwa, who had much influence over the Zarānīq and whose followers inhabited the region from Bayt al-Faqīh al-Ṣaghīr eastwards to Dhamār and Ibb, had escaped from Hodeida where the Ottomans had held him for the past year and was currently organizing his tribe against them. The telegraph line to Bayt al-Faqīh was cut. His influence was said to be second only to that of Ṣan'ā's imam. An attempt to blow up the *vali*'s house led to his neighbour's being destroyed by mistake. Hodeida's trade was halted and tribesmen allegedly were raiding the city itself, according to a report of 23 May. Plenty of arms were reaching rebels via Djibouti to Massawa. The revolt was attributed to oppression and the levying of exorbitant taxes on land and crops, even of poorer agricultural classes.[72]

Aptullah Paşa, commandant of the seventh army, reported on the rapidly deteriorating situation in Yemen and warned of the possibility of increasingly frequent outbreaks in the highlands spreading to the Tihāmah and 'Asīr, requiring additional measures and more troops to boost the morale of those under his command. Rather than face up to the difficult task ahead, Aptullah asked the *seraskeriyet* to relieve him of his responsibilities.[73]

As the events relayed in this chapter show, the Ottomans lost the military initiative and no amount of reinforcements could end the rebellion of the imam and his expanding coterie of supporters from tribes hitherto uncommitted to the struggle. The suppressive measures hated officials pursued only added fuel to the fire and led ultimately to the demise of direct Ottoman rule in Yemen. One must credit the hit-and-run tactics pursued by the rebels for the draining of morale among Ottoman troops. Add to this, disease, hunger and their being unaccustomed to the conditions of the land, and the beginning of the end was now in sight.

11. Smuggling and International Politics in the Red Sea

The rebellion in the highlands was not the Ottomans' only problem. Their administrations in the coastal regions faced equally serious challenges from bordering tribes determined to evade the controls to which the highland tribes were subjected and from the encroachment of rival European powers by sea. Detailed in this chapter are the challenges posed by the Zarānīq on land and sea, and by Italians off the coast who, with their warships, protected or even encouraged smuggling and illicit trading from the African coastal areas they controlled. Ottoman efforts to curb unwanted activities in this region and their success or failure in restraining the coastal tribes' involvement with the Italians' unlawful shipping are also examined.

While inhabitants of the Arabian littoral had engaged in smuggling and piracy since time immemorial, it only became a serious problem for the Ottoman state during the age of colonial expansion. When the Ottomans assumed control of the Red Sea region in the 1520s, it was the Portuguese they chased; two centuries later they were locked in struggle with the British; and, in the late nineteenth century, they engaged in what were often futile attempts to prevent the Italians interfering with their shipping in the Red Sea and encouraging sedition against their rule.

In the sixteenth and seventeenth centuries the Ottomans were fairly tolerant of smuggling and the resultant loss of customs duties, for these rarely contributed materially to the region's revenue or economy. But, in the nineteenth century, when the Ottoman administration became short of revenue and when the British ensconced themselves in the Aden region in an attempt to compete with Ottoman trade by promoting their own in the Yemeni highlands, the Ottomans began to tighten their controls over commerce in the Red Sea. With smuggling in contraband ever on the increase in the late nineteenth century and now directly affecting the security of their domains, the Ottoman government acquired an added incentive to put an end to it.

The matter became really serious at the end of the nineteenth century when the Ottomans lost control of the Eritrean side of the Red Sea to the Italians. Now that they had a firm foothold at Massawa, the Italians encouraged traffic in contraband. They used the fact that weapons were being smuggled to 'Asīri chiefs in rebellion against Ottoman authority to cement ties both with them and with the imam of Yemen, and to promote their own commercial and political interests there.

One might argue then that the increase in international political and commercial rivalry in the lower Red Sea corresponded with an increase in both private and state-sponsored smuggling and piracy.

The international setting

The British and the Italians were thus the two principal foreign powers jockeying for position in the lower Red Sea in the nineteenth century. As noted earlier, after decades of futile attempts, in 1839 the British at last acquired a foothold at Aden and, by the end of the 1850s, were seeking to expand their influence into the highlands to promote British commerce. Indeed, they became actively involved in the political struggles of the peninsula with the government of India encouraging arms shipments to allies such as the 'Ubūds of Kuwait against 'Abd al-'Azīz ibn Rāshid of Shammar who, with Ottoman backing, was locked in a struggle against both the house of Saud of Nejd and the Ṣabāḥs of Kuwait. They also supported Imam Yaḥya Ḥamīd al-Dīn of the Zaydi highlands in his rebellion against the Ottomans.[1]

In the 1880s the Italians were aiming for the Bay of 'Aṣab in present-day Eritrea while denying the Egyptians any legitimate claim to the area over which they had exercised influence, if not control, for some time. The British tended to overlook the Italian manoeuvrings because they entertained similar ambitions in the Bāb al-Mandab area.[2]

Menace of the Zarānīq

The Zarānīq, with headquarters at Bayt al-Faqīh but smuggling from Kamarān island, was the wildest and most defiant of the Tihāmah tribes. Divided into two segments, Shāmi and Yamāni, each under its own *shaykh*, they commanded between 5000 and 6000 rifles and were forever blocking routes to Zabīd and Hodeida and smuggling arms from Jāh. The Jarābīh was another rebellious tribe. Though four to six warships would have been required to patrol the long Yemeni coast to prevent gun smuggling on *sunbūq*s and customs evasions, the *bahriye* had to date authorized only two.

With Ottoman troops facing bleak prospects in Yemen, the Italian government, concerned about the administration's ability to maintain safety in the Red Sea, suggested that each European power take up the task of guarding its own possession opposite the Arabian coast to deter slave traders and pirates. A new commodore under Ferik Ferid Paşa, president of the commission of inquiry, informed the Italian consul general in Hodeida that three Ottoman gunboats (*Adramite*, *Yozkat* and *Kastamunu*) were scheduled to patrol the Red Sea — after an incident in July 1905 involving the Eritrean *sunbūq Azad* in the waters of Jāzān. Ferid made it clear to the consul that:

- only Turkish boats had the right to stop and inspect suspicious *sunbūq*s flying foreign flags;
- if an Italian *sunbūq* were to be stopped for possessing irregular papers or for any suspicion, it would be taken to the nearest Italian consulate; and
- if caught smuggling, its cargo would be confiscated and the *sunbūq*'s captain remanded to the Italian consulate's tribunal for trial.[3]

Impact of an unsecured coast

Improving port facilities was considered the key to expanding exports and earning more customs fees and income from trade. Yemen's agriculture yielded coffee, grain and other produce, shipped out of Mocha to Ethiopia, Zanzibar and Zayla'. Despite the hot climate, the coastal area was deemed suitable for producing up to five or six crops a year, but to handle exports the ports had to be widened, it was argued.

Hodeida's annual income was 200,000 *riyal*s, from which the troops were paid, but Hodeida's customs fees were used to postpone the expenses of half the troops in Hijaz; the *sancak* of Hodeida yielded more than 20,000 *akçe*s, while that of Ta'izz yielded 10,000 *kise*.[4]

With the rebellion widening, more manpower was needed along with 100,000 *lira*s for expenses in Yemen.[5] The explosion of the powder depot at 'Urr fort in the mountainous area east of Hodeida did not help matters.[6] Nor did the appearance of Italian warships and the notification of the cavalry units of this menace lessen Ottoman tasks.[7]

German concern

The informal rapprochement between England and Italy over operations in the lower Red Sea worried Germany, which suspected it might lead to Anglo–Italian control of the entrance to the lower Red Sea, ensure England of Italian help in expanding its influence in the Aden hinterland, and give Italy support to build a naval base on the opposite side of the sea.

Germany had treated Italy as a friendly country, but was soon disillusioned by it not supporting the Baghdad Bahn project.[8] Chancellor von Bülow notified his ambassador in Rome that Italy, as an ally of Germany, should make no commitment or concession to England in exchange for support in the Red Sea because of her negative attitude towards the railroad scheme. The Italian minister in Berlin alleged that no such deals were in the offing, but that it was simply rumour.[9]

The British, on the other hand, tended to exaggerate German movements, especially after the alleged 'German–Ottoman complicity to establish a coal depot in the Red Sea'. It was reported to London that *Marie*, a German collier, was surveying Farasān island with a view to establishing a coal store at Kumh island's Tibta Bay, where 17,000 tons were rumoured already to have been discharged with the Sublime Porte's permission for use in the 'Chinese War'.[10] Weakley, the British commercial attaché in Istanbul, alleged that the deal was facilitated by Sayyid Yūsuf al-Rifā'i, the 'very rich man of Farsan' and nephew of 'Shaykh Abu 'l-Huda (al-Ṣayyādi)', an influential confidant of Sultan Abdülhamid to whom the captain of the *Marie* handed a letter of authorization following a telegraphic exchange between Berlin and the sultan's circle after the *müdür* of Farasān objected to landing the coal. Soon afterwards he and other officials of Farasān and Kamarān were dined on board the *Marie*.[11]

There was no indication of serious political manoeuvrings, for in Weakley's own memorandum to his ambassador, the Ottoman marine ministry was offering to buy the lowest-priced coal from Galata (Istanbul suburb) merchants — 5000 tons of Welsh coal — and to purchase corrugated iron sheds from France to house the coal, even though they were intended for the use of German vessels. But to Weakley, why use

Farasān when the island of Jabal Zukr, south of the Farasān group, which provided harbours and with a lighthouse to be constructed shortly on neighbouring Abu 'Ali island, was just as convenient?[12]

Particulars of the transaction came from a 'respectable native at Hodeida, an employé (*sic*) of a well-known local firm at Aden Residency'.[13] On further enquiry, British officials in Istanbul learnt on the authority of 'Mr Black' (a British merchant who had been 'confidentially informed') that the Sublime Porte made the following arrangement with Germany: Germany would supply the coal and Turkey the buildings to store it. The whole establishment would be under the Turkish flag.[14] The pro-British *Levant Herald*, quoting the Turkish journal *Sabah*, stated that the coaling station was to be international, that English coal was already stored there and that no special advantage accrued to Germany, even if the new station was the result its efforts.[15]

If Germany gained at all by this undertaking, one might speculate it gave it direct access to the lower Red Sea, thus enabling it to keep a close watch on the activities of its rivals there: its alleged 'ally' Italy, as well as Great Britain and France.

Italian strategy

For some time Italy had been angling to gain control of Ethiopia. It saw it as a chance to extend its influence to Yemen by strengthening its naval presence in the lower Red Sea. Smuggling provided a pretext to make a military move against both sides of the sea and it could pay off in handsome trade benefits. Sudan's commerce passed through the port of Massawa and Italian military undertakings against the Ethiopians resulted in it seizing control of this key port.[16] Mobilizing troops from the Hijaz to defend Massawa and prevent Sawākin falling to Italian aggression did not seem to prevent the loss of Massawa.[17] Italy missed few opportunities to castigate the Turkish authorities in Yemen 'on the slightest pretext' (which it often created).

Exasperated by Italy's tactics, the British vice-consul in Hodeida wrote to his government urging it to endorse Ottoman efforts to checkmate Italy's overt designs and aspirations in Yemen.[18] Stopping piracy and smuggling called for a considerable increase in the number of patrolling gunboats, and to cover the stretch from Jiddah to Mocha required financial outlays the Ottoman treasury could ill afford.[19]

The Italians made demands the Ottomans simply could not meet without compromising their legitimacy and sovereignty. They encouraged or overlooked acts of piracy and smuggling to justify their unreasonable requests. They did not hesitate to dispatch units of their fleet to threaten and intimidate coastal areas like Hodeida, Kamarān, Perim, Mocha, and the island of Farasān.[20] The Ottomans responded as best they could, given that their fleet's units were on assignment from the Persian Gulf to the Mediterranean and could not react quickly even when gunboats were authorized to be dispatched to the Red Sea to counter piracy.[21] They also stressed the importance of Kamarān island in this regard, authorizing the reinforcement of its defences. The *vali* of Yemen was instructed to build military barracks there in accordance with the *seraskeriyet*'s recommendations.[22] To avoid the dangers of strong winds in the narrows of the island and to safeguard against damages to naval vessels, the council of Ottoman ministers authorized the dispatch of four floats and a pair of heavy anchors and chains, charged to the account of the ministry of marines.[23]

To speed up and improve communications with the lower Red Sea region, the Ottoman government agreed to lay a cable all the way from the Hijaz to Perim via Mocha, with an extension to Shaykh Sa'īd and Sawākin. It would be laid underwater to prevent sabotage.[24] The connection to Shaykh Sa'īd became important after the Ottomans evicted a French contingent that had occupied it momentarily in 1871.[25] The French coveted it for its strategic location, being conveniently situated opposite Djibouti, their possession on the Somali coast. The case the French foreign ministry presented to Münir Paşa, the Ottoman ambassador accredited to both Paris and Brussels, for renewing their demand for Shaykh Sa'īd in 1901 was that it would allow the Ottomans, with French help, to counter British ambitions in the Persian Gulf and their expansion in 'Basra Bay'.[26] Shaykh Sa'īd lay opposite Djibouti on the Somali coast. French control over it would have given them a strategic advantage in the Bāb al-Mandab narrows. The Ottomans responded by authorizing the reinforcement of troops in the nine districts bordering Aden. The Ottomans' inability to control traffic out of Massawa, with its customs revenue tied to Egypt's, complicated matters further, and they criticized the Italians for interdicting it.[27] The sultan's government also instructed its embassies in Europe to call attention to Italy's aggressive behaviour in the Red Sea and to protest to Rome against such encroachments on Ottoman coastlines.[28]

An Ottoman naval vessel arrested the captain of a *sunbūq* smuggling off Midi and held him prisoner for over 30 days in Hodeida. The Italian consuls in Massawa and Hodeida demanded his release, but to no avail. The chief *dragoman* of the Italian embassy then authorized the dispatch of an Italian war vessel to reinforce the demand after the Italian government had made the same representation to the Ottoman embassy in Rome.[29] The tobacco regime asked the Ottoman council of ministers to tighten control over the corridor between Yemen and Aden to intercept smugglers and evaders of customs payments. They also requested greater naval vigilance in patrolling the waters in-between by strengthening surveillance with more warships.[30] Responding to the Porte's instructions and the urgings of the *seraskeriyet*, the governor of Hodeida undertook to establish a customs house at Midi (a small coastal town of the Banu Marwān) where for some time arms and tobacco had been smuggled to the interior. He was transported on this expedition on the Ottoman warship *Zawar Deria* under the command of Hamdi Beg, accompanied by six other war vessels while a cavalry unit of 100 men travelled up the coast at the same time rendezvousing with the fleet at Luḥayyah, Midi and Jāzān. Troops were landed at Midi and the customs house was established.[31]

There were other complaints to Istanbul about unwelcome activities by foreign residents of Yemeni coastal cities. Some 100 Greeks resided in Hodeida and elsewhere and not only monopolized trade with Europe but were occupied also with smuggling. The foreign ministry laboured to find ways to curtail their activities, if not to expel them altogether and open up trading opportunities to natives. The Greeks' offer to meet the imperial army's supply needs there was deemed insufficient inducement to tolerate their activities.[32] Yet little was done or could be done to accomplish this objective.

Another matter of concern was the appearance of foreign ships at a place called Berke, located between Qunfidhah and Hodeida to pick up ancient artefacts sold to foreigners by local Arabs, which angered Feyzi Paşa, overall commander of Ottoman forces in Yemen, who demanded an explanation from the Hodeida commandant.[33]

Accommodating the Italians

With the Italians threatening to take matters into their own hands and to bombard the ports from which pirates and smugglers set out, the

Ottoman government felt compelled to go along with the Italian foreign ministry's five conditions to put an end to piracy. The terms were relayed by telegram to Commandant Arnone, stationed off the coast of Midi, with instructions to bombard it.

The first demand was for the destruction of the piratical *sunbūq*s[34] and for a joint Ottoman–Italian *zaptname* (restraining order) to that effect endorsed by both parties.

The second was that Italian corsairs held by the Ottomans were to be delivered within two months to Italian officials stationed at Massawa. A telegram of 27 October 1900, dispatched jointly by Kâmil and Rüşdi Beg, stated that the captives would be released one month after Arnone had destroyed the *sunbūq*s and the Italian fleet had lifted its siege of Midi. After their release, Arnone would then sail to Hodeida to receive the Italian captives.

The third was that the Ottoman fleet would track down and wipe out the piratical *sunbūq*s. The Ottoman navy would then assign the necessary warships to the Red Sea service. Pirates seized were to be tried and punished to the full extent of the law.

The fourth was that Italy's claim of MT$ 19,000 compensation for losses to pirates would be paid from the (Yemen) *vilayet*'s revenue as authorized by the central government on 6 October 1900. Compensation of MT$ 6500 for those killed had been authorized by the telegram of 26 October. These two assurances would be delivered to Arnone when he arrived in Hodeida.

And the fifth was that the west coast of the Red Sea was also to be rid of piracy and that the Italian government would protect *sunbūq*s of all nationalities equally according to established laws, particularly over non-discrimination in levying customs duties. These terms were approved in a special session of the Porte's ministers and communicated both to its officials in Yemen and to the Italian government.[35]

Not to be denied their pound of flesh, the French staked out a claim to Shaykh Sa'īd and clashed with the Italians when both sought to control Zayla'. The British supported Italy's efforts to gain control of the key port of Massawa opposite the Yemeni coast, then Egyptian territory and a key town for trade with Ethiopia and Sudan, even though they acknowledged that it formed 'part and parcel of Ottoman land'.[36]

On the surface, England and Italy gave the appearance of sharing a common interest in the region, though England had gained control of Egypt at this time and one might have expected it to defend the

Egyptian position over Massawa. Instead, it looked the other way, ignored the breach of the Treaty of Paris (1856) implied in Italy's occupation of Ethiopia, and allowed Italy to obtain the 'best plum of the pudding'.[37] Instead of defending it, the governor of the Egyptian Red Sea littoral, Colonel Chemside, handed Massawa to the Italians. There were protests from the khedive of Egypt, St Petersburg and Vienna, but Sultan Abdülhamid balked at sending war ships to undo the British action, even though he too had reasons to fear the presence of French, Italian and British warships in the area. The inhabitants of Massawa and of Benlil, from where Egyptian garrisons were forced out, had hoped the Ottoman government would challenge the action, but prudence and a weak naval presence decreed otherwise.[38]

Protests to all the capitals of Europe came to naught. Italy argued that the action was necessary to 'pacify' the land and counter 'the lack of security'. The German press vehemently opposed Italy's action and supported the sultan's sovereign rights, but to no avail. The Negus of Ethiopia was to be appeased with 'rich gifts'. The Italian press alluded to a deal between Great Britain and Italy: the latter would abandon claims to Mediterranean lands while Britain would allow it a free hand in the Red Sea.[39]

The Italians and piracy in the Red Sea

To the alarm of both the Ottomans and the British, Italian activity off the coast of Yemen intensified after 1881. By 1898 their warships were intimidating the authorities in Hodeida at the slightest pretext.

The Italian–Ottoman agreement to control piracy in the Red Sea did not yield immediate results. Within a year the German government was reporting increased piracy by both Arab- and Italian-protected *sunbūq*s. In October 1901 the *Dancoli*, an Italian *sunbūq* sailing with a load of camels from the Arabian coast to Massawa, was attacked and pillaged near the islands of Farasān and one crewman was enslaved. Shortly afterwards the *Marzūq*, a *sunbūq* carrying 27 pilgrims, was attacked while heading in the opposite direction and its entire crew was enslaved. The Italian embassy in Istanbul lodged severe warnings with the Sublime Porte over such acts of piracy emanating from Arabian shores. The protests of 19, 26 and 28 November and of 2 December 1901 pointedly blamed the chief pirate, Sa'īd ibn 'Abd al-Rāḥi and another, 'Abdallah ibn Awbash. The acts were allegedly perpetrated within sight of the Ottoman corvette *Beyrut*. It was further alleged that such piracy had been taking place off the coast of Jiddah. Moreover, the royal Italian embassy stated that if the Ottoman government failed to suppress piracy in the Red Sea, Italy would do so on its own.

In March 1902 a pirate *sunbūq* manned by 40 men armed with Remington rifles attacked the island of Dalak. The wife of the Italian *zaptiye* was killed, a *carabineri* was wounded and a number of native women were violated. The incident was reported in detail on 27 April in an *aide-mémoire* to the Ottoman embassy in Rome and to the Ottoman foreign minister Reşid Paşa.

In May 1902 two pirate ships attacked the Italian *sunbūq*s *Malac* and *Fulca*. The one escaped, but the other was captured and relieved of its cargo of camels. Three *sunbūq*s were thus attacked in less than three months. And not only *sunbūq*s bearing the Italian flag were assaulted. In the same month of May, pirates from the Arabian coast near 'Cos' captured an Ottoman *sunbūq* carrying 200 packets of merchandise belonging to Massawa merchants.

On 27 May 1902 the Porte told the Italian embassy how it would end piracy in the Red Sea. It would send four steamships of the *mahsusa* (special) class to the Red Sea, but by July nothing had been done. Then in September 1902 a pirate *sunbuk* with 19 crewmen and 14 rifles attacked the village of Dubell on the island of Dalak near Massawa and carried off booty worth MT$ 20,000, even making Arab fishermen help load it onto a *sunbūq* they had stolen that was anchored offshore.[40]

The Ottoman ambassador in Berlin, Tevfik Paşa, had sent an urgent ciphered message to his government stressing the need to delay Italian action because the Sublime Porte had been conciliatory in the face of the Italian ultimatum and stating that some pirates had been apprehended.[41]

Germany negotiated with Italy on behalf of the Ottoman government to settle the problem of piracy peacefully, assuring its ally that more Ottoman gunboats and a cruiser would be sent to the Red Sea to stop the smuggling of weapons. The kaiser's government alleged that there was no proof that weapon smuggling was from the Eritrean coast or that Italy was involved in it. Nevertheless, the German ambassador in Istanbul was instructed to tell Foreign Minister Rifat that his country and the other three countries involved in the Red Sea (France, Italy and England) were opposed to any form of arms smuggling.[42] The Italian government, however, was no longer prepared to delay executing its ultimatum of direct intervention to end piracy. In May 1902 pirates captured an Ottoman *sunbūq* carrying 200 barrels of petrol and 35 packets of merchandise belonging to Massawa merchants operating off the Arabian coast near Cos.

The Ottoman governor moved quickly to arrest Ibrāhīm, Adham and 'Uthmān, as well as the eldest son of Shaykh Ṭāhir, and to give chase to their *sunbūq*.[43] The arrest followed an ultimatum in which the Italian commandant threatened to bombard Midi. Riza informed Arnone that he could not deliver Shaykh Ṭāhir to him because it would have grave consequences for Ottoman troops, but that he was prepared to have him punished as stipulated in an imperial order from Istanbul. Shaykh Ṭāhir wielded considerable power in the region and the rebellion that might result from his being handed over to the Italians would prove disastrous to the Ottoman presence in Yemen. But Arnone insisted and told the grand council of the *vilayet*'s admiralty that if Ṭāhir were not handed over with MT$ 6500 in blood money for the Italians of Massawa killed and wounded, he could not guarantee that his ships *Nourallah* and *Césare* would miss Ottoman troops when they opened fire.[44] Their fleet bombarded Midi north of al-Luḥayyah in October 1902, a month before the targeted date, because the Ottomans had been too slow to indemnify them for the losses they and their protégés had sustained from Banu Marwān raids on the Eritrean coast off Massawa.

The Porte sent a telegram to Rome restating that the Ottoman government, not the Italian commander, had the right to punish and urged that he be so notified in the interest of avoiding belligerency.[45] But before any action could be taken, the Ottoman government received a telegram of 'great urgency' from Aptullah Paşa, commander of the Ottoman forces in Yemen, saying that Arnone had bombarded and levelled Midi, forcing all the inhabitants to flee with only imperial troops remaining behind. The Italian government viewed the whole matter as a natural result of hostility rather than as a gross violation of international customs. The Ottoman foreign ministry instructed its ambassador in Rome to notify the Italian government of the event and to urge it to put an end to such outrages. However, according to a report in *L'Eclaire* (3 November 1902) relayed from Aden the day before, the Italian government considered the Ottoman guarantees insufficient and had issued orders to its commander to attack Midi on 2 November.[46] An angered Ottoman commander sought to head off the attack by having enough time to reinforce his Midi garrison with four additional battalions and one battery, hoping in so doing that the Italian flotilla of four warships would sail away.[47]

The Ottomans were caught in an awkward position. Following their attacks and notwithstanding that some of the pirates had been captured, the Italians still insisted this was not enough. They had proceeded to bomb the littoral, only an hour away from Midi, three days before they bombed Midi itself. The argument they used was that the powerful Banu Marwāns were attacking *sunbūq*s carrying the Italian flag off the Yemeni coast and that they were now sufficiently aroused even to attack the Ottoman camp that same night.[48]

Angered by such highhanded action and by the Italians' refusal to accept Ottoman assurances, the sultan's government dispatched urgent messages to its embassy in Berlin instructing Tevfik Paşa to entreat the German chancellor to intercede with the Italian government to obtain the withdrawal of its fleet and to negotiate areas of disagreement.[49]

The Ottoman government was fully aware that the Italians were seeking any excuse to encroach on the Yemeni littoral. Though they used piracy now as their main pretext, they themselves were equally guilty of sponsoring it from their possessions on the opposite side of the Red Sea. The ultimatum, scheduled to expire on 18 October, gave little time, as designed, for the Ottomans to respond. Instead, they called on the German kaiser to put pressure on the Italians to hold off until a full investigation could be held, the corsairs had been interdicted and the goods they had taken restored to their rightful owners.

Germany was unable to restrain Italy's coercion because Italy clearly aimed to extend its influence to Yemen. Promoting their own brand of piracy, in which Italian agents played no small part, was designed to provoke the powerful Arabian tribes of the littoral into retaliation. It was part of Italy's overall objective to drive a wedge between them and the legitimate authority.[50]

On 21 October the Ottoman ambassador in Berlin, Tevfik Paşa, relayed to German Chancellor von Bülow his government's request that Germany put more pressure on Italy to desist.[51] But the commander of the *Pièmonte*, an Italian cruiser stationed off the port of Hodeida, claimed he had not received instructions to discontinue, further alleging that corsairs had taken loot from the island of Dalak.[52] The amusing side of it was that the pirates were able to take the loot in *sunbūq*s to Massawa right past the Italian warship and to get MT$ 19,000 for it.

The Ottoman predicament

A marine officer who spent many years in the Red Sea countering the slave trade perhaps best states the Ottoman government's predicament. In his report he described Midi as nearly inaccessible by land or sea and with its chief able to call on 20,000 warriors if need be. He also noted that there was no Ottoman post in the area and to come upon it by sea would involve passing through a narrow, winding, three-and-a-half mile waterway. In approaching by land, the Ottomans would be able to get no nearer than 50 miles of it.[53]

To compound the woes of the Ottoman navy in the Red Sea, envious French reporters with no love of Germany were asserting that the Italians, in gaining terms from the Ottomans by which they did not abide, were able to accomplish what a French naval squadron (five large ships and two counter torpedoes) was unable to do, namely to win compensation for French losses to Midi pirates. Italy's success was attributed to its friendship with Germany and the kaiser's intercession.[54]

After the Italians had pointed the way so boldly, the British too began to ask whether it was time for all the powers trading in the Red Sea to act in concert to counter piracy. British shipping had also suffered from piratical raids and it was recognized that the Ottomans were either too weak or too apathetic to counter them. The British had extended protection to Ḥaḍramī shipping and to merchants stationed in Hodeida who could prove they were born in Hadramawt or had been established in Aden beforehand. The Ottoman authorities, however, refused to acknowledge Britain's right to protection and the argument between them and the British authorities lasted for three years.

In the meanwhile, the Ottomans took great care to protect Ḥaḍramī trade out of Hodeida, though they were unable to extend protection to al-Khawkhah from where, in the absence of official surveillance of the area, Ḥaḍramīs transported coffee to Aden without paying their share of customs. Goods of all kinds, especially tobacco, reached Aden without the Ottomans being able to stop contraband or collect customs dues. Moreover, there was an understanding with the *müdür* of Hodeida that he could let goods slip through without customs being collected on them. Worse yet, every week large quantities of Maria Theresa *thaler*s, whose import was prohibited, still managed to reach the Yemeni highlands via the ports of Hodeida and Mocha, where they were still more popular than the Ottoman *mecidiye*s.[55]

The Ottomans had to patrol 400 miles of Yemeni coastline, yet at the same time match and overcome the power of the tribes engaged in smuggling. A reporter commenting on the strength of the Banu Marwān and their ability to muster 20,000 men armed with Martini-Henri rifles and good breechloaders, argued that the time had come to mount a strong military expedition against them and that Great Britain should perhaps support the Italians in doing so.[56] Within half a decade Italy and Great Britain found it in their mutual political interest to support each other's ambitions in the Red Sea, an undertaking that lasted until the end of the First World War.[57]

Attempts to remedy the situation

With European encroachments on Yemeni territory and commerce precipitating the need for a formal study and assessment of the situation in the Red Sea, in May 1889, the Ottomans sent Mehmed Ziya to evaluate the situation at close range. In his report of 27 May he asserted that with Britain and France enjoying footholds on the Yemeni coast and Italy at the opposite end of the Red Sea, new measures were now necessary to deal with the situation in the interests of stabilizing and strengthening Ottoman coastal establishments and developing the mineral and agricultural resources of the Tihāmah.

Ziya attributed the deterioration to the near absence of an Ottoman presence in the region, which in turn was due to lack of funds to pay for officials and troops. This, in his view, had brought anarchy and lawlessness to the region, thus inviting intervention by foreign powers, which seized the opportunity to cultivate the tribal chiefs. Intrigue went on with the disaffected inhabitants who were wooed with arms. England, he argued, had taken control of Aden by converting it into a coal depot and fortifying it. The emir of Laḥj had received a battery of artillery from Britain whose ships sailed at will to Mocha, Hodeida and other coastal areas, in and out of Ottoman ports as if they owned them. Italy was in Massawa and 'Aṣab and from these ports its nationals smuggled arms into Yemen. It had two to three depots in Mocha. France so far was inactive, though for a century or so it had kept an eye on British activities in the area.

Having assessed the situation, Ziya proposed 15 remedies, a number of which were designed specifically to stop foreign intervention and coastal activities affecting the interior. One of them recommended replacing the Ottoman *mecidiye* with the Austrian *thaler* and removing English currency from circulation. Another urged stationing warships from Istanbul in the Red Sea to patrol the coast.[58]

A more impressive set of recommendations for reforming Yemen in general and for addressing the situation in the Red Sea in particular was submitted in a 38-page report by Mahmud Nedim.[59] He stated that for a number of years Yemen had been insecure both by land and sea, especially since the introduction of new arms into the country. Unless the inhabitants were stripped of them, he argued, the land would never be secure. He recognized how difficult it was to patrol a 400-mile coastline with an average depth of between four and five feet. Large ships could only anchor two to three miles from the shore; only *sunbūq*s could come nearer, the vessels used for smuggling arms and other goods past customs stations with much loss of revenue to the treasury. To stop them they would need piercing devices, 250 imperial troops, a small artillery piece and eight steamships to patrol the coast. Smuggling by land from Aden could be stopped, he argued, by constructing four customs posts along the border with a military outpost at Ḥujarīyah to intercept smugglers using the Ḥujarīyah–Ta'izz road.

Nedim claimed that each September large commercial ships laden with goods from Zanzibar, Java, Basra and Iranian coastal cities entered the Red Sea and, after telling Ottoman officials they were simply passing through but staying long enough for local merchants to learn the contents of their vessels, anchored for a few days at the Yemeni ports. They then sailed to the opposite shore where merchants' agents bargained to buy the contents, then smuggled them across into Yemen and Hijaz at a great loss to the *vilayet*s' customs revenue.

Placing warships on patrol would prevent this type of traffic. Moreover, if they were allowed to anchor at all, it should only be after they were made to unload their cargo and pay customs fees on it.

Being uninhabited, like 20 other localities along the coast, the islands of Farasān and Kamarān posed a danger in that some day they could suffer the same fate as Perim, with the English and Italians using them to offload close to the Yemeni shoreline. Nedim recommended that they pump water to them and encourage natives from the mainland to settle there to till the soil by providing them with implements and tools and, where the land was unsuitable for cultivation, encourage them to take up fishing; the same policy could be applied to the islands off Hijaz. Moreover, Farasān and Kamarān were rich in high-quality cement, where it could be produced far more cheaply than importing it, which, in itself, would be a great saving.

Each year, continued Nedim, Hijazis exploited mother-of-pearl and pearls, which they transported to Aden to sell to British merchants, thus bypassing Yemen and losing out on another source of revenue. He suggested that, to benefit Yemeni merchants and the local treasury, these merchants be granted a five-year customs exemption in exchange for unloading these commodities at either Luḥayyah or Hodeida.

Nedim's report dwelt on the commercial value of Mocha as a port, which he claimed only the smaller *kayak* vessels could enter. The annual value of imports and exports was placed at 20,000 Ottoman *liras*; besides woven mats and containers, no other noteworthy industry was located there. The Ẓahari and Mashliḥah tribesmen of the area earned their keep by transporting commercial goods and salt from the salt mines of the region; the mines in the area yielded up to 1.5 million kilograms. The salt was carried by camels into the highlands and across the sea to ʻAṣab, Massawa, Ubukh, Zaylaʻ and Zanzibar.

Villages between Mocha and Hodeida (100 miles apart) engaged mostly in fishing. With 45,000 inhabitants and its commerce valued at approximately 2 million Ottoman *liras* annually, Hodeida was the port *par excellence* on the Red Sea.[60] The export value of coffee beans and their skins alone was listed at 1.5 million *liras*, and most of it was in the hands of foreign traders.

The coinage problem was again noted in his report, in which he stated that the country's currency consisted of 'gold coins and Selim Mecidiyes' (*sic*) only. The need now was for the equivalent of 5 million *liras* of silver.

Proposed measures to control and interdict

Another proposal to control the Arabian littoral of the Red Sea from ʻAqabah to Bāb al-Mandab and to prevent smuggling, piracy and contraband traffic was discovered in the naval museum library in Istanbul by William Blair of Princeton University.[61] According to this 22-page draft report, undated but most likely presented after 1906 since it refers to the Hijaz railway, the distance to be patrolled was put at 1000 miles, with a shoreline fraught with natural barriers. At the time of the report there were only a few scattered posts for patrolling and officials appeared helpless to do much about preventing illegal traffic in the Red

Sea. The area, furthermore, was largely undeveloped and, where inhabited, there were fewer than 1000 residents in any one locality.

Existing posts were located at 'Aqabah, Yunbu', Jiddah, Layth, Qunfidhah, Farasān, Luḥayyah, Kamarān, Hodeida, Mocha and Bāb al-Mandab. Arabian tribal chiefs controlled the areas in between and dominated the shoreline and the traffic, commercial or otherwise, up to Aden and Massawa. Enriched by such illicit traffic, their sons travelled to Egypt, Sawākin and centres of foreign trade with motorized vessels further to extend their trading operations.

The report recognized that legal traffic in the Red Sea required security of transport to the key centres of trading, namely Massawa, Djibouti and Aden. To provide protection and security it was necessary to control the shores and to bar the entry of weapons and other contraband. It also meant preventing the periodic uprisings of the tribes settled off these shores. To date there had been no evidence of such control. It was imperative at this juncture to dispatch both naval and military forces to put an end to defiance on both land and sea. Such undertakings were all the more urgent in view of the fact that the British, Italians and French had banded together against the Ottoman government and were capitalizing on every opportunity to benefit from any turmoil facing it. Stabilizing the region of the Red Sea was now of utmost importance to ensure the security of both the inhabitants and the sultan's possessions.

Proposals for controlling illicit traffic

The Zarānīq, Banu Marwān, Idrīsis and their various followers were the most influential tribes of Yemen and the Hijaz littoral. Their most important political and commercial ports were al-Khawkhah, Ibn 'Abbās, Ḥabl, Midi, Jāzān, Shaqīq, al-Nadīm and al-Barq. There were proposals to establish official posts to control imports at these points.[62] It was considered essential to assign steamships to patrol the area, for at the sight of a steamship or its smoke on the horizon, smugglers and their *kayak*s were more likely to return to shore and safe havens than to continue sailing with illicit loads of female slaves and tambourine cymbals. To catch up with them, 30-ton draft motorboats equipped with 37-millimetre artillery would need to be stationed at or near Qunfidhah.

Given the nature of the coast, which stretched for 1000 miles, policing rather than administrative posts, such as the one at Hodeida, were best suited to patrol it. Policing posts should be located at 100-mile intervals with a warship stationed at each one. Ideally, the post should be located in a natural place of safety, but unfortunately such places did not exist; hence the need to build them.[63]

The report recommended establishing a naval base to keep track of ship movements and prevent disturbances, but details were not spelled out. The Red Sea was especially in need of such a base to patrol shores. The port of Abkhur was considered suitable because the entrance to its harbour was in the shape of the eye of the bridge.[64] It was curved in form, and the curved length measured six-and-a-half nautical miles; 20 at the entrance, 25 in the middle and three-and-a-half fathoms deep at the end: it was 8500 metres from entrance to end. Its coast was shaped like a quay, straight up (literally like a pole) from the water. If needed, a prefabricated dock could quickly be brought in. It was only three to three-and-a-half hours by camel from Jiddah and the climate between Jiddah and this place was judged to be suitable.

According to the report, establishing the port presented no difficulty. It was easily defensible because it could be connected to the Hijaz railroad and it was important for the Ottomans to have a protective base halfway down the Red Sea. As a precaution, it was equally important to have such bases at ‘Aqabah, Jiddah, Qunfidhah and Kamarān. A facility at ‘Aqabah could have been linked to the Hijaz railway system; its entrance could have been protected with fortifications above and on the opposite side of the sea inlet, but it would have been difficult to build it a potable water facility. Jiddah was an important location for the Hijaz on the Red Sea, but to establish a port there would have meant exposure to natural barriers and transport to it would have been extremely difficult and expensive to provide. It would have been impossible to establish a naval base there. Qunfidhah in ‘Asīr was a good location for constructing a base; the weather, water and shore were fine and an iron works facility could conveniently have been put there, but it might have been difficult to locate a naval base there. Kamarān was an adequate place for a naval base, given its pleasant climate, but it would have been difficult to defend in the event of a war.

Locating the naval base

If one of the locations chosen materialized into a base, then a number of facilities would have to be established, namely army barracks, docks for warships and sleeping quarters for up to 15 persons. Additional space would be required for an up-to-date hospital; for iron and ceramic works facilities; a foundry; a boiler room; and a factory for building tools. The base should be able to handle gunboats and postal steamers, which would require a large floating dock, depots for storing oil, gas and other similar combustibles, besides storage facilities for combat equipment and machines. Water depots would be required, as well as water distilling facilities and machines for making ice.

In the interests of conservation, machinery and supplies generally (with the exception of brass) could have been shipped from Istanbul. Because Red Sea trade for the most part was in the hands of Greek merchants, they would have to deal with the one who offered the lowest bid for locally obtained supplies. Communications between Jiddah, Yemen and Istanbul would be through a cable company arranged via Sawākin. To avoid delays and minimize annual expenditure, a telegraph station could be established.

A model would be made to facilitate the process of establishing boardwalks and of locating suitable positions for ports, naval construction facilities and lifts for heavy loads. To facilitate entry and departure from ports, suitable lighthouses and lit buoys would be planted at proper intervals.

End results?

The observations contained in the report and the recommendations it offered made perfect sense. However, time was running out on the Ottoman Empire and political events, namely the revolution against Sultan Abdülhamid in 1908 and the intensification of international pressure on a much weakened Ottoman state, put an end to the realization of such elaborate, extensive and time-consuming projects.

Two powerful Yemeni leaders worked against Ottoman control of the coast, Sayyid Muḥammad al-Idrīsi of 'Asīr and Aḥmad Fatīni of the Zarānīq. The former proclaimed in 1906 his mission to undo what he termed Turkish misrule. In this he had the support of other Tihāmah tribes, namely the Banu Jumi', Wā'idāt, Banu Qays, Zal'īyah and Banu Sulayl.[65] By 1907 the powerful Zarānīq tribe of the Tihāmah had been won over not only to the Idrīsis but also to the Italian cause. Rising in revolt in the name of religious reform, Idrīsi movement attracted support as far north as Qunfidhah. With the capture of the key stronghold of Mahāyil, Abhā, the capital of 'Asīr, was cut off from Qunfidhah's port. The Ottomans now were engaged in a struggle to put an end to a revolt encouraged and supported by the Italians.

With major shuffling of top military and civil officers[66] on the eve of the Young Turk revolt, the situation along the Yemeni coast was as unstable as ever. When Ferik Hasan Tahsin arrived on 30 December 1908 as *vali* and commander-in-chief, prominent local merchants who met him on disembarkation complained of loss of trade because of Zarānīq attacks on caravans passing Bayt al-Faqīh and Zabīd, two important trade centres. British Vice Consul Richardson also met Tahsin and told him of the Zarānīq's eight-year record of disruption, cutting telegraph lines and piracy against British shipping off the Yemeni coast. Recently arrived Ottoman officers and troops mobilized against the Zarānīq suffered disastrous military reverses, necessitating reinforcements from Ṣan'ā'. At sea, however, they enjoyed some success. On their way down from Kamarān, the newly arrived Ottoman gunboats *Taşköprü* and *Nevşehir* encountered two *dhow*s near Cos running arms; they sank one, captured the other and confiscated 350 rifles and a quantity of ammunition. Richardson reported further that the gunboats were now cruising and patrolling south of Hodeida, cooperating with troops operating against the Zarānīqs.[67]

In the highlands, Imam Yaḥya's revolt nearly ended Ottoman rule in 1911. No sooner had the Young Turk government come to terms with him than the war with Italy broke out. With a constantly menaced coastline, the Ottomans could hardly be expected to proceed with the measures recommended for reinforcing their military positions along a 1000-mile shore with rebellious tribesmen threatening the Yemeni coast.

The question of how to control piracy and smuggling was superseded by the more urgent one of how to maintain an Ottoman presence in the Red Sea. The Italian invasion of what became Libya, an Ottoman province in North Africa, proved costly in terms of resources (financial and material) for an already exhausted Ottoman state. It diverted attention away from the Red Sea area and there was a momentary reprieve when the contending tribal and ideological forces in Yemen and 'Asīr enthusiastically supported the Ottoman position in the war. However, no sooner had it ended unfavourably for them than they found themselves dragged into the First World War, which culminated in the final demise of the empire altogether, rendering the question of how to control disruption in the Red Sea area a moot one.

12. The Last Phase of Rebellion, 1905–11

The newly appointed Zaydi imam, youthful energetic Yaḥya Ḥamīd al-Dīn, who succeeded his father al-Manṣūr bil-Lāh in 1904 at the age of 35, launched the last phase of the Yemeni rising against the Ottomans, with its successes, reverses, then ultimate triumph. In this chapter we see how his skill and leadership brought about the truce of Da'ān in 1911 and the concessions he won from a recalcitrant Young Turk leadership ended in Yemen's confirmed loyalty to the Ottoman state during the First World War and the final evacuation of the Ottomans from Yemen in 1918.[1]

The imam sought official recognition of his leadership from the central government and the right to administer his affairs in accordance with Islamic laws and Zaydi rites.[2] Yaḥya had learnt a lot and made good contacts with Yemeni leaders while accompanying his father on expeditions, but the Sharaf al-Dīns, who enjoyed both Zaydi and Shāfi'i support in a number of quarters, challenged his claim to the imamate. The Ottomans' general weakness in Yemen at this time encouraged tribal chiefs and heads of villages to challenge the imams for leadership and to assume the lucrative task of gathering taxes, including the mandatory *zakāh*, from both Zaydi imams and Ottoman officials.[3]

The 1899 insurrection had been suppressed, but with Ottoman officials more interested in amassing wealth than in good administration, the discontent continued. A reporter in Yemen informed the *Times of India* that the main causes of the insurrection had been corruption, extortion and the oppression of natives. Fortunes gathered by illicit means were changed to British sovereigns through an agent in Aden or Hodeida, and the recipient official would return to Turkey rich. Two successive years of drought, however, rendered these acts of extortion less endurable. People were in great distress and supplies of grain from India were sold at famine prices. Moreover, they had great difficulty transporting it to the highlands, often at the cost of ten rupees a bag. More than 100 people died of hunger at Ibb and Jiblah; many more fled to the Red Sea ports and Aden to escape death. The authorities provided shelter, raised subscriptions and supplied food and medicine, but in insufficient quantities to meet the need.

The 1904 insurrection

When insurrection broke out again in 1904 the Ottomans were taken by surprise. The few troops they had were scattered over the country at a time when the imam's forces, rumoured to number close on 100,000, were armed with rifles and equipment, including artillery taken at the capture of Ṣan'ā'.[4] The first serious incident took place on 8 November 1904 when a garrison of 400 troops was attacked and completely destroyed at Ḥafash. This was a blow to Ottoman prestige. The nearest reinforcements, the Adana Redif brigade, had been held up for a year at Qunfidhah on the coast of 'Asīr. British Vice Consul Richardson reported from Kamarān that the departure of unpopular *Vali* Aptullah Paşa gave the tribes their opportunity to rise. Sūq al-Khamīs and Manākhah, he stated, had always been in rebellion. Outbreaks followed at Ḥajjah, where the new imam's adherents were constantly active. The Zarānīq along the coast were also defying the administration.[5]

The new imam had been expected to give the Ottoman *vali* trouble after Aptullah's departure, and quickly the Ḥāshids and Bakīl tribes north of Ṣan'ā' rose in rebellion and caused trouble at Ḥajjah and Ḥajūr. Reinforcements were called in from 'Asīr.[6] Meanwhile, the British expressed concern that the rebels advancing on Qa'ṭabah in the south might attempt to cross into al-Dāli' to engage fleeing troops. Refugees would be acceptable but not a military engagement, and the *shaykh* of the area was so informed by Major Jacob, the political agent at Aden.

Both the Ottoman authorities and the British found the situation in the south disquieting. Rebels had occupied Dhamār and Yarīm and were marching on Ta'izz and Qa'ṭabah, where a garrison of 500 Turkish and Syrian soldiers armed with 1200 rounds of Mauser bullets had dug in. This alarmed the Aden authorities, who feared that rebels might enter the territory of their protégé, the Shaykh of al-Ḍāli'; so they sent troops to protect their frontiers.[7]

A telegram from the *mutasarrıf* of Ta'izz claimed that rebels were invading the *kaza* of Yarīm, and Qa'ṭabah and Ibb were under siege.

The Times of London reported on the basis of reports from Istanbul that the whole country south of Ṣan'ā' to Qa'ṭabah and Ta'izz was in revolt with much of it having fallen into rebel hands.

Within a month of the imam's rising, wire lines had been cut between Ṣan'ā' and Ta'izz, and supplies for the troops had run out and had to be imported from India. On 12 December Ṣan'ā' was reported under siege, as was the road to Hodeida. On 24 December a *redif* division from Syria finally got under way, by rail via 'Aqabah rather than by sea, to save canal dues, despite the *vali* of Syria having protested against sending troops by land because of the shortage of potable water at Ma'an and 'Aqabah. On 26 December the rebels captured the Sinan Paşa post on the Ṣan'ā'–Hodeida road with some small guns. More troops were requested. Then, on 31 December, the *müdür* of the *nahiye* of al-Maḥwīt, a dependency of Kawkabān, was captured and Colonel Edhem Beg was forced to surrender at Sūq al-Khamīs. On 10 January 1905 Ṣan'ā' was besieged and attacked steadily for six days and nights. The *vali* notified headquarters that unless the rebellion was suppressed quickly it would take 50 to 60 battalions to do so later. On 16 January 1905 a special order was issued to mobilize three brigades for service in Yemen, two from the Syrian *redif*s and one of eight *nizam* battalions from the fifth (Syrian) corps, and to set their salaries.[8]

On 29 January, a Greek vessel full of troops from Qunfidhah, the *Hagion Oros*, was seized by mutineers and forced to head back; they arrived at Suez in a state of starvation, paid canal dues and reached Mersin, their home port. Orders were issued to punish them severely, but there is no evidence that these were carried out. The urgency of the situation demanded that troops be siphoned away from regular units and dispatched quickly to Yemen. The fourth army reported that 250 of the *redif* battalions of the Malatya command had fled. Some were rounded up and dispatched south towards Urfa. Serasker Riza ordered the others to be retrieved and chastised harshly.[9]

The second siege of Ṣan'ā'

After declaring war on the Ottomans and expressing his determination to end their control over ZayditeYemen, Yaḥya led a force of 20,000 Zaydis and Shāfi'is to lay siege to Ṣan'ā'. The defending garrison consisted of seven battalions (3500 men) led by former commandant Tevfik Paşa. The siege lasted six months and had a devastating effect on both the inhabitants, more than 1600 died of starvation, and the countryside, where people had next to nothing to eat after selling what few belongings they could muster to purchase scarce foodstuffs. It is also alleged that, being pro-Ottoman, the *mufti* of Ṣan'ā' confiscated the wealth and belongings of well-heeled people to ensure the survival of the troops during the siege.[10]

The *vali* and commandant of Yemen's seventh army desperately needed reinforcements. He appealed urgently for immediate help from nearby Qunfidhah, where fourth and fifth army auxiliary units were stationed. Without help he could not match the new challenge of insurgents now armed with Martini rifles, which the French and Italians had smuggled through British-held areas in the south.[11] They needed immediate relief but it was considered unwise to arm Arabs loyal to the Ottomans to counter the rebels' assault.[12] Ṣan'ā' was virtually isolated. Some 150 residents with Turkish backgrounds were given arms to withstand the assaults of rebels surrounding the city and preventing food and other supplies entering it. Only a quarter of what was needed for the troops was available. It was dangerous to venture into the countryside to find food because rebels immediately pounced on them. On one occasion when troops set out from Ṣan'ā' in search of provisions, rebels attacked them and they lost one officer and a dozen men.[13] Leland Buxton, who had just returned to London from a tour of the Persian Gulf and Yemen, reported that conditions in Ṣan'ā' and in Yemen generally were dreadful. The city's population had dropped from 70,000 to 20,000; Turkish artillery had destroyed villages; skeletons were strewn everywhere; and dogs and cats were being killed for food.[14]

On 5 March Riza set out from Hodeida with 4000 men to relieve the siege of the city, but the contingent was too small and Syrian reinforcements were too slow to arrive. The insurgents were said to have fielded 40,000 men. The 'Akka relief brigade consisting of eight *nizam* and 24 *redif* battalions was still on its way to Hodeida. Transport was the problem. Three Egyptian Khedive Mail Line vessels were embarking troops for Hodeida. Some 5000 recruits and draftees from Antalya and the Syrian ports were assigned to service in Yemen, together with two field batteries, a mountain mortar and 30,000 large-calibre Mauser rifles. Substantial quantities of food and flour were also shipped.[15]

Serasker Riza mobilized the fifth army's remaining battalions and 274 animals to send to Hodeida as soon as ships could be found.[16] This was partly in compliance with the *sadaret*'s decision of 3 S 1323/9

April 1905 to send 5000 troops, with 2000 additional *redif*, to Yemen. The commander of the second imperial army sent a telegram saying it was easier to embark recruits from the Isparta and Karahisar region at Izmir on the Aegean Sea than at Antalya on the Mediterranean and that the 2000 from the Antalya and Konya brigades (*liwa*s) could also leave from Izmir.[17]

Meanwhile, a relief column led by Arif managed to reach Ṣan'ā' on 7 February, but too late to prevent its surrender. The rebels suffered a momentary setback, but in the fighting to get there Arif had lost his guns, victuals and other stores. Five days later the rebels attacked the city again. The post of Jabal al-Sharqi in the *kaza* of Ānis surrendered on 12 February, as did the fort of Ḥufāsh in the *sancak* of Hodeida. Guns and ammunition were captured and the commandant killed. A week later troops withdrew from important posts at al-Ḥajūr and Tabjīl. Within another week, the lack of provisions had forced Ottoman troops out of the *kaza* of 'Ans and three companies at Manṣūrīyah in the *kaza* of Ḥarīb had surrendered. Shaykh A'iḍ, the *shaykh* of Ahl Shamīr's brother, wrote to Sir Aḥmad Faḍl al-'Abdali, who relayed the message to Mason at Aden,[18] that the imam's *muqaddam*s wrote letters to most of Yemen's Arab chiefs asking them to come and submit to him, but most replied that they could not do so as long as the Turks held Ṣan'ā'.

A delegation of Ottoman representatives was sent to the imam, who was then in Kawkabān, to negotiate terms of surrender. He agreed on condition they leave behind the possessions of the state and its treasury in return for which he would help transport them to Ḥarīb *en route* to the port of Hodeida.

The final surrender of Ṣan'ā' allegedly took place on 5 March 1905 and the imam entered the city the next day.[19] He allowed the *vali* and commandant charged with the city's defence to leave under his personal guarantee. His lieutenants then took possession of all forts, guns, rifles, ammunition, military stores, transport animals and public buildings. The insurgents captured 30 guns, 20,000 rifles and a large quantity of ammunition; they were believed to have taken 40 cannons and 7000 cases of rifles, including big gun and rifle ammunition. Foreign and native merchants were allowed to carry on their trades.[20] For £5000 sterling the imam agreed to provide transport for troops and officials who had surrendered. Lines out of the capital were cut and Commandant Izzet Paşa's life was spared.

For some obscure reason the *mutasarrıf* of Hodeida, who had been accompanying Izzet, disappeared from his company then surfaced three months later in Manākhah when his presence there was indispensable. The Syrian *redif* garrisoning Manākhah moved south to Ḥujaylah and 2000 Albanians took their place. Many people in the countryside acknowledged the imam's leadership. The insurgents then headed for Manākhah, where 500 troops in a state of semi-mutiny were garrisoned, to lay siege to it.[21] Then, early in March, there was a serious disaster. Ḥajjah was captured and, while defending it, Commandant Tevfik Beg allegedly committed suicide.[22] The rebels captured four officers, one 12-centimetre, five 6–7-centimetre and six 4-centimetre guns, 2500 Martini rifles and 3000 cases of ammunition; only 500 of the garrison survived to reach Hodeida — disarmed, naked and foot sore.

On 22 February rebels besieged Qa'ṭabah and Ibb in the south and, with 2800 insurgents fortified on top of the Ba'dān mountain, they cut off communications with the *sancak* of Ta'izz.[23] The *mutasarrıf* of Ta'izz, Brigadier General Riza, was trapped at Ibb with his 1000-man force after failing to alleviate the insurgents' assaults on it. The British feared that if both fell and the Yāfi'is joined in, their own troops would be threatened, especially since the anti-British Shaykh Muḥammad Nāṣir Muqbil, head of the Ḥumar and al-Qanā'irah, had joined the insurgents and the imam had asked him to withhold revenue in the Ta'izz area. Agent Mason told the 'Abdali sultan that he had heard that a large Ottoman force was being rushed to Yemen and that he doubted that the imam would be foolish enough to send his supporters into Ḥawshabi and Yāfi' country.

Ḥusayb was next to fall despite the brave defence of Colonel Sadik Beg and his 150 men. The rebels got two 6.5-centimetre guns, 1500 rifles and large quantities of provisions, then marched on Qifl in al-Juḥur district, defended by Ferik Yusuf Paşa, but were unable to take it. Riza was beaten back from Ma'bar and Ḍawrān on returning to Hodeida with 1500 men via Ḥujaylah.[24] The *vali* sent a telegram requesting more troops. Six transports were on their way, but trouble was expected from Zarānīq tribesmen whose *shaykh* was imprisoned at Hodeida.[25]

Only 2000 of the 13,000 soldiers available were recruits; the majority were *redif* from Syria who had served in Yemen before and two of the eight officers promoted to the rank of general were from Syria. The relief expedition for Ferik 'Ali Riza arrived in Hodeida on 3 March 1905. Riza was considered a good soldier with lots of energy, the right man for the post according to British intelligence.[26] Brigadier Riza broke through the siege of Ma'bar after four days of fighting in which 17 of his men were killed and 58 wounded. He joined Commandant 'Ali Riza who was moving quickly to Ta'izz with his whole force. The British ambassador thought that he might have been prompted by the *mutasarrıf* of Ta'izz's report that should Qa'ṭabah fall, the British might use it as an excuse to invade to block land transport.[27]

The garrison was holding out at Manākhah. The *mutasarrıf* of Hodeida, Ferik Ahmed Fehmi Paşa, a Circassian who, having served in Yemen twice before (once as *mutasarrıf* of 'Asīr), was well acquainted with the *vilayet*'s problems, out of desperation urged the Sublime Porte to inform the sultan — hitherto kept in the dark about the gravity of the situation — of the reality in Yemen, namely that there were insufficient troops to cope with the rapidly deteriorating situation, even submitting his resignation out of frustration and anger.[28]

In his palace at Yıldız the sultan took note of the seriousness of the situation and decided that force of arms alone would not end the rebellion. His first reaction was to ensure that troops destined for Yemen received adequate salaries and provisions. Special orders authorized both for up to three months.[29] At this juncture, 28 battalions had to be provided for at 50,000 *lira*s a month,[30] along with the cost of their transport and Suez Canal transit fees.[31]

Recognizing the need for a peaceful settlement, Sultan Abdülhamid opted for radical changes in Yemen's administrative procedures. He decided to appoint Ferik Şâkir Paşa to lead a commission of inquiry to Yemen to investigate how needed reform could be introduced.

The reappointment of Ahmed Feyzi

Unable to quell the rebellion with his limited resources, Riza was replaced on instructions from the Sublime Porte by Ahmed Feyzi, who was now more than 75 years old and serving at this time in Nejd.[32] Feyzi received orders to move rapidly to Yemen to take charge of its armed forces. He was assigned a staff that included Ferid Beg and Mustafa Efendi, both of whom had been serving at the time in Damascus. They rushed to Beirut on their way to Yunbu' to join a major-general (*liva*) and colonel from Istanbul,[33] all to join Feyzi in Nejd, where he had been serving since his transfer from Baghdad, to quell the Saudi uprising.

He reached Hodeida on 8 June 1905 and awaited the arrival of reinforcements before commencing his mission against the imam's forces. Meanwhile, 18 battalions had arrived from Prevesa,[34] including the eight *nizam* battalions 'Ali Riza had requested and the sultan had authorized be withdrawn from Yanina. The *vilayet*s of Aleppo, Beirut and Syria were to supply 40 mules per battalion; a special steamer was to convey 6600 Mausers and 27,000 more for troops already in Yemen, for a maximum of 37 battalions.[35]

According to the British consul at Damascus, the Ottomans decided to call up eight more battalions of *redif* from the 'Akka brigade to bring up to 32 the total number of battalions on their way to reinforce the Ṣan'ā' relief expedition under 'Ali Riza Paşa. These units were part of the fifth Syrian corps, which, when they arrived, would add another 25,000 men to the expedition. A further 5000 recruits for the *nizam* battalions were to come from Adalia and various Syrian ports.[36] From Germany, Krupp Industries supplied 20,000 large-calibre Mausers and one mountain mortar for trial in Yemen.

However, there were too few serviceable ships to transport them. They needed six transporters to load the stores, including the two field batteries, one mountain mortar and 20,000 large-calibre Mauser rifles on trial from Krupp. Also, besides the large quantities of food that needed to be transported, they had to collect men at various Syrian ports, which compelled the government to contract steamers from private companies.[37]

The imperial government authorized the finance commission to grant 500,000 *piastre*s to the commandant of the fifth army to finance sending reinforcements to Yemen.[38] Other costs included troops' salaries, monetary aid to drought-stricken areas around Ta'izz, and 50,000 *lira*s to unpaid units stationed at Hodeida. In addition, 20,000 *lira*s had to be borrowed to pay for supplies and more than 12,000 *akçe*s to meet deficits incurred in sending and supplying a light cavalry regiment commanded by Ahmed Efendi to serve as a mobile police force, all of which taxed the capacity of the central administration to the limit. Moreover, roads had to be built to allow for the quick movement of troops. An additional 60,000 *lira*s were required to pay and provision troops while being dispatched to Yemen. Then there were the costs of preparing quarters for troops, and arranging transport and expenses for 14 battalions, all within the first two years of the outbreak of the insurrection. It was not an easy task for an administration confronting uprisings elsewhere, even in the Balkans.[39]

The authorities found it difficult to mobilize units for Yemen from Rumeli and Anatolia, with only two of the Yanina brigade's eight *nizam* battalions embarking for Suez. They had partial success in mobilizing four battalions of *redif* in Albania, where men were clamouring for arrears of pay while others took their rifles and returned home. In mid-May a French steamer carrying 2553 troops reached Port Sa'īd on its way to Hodeida from Izmir. The ministry of war lacked details on the fall of Ṣan'ā' and continued to charter steamers and mobilize troops to send to Yemen. After lengthy delays, the remaining six battalions of the Yanina brigade of *nizam* troops left Prevesa for Hodeida; 6400, forming the Isparta brigade of *redif*s of the second army corps of Edirne, were waiting to embark at Izmir.

It was also very difficult to mobilize *redif* brigades in Elbasan and Rize because men were refusing to answer the call to the colours. Orders went out to mobilize a division of Ankara *redif* consisting of 16 battalions of the first army corps headquartered in Istanbul for service in Yemen. The Russian volunteer fleet's *Nijni Novgorod* was chartered to fetch troops from the Albanian coast; and two French vessels arrived in Izmir to pick up troops waiting there for transport to Hodeida.[40] Large-scale mobilization of reinforcements to Yemen followed news of the fall of Ṣan'ā'.[41]

The British embassy in Istanbul received intelligence that the Ottoman government was no longer certain that the insurgence, which had reached a critical stage, could be ended militarily. If one were to reflect on how rebellion was dealt with in the past, the following would be worth noting: resistance to the return to the highlands in 1872 was dealt with decisively by the government that ended the imam's rule; the 1892 revolt was quelled with lavish expenditure of troops and money; the 1903 outbreak spread to 'Asīr and the Ottomans had to confine their rule to the coastal area; the 1904 insurrection led to serious losses of key areas including Ṣan'ā' and Manākhah, an important artillery depot, and its garrison of 5000.

Meanwhile, Ferik Arif Hikmet was proceeding with a court martial to try officers and men implicated in the recent surrender of garrisoned towns. *Vali* Tevfik resigned and Feyzi succeeded him temporarily.

Conditions in Hodeida

To add to the authorities' woes, locusts destroyed the Tihāmah maize crop, but shiploads of grain and food were unloaded at Hodeida every week while demand kept on increasing. Conditions in the city were bad because of the large presence of troops who were given prior access to the limited water supply; then Albanians landed by force and illegally sold 5000 kilograms of tobacco and a large quantity of spirits.[42]

The British Foreign Office and the foreign and Ottoman press began to focus more keenly on the turmoil in Yemen and on the intensification of the rebellion now led by Imam Yaḥya, allegedly commanding a force of 20,000 men armed with 30 field guns, Martini rifles and large quantities of ammunition captured from the Ottomans.

The incompetent *vali* and commander-in-chief, Aptullah Paşa, was forced out in December 1904 when Yaḥya became imam and strove to bend the Ottoman government to his will. Few Arab traders were about and an Italian merchant was seen storing up provisions in advance. For six weeks postal communications between Ṣan'ā' and Hodeida were cut off, and telegrams could be received only by a circuitous route and with difficulty. The caravan route between Manākhah, the first garrisoned town in the mountains 55 miles northeast of Hodeida,[43] and Sūq al-Khamīs, 25 miles to the east, was unsafe because the tribesmen of this region were hostile to the Ottomans. Rebels commanded the heights between Manākhah and Sūq. At Bu'ān, to the northeast, the Ottomans kept two blockhouses and a small garrison. That area too was unsafe.

The plight of both soldiers and natives was most wretched, wrote the British consul. A sack of flour now cost MT$ 30 compared with the normal price of between $10 and $15. North of Ṣan'ā', the Ḥāshid and Baqīl had risen again and were threatening Ḥajjah and al-Ḥajūr. Out of desperation the *mutasarrıf* of Hodeida had left with a few Arab *shaykh*s for Bājil to enrol the 2000 armed Arabs who had pledged to help force a passage through to Ṣan'ā' and provide for its starving garrison. Two battalions of *redif* were expected to arrive from Qunfidhah in 'Asīr via Luḥayyah on their way to Manākhah with more expected from Istanbul. A force of 600 men was being raised locally at Hodeida by the head of the local municipality.[44]

The situation was becoming desperate. Vice Consul Richardson reported the imminent fall of Jabal al-Sharqi, the mutiny of *redif* soldiers and the need to arm native conscripts such as Yām tribesmen, not known in the past for their loyalty and reliability. Meanwhile, a unit of 1251 soldiers arrived at Hodeida via Yunbu' on 4 January and the next day the Egyptian Khedival Mail Line's *Miniah* landed another

1750 troops, who were quickly dispatched to the interior with two big guns and 120 camel loads of equipment. When the *Sakaria* went to fetch the *redif* from Qunfidhah to bring them to Hodeida, they mutinied and refused to embark because they had neither been paid nor received enough rations. They had been detained for over a year. The vessel *Çozlu* arrived from Qunfidhah on 6 January with 400 *redif* but they too mutinied and refused to march towards al-Zaydīyah via al-Shalīf.[45]

More bad news came from the *mutasarrıf* of Hodeida, who cabled that the battalion of troops at Ḥajjah had refused to surrender to the insurgents even after suffering great losses. The garrison was still holding out after having eaten all its cattle and food and was in dire need of relief. If they surrendered, the rebels would capture four guns, 2000 rifles and more than 1000 cases of ammunition. Another cable from Hodeida stated that the insurgents had captured three companies of troops at Manṣūrīyah in the *mudīrīyah* (canton) of ʻIrr, *kaza* of Harīb, together with their officers after sustaining a number of losses and that the *müdür* of the canton in the *kaza* of ʻAns had been blockaded.[46]

The Ottoman government was frantically mobilizing units for Yemen from a number of quarters. Consul W. S. Richards reported from Damascus that reinforcements — 7000 troops dispatched via Damascus and Maʻan by the Hijaz railway — would soon be on their way.[47] He said that two battalions of *redif* from Jafa were coming via Beirut to Damascus and another from Hama, that Ferik ʻAli Riza Paşa, chief of staff in Tripolitania, had been appointed commander-in-chief for Yemen, that the expedition to Yemen was being assembled in Damascus, and that a *nizam* battalion stationed in Ḥawrān had left for Maʻan. He also reported that there was considerable anger in Damascus because the authorities had commandeered 150 camels and 90 horses from various citizens for transport from ʻAqabah to Maʻan for Yemen, a situation rendered more difficult by the lack of a rail connection, at which juncture the Sublime Porte decided on the need to connect the two by rail.

The contractors had not been paid, so they refused to provide meat and other supplies to the troops. The men's diet, he reported, had been poor for the past three weeks.[48] Because of various difficulties, the land route to Yemen had been abandoned in favour of sea transport, but it became impossible to embark troops from ʻAqabah because of rough seas and the intense drought that had caused the deaths of many camels and transport animals. ʻAli Riza, head of the contingent there, was held up in ʻAqabah unable to leave for Yemen.

The British surmised that the delay would have a negative impact, especially when news of Ottoman reverses reached the troops, most of whom were Syrian and basically sympathetic to their fellow Arabs' cause. Rumours had been circulating in Damascus that the British were helping Ibn Saud's uprising in Nejd, where it was alleged that British officers disguised as Arabs had been directing his campaigns. A report from Damascus claimed that there was 'another absurd rumour about the alleged connection between the Yemenese insurgents and the Aden authorities to show you the trend of popular opinion'.[49]

Because of deficient transport, troops could not be sent there except with extreme difficulty. Even getting troops to Yemen was difficult. Many camels perished while getting to the railhead at Ma'an from 'Aqabah, not to mention the high rate of desertion.[50] Insurgents increased their pressure on Ṣan'ā' where stubborn fighting raged for days, with many troops refusing to fight. Near Ibb in the south, the rebels surrounded a contingent of 2000 troops and four guns and what had been reported as a victory for Ottomans at Manākhah turned out to be a victory for the insurgents.[51]

Four battalions of reinforcements were put on trains from Damascus and Ma'an; and eight fresh *redif* battalions were called up as part of a plan to bring the number of battalions serving in Yemen up to 32. The seventh army corps' original garrison in Yemen plus reinforcements would have brought the total up to 76,000 men.[52] As the British military attaché put it: 'It is impossible to say how many will live to return home after this disastrous campaign.'[53] The ministry of war was negotiating with various steamship companies about conveying troops, provisions, ammunition and three batteries from Istanbul. Meanwhile, with seven battalions and a battery of artillery, 'Ali Riza left Hodeida for Manākhah, to which only the road was still open.[54]

Ottoman troubles were not confined to Yemen. According to *The Times* (London) of 18 March 1905, while four battalions were heading to Hodeida from 'Aqabah, another four left Medina for Qaṣīm south of Ḥā'il to join seven battalions from Baghdad to fight Ibn Saud in Nejd. Meanwhile, the insurgents had captured Yarīm and other areas nearby and surrounded Ibb.[55] By the third week of May they had captured the town together with Qa'ṭabah and the seriousness of the threat to the south induced the Ottomans to rush troops to the area.[56]

The central government continued its frantic efforts to find troops to send to Yemen, depleting units in Anatolia and Rumeli. Over 15 such authorizations were made in a 16-month period, which was an index of the seriousness of Ottoman reverses in the field.[57] The problem was not only that the Ottomans were unable to dispatch troops in time, but that the bulk of those serving in Yemen were Syrian and had no stomach for fighting fellow Arabs, which would explain why they mutinied and made it impossible to hold onto Ṣan'ā'.

Failed negotiations and resumption of hostilities

On 19 May 1905 Signor Crapotti, a man equally trusted by Turk and Arab and the only foreigner except for a few Greek shopkeepers in Ṣan'ā', left via Hodeida for Istanbul bearing a letter from the imam to the sultan, which summarized the history of the revolts in Yemen and suggested how peace could be achieved. But attempts at a negotiated settlement with the imam's envoy to Istanbul failed and it became clear that the Ottomans would have to retake Ṣan'ā'. Feyzi, who had spent half a lifetime in Yemen, awaited the arrival of reinforcements in Hodeida — he expected 25 battalions and ships were already discharging guns and ammunition — before advancing simultaneously on Ṣan'ā' and Ta'izz. In mid-July, with three battalions of Albanians, he launched a three-pronged drive on Ṣan'ā' from a stronghold near Manākhah. Feyzi had moved to Manākhah that month because troops were being sent to 'Asīr from Hijaz and Hodeida. He feared that the rising might become general before he could suppress the insurgents.[58]

By mid-August Ottoman forces had taken the offensive and by the end of the month they had recaptured Abhā in 'Asīr, inflicting heavy losses on the enemy. It was rumoured that more than 1000 were killed and that many prisoners were taken, including 50 chiefs, with only four killed and ten wounded on the Ottoman side.

In the south, a unit from Ta'izz recaptured Yarīm after heavy fighting and Feyzi advanced to Mafraq where he established a base.[59] After an all-day battle, he beat the insurgents at Sūq al-Khamīs, inflicting heavy losses on them, then moved towards Ṣan'ā' and occupied the heights on the road to the city and all strategic positions as far as Khawlān, routing the rebels wherever he encountered them.[60] On the road to Ṣan'ā', he dislodged 3000 insurgents from strong positions with heavy losses and prisoners taken. Feyzi reported 24 villages retaken, including Jiblah and Ba'dān. He next recaptured the junction town of Sinan Paşa, 15 miles southwest of Ṣan'ā', then routed insurgents at Sūq al-Khamīs.[61]

Recapture of Ṣan'ā'

On 30 August 1905 Ṣan'ā' was retaken without firing a cannon shot on its walls and Ottoman troops entered the city the next day without opposition. The insurgents had plundered Ottoman property and much of the city was destroyed in the process. Chiefs from the vicinity came in and surrendered their arms to Feyzi.

Syrians were used all along to suppress revolts because they knew the language, were supposedly better able to handle the climate and were more sympathetic to each other because most of them came from the same villages. Even though Feyzi declared he was going to fight with Albanians, Kurds, Turks and Lahzs, most of the troops he commanded in the campaigns were still Syrian. They endured hardship and famine, with a death rate of two-thirds to three-quarters in each company.

Before launching his reconquest campaign, Feyzi tried to win back the chiefs with flattery, promises of remedial action and, while extolling the virtue of loyalty, granting full amnesty to tribes and chiefs who surrendered. Though he spoke Arabic well, he preferred to address the Arabs in Turkish, insisting they should learn it. Temperamental as he was, he could still join chiefs in a *narguila*-puffing session as if he were one of them. Natives were allowed to carry arms, even though all were involved in the insurrection. He also understood European politics well. It took him six weeks after arriving in Hodeida to prepare for military action and the Ottomans at that time controlled no more than a stretch of an area between Hodeida and Manākhah. Roads were carved out and flanked by stones to facilitate movement. Ottoman soldiers — despite being poorly tended, ill paid and badly clothed — managed to get heavy guns to Ṣan'ā' in eight days. Conditions in the camps strewn along the main road were usually unsanitary; drainage and waste disposal were inadequate with famine, fever and disease taking a toll — up to 85 per cent of the troops according to correspondents allowed to enter them.

Two weeks later, sizeable reinforcements landed at 'Asīr under the command of Ferik Emin Paşa. Meanwhile, Feyzi had retaken 'Amrān, Thulā, Kawkabān and Ḥajjah without resistance, capturing several thousand rifles in the process. By mid-November the situation in Yemen appeared to have improved markedly for the Ottomans, and several troop units were recalled to Syria via Hodeida and the Gulf of 'Aqabah. The sultan decorated Feyzi for his valuable services.

From triumph to defeat

In his determination to capture the rebellious Imam Yaḥya, in December 1905 Feyzi sent Colonel Riza north to al-Sūdah. Ḥāshid tribesmen attacked him and stripped him of his supplies, *thalers*, ammunition and other provisions. Four more battalions were sent against them, but they too were beaten. Then, with two battalions of Albanians, Feyzi rushed to his aid from Ṣan'ā', recovered all that was plundered, destroyed al-Sūdah and slaughtered 200 for breach of faith.

Before leaving with Riza for Ṣa'dah, via the imam's stronghold at Shahārah, Feyzi awaited the arrival of eight well-equipped battalions.[62] He needed them because 14,000 troops had been sent home after his earlier triumphs. He and his troops then marched north towards Ṣa'dah without realizing that, by retreating to unknown mountainous regions interspersed with narrow ravines, the rebel forces were drawing them into a snare. This time the Ottoman force suffered heavy losses in men and materials because, once trapped in Shahārah's narrow ravine, the insurgents attacked them mercilessly. Feyzi was forced to retreat towards 'Amrān and to await fresh reinforcements after failing to capture Shahārah and its surrounding country.[63]

The defeat at Shahārah cost Riza Paşa his life, for he perished at al-Sūdah. Another high commander, Yusuf Paşa, was wounded and many soldiers lost their lives. Feyzi had only a few prisoners to show for his efforts when he got back to Ṣan'ā'. Within two weeks he and his troops had to retreat from there towards Ta'izz with the imam's forces in hot pursuit.[64] Weather conditions were also harsh, with abnormal rainfall having caused flooding in the Mocha and Dubāb districts. Meanwhile, tribesman with headquarters at Khamir in the north surrounded 'Amrān and occupied Jabal Dharwah and al-Ya'ābir.[65]

To compound matters, as commander of the expeditionary force Feyzi found himself locked in conflict with the special commission of inspection headed by Ferik Ferid Paşa, who had succeeded Şâkir Paşa. The commission attempted to interfere in Feyzi's military operations; he forced them to retreat to Hodeida and would not let them back.[66] This occurred before the retreat from Ṣan'ā'. He cabled the *sadrazam* on 13 February 1906 stating that Ferid was sick and recommending that he should stay in Hodeida for his health, where he should address matters like the proposed railway line, the ice factory and the cantonments.[67]

Reliable reports from Istanbul by Reuters' correspondents claimed that, despite prolonged sorties by 10,000 men, Feyzi failed to gain his objective because the transport system broke down and failed to keep up the delivery of supplies to the troops, so no sustained campaign was possible. Exasperated and frustrated, Feyzi begged to be relieved of his command in favour of a younger man, but the government would not allow it, promising to keep him supplied with men and munitions. However, lack of money, the soldiers' reluctance to serve in Yemen and the Turkish administration's inefficient methods negated all efforts.

Unverified press reports put troop losses at between 25,000 and 30,000 out of a total of 110,000. The greatest losses in Yemen were attributed to famine, misadministration by incompetent officials, and the greed and ambitions of the *shaykh*s. With 54 villages around Manākhah deserted, soldiers were saying that once Feyzi went so would Yemen.[68] Correspondents reporting from Istanbul admitted that it was impossible to get authentic news from Yemen, but what filtered through was not good.[69]

Reverses on the battlefield and heavy losses in materials and men, including the death of Brigadier General Riza, drove some Syrian *redif*s to desertion, especially after Jabal 'Iyāl, Yazīd and Ḥāshid tribesmen attacked their units while they were retreating to ‘Amrān. In Istanbul, Serasker Riza Paşa alleged that only 250 soldiers had been killed at Shahārah, not the one-and-a-half battalions as reported earlier.[70]

Troops mutiny

Exhausted and unpaid, the Syrian officers of Feyzi's contingent withdrew to Ṣan‘ā’ and demanded they be compensated and repatriated to Syria.[71] Some camped at the Farwat ibn Masār mosque northeast of the city and plundered the homes of natives in the area when the *vali* refused their request to be repatriated. Three other Ottoman battalions made similar demands and, to underline these, they stormed the great mosque, forced everyone out, including *shaykh*s, students and ulema, closed nine out of ten gates and remained there for half a month, compelling the *vali* to meet their demands and ship them home. Meanwhile, rebel forces surrounded Ṣan‘ā’ once again. The officers manning post and telegraphs rebelled, demanding their back pay, but Ottoman units quickly surrounded them and forced them to back down.

Syrian and non-Syrian troops that rebelled had served their time and received no pay. Their revolt, coupled with reverses on the battlefield, forced the government to consider negotiating once more with Imam Yaḥya. He, meanwhile, had been winning over more Yemenis, including *sayyids* and ulema, and had been encouraging them to persuade the natives to stop paying taxes to the imperial government. He had been arming them and sending them with equipment captured at Shahārah to dislodge the Ottoman forces at Firkat al-'Idhar (of the Ḥāshid).

The *vali* and the commandant each asked for a division of *nizam* troops with fresh draftees, a battery of the new pattern guns (20,000 rounds) and four howitzer guns, bringing the number of serviceable troops to 12,000.[72] Feyzi was unable to launch more attacks on the insurgents until he received 8000 troops from the Anatolian command, 2500 *redifs* from the second army corps, 1000 from the Aydin division of the third army corps and 1000 from the Adana command, all of which he had been promised. The minister of the marine was ordered to secure transport for the troops as quickly as possible.[73]

Feyzi launches an offensive

After regrouping in the Hodeida area, Feyzi's troops marched north, recovering control of Manākhah and much of the lost arsenal and, more importantly, 80,000 *liras* in cash and gold, which he insisted went to the troops. He then continued northwards. Şâkir was operating out of Ḥujaylah along the Ṣanfūr road below Manākhah, past Jabal Ānis, creating a junction at Mafḥaq with Feyzi's units. Eight battalions of *redifs* under Yunus Paşa were advancing from Zaydīyah to relieve the garrison at Qifl. The main objective of this division was to recapture Ḥajjah.

In the south, three divisions (12 battalions) under Ğâlib Paşa were moving north with eight guns from Ta'izz towards Yarīm after the recapture of the strategic Sūq al-Khamīs, which may have occasioned the imam's offer to hand back Ṣan'ā' to the Ottomans in return for keeping Dhamār, Yarīm, 'Amrān, Kawkabān, al-Ṭawīlah and Ḥajjah.

The deaths of 24 *shaykhs* aroused native concerns. It was unclear how many either the imam or Feyzi had killed. It was at this point that the imam allegedly sent a letter to the King of England asking the British to come to his military aid.[74] The Bombay government agreed to forward his letter to the king.[75]

With the military unable to end the insurgence, with the garrison in Hodeida refusing to move up to relieve Ṣan'ā', with uncertainty over troops scheduled to arrive from ‘Aqabah, with telegraph lines cut and with imperial troops hard pressed by tribesmen, Feyzi threatened to resign unless reinforcements and provisions arrived within eight days, for otherwise he would be unable to hold out at Ṣan‘ā’.[76] A subsequent report from Hodeida claimed that the Ottoman force of six battalions had suffered a severe defeat near Ṣan‘ā’ after having retreated from the city, that it had mutinied and that there was no secure way to communicate with the city. Even Hodeida had a mutiny; its water supply was cut off for two days with the insurgents threatening to bombard the city unless their demands were met. Units from Uskub (Skopia) and Izmir also mutinied at the end of May, insisting that they did not have to serve beyond their agreed time or even to serve in Yemen at all. This was a very disquieting sign for the Ottomans.[77]

If any Ottoman commander could check the insurgents Feyzi was that person, but letters to Istanbul pointed to the helplessness of the situation. Feyzi recognized the great sacrifices his troops had made. Officers and men were sent out on a mission only to lose their way, often due to the lack of roads and maps. Sickness and starvation took their toll. In the past they could count on Arab friends; now the very ones who had guided their way became enemies. The insurgence was gaining adherents in the Hijaz and Nejd, further threatening the Ottoman presence in Arabia. The imam's followers treated their prisoners kindly in an attempt to win them over.

Refugees reaching Suez claimed that the rebels could move at will against outposts — they could forage and retreat — whereas the Ottoman troops had no transport. Informed sources in Cairo blamed neither Feyzi nor the troops, but rather the imperial ministries of war and finance for failing to organize transport and a commissariat, for even Ottoman soldiers required food, clothes and pay to fight with a will.[78]

A force of 6000 troops had assembled at ‘Aqabah before moving on to Ṭābah on the Gulf of Suez, from where they were to embark for Yemen. Unlike those enduring hardships in Yemen, these men were well fed, well armed and well trained. Numerous rail accidents had failed to prevent the transport of more than 12 mountain guns, which had reached the port from Damascus. More extraordinarily, reported the *Egyptian Gazette*, four heavy pieces (47-inch calibre) had been hauled over the desert from Ma‘an to Ṭābah without a mishap.[79] The ship *Abd-el-Kader* left Port Sa‘īd for Hodeida on 7 May with 1380 troops.[80]

Reinforcements were not expected to change the equation because the disorganization of the commissariat service finally induced five battalions of troop reserves to mutiny and set out for Ṣan'ā' demanding they be sent home. Feyzi ordered the regulars to open fire on the mutineers, which lasted a few hours and ended with 300 being killed and wounded, with several hundred escaping and the rest surrendering. The officer who led the mutiny was later captured, court-martialled and allegedly shot.[81] They were then sent to 'Amrān to reinforce Yusuf Paşa's troops. After a quiet interval, the imam's forces advanced and in a battle with Ottoman forces both sides suffered heavy losses.

The mutineers were mostly Muslim recruits from Jerusalem *sancak* and other Syrian provinces who felt resentful that those exempted from service — Christians, Jews, Druzes and 'Alawites — went to America, Africa and other lands to make money and prosper while they were shipped off to Yemen to die. They had first served in the Hijaz division of the seventh army corps; the 22 *redif* battalions sent from Syria to serve under the ill-fated Riza came back after the fall of Ṣan'ā' 50 to 70 per cent below strength. Coming mostly from Hama, Damascus and Jerusalem, they had been transported by rail from Damascus to Ma'an and 'Aqabah, and from there by ship to Yemen.

One observer noted that the sultan risked depopulating the Muslims of Syria because those who returned were disease infested (with malaria), aged beyond their years, married late and had fewer offspring, while 30 to 40 per cent of the Christians who left returned relatively healthy and wealthy, and were able to prosper. One correspondent saw this as bad news for the sultan's pan-Islamic policy, hoping that he would now stop claiming that the British were behind his woes in Yemen 'for selling for one shilling a rifle to Yemenis'.[82]

Reports and letters sent to Damascus claimed that Feyzi was naive to think that reinforcements would relieve the siege of Ṣan'ā'. Syrian troops held out well at the siege of the city but their sympathy for the Yemenis led them to give out intelligence to rebels. The imam would withdraw, it was argued, and then attack later. His forces were more mobile than the Ottomans'. Blockading the coast to stop contraband and gunrunning from Djibouti and Massawa posed a minimum risk, for the capture of thousands of rifles did not seem to disturb the imam. He did not fear fresh troop arrivals in Hodeida, for they tended to mutiny in demand of their pay.[83]

The government, however, was still bent on carrying the battle to the imam. Two new steamers bought in England were ordered to Beirut to transport eight battalions to reinforce the garrison at Ṣan'ā'. This was happening while they were facing an uprising of tribes in Mesopotamia who were denying the authorities a ten-day truce to investigate their grievances and were holding up navigation on the Tigris.[84]

Feyzi's role was further diminished when his alliance with Ḥusayn Yaḥya, the rival imam at Ṣa'dah, came to an end. The latter, with his 12,000 men, was alleged to have joined Yaḥya Ḥamīd al-Dīn, the leader of the insurrection, but evidence of this is doubtful. Reporters were not always accurate in assessing facts on the ground and were sometimes forced to retract. A report in the *Egyptian Gazette* stated as late as 23 October 1906 that Yaḥya's rival was pressing him hard and was still supported by the Ottomans.[85] If this were true, it would have meant that Ottoman troops could no longer threaten to get to Shahārah, or past it.

The international perspective

First World War European alliances were already in place with their propaganda machines operating at a stepped-up pace. The semi-official German press asserted that British government plans to pave the way for British supremacy in the Arabian Peninsula, and eventually to proclaim a protectorate over Kuwait (as came to pass) and Basra, were the cause of the Arab revolt against the sultan. Maunsell, the British military attaché, reported to informed sources in Cairo that:

> no opportunity of impressing the Porte with this view has been wasted, a proceeding which may be attributed to the fact that an independent or semi-independent Arabian Empire would certainly menace German interests in connection with the Baghdad Railway Scheme … should the present revolt succeed, spread to Hejaz and should the Imam proclaim himself the true Kaliph (first time brought out openly in official British thinking) in opposition to the Sultan of Turkey — a not impossible contingency, for the Imam is a more direct descendant of the Prophet than the Sultan — it is difficult to see how far the wave of fanaticism may not carry him.[86]

The English press, however, argued that Britain should stay out and not offer the Ottomans help lest they themselves lose influence with the Arabs in the Gulf and elsewhere, whom they argued had a better claim to Mecca than some 'Mongol tribe' (reference to the Turks). There was no fear of Germany coming to the rescue because it could not move troops fast enough.[87]

On the other hand, the press did not see it in Britain's interests for Arabia to fall into a whirlpool of international jealousies if Mecca fell to the rebels. The Foreign Office was advised to approach the sultan with a suggestion that he recognize the *de facto* situation in Yemen and surrender all claims on the province to a ruler selected from the old imam's family, but the author doubted the sultan could be persuaded to do so; the arrogance of the English surfaced in the reporter's next statement suggesting that an Anglo–Turkish commission escorted by a small well-equipped force proceed to Ṣan'ā' (from Aden) and select from the old imam's descendants the most capable candidate to rule. 'The commission then would delimit the border of his kingdom and Turkey and England would enter into a formal agreement to secure the new king from internal and external enemies, and to guarantee the integrity of his kingdom.' He further asserted that 'the mere approach of a force from Aden would dissuade Yemeni warriors from marching onto Mecca.' He concluded it was 'best for Britain to espouse a policy in Arabia that would localize disturbance and inspire confidence in British policy throughout the Muhammadan (*sic*) world'.[88]

The French were doubtful about British intentions. An editorial in *L'Echo de Paris* (17 July 1905), based on an interview with a 'high-ranking Turkish official', asserted that Yemen had always been difficult to govern and the fact that most troops stationed there were of Arab origin merely compounded matters. It stated that every year England sent more than 75,000 Indian and other Muslim ethnics on pilgrimage to Mecca and Medina to spread propaganda on its behalf, alleging that great benefits had accrued to them and the same would accrue to Arabians were they to become independent of the sultan's government and come under British suzerainty. He told the *Echo de Paris* correspondent that the situation was very serious, that most parts of Yemen and 'Asīr were under the sway of the imam and that Germany was trying to get Italy to intervene on the pretext of avenging the murder of an Italian subject.[89]

To woo the Arabs, the pilgrims were asserting that England could deliver by virtue of its example in India and because it did not need to ship rifles to Arabia, where allegedly not one of British make could be found. Besides, 'by casting her protecting arms' around the proposed terminus of the Baghdad railway (Kuwait), had Britain not proved its friendship? The chief of the insurgents, the correspondent further asserted, 'is not interested in just autonomy and paying tribute but in the title of caliph as well'.[90]

Railroad politics

It was an open secret that the British did not want the Germans to have access to the Persian Gulf to boost their commercial enterprises.[91] To that end they courted Shaykh Mubārak al-Ṣabāḥ of Kuwait and, through him, the Sauds of Nejd who, under 'Abd al-Raḥmān's leadership were encouraged to revolt against Ottoman rule, hence Feyzi's role in suppressing them before being assigned to Yemen to quell that revolt.

The Ottoman government was under increasing pressure not to let anyone but the British build a rail line south of Basra, which meant they could influence it completely and deny its German character; the kaiser found this unacceptable.[92] German annoyance with British antics was evident in another communiqué from their embassy in Constantinople, which appeared in an article in the *Berliner Tageblatt*, accusing the British of meddling in the affairs of Yemen and of encouraging the revolt.[93] They also accused the British of backing the khedive of Egypt in his 1905 dispute with the sultan's government in which he tried to claim the strategically located port of Ṭābah on the Gulf of Elat as part of his territory. The Germans, however, decided to show no more than a keen interest in the affair. Their concern was over England's alleged long-standing strategy to control Arabia and the holy sites, which would explain Britain's interference in Yemen and its efforts to block the Mecca–Medina rail extension.[94]

Concessions and charges postponed the connecting of other railway lines, such as the one from the capital to Izmit, where it was to link up with the Adana line — a 100-kilometre project known as the Wa'di 'Ali, which Izzet (al-'Ābid), the sultan's second secretary, had pushed through at a cost of 1,200,000 *liras*. The 640-kilometre Haifa branch had been completed but not connected to the main line.

To justify his petition to the sultan and reinforce his credibility, Izzet listed the various official projects he had supervised that had saved the state money. He had overseen tribal resolutions; disrupted meddling by foreign envoys; exposed encroachments on the sultan's sacred rights and territorial possessions; resisted Armenian attacks; salvaged half Bulgaria's taxes (at the Berlin conference of 1878); reduced foreign borrowing through well-planned projects like extending the telegraph line by 3050 kilometres to Hijaz and Benghazi; and established a factory to produce German Mauser guns and sanitation equipment — all as proof of his competent and loyal services.[95]

The search for remedies

Having concluded that they were not going to suppress the insurgence by force, Feyzi was now convinced that some sort of autonomy was the best solution. But, as one observer put it, 'who dares recommend it to the sultan?' Sending Şâkir Paşa, *vali* of Uskub (Scopia in Macedonia), with 50,000 *lira*s to bribe Arab chiefs to abandon the insurgence yielded no results, so the Ottoman government decided to consider other ways and means of dealing with Imam Yaḥya. Sizeable funds were set aside to buy the loyalty of principal tribal chiefs while the council of ministers ordered an inquiry into the various abuses committed during the collection of taxes and other complaints to the sultan.

By imperial decree, in 1904 the Sublime Porte summoned Sayyid Aḥmad ibn Yaḥya al-Kibsi al-Yamāni[96] and his father Sayyid Yaḥya from their exile in Rhodes to Istanbul to discuss the outbreak of rebellion and consider how to remedy the situation in Yemen. Sayyid Yaḥya al-Kibsi was at that time advising the foreign ministry to work on a new set of regulations for solving Yemen's problem.[97]

In his petition of 18 August 1907, al-Kibsi intimated that it was on his advice that a military commission under Şâkir Paşa had been sent to investigate. 'The tyrant Ahmed Feyzi, that Tatar descendant of Timur Lang, the betrayer of country and faith' followed him, but no reforms were introduced. 'That deceitful oppressor is now (in Yemen) for the fourth time,[98] as *vali*, and the Arabian peninsula will remain in turmoil.' Furthermore, 'we are again accused unjustly; both father and uncle are imprisoned in Hodeida following false accusations arriving by Italian pouch from Hodeida relaying word from the Italian consulate in Egypt. Our home was ordered destroyed in Ḥajjah of the Khawlān tribe.' 'It is completely untrue,' they argued:

> that Imam Yaḥya is claiming an Arab caliphate for himself. All this is part of the dissension perpetuated by Ahmed Feyzi. All the Imam wants is to apply Islamic law, no less, no more. Officials here do not even honour Islamic laws. What privileges

granted by Sultan Selim (1517) to the Ashrāf [descendants of the Prophet] when they were integrated in Ottoman domains have been lost. Traitors around the Sultan are trying to camouflage the financial pillaging of Yemen by falsely accusing us. Send two emissaries to assess accurately the situation. We are placed in Rhodes [exiled there] but have not received any allowances promised to pay for our expenses, and have to watch our *para*s [small coins] for subsistence. Put an end to the ugly acts of Feyzi at Ṣan'ā' and let peace prevail in the Arabian Peninsula.[99]

Whom to blame?

Disgruntled Yemeni chiefs blamed Hussein Hilmi, currently serving as inspector general of Macedonia, for the insurrection. When he served as governor general of Yemen he had sought to centralize the administration, whereas until then local affairs had been in the hands of *shaykh*s. Hilmi was judged an excellent governor for Europe but unsuited to Yemen. He wanted to abolish the role *shaykh*s played as links between the government and tribes and replace them with Turkish officials. The *shaykh*s were prepared neither to lose their dignity nor be reduced to poverty. Their exasperation, not popular discontent, had led to revolt and, they claimed, no religious question was at stake.

The imam was falsely accused of laying claim to the *sherifate* (of Mecca). He was able to rally the support of discontented *shaykh*s because Hussein Hilmi Paşa's reformist tendencies irritated them and drove them to rebellion. There was a tendency to blame everything on the Turks' bad administration, but outside a few centres there never was much of an administration in Yemen, good or bad. There was, however, abuse in the collection of taxes. The *shaykh*s collected them and from them paid out a certain amount as tribute to the government. Officials then ignored the *shaykh*s' authority and sent out troops to collect taxes directly. The Yemenis, however, were accustomed to that sort of thing, so they played a very small part in provoking the rebellion.

The English author of the report to *The Times* scoffed at the idea that the English had incited the Yemenis to rebellion, as rumour in Istanbul alleged. He claimed to have lived a long time in Yemen and was aware of not the slightest intrigue on their part.[100]

Reshuffling officials and officers in Yemen

With a new government led by rebellious Young Turks, in 1909 there were some major reassignments to Yemen. Feyzi, who had grown exceedingly unpopular with Yemenis, had retired and was replaced by Ferik Hasan Tahsin as *vali* and commander-in-chief. Necip Paşa was made *mutasarrıf* of Hodeida; Ferik Rifat was placed in charge of the seventh army corps' thirteenth division at Ṣan'ā'; Recip Beg became adjunct of the governor general (he had served earlier as the *mektupçu* of the *vilayet*); and Mahmud Emin Efendi was appointed deputy governor of Hodeida. Tahsin, who lasted less than a year, was replaced by Izzet for a year or so, then by Muḥammad 'Alī (former commandant at Adana) in lieu of Kâmil Beg (temporarily appointed) as *vali* of Yemen and commandant, proof not so much of incompetence but of frustration in combating large insurgent forces with inadequate troops.

Rebellion of the Zarānīq

Two factors were responsible for the rising of this tribe in 1910: opposition to the extension of telegraph lines through their territory and the unmet demand that the sons of their leaders held hostage in Hodeida, Bayt al-Faqīh and other localities be released from 'prison'. When the newly arrived *vali* disembarked at Hodeida, local merchants met him and told him of the loss of trade due to the Zarānīq attacking caravans passing by Zabīd and Bayt al-Faqīh, two important trade centres. The British consul told the newly arriving *vali* of their eight-year record of disruption, cutting telegraph lines and piracy against British shipping off the Yemeni coast.

Tahsin received orders from Istanbul to punish them and a battalion of infantry led by Major Recip Beg arrived from Ṣan'ā' on 7 February 1909; another landed at Midi; two more companies (800 strong) under the local *mutasarrıf* Hacip Paşa joined them and they all moved on to Bayt al-Faqīh.[101] The Turkish garrison at Zabīd led by Riza Beg captured the Zarānīq stronghold at nearby Ḥusaynīyah, but the rebels ambushed him as he moved south to join Necip, killing about 30 and capturing his transport. He was forced to retreat to Bayt al-Faqīh. The convoy from Hodeida to Bayt al-Faqīh was held up two days later and about 30 Turks were killed and their camel-loads of supplies captured, while the *mutasarrıf* was trapped in Bayt al-Faqīh.

It was suggested that one way to deny the Zarānīq their operational base would be for the Ottomans to place a coal station there for ships. For 20 years the tribe had paid no taxes to the state and, to add insult to injury, had harassed passing *sunbūq*s, stripping them of their commercial and personal goods. This finally made the *mutasarrıf* of Hodeida request help from Ṣan'ā' to take their stronghold at Bayt al-Faqīh and suppress them. They had attacked Kaymakam Mahmud Riza at Ḥusaynīyah after he had captured it, at a cost of 80 Zarānīq and allegedly three Ottoman deaths.[102] The force was not strong enough to handle them. Riza had only between 1500 and 1600 troops and two mountain guns at Ḥusaynīyah.[103]

Clearly, a larger force was needed to relieve the trapped troops and Ferik Yusuf Paşa was called upon to lead the operation against the Zarānīqs. He left Ṣan'ā' at the head of three battalions of infantry to confront about 10,000 mobile Zarānīqs, who were good marksmen and well armed. It was not easy for Yusuf to hunt down these truculent tribesmen. Preferring to negotiate a peaceful settlement with them, he laid down the following five conditions. They must:

- pay all taxes in arrears;
- return the loot taken from Zabīd and Hodeida merchants over the previous five years valued at between 5000 and 10,000 *lira*s;
- surrender all their arms;
- destroy the thick brush they used to fortify themselves against Ottoman troops; and
- hand over 57 hostages from various sections of the tribe as sureties.

They only, however, accepted the first two conditions and combat ensued. Yusuf attacked them from al-Maḥwīt, but neighbouring tribes made common cause with them and the results were inconclusive.[104]

The Zarānīq and Banu Marwān tribesmen had created a crisis for Aptullah with the Italians, for they had been raiding their shipping for some time and the Italian admiral was threatening to bombard the coastal area from north of Midi to Hodeida.[105] Aptullah not only had to stop piracy in the Red Sea but also had to devise ways of preventing the Italians smuggling arms to the imam through intermediaries.[106]

On 21 February, when two Turkish gunboats, the *Taşköprü* and *Nevşehir*, sank one and captured another *dhow* carrying arms near Cos while on their way down the Red Sea from Istanbul, the two gunboats, having confiscated numerous rifles and ammunition, began to patrol the coast south of Hodeida, cooperating with troops fighting the Zarānīq.[107] Yusuf attacked them again and defeated them badly, supposedly killing and wounding more than 750, then refused to grant them amnesty until they laid down their arms.[108]

European spying activities

Meanwhile, the British, Italians and Germans, eager to assess the effects of the oncoming demise of Ottoman rule, stepped up their spying activities. In November 1911, an English army captain disguised as Ḥajji 'Ali and carrying a false passport, arrived on the khedival steamer to stay for a while with the British consul in Hodeida. *Vali* Muḥammad 'Alī sent an enciphered telegram to Istanbul containing information about him, which was passed on to the secret police. He had obtained a visa from the Ottoman consul in Marseilles, had served as an officer in the Transvaal regiment, and had come to Mecca and Medina on a 'pilgrimage' three years earlier. He had also visited Damascus and Tripolitania where he met Ferik Hasan Edip Paşa.[109] The chief of police in Hodeida could neither remove him by force nor imprison him without cause. It turned out that he had paid one Salih of the Bani Hāshish 30 *lira*s to smuggle him out of Ṣan'ā', where he intended to go to observe Ottoman troops and seek an exit via Aden. Instead, he was forced back to Hodeida when Salih brought a case against him in court for his 30 *lira*s and left for Aden on the Egyptian steamer.[110]

Another Englishman 'explorer' named A. B. Wavell was discovered spying in Ṣan'ā', but the *vali* seized him as he attempted to slip out disguised as an Arab. Izzet had him delivered under escort to the British consul in Hodeida.[111] The consul himself was accused of spying on Ottoman troops.[112]

A year earlier tribesmen had murdered Marchese Benzoni, an Italian consular agent at Mocha, and Herman Burckhardt, his German companion, near Ta'izz. They had travelled into the interior from Ṣan'ā', allegedly against the advice of the authorities, and had fallen into the hands of rebels. Benzoni, formerly a colonel in the cavalry and for some time commander of troops in Eritrea, was well known for his adventurous journeys in Africa and Arabia, which were sometimes for official purposes. This last time he had ventured into a dangerous area without the Italian government's permission and allegedly despite its remonstrance against it. The minister for foreign affairs in Rome instructed his ambassador in Istanbul to ensure that the guilty parties were captured and punished.[113]

To compound the Ottomans' problems, the Italians, who were becoming deeply embroiled in the turmoil of Yemen, demanded satisfaction for Benzoni's murder, even though the Ottoman authorities believed he had been spying in the south. They sent an armed unit of eight men and an officer to Ta'izz to investigate the murder and threatened to use units of their fleet to bombard the coast.[114] The *serasker* in Istanbul requested permission to respond and the Sublime Porte replied by denouncing the action as a violation of international law. Only the local government was authorized to conduct such an investigation, it stated, and Tahir Paşa at Hodeida was to be so informed. The Italian consul came to Ta'izz with a military escort, allegedly on an official visit, and the Sublime Porte decided to overlook the illegal act.[115]

Burckhardt, on the other hand, had entered the country two years earlier and was under suspicion. It turned out that the German consulate general in Cairo and its notorious spymaster Max von Oppenheim had indirectly commissioned him to go to Yemen to report on general conditions there. His report to his handling agent, the German director of the Khedival Library in Cairo, appeared in a series of dispatches to Berlin.[116] His assessment of the situation was sound in terms of what has been discussed so far. Of particular interest was his outline of all the peace missions sent to conciliate the imam but without success.

Abdülğani Senni recorded the full story from Ṣan'ā' on 10 December 1909. He alleged that Joseph Caproti, an Italian coffee and leather merchant, had befriended Herman Burckhardt, who described himself as 'a free citizen of the world', after several encounters. Burckhardt had spent two months learning Arabic and often travelled between Ṣan'ā' and Hodeida carefully observing everything and taking numerous photographs, which he often showed Senni. Indeed, Burckhardt had allegedly assisted the *vali* in his travels inside the country, even though conditions did not favour travel by foreigners. Nevertheless, he got the *vali*'s approval to travel to Ta'izz, where he stayed with 'the honorary vice consul' Benzoni, who apparently failed to secure the consul general's permission to venture into the interior. So he resigned and decided to accompany Burckhardt back to Ta'izz after heading for Mocha, then to Ibb, where they spent a few nights. It was while they were travelling towards 'Udayn and passing through Wādi al-Dīn that a few rifle shots were fired and both were killed, as reported later to the *kaymakam* of Ta'izz. The police sergeant and one or two others accompanying them were wounded. It was alleged that the bandits who shot them wanted to rob them and had killed others the year before.[117]

Renewal of rebellion in 'Asīr

In 1907, just when the Ottomans thought they could settle the fighting side of their engagement with the imam, Muḥammad ibn Idrīs, a claimant to the mahdiship of Maghribi origin who had been preaching strict obedience to the laws of Islam *à la* Wahhābi doctrine in next-door Arabia, arrived in 'Asīr and began to incite the tribes against the sultan's government. Şarâ'i Paşa at Hodeida, who misjudged the claimant's capacity for mischief, challenged him. Ibn Idrīs, though still without a solid base of followers, was talented enough to rally support from the tribes with his appeal for reform and restoration of 'true Islam'. He rallied enough people in the Tihāmah to defeat Şarâ'i, so thus began a new front of uprisings against the Ottomans and a serious threat to Hodeida, which at that moment in time had no troops to defend it.[118]

There was concern that the imam might make common cause with the 'Mahdi' of 'Asīr, but the religious difference was too great to match a Zaydi with a Wahhābi. Whatever brief alliance had been struck up between them ended as the imam awaited the outcome of negotiations with Talaat, minister of the interior in the Young Turk government, by his representatives in Istanbul.[119] The arrival of much better prepared Ottoman troops from the first and second army corps convinced the imam that he had closer interests with the sultan than with the mahdi.[120]

Talaat, however, was determined not to introduce any reforms in Yemen until all rebellion had ended. He ordered a new force of 12,000 men from Istanbul to combat the claimant and his 'Asīri followers and had the treasury allocate 30,000 *lira*s for the task. Yavur Paşa replaced Muhtâr as commandant of the first army corps and the first contingent of 3000 left for Hodeida on 29 August, followed the next day by a detachment of cavalry.[121]

In an interview with the Turkish newspaper *Sabah*, Talaat declared that all defiant and rebellious tribes throughout Yemen and 'Asīr had first to be punished, then suppressed. But this was easier said than done. He had been banking on newer and faster warships in the Red Sea for they had first to control the coast to prevent arms reaching the interior before combating the defiant tribes and impressing them with the power of the central government. The Ḥamdān, Khawlān, Dhu Muḥammad, Dhū Ḥusayn, Ḥāshid, and the tribes of Bilād al-Bustān and Khawlān around Ṣan'ā', the bold mountain tribes that had caused many losses in men and materials, between them had at least 100,000 weapons, which posed severe problems when it came to stationing troops to control them anywhere in the highlands.[122]

His strategy had little effect. He came under attack in Istanbul's chamber of deputies for entrusting the task to the unpopular former policeman Şarâ'i, who was renowned for incompetence and corruption. Angry members argued that they had been promised change when the constitution was set up, yet the same low-grade officials were still being sent to Yemen to govern.

Zarānīq defiance was still unresolved. The treasury had dispatched 15,000 *lira*s to establish a truce with them, but to little effect. Robbing and killing went on. Fewer than 1000 *lira*s were collected from them in unpaid taxes and they surrendered no arms. Şarâ'i had misled the government when he told them not to worry about Ibn Idrīs, who in the meanwhile had rallied 150,000 fighting men to his cause. A governor adhering to the re-established constitution was needed to replace the dishonest governor who had enriched himself with bribes for years and misrepresented realities to Istanbul, argued the press.[123]

For the next year, reinforcements poured into Yemen as the forces of both the imam and Idris continued to fight in Talaat's futile attempt to put down all rebellion by force. It was obvious that he had been misled and ill-informed of the magnitude of the uprising in 'Asīr and wanted an accurate assessment of it.[124] Meanwhile, authorization was given to rush more troops to Yemen to counteract the mahdi's forces.[125]

Most mobilization was in January 1911. At first, 11 battalions were sent to Yemen, with five more being prepared for dispatch.[126] Izzet Paşa was in charge of nine battalions from the first and fifth regiments. Serious fighting took place around Ta'izz in which 63 Yemenis were killed and 113 wounded as against 40 Ottoman deaths, with 16 more killed and 41 wounded in the surrounding area. There was also fighting when the insurgents attacked Ottoman outposts around Ṣan'ā'. Being under siege and attack off and on for months created hardships for the citizens of Ṣan'ā'. By way of a contribution, the government decided to allocate 6000 *piastre*s to those in need and when the *vali* reported it was insufficient, it increased the amount by another 2600 *piastre*s per individual.[127] The *sadrazam* authorized that one *lira* a month be paid as a living allowance to each individual of a battalion returning to Istanbul and that they also be provided with necessary clothing.[128]

Idris and his rebels were moving south into the Tihāmah in an attempt to cut off Hodeida from the interior. They killed 45 and wounded 84 Ottoman troops. Four *nizam* and four Izmir *redif* battalions were sent to Yemen. Reinforcements were also ordered from Syrian and Istanbul army corps. This was still not enough, so 30 more battalions and a strong force of artillery were ordered to crush the opposition in 'Asīr and Yemen once and for all.

The Turkish force was composed of 35 *nizam* and ten *redif* infantry battalions; three batteries of field guns and two machine-gun companies, all organized into three divisions under the command of either Çerkes Yusuf Paşa or Kara Saïd Paşa. More *redif* units were recruited in Macedonia with horses and mules being brought up for transport to Yemen. But then Yemen was not a safe place in which to serve; the Albanian units refused to serve abroad and the surging unrest there made the Ottomans fear that they might soon face additional insurrections in Albania and Macedonia.

Expenditure for increased military operations was mounting because troops in Yemen had not received compensation for a while and the Sublime Porte was eager to reduce the number of forces, but was compelled, rather, to increase them for the 'Asīr campaign. Sending back the fourteenth army *kul* battalion, even by the least expensive route, meant an increase in expenditure to the tune of 324,000 *lira*s, which the war ministry urgently requested.[129] Machine guns, cannons and other types of modern weaponry were to be prepared in Syria to accompany the Tabuk *redif*s to Yemen.[130] Keeping the troops paid was critical and the *vali* sent a ciphered telegram to the *sadaret* asking urgently for 13,000 *lira*s to meet the deficit.[131] *Nizam* troops were falling behind in pay and requests for more funds were constantly being cabled to the central government, in addition to having to finance new recruits.[132]

Increased fighting in 'Asīr, coupled with military engagements in Tripolitania and before that the Balkans, gave rise to rumours that the Young Turks were about to abolish parliament and replace it with a dictatorship, as proposed by Minister of War Mahmud Şevket Paşa, with the latter being put in charge.[133]

This consideration was important in the decision eventually to meet Yemeni demands, but it was considered illogical to agree to the imam's request to govern Shāfi'i-Sunni regions like the Tihāmah or 'Asīr. The

Young Turk government decided to implement a reformist policy for one *vilayet*. In 1900 it had drawn up and submitted a scheme to the chamber that would have divided Yemen into two provinces, made the imam governor of the *jabal* (highland) province with powers to appoint civil and military functionaries but retain a portion of the internal revenue for administration and withdraw the greater part of the garrison from Ṣan'ā', which would become the imam's capital. The idea of one *vilayet* was abandoned when Idris, the *mutamahdi* (claimant to the mahdiship) appeared on the scene in 1909 and rendered the idea of an autonomous Yemen hazardous. So the scheme was withdrawn in favour of one that promoted local reform, namely applying the Sharī'ah, remitting TL 80,000 in taxes, creating schools (a number had already been built by 1911) and constructing public works.

The proposed scheme calling for the autonomy of the *jabal* was the work of Hussein Hilmi when he was grand vizier. Seven years earlier he had served as *vali* of Yemen; he knew the country and its people well and admired Yemeni intellectual and commercial skills. But when Talaat became minister of the interior, he shelved the scheme, having opposed it before the chamber of deputies and got the majority to support him. He had no knowledge of Yemen, so the government now faced a long and costly road to peace.

Last phase of the insurrection

In the meanwhile, the war intensified and the situation became graver. The imam launched several attacks on Ṣan'ā', where the besieged *vali* desperately awaited 36 battalions from Istanbul to counter the imam's 60,000 fighting men. Miralay Riza Beg warded off attacks near Hodeida, but by blocking the road to Bājil the rebels had stopped him going to Manākhah's rescue. The imam's levies attempted to seize the heights above Manākhah to prevent reinforcements reaching the highlands; 1200 soldiers had arrived in Hodeida but were put in quarantine.

In a frustrating effort to achieve results by continually reshuffling high ranking officers, Muḥammad 'Alī soon replaced Izzet Paşa, chief of staff and commander-in-chief of the first army, as overall commandant in Yemen. The sultan met Crown Prince Yusuf Izzedin, and heads of the departments of war, navy, army and the interior to plan his orders and elicit support. The steamship *Hilal* was commissioned to transport a battalion of troops, two batteries of mountain cannons, a company of telegraph specialists and a number of health officials for disinfecting purposes.[134] Other transport ships bought from Germany were preparing to load troops for Yemen and eight German Torpil destroyers were ready to enter service in January 1910.

Though the snow conveniently held them up, the Istanbul government could not get Kurdish *redif*s to go because they had not received back pay since Abdülhamid's days. It was a constant battle for the government to find salaries and allowances for unpaid and underpaid troops.[135] The restored telegraph to Ta'izz relayed the bad news that the Ottomans had lost a machine gun at Dumak and that the 30 battalions forming the Yemen garrison were to be supplemented by 34 infantry, three batteries of field guns and 12 Maxim to bring the total to 50,000 men. However, the difficulty getting transport held them up. It had become much harder to secure land transport because the insurgents controlled the strategic pass of Manākhah, but in seeking to seize it with 2000 attackers had repeatedly been repulsed, losing 130 lives to 61 Ottoman soldiers and friendly Yemeni supporters. Morale, however, was holding up at Ṣan'ā' and the steamship *Cambridge* was able to convey 653 Turkish troops from Kamarān to Mocha.[136]

Idris, meanwhile, had surrounded Abhā and was threatening Hodeida. This galvanized the grand *sharīf* of Mecca into action. His destination was Qunfidhah where 6000 troops allegedly awaited him, with another 6000 to be collected along the way. His son Fayṣal, who planned to join him, was taking the Hijaz route to help Süleiman Paşa defend Abhā with the additional 5000 men he was to bring with him. Idris, who had gathered a large force, was attacking Abhā and cutting communications to Qunfidhah.[137]

There were rumours that Idris had sent the imam reinforcements, including 80 camel loads of supplies, to aid in his attack on Ṣan'ā' and that he was dispatching agitators to stir up the Abu 'Arīsh and Ḥusaynīyah. Hitherto neutral Shāfi'is were now attacking villages in Jabal Raymah and anxiety was spreading in the ministry of the interior, which sent another representative to negotiate with the rebel leaders.

A report to Damascus newspapers alleged that had the government moved quickly at the start of Idris's uprising, it would have taken no more than four battalions to suppress it. Now not even 40 could do so because the whole of 'Asīr was under siege. Süleiman Paşa was virtually a prisoner in Abhā and whenever he sent a messenger to Hodeida to inform its *mutasarrıf* of the situation, Idris's agents seized him. His aim was to establish an independent emirate in ʻAsīr, stated the editor.[138] Reuters' correspondents alleged also that more than 100 of the experienced military officers the Young Turks had dismissed had returned to Yemen to join and lead the uprisings.[139]

An outbreak of yellow fever in Yemen's ports compelled the Turks to land their expeditionary forces in three units, the first of nine battalions and two batteries of light artillery and a number of machine guns; the second of six battalions of *redif* and 13 battalions of *nizam* troops along with a battery of rapid-fire cannons and a number of machine guns; and the third of three battalions from Tripolitania, six others from elsewhere, two batteries of the fourth army, and four battalions of *redif*s with two batteries of guns transferred from Albania. All this was to be under the command of Müşür Aptullah Paşa. Saïd Paşa, who served as governor of ʻAsīr and was its military commandant, arrived in Hodeida and was awaiting instructions.[140]

There was serious concern over news to Istanbul being blocked by disrupted telegraph lines. The inhabitants of Ibb, Taʻizz and Abhā declared their loyalty to the Ottoman administration in a telegram to the minister of war Şevket who cabled back his appreciation on the same day. This was reassuring, but the status of the strategic town of Manākhah was still unclear. It was questionable whether it could hold out for long, despite Riza having declared a great victory in the area and alleging to have forced the rebels to flee.[141]

The long-alienated Zarānīq came to Hodeida offering to help transport equipment and supplies to Ṣanʻāʼ. Abhā was still under siege and the army was accused of not reporting the truth about the military operations.[142] Within days of alleged victories, word reached Istanbul that Riza had been defeated in the Manākhah area and that three battalions of troops from the fourth army were being sent on board the steamship *Shâm*, and two from the sixth army on the steamer *Kara Deniz*.

It was disconcerting to learn that the *sharīf*, allegedly on his way to relieve the siege of Abhā with his Bani ʻUtaybah warriors, was still held up well into April at Mecca's resort of Ṭa'if. When contact was finally made, the *sharīf*'s forces had been badly mauled by Idris's before they got near to Abhā, which had fallen to him, as reported in *The Times* on 2 June 1911. There was scepticism over the losses inflicted on the imam's forces (estimated at between 500 and 1500).

Turkish guns were fired at Shaykh Saʻīd to celebrate the news of the imam's alleged capture at Ṣanʻāʼ. Insurgents surprised Muḥammad ʻAlī

Paşa's advance guard at Jāzān, killing 1000 and wounding 500, mostly with daggers; the rest of his troops fled in disorder. The gunboat *Entebe* then shelled the town, killing and wounding several hundred soldiers. The insurgents returned with the booty — four guns, two Maxims, 2000 rifles, ammunition and 100 mule-loads of supplies. The Turkish commander was missing; the expeditionary force's water supply had been cut off; 80 cases of cholera were reported with 34 deaths; and the epidemic was raging among the troops at Jāzān and Qunfidhah. Reinforcements consisting of ten battalions and six guns under Nihât Paşa were reportedly being got ready for a large-scale operation to help the *sharīf* rescue Abhā.

It would appear that too few forces were sent to quell all the rebellions at the same time, so eight more battalions, half *redif* and half *nizam*, were recruited from Adana. Large quantities of ammunition and supplies were to be rushed in because by mid-July 1911 'Asīri insurgents were ready to seize Luḥayyah and Jāzān, having cut off their water supplies, and the commandant of Hodeida prepared to shore up the city's defences while anxiously waiting for reinforcements to arrive.

Muḥammad 'Alī met disaster at Abhā. He lost about 1600 troops in the battle of Jāzān, of whom 1100 lost their lives. At the beginning of August it was announced that troops under Hussein Paşa had recovered Abhā with the assistance of the *sharīf*'s Arabian forces, but that did not stop Idris striking back three days later. By the third week of August it was reported that Idris's followers were abandoning him and the warring tribes were surrendering to the *sharīf*. However, by February 1912, with help from the Italians, it was reported that Idris had attempted to occupy Farasān island with the aid of two machine guns.[143]

Unable to contain the ongoing insurrection whether in the Tihāmah, 'Asīr or Yemeni highlands, Talaat finally gave in to reason and sought to negotiate in earnest a settlement with the imam and other adversaries.

The Ottoman attempt to suppress the revolt in Yemen failed — under the old regime and the new one of the Young Turks — because the rebels had gained allies from non-Zaydis in the highlands and from the tribes of the Tihāmah: hence, the ultimate realization that the only alternative to ending the upheavals was a compromise truce. In the next chapter I focus on repeated efforts to reach this compromise through negotiators on both sides and the final realization of it.

13. The Search for and Arrival at a Settlement

Early in 1911 it became obvious that Talaat was not going to defeat the rebel forces, which, through the astuteness of the imam and the harshness of the Young Turks' failing military policy, had grown to encompass more than just the Zaydis. In view of the military losses and growing European imperial assaults on Ottoman possessions elsewhere, the compromise the imam and his allies sought appeared so reasonable that the Young Turks were left with no choice but to compromise.

The imam's negotiating position

In this chapter we see how the imam succeeded in pressing the Young Turks to see matters his way and to agree to terms that left the Yemenis in the Ottoman fold on the eve of the First World War.

Explaining his position, the imam said that had reform decrees issued earlier been honoured and implemented, the unrestrained killing and plundering of Yemenis would have been averted. He insisted the Yemenis rose not against the sultan but against oppressive officials when their complaints went unheeded. 'We are descendants of the Prophet,' declared Yaḥya, 'and we take seriously honouring the injunctions of our religion; those who dishonour our faith by killing, looting, oppressing will not be tolerated because we preach what the holy text teaches: do good and avoid what is forbidden. We also defend the Sharī'ah.'

He then asked the sultan to issue an imperial order authorizing him to send three of his followers to Istanbul to explain the bad situation in Yemen. The three proposed were 'Abdallah ibn Ibrāhīm ibn Aḥmad ibn al-Imām, Aḥmad ibn Hāshim al-Shāmi, and al-Qāḍi Sa'd ibn Muḥammad al-Sharqi. They were told not only to explain his position and present the facts, but also to stipulate what reforms were necessary to correct the situation.

'The sultan,' he stated, 'should be the supreme enforcer and defender of the high principles of Islam and be aware that Christians always seek to sow dissent among Muslims.' He urged Abdülhamid to follow the precedent of the early sultans to enforce the decrees of the Sharī'ah in Yemen and honour the commitments of the past and abide by them. 'We requested a *ferman* be issued to that effect so the situation in Yemen might be improved and the Imam return to obedience.'[1] The *sadrazam* received the imam's Arabic petition, which appealed for the institution of reforms to ensure the security and peace of Yemen.[2]

Ẓafār Amīri's father, the late Sayyid Fazıl Paşa Zadé, had submitted a petition to the *sadaret* stating that the people of Yemen, Zaydis and Shāfi'is alike, wanted equal justice and good administration. 'Officials sent to date,' he argued, 'have been self-enriching, oppressive, plunderers, and enemies of the faith.' Most Yemenis were Ashrāf (*sharīf*) or Sūdah (*sayyid*), descendants of Imam Ḥusayn, grandson of the Prophet Muḥammad, and very dedicated to Islam and to its teachings and decrees. 'We cannot tolerate those who violate its decrees,' they argued. 'To keep them down unjustly will take much money and many troops. Conscientiousness and justice is what we expect from our administrators. Yemen has become now the graveyard of Muslims and money.'

'The task of the Ottoman government', he stated, 'is to reconcile to it three million Yemenis of all tribes. We suggest increasing the pay of officials in Ṣan'ā' and court heads of tribes who have residences in the city and who are being courted presently by the British by:

- offering them hospitality by building a hospitality house in the city and allocating a monthly stipend for them of 20,000 *piastre*s;
- appointing a *vali* who is honourable, conscientious, responsible and grounded in the teachings of the Sharī'ah;
- appointing a *vali* who can communicate with heads of tribes in the city and who should receive gifts and pelisses to cultivate their loyalty to the Ottoman government;
- applying decrees drawn from the Sharī'ah, not derived from foreign inspired constitutions;
- setting up Islamic schools;
- using Arabic as the official language of communication;[3] and
- acknowledging that feuds in the region of Ṣan'ā' are the result of

inter-Zaydi conflicts; hence troops stationed there should be Yāfi'is Shāfi'is led by a just commander'.[4]

The imam's proposals for a settlement

At this point, the imam held out a peace offer to the government: he would pay tribute and accept Ottoman suzerainty provided he was granted autonomy in dealing with Zaydis. He made a similar offer in 1905 through the intermediation of Shaykh al-Ḥarīri, grand *mufti* of Hama (Syria), but without results.[5] A year later the central government decided to send a delegation to make peace with the imam and his two powerful *shaykhs*, Qaşīm and Mikdād. The Ottoman government returned two Yemeni chiefs, in exile on the island of Rhodes, Sayyid Mahmud Mu'aykar and Sharīf 'Abdallah ibn Ḥasan al-Mutawakkil, to Yemen to induce the imam to send deputies to Istanbul to voice their complaints. The imam selected 'Abdallah Ibrahim, Qāḍi 'Izz al-Dīn al-Sharqi and Sayyid Muḥammad al-Shāmi, all of whom enjoyed great influence with the imam and the tribes. They sailed to Istanbul on a khedival steamer, but the question to address was whether the Ottomans could heed their views without compromising suzerainty over Yemen.

The commission the Porte sent earlier had no chance of success, for it had failed to establish contact with either of the rival imams (Yaḥya and his challenger at Ṣa'dah) or with the key *shaykhs*. The cost of fighting rebels was getting too high and there was now a more urgent need for peace. Feyzi had requested TL 30,000 with which to placate and pacify tribal chiefs and did not think sending TL 20,000 was sufficient.

So the government decided to make a fresh attempt to conciliate the tribes by dispatching another special mission to discuss terms of settlement. The commission consisted of two generals and two ulema. They left for Yemen on 7 April 1906, but foreign observers were sceptical about the likelihood of a settlement that failed to grant full autonomy to the tribes.[6]

The petition addressed earlier to the *sadaret* presented the imam's conditions for peace and security in Yemen and pleaded for action.[7] His main aim in renewing negotiations was to gain government recognition of his religious leadership over his people with some official responsibilities to go with it. He did not object to continual Ottoman suzerainty because it made the government responsible for defence against outside aggression, which he himself was incapable of mounting.[8]

The government did not respond immediately to the imam's terms partly because its officials had failed to inform it of the seriousness of the military situation in the land and it did not wish to demean local government or its representatives, and partly because it did not wish to detract from the sultan's authority. Abdülhamid, on the other hand, was deeply interested in Yemen's security. He realized that if the country was to remain loyal to his caliphate there was a need to improve its administrative policies.[9]

In 1891 the *sadrazam* sent a *mazbata* to the imperial *divan* with a proposal that Yemen's administration be put in order and recommending that a commission of inquiry be sent to investigate the means to that end. The *divan* recommended in 1894 that such a commission be appointed to investigate how to improve Yemen's administration and military structure.[10] One of the commission's functions was to recruit native Yemenis for service in the *vilayet*'s police force and soldiers for the army. The commission was instructed also to enquire into ways of improving the commerce, economy and agriculture of the land, and of installing competent civil authorities.

The *tâlimat* (instructions) the sultan's head scribe drafted for the commission recognized the presence of three million Muslims in Arabia who, due to neglect, did not enjoy the full potential of their resources, hence the need for this investigative commission. The area suffered from disease and foreigners occupied it in the south. Inhabitants argued that they were members of the Muslim community who, according to the Sharī'ah's provisions, were entitled to military service and to serve under their own officers. Criminal law should be strictly enforced, criminals should be punished and no infraction should be overlooked.

The *vilayet*'s annual income of 450,000 *lira*s had to be collected; no siphoning away should be allowed and no pressure should be applied to the inhabitants to make up the difference. Neither officials nor their own *shaykh*s should oppress them for financial gain and their security must be safeguarded. Misgovernment, either by officials or the military, should be punished; those who made fortunes by illicit means should be held to account and incompetent officials transferred out. Honourable men of stature should serve on the *vilayet*'s administrative council and be charged to look into civil infractions. Not a *para* was to be squeezed out of the inhabitants by any means, open or secret.

The investigative commission was empowered to arrest guilty military officers and remand them to the war *divan* for court martial.

Yemenis were to be recruited for military and police service. Military personnel were to be adequately paid and rotated at set intervals. Instead of appointing *kaymakams* from Istanbul, competent members of the *mashāyikh* would be selected to serve in that capacity. Finally, the commission should make careful and judicious recommendations.[11]

The *sadrazam* proposed the commission consist of Ahmed Eyup Paşa, head of the *maliye meclis*, Ibrahim Efendi, and Aptullah Beg Efendi, a member of the *Şura-yi Devlet*.[12] His advisers had recommended as early as 1897 that the military and administrative posts be separated to provide checks and balances between the two top posts. This was the recommendation of former *vali* of Adana, Hussein Hilmi Efendi, as taken up in a special session of the ministers.

Hilmi submitted a memorandum to the government outlining ways to improve the situation in Yemen and to avoid the excessive cost of constantly having to suppress rebellions caused by the misadministration of self-serving officials. Justice could only be served, he argued, with decrees that were derived from the Sharī'ah and strictly implemented. Taxes should be equitably levied and collected, but not by military officers using force. To increase revenue the state should promote trade and economic growth, secure the roads, build more technical, trade and craft schools, and recruit Yemenis for police duty to lessen resistance. These were the sultan's recommendations to his *sadrazam* Rifaat[13] who was not to compromise the sultan's suzerainty in Yemen.[14]

The country was divided into four *sancak*s.[15] Hilmi proposed increasing by 150,000 *lira*s the income of these administrative units, which to date had been bringing in up to 500,000 a year, mostly from customs and various fees. He suggested conducting a land survey to determine land ownership and set taxes properly. The problem, he noted, was how to come up with the 4000-*lira* cost of the survey. Each village's *shaykh* was to be in charge of collecting taxes. Hilmi was persuaded that if control could thus be established, revenues from taxes, customs fees, agricultural yields and debt collection would increase to 600,000 *lira*s compared with 400,000 at present. 'If we can collect 250,000 more and net 150,000, we can serve Yemen better; perhaps even having two instead of one *shaykh* in charge per village, who will not oppress citizens.' The annual military expenditure was put at 350,000 *lira*s; with present revenues insufficient to meet this expense, the central treasury was compelled to shoulder the difference.

Once the land was secure, he argued, fewer troops would be needed to patrol it and military expenditure would decrease. There were eight regiments serving in Yemen at the time, which could be reduced to four with a considerable reduction of expenses.[16]

Land and population surveys were vital for recruiting troops. Rebuilding the Ma'rib dam would increase agricultural production, and constructing a harbour at Mocha would increase shipping and revenue from it. Opening up coalmines in the *kaza*s of ‘Udayn and Ḥujarīyah would provide another source of income, while upgrading road communications and expanding trade would improve access to Hijaz.

With the situation stabilized, troops could be recruited from Yemen who would be cheaper to maintain. The *shaykh*s, who were giving the Ottoman authorities false information, needed controlling. They may need to maintain the present force for up to a year-and-a-half, incurring huge expenses they could offset with income from increased production. One could not be sure that the Ṣa‘dah and Shahārah regions would be free of troublemaking, but if administrative responsibility were delegated to competent and honest officials and a good *vali* like Ahmed Muhtâr,[17] Mustafa Asim (five–six years service) or an Ahmed Feyzi (15–16 years), then political affairs could be straightened out.[18]

It was vital to increase revenue and, to this end, winning over defiant chiefs was a key issue. To look into how to do so and to straighten out Yemen's finances, Minister of Justice Sayyid Hussein Riza appointed a commission headed by former finance counsellor Namik Efendi. Chiefs were to be won over with gifts and better relationships. Rifaat Halil, minister of the interior and imperial documents supervisor, endorsed the commission following approval of a *mazbata* of instruction from the *Meclis-i Mahsus* to Namik on 16 June 1892. Specifically, 100 robes of honour were to be given to tribal heads and *shaykh*s, 15 silver *mecidiye* coins, 100 silver watches and 3000 *piastre*s in monthly allowances to Namik and an accompanying secretary.

More specifically Namik was instructed to:

- execute all just military, administrative and financial measures fairly and properly;
- reconcile Zaydis with Ottomans, being careful not to insult their beliefs;
- take no measures to antagonize tribes that might be reconciled to Ottomans and pay their taxes;
- introduce just measures to levy and collect taxes peacefully;

- keep careful records of surplus revenue once army and administrative expenses were paid;
- take firm measures to ensure that customs fees were collected in Hodeida and used to pay the seventh army; if these were insufficient, then the central treasury should provide the balance;
- make any changes in official appointments that were necessary to improve the administration of the *vilayet*, and
- consult the *vali* and, if need be, defer to his judgement on how to improve the situation, then recommend whatever authorization was needed to effect the ends of his mission.[19]

To counter propaganda against Sunni ulema, it was recommended that a *medrese* (religious school) be established to teach Shāfi'i and Ḥanafi *fiqh* (jurisprudence) and consideration be given to the frequently suggested establishment of a rail line between Hodeida and Ṣan'ā'.[20]

On 11 S 1325 (26 March 1907), 15 years after submitting his first memorandum to his government, Hussein Hilmi Paşa presented another that assessed the situation in Yemen during the period of his service, which began in 1887. His review of the record of administrative procedures in Yemen after the Ottomans returned to the highlands in 1872 shows that from the very start the government had been aware of the need to establish good administration for the country.

The measures Muhtâr Paşa introduced to ensure stability after peace was restored in 1872 proved inadequate. A problem was the presence of Zaydis along the *Hatt-i Yemen*; also local notables treated theirs as a heretical *da'wah*, hence the frequent uprisings against them and the havoc wreaked on agricultural production as a result.

The government, he argued, tried to win over the imams and *shaykh*s by giving them stipends, payable out of local production, and by allowing them to do military service in lieu of paying a *bedel*. The government collected various taxes and fees but made no specific allocations to tribal heads or imams.

Yemeni tribes were organized as follows: *mikhlāf*s, the largest unit, were divided into *'uzlah*s, which were made up of a number of villages each headed by a *muhtar* (mayor), a resident who was wise, mindful of the welfare needs of the inhabitants and responsible for allocating the *miri*. The abuses that took place during the levying and collecting of this tax, for which the Ottoman government was blamed, alienated the subjects who lost faith in its fairness.

Order was introduced for a while after the Ottomans returned and the wealth of the state increased. Then appointed officials began to act irresponsibly and Aptullah Paşa had to be recalled for catering to his own rather than to Yemeni interests. The military could not suppress resistance by force, which only served to alienate the inhabitants from their caliph.[21] To relieve the financial pressure on the inhabitants, the *divan*, responding to imperial instructions, decided to exempt them from paying the personal *vergi* and on 21 January 1904 the sultan recommended it not be levied for that fiscal year.[22]

There was a strong awareness of the need to introduce proper measures and to enforce them vigorously. Early on, the inhabitants only had Vitelli muskets, which Ottoman troops could easily confiscate, but oppression, which the narrow views and ambitions of their imams exacerbated, forced them to acquire more modern arms. Ottoman officers and officials thus indirectly contributed to the problem by inflicting abuse on the inhabitants in defiance of the Islamic Sharī'ah. And this abuse partly came from having to deal with defiant tribes led by the imams' *sayyid* and *shaykh* followers.

In 1889–90 (1307) a unit of irregular troops was deployed to force the tribes to recognize the local administration. But, between that year and 1898, the imam bought new weapons with the *miri* taxes he had withheld from the state. Once again a unit of *redif*s was sent against them, but this time the state took the opportunity to introduce reform, dismiss and punish bad officials, ensure that taxes, fees and *âşâr* were collected village by village and that each received its proper share, introduce education, establish schools — particularly from 1899–1900 (1317) onwards — and enforce reform measures to ensure the inhabitants' peace and security.

Officers assigned for service in Yemen, asserted Hilmi, had to be above reproach and measures taken to ensure they stayed that way if agriculture was to prosper. To that end, land had to be irrigated and dams built. The country had four million intelligent, bold and hard-working inhabitants who needed the security of a caring administration. Peace and order could be assured only after the rascal (Imam Yaḥya) was suppressed and replaced by a decent relative or *sayyid*. If tribes could be involved in the administration, they would abandon the imam and lessen his capacity for troublemaking. It would take five imperial divisions to end the Zaydi-led rebellion and throw fear into their hearts.

Local income for 1895, 1897 and 1898 was 360,000 *lira*s each year, but after 1901 it was 200,000 *liras* lower. This was not enough to support the troops, so the central treasury was obliged to provide the balance. The government could not afford to confront an uprising by the 'rascal' every five years or so, so he had to be put down by force once and for all and punished. If the state could not afford to send troops and money to Yemen to do it, then it should withdraw from the country. On the other hand, if proposed reforms for the military and administration were implemented, the treasury could have a surplus.[23]

The 1898 recommendations were for a military solution with forcible action to quell revolt in the Zaydi-controlled tribes and areas. Emphasis on military action was central to the reports received from Yemen and endorsed at first without much challenge or long-term success.

Yaḥya's 1904 insurgence posed another problem and signalled the start of a policy shift in Istanbul. Memduh Paşa, then minister of the interior, led a commission to seek a non-military solution with a view to bringing Yemen in line with other Ottoman provinces enjoying progress and development. The commission reviewed recommendations made during the 1898–1904 period. Among the documents studied were those that the Reform Commission of 1898 presented to the Council of State. They dealt with a range of suggestions from the proposed construction of a railroad between Hodeida and Ṣan'ā' to criminal law procedures and the organization of Sharī'ah courts, as well as steps needed to establish peace through enforcing law and order.

Other items of discussion included a proposal by the *vali* in 1898 to restructure Yemen into four provinces and a report by him the same year to improve agriculture and state income; the Council of State's civil service office report on administrative reform; dispatches to the palace from Yemen in response to the sultan's queries about delays in settling Yemen's problems; and dispatches on the implementation of orders to separate the police from the military.[24]

In response to Memduh's recommendations, the *mutasarrıf* of Ta'izz was relieved of his duties because of incompetence and replaced by Alâeddin, the *vilayet*'s *mektupçu*. He in turn was to be replaced by competent Recep Efendi of the correspondence bureau in Istanbul, at a salary of 5000 *piastres*.[25]

Following a petition to the *sadaret*, an imperial order was issued on 15 August 1902 to authorize implementation of measures to improve the administration of Yemen. Instructions as outlined in broad terms were as follows:

- appoint a *vali* and an experienced military commander with the rank of *ferik*;
- appoint competent officials at all levels of administration from municipalities to districts;
- give preference to competent local personnel; if not available, then appoint suitable ones from Istanbul;
- central government to review and approve appointees;
- appointees must be tactful, able to speak Arabic and competent to deal with tribal leaders;
- administrative, legal and financial officials should be paid adequate salaries; and
- for good work promoted in the third and final year of service.[26]

On 8 February 1905 Kaymakam Ismail Rehmi submitted a memorandum to Istanbul reviewing conditions in Yemen, the disturbances of which every three to five years he attributed partly to Zaydi disaffection and partly to mismanagement of the country's affairs. He considered the measures that Müşür Muhtâr and Defterdar Edip had introduced in the past irrelevant for the present. Besides, Edip[27] was unfamiliar with the nuances of the prevailing order. All ordinances passed and enforced to date had had a negative impact, he argued. The recommendations were deemed faulty. The continuation of defiance was attributed to:

- army officers and officials failing to obey instructions, so angering tribes into reacting against the administration; and
- when trouble broke out, no effective means adopted to avert it.

Following in the footsteps of his father's rebelliousness, Yaḥya took advantage of the situation to rally the tribes around Ṣan'ā' and impose his influence by force on the inhabitants.

The *sadrazam* sent out a commission of inquiry in April 1906 headed by Ferik Ferid Paşa and including Hüsnü Efendi, head of the inspection court, and another unspecified person.[28] Ferid's report of 7 March 1907 recommended rearranging the *vilayet*s, standardizing tax distribution and promoting education.[29]

Government ministers held a special session to ponder the imam's peace proposals[30] and sought directives from the sultan to attempt to improve relations with the imam by addressing his complaints and making their own recommendations.[31]

The *sadrazam* took the imam's recommendations into consideration and added his own from the advice Ẓafār's late emir, Seyyid Fazil Paşa-Zâde, had given him in his petition to the *sadaret*.[32]

Unable to determine what was needed to ameliorate conditions in Yemen and ensure good and safe administration there in keeping with imperial decrees, the *sadaret* decided to call on the services of an outside expert who was familiar with the country. Their choice fell on Eduard Glaser, an Austrian who two decades earlier had worked as an ethnographer in Yemen, knew the country well, spoke Arabic, and was on friendly terms with Ottoman military officials in Yemen.

On 7 March 1907, Mehmed Ferid, son of Sa'd Paşa, submitted his proposal, which was to wed the increase of agricultural productivity and commercial activities to administrative reforms.[33]

Imam's proposal to Sadrazam Kâmil Paşa

Dissatisfied with the earlier response, the imam submitted a petition dated 10 Ra 1327 (2 April 1907) embodying the terms he sought. His envoy Sa'd ibn Muḥammad al-Sharqi and his two other companions delivered it personally to Sadrazam Kâmil Paşa with the message that Imam Yaḥya would honour whatever the government decreed to stop bloodshed once the government and the people of Yemen had reached a consensus. He proposed that

- communications be secured;
- legal matters be handled by judges of the respective rites;
- the imam's privileges be allowed to continue;
- the turbulent tribes be placed under his jurisdiction for better control;
- more primary schools be established; and
- the system of adjudication in Yemen be unified.[34]

The imam concluded that acceptance of these terms would let the country revive and peace prevail. Ottomans, consequently, would be spared the expense of sending more troops to Yemen and the Yemenis' loyalty to the sultan would be assured, encouraging stability and a chance to progress. He urged the sultan's government to accept them.[35]

The response was not immediate because Ottoman forces meanwhile were able to hold off rebels threatening Ṣan'ā' and Manākhah. The rebels had withdrawn, but probably, it was stated, to await the delegation's return from Istanbul. There was great relief in Ottoman circles when it was reported that two officers sent to Yemen, Hüsnü Paşa and Mustafa Paşa, had been exiled to Aleppo and Damascus respectively for mutinous behaviour.[36] Rumour had it that the Ottoman military and civil authorities escorting Yemeni *shaykh*s home were ordered to form themselves into a commission to examine the charges of misconduct brought against Feyzi. The delegates had gone to Istanbul with the imam's message.[37]

Negotiating a peace settlement was still causing difficulty. A report in the *Egyptian Gazette* from a correspondent in Aden claimed that the peace commission had left Hodeida for Mecca to negotiate with the rebels, but the mission was believed to have been fruitless because the imam would accept no terms short of complete autonomy and 'to his arrogation of the title Commander of the Faithful' to which the commissioners took strong exception.[38]

The imam was not about to let up. He raided districts still under Ottoman control, and collected both provisions and recruits for a new offensive. Even hitherto unresponsive Sunnis of Ta'izz and Zabīd now took up arms against the Ottomans. Communications between that city and Hodeida were cut, and the coffee growing district around Ta'izz was the scene of constant disturbances.

Yemeni merchants also had their complaints. They incurred considerable losses by having to change the *riyal* into *rupee*s at a 15 per cent discount to pay for imports. They also felt that the government should lend them a hand by easing the collection of fees.[39]

Impact of the Young Turk revolt

The restitution of the constitution in Istanbul in 1907 brought hope of a new era in Yemen, and was well received in Ṣan'ā'. Excitement among the troops ran high over the prospect of a settlement at last, and Feyzi had to use much tact to keep his 6000 troops calm over it. With the Young Turks and their Committee of Union and Progress staging a successful revolt, some Yemenis expected a change of policy. No terms were reached with the imam, but the *shaykh* of the powerful Ḥāshids submitted to the new regime. The imperial commissioners reaching Hodeida on 16 October 1908 would, it was hoped, work out a settlement, especially since a new governor general and commandant,

Hussein Tahsin Paşa, was to take charge. Angered by Feyzi's arbitrary behaviour, some officers were rumoured to have plotted to arrest and imprison the old field-marshal, but Feyzi was onto them; he sent the undesirable characters to Istanbul (60 to 70 from Ṣan'ā' alone).

The old *mutasarrıf* of Hodeida, Ahmed Izzet Beg, fared less well. He was kidnapped and put on the Italian Rubatino Line's *Delora* for Suez. Officers behind the coup put up their own local puppet, Commandant Arif Hikmet Paşa, deemed as incompetent as Izzet for the post. About 30 or 40 of them then formed themselves into the 'Hodeida Ottoman Committee of Union and Progress' and began to interfere in *sancak* affairs. They dismissed the *kaymakam* of Jabal Raymah and appointed an army officer in his place. The *qāḍi* and *muhasıpçı* both resigned and left for Istanbul without permission. The post of *müdür-i tahrirât* (chief of correspondence) and the court of first instance were left without a president. In short, no responsible officer remained in Hodeida.

In Ḥajjah, troops instigated by their officers arrested and imprisoned Ferik Hakkı, the commandant of its military post. There were rumours that Feyzi, now 75 and still in control of his physical and mental faculties, had resigned. It was feared that news of this, if it were true, might give the imam, whom he had neutralized for some time, an excuse to rise up again. In his judicious way, Feyzi had won over formerly rebellious *shaykh*s. There were altogether 23,000 troops stationed in the *vilayet*, including those garrisoning 'Asīr, a force considered sufficiently strong to meet all emergencies.

Council of State recommendations

Imam Yaḥya sent delegates to Istanbul to propose a peaceful settlement amid fresh attacks by his followers on tribes that had not joined the insurgence, which made the situation more critical for the government, especially after a lull in the fighting necessitated the dispatch of more reinforcements.[40] Earlier, emissaries had presented the imam's petition to the *sadrazam* reminding the government that the Prophet and many of his traditions stipulated that rulers must be good to '*ahl al-bayt*' (Prophet's family) as exemplified also by the conduct of the Orthodox caliphs (632–61) and the 'Abbāsids (750–1258), implying that he, as one of those descendants, deserved similar consideration.[41]

The Council of State decided to appoint Hasan Tahsin Paşa *vali* of Yemen rather than Mahmud Nedim, who was known in Yemen and respected by the imam (but distrusted by the *shaykh*s) as the *Egyptian Gazette* had speculated. Tahsin came from southern Albania and was considered to be upright and energetic. Many of the seasoned officers had resigned and left Yemen and the new officers did not know the country as well as their predecessors. The old field marshal (Feyzi) was exasperated and frustrated and in April 1906 he offered his resignation. Short of money and supplies, he was in Ṣan'ā' awaiting the promised *nizam* troops he had requested while his forces were being besieged at 'Amrān, Ḥajjah, and al-Ṭawīlah. He also sought new rapid-firing guns. He mistrusted the special commission of inspection headed by Ferik Ferid and would not cooperate with it.[42] Had Feyzi's resignation been real and acted upon, it would have been an irreparable loss to the seventh army corps, which would have become even worse.[43]

The next important question in the ministers' minds was whether the imam would settle for Ṣa'dah as a sphere of influence or insist on having Ṣan'ā' as well. The Committee of Union and Progress contacted the Sultan of Laḥj to serve as intermediary with the imam, urging conciliation with the new Ottoman government run by the Young Turks on the grounds that it now stood for equality and justice.[44]

Sayyid 'Abdallah ibn Ḥusayn ibn Mutawakkil and Sayyid 'Abdallah ibn Muḥammad al-Sharafi brought letters to the imam (from the Sublime Porte) stating that bloodshed among Muslims must cease and that decrees of the faith must be honoured. But the imam had complaints about 'the troublemakers of Ṣa'dah' who had driven him out of where he had been born and in his view they had to be taught a lesson.

When the council proposed the above reform measures, it was unaware of the imam's determination to exact vengeance, so offered him the administration of Ṣa'dah, which he had not had since his father's death in 1904. The father's sphere of authority over the past four to five years had been limited to the Shahārah and Qaflat al-'Adhar area. Three months before he died, the old imam had been afflicted with a paralysing stroke of the upper extremities and since Zaydi law said that the imam had to be sound in every limb, a notable of Ṣa'dah, Sayyid Ḥasan al-Qāsimi al-Dhayyāni, claimed the imamate for himself but had no following to back his pretensions. When Ḥamīd al-Dīn died, al-Dhayyāni was able to hold his own at Ṣa'dah against his son Yaḥya. Feyzi supported him with a view to crushing Yaḥya's power; indeed, al-Dhayyāni defeated Yaḥya more than once, capturing a couple of cannons from him.

The question that befuddled the Young Turks now was how to make Yaḥya administrator of Ṣa‘dah. Worse still, the *shaykh*s and tribes in Ḥāshid territory were unlikely to settle for less than full autonomy of the whole mountain area. Moreover, the Ottomans feared that again they were likely to have to face five or six claimants to the imamate, each seeking control over the same area as was the case before Muhtâr Paşa consolidated Ottoman control in the highlands shortly before the Ottomans returned in 1872.

The problem was compounded by the fact that the districts of Ḥarāz, Ḥāshid, Bilād al-Bustān, Ānis, and Ta‘izz never belonged to the forebears of the present imam, even though their chiefs made common cause with him and his father before him to drive out the Turks.

Chamber of Deputies' proposals for a solution

Immediately after the Young Turks' revolution and ousting of Sultan Abdülhamid in 1908, appeals for reform were renewed in the belief that the new administration would be amenable to such improvements. During its February 1909 session, the Istanbul Chamber of Deputies agreed to implement a policy that would empower competent officials to administer Yemen, resolve complaints about revenue collection, provide security, increase Qur'anic schools, and abide by Islamic laws of good administration.[45] The Council of State had already recommended substantially the same at its 3 December 1908 meeting.[46]

The chamber had not counted on Talaat, the new interior minister, being hard-nosed about making concessions or agreeing to the terms of a settlement until the country had been defeated militarily. His proposal for a solution to the chamber failed to receive its approval. He had stated that the government was committed to its committee's principal recommendations to divide Yemen into two provinces, with the imam governing the mountain one and allowing the inhabitants to elect certain officials. Even if agreed, the plan could not be implemented now that the ‘Asīris had risen in rebellion.

Talaat favours a hard line

An editorial of 7 August 1909 in the leading newspaper *Sabah* proposed turning the highlands over to the imam to administer and leaving the Tihāmah (coastal area) to the Ottomans.[47] This would control tribal turmoil resulting from poverty and offer highlanders a better life without having to resort to banditry to survive. The practice of having to exchange the Yemeni *riyal* for Indian *rupees* at a heavy discount to pay for goods irked the merchants, who appealed to the government to allow the *riyal* to serve as legitimate currency for commercial dealings and relieve the merchants of heavy duties.[48]

The chamber had authorized a commission to investigate the central government's plan for Yemen. It suggested that building a railroad (75-centimetre gauge) would be much cheaper than constantly dispatching troops to control Yemen. In a subsequent issue of 21 August, the editor accused Interior Minister Talaat of stalling when he asked for a delay of three months until the next session was held before approving a list of commissioners the chamber had proposed to negotiate with the imam. He still adhered to his motto of 'first force, then supremacy', without consideration for the peace of the inhabitants.

In a lead editorial in *Tasviri Efkâr*, the editor Abu al-Ḍiyā argued that force and treachery would not make the people of Yemen and 'Asīr obey government directives. He reviewed acts of governors going back to Redif Paşa, whom he accused of robbing people of their wealth and killing the 'Asīri chief Muḥammad 'Ā'iḍ after granting him security, a principal cause of rebellion. The Arab bedouin temperament would not tolerate bad administration and lack of justice, he argued.

> We gave assurances 38 years earlier (1873) of a new era of Muslim brotherhood, then a *vali* here and a commandant there negated such assurances by oppressive acts, ignoring legitimate complaints of far off provinces like Yemen and 'Asīr. We have only a few provinces left that are Muslim; we cannot afford to lose them. Several hundred thousand troops might keep them in line for a while, but then what?

Citing a reporter of the newspaper *Tanin*, Abu al-Ḍiyā continued: 'we have always maltreated Yemen and today it has turned into an Ottoman cemetery. We have among us those who preach unity and brotherhood but do not get at the root of problems; insisting on all speaking one language [Turkish] will not do, nor will the appeal to Islam as a binding force under such circumstances.'[49]

Talaat's notion of *ta'dīb* (teaching a lesson) would not work; it would only backfire. To what kind of *ittihad-i Osmani* (Ottoman unity) was it conducive? Local chiefs were not against the government; they only wanted their privileges safeguarded. Without decent structuring one could not improve the administration or lot of the Yemenis. Force would not do it. Social justice would. The spirit of the constitution was supposedly anchored in justice. That is what they needed to apply.

Unfortunately, the cabinet endorsed Talaat's wish to subdue the Yemenis by force before implementing changes. The inhabitants, he argued, must feel the weight of the government. As a demonstration of force, two gunboats and two cruisers were to be dispatched to the Yemeni coast, and two more vessels were ordered to transport nine additional battalions of troops to Yemen.

The coast was too long to put a stop to gun smuggling and, as one observer said, it was questionable whether local chiefs could be relied on as administrative officials. Both Wahhābis and Shāmis (inhabitants of 'Asīr and the Tihāmah) would resist the imam's administration were he to be appointed over the whole land. Three administrative heads with an Ottoman administrator supervising and directing them might be a better solution. 'It is a known fact,' the editorial in *Sabah* continued, 'that injustice is behind resistance to the present administration.'

The delegation the imam sent to Istanbul to discuss peace terms was well received by the president of the Chamber of Deputies. The *vali* of Jiddah authorized the dispatch of a representative to Hodeida to discuss terms.[50] One of the imam's delegates, 'Abdallah, informed its members that 'the Imam does not seek the *vali*ship of Yemen and will not accept it if offered to him.'[51]

Facts on the ground lent no credence to the efficacy of Talaat's show of force. On the other hand, Idris's position had been clarified when he vehemently opposed the Tanzimat laws, which he considered un-Islamic. Talaat was correct in assuming that the revolt would have to be suppressed by force before any reforms could be introduced. He supported the idea of organizing a cavalry unit to patrol the coast with recruits from among the inhabitants to police the area. This conformed to the policy introduced after the proclamation of the constitution in Istanbul of reforming the police force in the Balkans and elsewhere, but it had not been applied to Yemen.[52]

For a brief period after a major force of ten battalions (principally from Tripolitania) landed at Hodeida and four warships arrived with six more promised for the following year, the rebellion quietened and, it is alleged, Idris sent word to Istanbul that he was loyal to the Ottoman state. Talaat, however, disagreed with members of the chamber that

Idris would submit to central authority if administrative reforms were introduced and he were given some formal authority over 'Asīr.

Talaat opted to suppress both Idris and Imam Yaḥya by force before sending a high functionary to determine the type of government suitable for Yemen. The Ottoman press took exception to Talaat's strategy and called attention to the real danger the two leaders posed in combining efforts to combat the Ottomans. Still, nine battalions from the first and fifth regiments were dispatched under Izzet Paşa to Yemen.[53]

In chasing 'Asīri rebels, an Ottoman contingent was ambushed in Ṣabyā and 450 were killed. They had been able to intercept only two *sunbūqs* bearing arms to 'Asīris. It was rumoured that Idris, 'the false Mahdi', had fled to Massawa for protection, which was untrue; but of the tribes inhabiting the coast only a few of the Banu Murr and Banu Marwān offered their allegiance.[54]

In an article entitled 'Defiance in Yemen', Dr Ismail Ibrahim attributed the uprising to neglect, abuse, exploitation and hardship, the likes of which had not been experienced in other provinces like Syria, Anatolia and Mesopotamia. He criticized the government for sending incompetent abusive officials and for periodically massacring the inhabitants when they resisted, as well as for devastating rich productive lands through neglect. He asked 'why the uprisings?' and answered by describing Yemenis as a proud people with a bedouin mentality whose leaders had to earn their loyalty by hard work. Yemen, he argued, had been in a state of rebellion 38 years earlier and had complained to the Ottoman government of the then imam's misrule. Redif Paşa had been sent to 'Asīr with an army and he tore down towers and fortresses. Ahmed Muhtâr followed him and left good order behind. He then decided to put an end to direct rule by the imam in the interests of security. Poor rule had ensued since Osman Paşa, who is still remembered for his just and good administration, governed. The inhabitants eventually acquired firearms, but the government failed to cultivate imams and, through them, their loyal followers. Instead, they incited bedouin chiefs against them; the former were ill mannered; the latter were cultured, strong leaders for resistance, and fearless in facing the armies sent against them.[55]

The causes of rebellion, according to Ibrahim, were due to:

- the imam being unable to collect his share of *zakah* taxes once a year and the Shāfi'i tribal chiefs seeking to make personal gains by threatening to revolt even if in past years they had professed loyalty to the local government;

- the abundance of modern weapons, including even Vitelli guns, besides all sorts of swords and daggers, with weapons flowing in via Djibouti and Massawa. Pirates waylaid traffic around Ṣūr al-Waḥlah and Ṣubayḥah, robbing and killing. They smuggled in Martini and Winchester rifles, as well as Remingtons and Mausers; with more than 300,000 new weapons, there were plenty of Manlichers and Mausers to go around. Eagerness for new weapons had encouraged Djibouti merchants to provide them secretly and they were sold openly in the bazaars of Midi at Banu Marwān and Wādi Ḥār, Sūq al-Jum'ah, Sūq al-Khamīs, Baw'ān, Ḥajjah, Ḥajūr, Khawlān, Ṣabīḥah, and Sūq al-Ḥarwah. In the Tihāmah, there were various new weapons, including English cavalry Martinis. They were smuggled through Hadramawt and Aden, but mostly by *sunbūq*s. With such weapons tribes could match the Ottoman soldiers' firepower;[56]
- officials and soldiers were often incompetent and lacked manners; they exploited subjects, most of whom were poor and had little to live on. They antagonized the *shaykh*s they could not control, hence defiance and resistance mounted. Tribal heads levied taxes as they saw fit and divided them among themselves; officials could not solve the problem and the income of the state was dwindling because of their inability to collect their share of the taxes. Chiefs were not afraid to use weapons against government agents; and
- the government had been indifferent; in 40 years there had been no beneficial acts on its part; local commerce was drastically reduced; even coffee planting and harvesting were ignored.

So Aden thrived while Yemen suffered. The people were treated like milch cows, yet were obliged to pay taxes. There was no justice in the local courts. Foreign relations also played a part. With nine different border points at their disposal, the English, who were forever inciting tribes to defiance, sought to divert trade to Aden for export, channelling coffee to Europe and manufactured cloth, spirits and other goods to Yemen's highland via Aden.

Five years earlier, Aptullah, the deputy governor at Hodeida, had submitted a memorandum on the inadequacy of its port for ships and on the consequential losses this implied in commerce and customs duties. Accident insurance claims were mounting, with ships carrying coffee being turned back or diverted to Aden, when only a few years' earlier 120,000 sacks had been shipped from Hodeida. The English were even thinking of building a railroad from Shaykh Sa'īd, opposite Perim, to al-Ḍāli' and Aden to facilitate the transport of commercial merchandise and siphon off goods from Yemen. Hodeida's commerce was gradually being smothered and Aden's increasing commensurately.

To stem the tide, a good port and modern docking facilities were needed.[57] Shipping lines, like the Austrian Lloyd, were eager to use the facilities. Increased and improved commerce would expand the potential of the Tihāmah. As stated in Aptullah's report, there was a need to deepen the port to handle bigger ships, whereupon 800,000 *lira*s in revenue from coffee could then be assured Yemen; also grain could be cultivated to increase revenue.

Senni's observations

Abdülğani Senni, who had been assigned to Yemen as the *mektupçu*, left a diary of his trip to Hodeida while on his way to Ṣan'ā' to take up his assignment. He noted that Hodeida was inadequate for a port facility. He described the city as humid and exposed to strong winds, which made it difficult for ships to enter, while two hours away to the north of the city, at Jabānah, there was a protected harbour with a suitable climate. He described it as a good location for a city to serve as a seat of local government and a railroad terminal. He would locate a customs house there and an administrative centre with military barracks and a hospital. He suggested that the coast be cleaned up and the inhabitants of Hodeida moved to it. In no time, he argued, they could have a city plan and development along European lines. He promised to inform the *vali* when he reached Ṣan'ā' of his idea and have his proposal forwarded to Istanbul.[58]

Senni found British consuls at Hodeida actively engaged in anti-government activities to increase their influence. Italians, who were also eager to expand their power in Yemen, smuggled tobacco, hashish and drugs into the country; stricter customs officials were needed to stem such trafficking and bureaux to improve the lot of the inhabitants. Foreigners had trading establishments, and even honorary consuls at Hodeida eager to please. The Ottomans needed to win the local support and discourage merchants shipping through foreign establishments by cutting commissions and keeping up with world market prices.

Foreigners were seeking to control local commerce, he argued; hence the need for policy directives to stem this tide. Five to six trading firms in Yemen and Aden had set market prices. Then, 100,000 *riyal*s were needed for a fish basin. Natives wanted payment only in *riyal*s; the pressure thus induced brokers to raise the price, which in turn increased the cost of coffee, sometimes above world market prices. Big commissions were made because Hodeida merchants had to purchase *riyal*s in Aden through agents, which in turn affected the price of imported goods, which could exceed market values.[59] Furthermore, no matter how much coffee was exported, income remained half the cost of gas and cloth, which was harmful to them and of great benefit to foreigners, continued the editorial. They had to substitute *mecidiye* currency for the *riyal* at a premium rate and often with interest.[60] A French exchange company had been charging ten *piastre*s on the exchange of a *riyal* to an Indian *rupee* to pay for goods from India.[61]

There was a need for better control of the Yemeni coast. Hodeida had between 46,000 and 50,000 inhabitants and was the key port of Ṣan'ā', 50 hours upland. It had 50 trading houses, so with improved customs controls it could have been assured an income of nine million *piastre*s, hence the need for more naval activity to stop smugglers, to ensure sea traffic from Basra, Massawa, Jiddah and Suez and to protect it. The *sunbūq*, known as a Muscat boat, was the commonly used ship for transport, but the high winds often made it impossible to dock.

Senni talked to the *mutasarrıf* about the use of steamboats and was told that it would not be difficult to start such a company. A steamboat would earn ten *piastre*s more than a *sunbūq* (60 versus 50) because of its increased seating capacity; moreover, even if an average of eight *sunbūq*s tied up each month at Hodeida, steamboats could earn 900 against 300 for *sunbūq*s, and the cost of a steamboat was no more than 1000 *lira*s. This would be added income to an operation out of Hodeida argued the *mutasarrıf*.[62] Moreover, a journey from Hodeida to Istanbul by steamboat would take no more than seven days.

Luḥayyah was next to Hodeida in importance, located 24 hours north of it. A local *shaykh*, 'Abd al-Wadūd Efendi, controlled the traffic by *sunbūq* to India. There was a need for inspection points in its area, especially the islands opposite it, like Kamarān.

Mocha was third in importance. At that time its imports and exports were much reduced. It had once been the chief centre of trade for Arabia, Africa and Asia. Then, a handful of houses and a few hundred inhabitants were to be found there. There was a time when the coffee of Ta'izz, Ḥujarīyah, Ibb, Qa'ṭabah, al-Ḍāli' and Perim had been exported from Mocha, but transport facilities had deteriorated and pro-British tribes in its neighbourhood had used Mocha for arms smuggling. After Mocha came Jāzān, Midi, Shaykh Sa'īd, Qunfidhah, Hilla, al-Wasīm, and Shaqīq, but only Jāzān and Qunfidhah were important as ports.[63]

The coast needed closer watching to stem the flow of weapons. There were too many pirates and not enough warships to stop them. Six years earlier they had seen the shameful episode with Italy over piracy in the Red Sea. Control at Hodeida had to be strengthened and its governor further empowered. Ten to fifteen fast gunboats armed with Hodgkis cannons were needed to chase pirate boats and inspect British and Italian *sunbūq*s. A ship repair and maintenance facility stocked with necessary equipment and parts was needed on the island of Kamarān.

There was also a general breakdown of the legal process. Cases were heard not in courts but by local *faqīh*s, and Ottoman courts had limited authority to hear and adjudicate. Sharī'ah and commercial courts required revamping. There was a need also to control and guarantee education, to establish schools and bring teachers from Istanbul. 'Yemenis are intelligent,' one observer noted, 'but education is lacking.' They needed a teacher-training school in Ṣan'ā' for primary and secondary education, and Rüşdiye schools as well; the same applied to Ta'izz. Yemenis had to be taught how to improve agriculture; the land was rich and they should develop its full potential. If they were eager to have weapons, then they should have a school to teach them their use. Perhaps they could be recruited later for the army. Yemen's lot was too important to be ignored. 'If we are to command the loyalty of these subjects, then changes must be made, and soon.'[64]

The sultan's Arab advisers were concerned about the potential loss of Yemen and they tried to persuade him to come to terms with the imam. Abu 'l-Huda, a spiritual adviser to Sultan Abdülhamid, had his son lead a mission to Yemen in 1898. In 1901, when the drive was on to oust the Ottomans from Yemen following the siege of Ṣan'ā', a second mission came under Şâkir Paşa. More missions followed the recovery of the city with more ulema involved. A nephew of Sharīf 'Ali of Mecca led one in October 1906, but it yielded only a religious result; another by exiled Yemenis on Rhodes yielded no results. Two generals, Sabet Paşa and Hadi Paşa, accompanied by a number of officials and spiritual leaders from Istanbul, led a noteworthy mission in April 1907, but again without results because all such missions failed to achieve personal contact with the imam.

The third mission visited the whole of the south and selected 48 notables to accompany them to Istanbul. They were all Zaydis, but they had no influence at all with the imam. The only positive result was the establishment of a finance commission in Hodeida under Sabet Paşa. In autumn 1907 a strictly spiritual mission, consisting of ulema and *sharīf*s of Mecca, came to Ṣan'ā' from Hijaz. This too yielded nothing because the elderly *shaykh* who was serving as the go-between died and they returned empty handed.[65]

Campaign for settlement in the Ottoman press

Appalled at the increased commitment of troops and scarcity of funds in what appeared to be a no-win situation, the press increased its clamouring for a peaceful solution. This was evinced in a lengthy article published in *Sadayı Millet* (Echo of the Nation) entitled 'Yemen Ahvalı' (Conditions in Yemen),[66] which stated that despite the troops making a 100 per cent effort, the insurgence could not be put down by military force. It argued for concrete reforms, as recommended in a report by Sayyid 'Ali Maqḥafi Efendi, specifically:

- improve first and foremost the quality of the officials themselves;
- be familiar with Arabic to learn about local conditions at first hand;
- establish technical and vocational schools;
- reform and reorganize the court system;
- levy the *mīri* tax with fairness;
- entrust the collection of taxes to chiefs of tribes, not the police;
- consider the establishment of a railroad between Ṣan'ā'and Ḥajjah;
- establish a telegraph line between Hodeida, Ta'izz and 'Asīr; and
- protect and promote agriculture by abolishing internal customs dues.

The minister of the interior's secretary promised to discuss these suggestions at the next session of the *Mebusan* (Chamber of Deputies). Süleiman Efendi (Bustāni), an Arab deputy and agriculture minister,[67] proposed inviting a few Yemenis to Istanbul and sending some officials to Yemen to discuss plans. During the session of the chamber Ismail Hakkı Beg said that the proposal had been taken up for discussion the year before but that, with the downfall of Sadrazam Hilmi Paşa, the matter had been dropped. Süleiman retorted that they decided to do something the previous year but nothing came of it and he suggested the president of the Chamber of Deputies take up the matter again with the minister of interior (Talaat), who had been stalling.

There was a heated debate in the Chamber of Deputies on 12 February 1910, with the deputy from Ṣan'ā' demanding to know why Talaat had failed to respond to the various recommendations for change in Yemen. Muḥammad Maqḥafi Efendi bluntly stated the position of his country in an animated speech, declaring:

> We want to be part of the Ottoman state; if we cannot have independence, then to live as Ottoman subjects; changes are necessary; we have been neglected and abused and ignored for too long; this is why the revolt is on. Officials sent us are ignorant, negligent, abusive; they do not even mix, as in Hodeida, with local notables. They do not know Arabic, and most do not know Turkish. So Yemen becomes the place for them to get rich and forget the needs of the country. We need a commission of inquiry to investigate and recommend means for improving Yemen. We need roads, rail, better social and moral building facilities, security against marauding tribes, a police force. Soldiers and officers sent [to Yemen] do not know our traditions; those who are in authority do not know Arabic, let alone our customs. This must change.[68]

Under mounting pressure, Talaat acknowledged that he had received the memorial but argued that the time was not right to act on the scheme to reorganize the country's administration, citing tribal attacks on caravans, the uprising in 'Asīr, the threat to Hodeida by Idris, and the capture of 80 posts by insurgents. Talaat had promised that once pacification was complete, he would send a high functionary to determine the type of government suited for the country.[69]

Final negotiations with the imam

By the end of August, negotiations between Izzet and the imam were being conducted in earnest and they finally bore fruit after several months of exchanges. With the Chamber of Deputies' approval the Council of Ministers in Istanbul put together a special committee of high-ranking officials and military officers led by Tevfik Paşa to work out the terms of an agreement. These were relayed to Vali Izzet, even though military encounters between 4000 insurgents and 7000 of the Ottomans' Arab allies had been going on since February 1911. Izzet's persistence and his top military advisers' wise support yielded results. The imam at last decided to settle for a truce rather than continue a no-win battle with the Ottomans. His decision was at the urging of the Egyptian Aziz Paşa, who convinced him that he stood to gain more through a settlement than through an endless battle.[70]

On 11 September 1911, Izzet invited all the principal *shaykh*s of the Yemeni highlands to Ṣan'ā' and lavished expensive gifts on them. The negotiations for a lasting peace went well. The imam had already released 500 Ottoman prisoners, but many of the freed captive officers decided not to return home.

A truce at last

The imam and Izzet, *vali* and commandant of Yemen, concluded the truce on 9 October 1911 at the village of Da'ān and Sultan Mehmet Reşat approved and countersigned it on 2 S 1330/22 January 1912.[71] The terms of the truce were to apply to all the areas the Zaydis inhabited from Ta'izz in the south, 'Amrān and Kawkabān in the north and Ḥarāz to the west.[72] The imam appointed judges, scribes for the district centres and supervisors for *awqāf* and *waṣāya* (bequests) in keeping with the provisions of the truce.

Events requiring the diversion of Ottoman troops at a time when resources were scarce, for example the Italian invasion of Tripolitania that year and the problems brewing in the Balkans that led to the war of 1912, may have hastened the truce. The war with Italy prevented the repatriation of Macedonian troops whose period of service had ended; given the unsettled affair of 'Asīr and because the war had blocked the exit from the Suez Canal, Commandant Izzet was not prepared to dismiss them before replacements could be sent.[73] While the war on Idris had not been terminated, that with the imam had. Imam Yaḥya was henceforth content to exercise the religious authority he sought over the Zaydis under the auspices of the Ottomans, and even the Shāfi'is henceforth tended to look to him for guidance, especially over settling disputes.

Conclusion

The imam had taken an opposite position to Idris, who declared his revolt against the Ottoman state just when the imam was concluding the truce of Da'ān with it, and had captured Abhā, the capital of 'Asīr, though it was recovered later with the Sharīf of Mecca's help.[74] The imam stood by the Ottoman state while Idris continued to oppose it. The truce of Da'ān was the point of departure, for it brought out his loyalty to the Ottoman state. In a letter to Sultan Aḥmad of Laḥj he described the truce as the fruit of his ancestral efforts and expressed his determination to help preserve the greatness of the Ottoman sultan and to offer all his cooperation to defend the unity of Islam and to resist every foreign aggression, including Italy's against Tripolitania.[75]

The imam proved his loyalty by remaining neutral during the First World War, though he moved quickly to consolidate his authority over the entire country after the Turks had evacuated it, having taken possession of the arms and ammunition they left behind and thus negating also the boundary with the Aden protectorate.[76]

What might we conclude from the entire involvement of the Ottomans in the politics of the highlands? It became a prescription for disaster in terms of the huge losses between 1872 and 1911 in men, materials and expenditure. The fault was not entirely their own. Feuding among rival claimants to Zaydi leadership induced the Ottomans to return to the highlands to pacify the land. Ottomans could ill afford to jeopardize the security of this important corner of Arabia, and the southern gateway to Islam's holiest cities, given the increased pressures on the empire from European quarters.

Because the rivalries continued, the good administrative measures introduced in 1872 failed to stabilize the country. Incompetent, selfish officials who were ignorant of the land, its people and culture did little to ameliorate poverty by neglecting the country's most important asset and source of income: agriculture and commerce.

Ministers afraid to admit their failure in administering the affairs of Yemen kept Sultan Abdülhamid in ignorance for far too long, which not only compromised his authority but also magnified the problems confronting the Ottoman state. In retrospect, one might argue that this was the tragedy of both Yemen and the Ottomans.

Ironically, as it was proven in the end, the imam sought autonomy only over the affairs of his Zaydi communicants and not over the whole land. As the final truce indicated, the imam wanted to remain within the Ottoman fold and have the state defend the land against foreign aggression. Had all Zaydi leaders been of one mind on this, the tragic events that engulfed the country for decades might have been avoided.

To be sure, the imam resented the laws of the Ottoman Tanzimat being implemented in his domains, arguing, as he did, and successfully in the end, that only the laws of the Islamic Sharī'ah would be tolerated. In the end, the Ottomans simply conceded what one might construe as reasonable demands. The imam certainly did not seek to undo Ottoman sovereignty in Yemen as Idris endeavoured to do in 'Asīr, once an integral part of Yemen. Once the compromise agreement was concluded, the imam remained loyal to the state until the final demise of the Ottoman Empire and the emergence of Yemen as an independent country in 1920.

Annex A

Sırrı's Proposal to End Instability in Yemen

- Station 2600 cavalry and *başıbozuk*s at strategic locations in mountain region since half of those available at present were servants of various tribes and are not around all the time. There is need to have reserve troops to move around as required since they may have to cover distant area. Hodeida is surrounded by hostile 'Asīri and Yām tribesmen with a record of pouncing on the area.
- Need another 1500 mounted and foot *başıbozuk*s to secure this area and two additional battalions of regulars to keep an eye on the 'Asīris and Yām alone; have now only three altogether; the irregulars can be recruited, if need be, from the blacks of the Tihāmah and distributed among the towers in the mountain; must protect and encourage agriculture in the Tihāmah, often neglected because of hostile tribal raids. Muḥammad 'Alī had 10,000 in the area; today we need up to 20,000 to police the Yemen.
- Badly-needed supplies might be purchased at local auctions; hitherto wheat, barley, rice, beans and meats came from Egypt and Jiddah warehouses, but they have been slow in coming for over a year; supply expenses exceed 11 *yuk.*[1] Some 50,000 *piastres* could be made available from local revenues — which were expected to be good this year — until Jiddah's *defterdar* expedites shipments.
- Fiscal year 1266/1849–50 income was over 11 *yuk*s, over 11 *yuk*s less than 1267s/1850–51; so the expenses of 1265 and 1266 cannot be met fully from local revenue; troops assigned from Hijaz, therefore, will have to be paid from the Hijaz treasury, as only a third can be paid from Yemen's.
- Need Ḥijaz or Egypt's treasury to pay for draft animals — camels, mules — to pull 16 artillery pieces, mountain, light and heavy — and to transport supplies — which can be purchased at auction in

Egypt, Hijaz or across the Red Sea from Yemen. Estimated cost: 200,000 *piastres*.

- To carry out duties and assure the inhabitants, the central government must clarify my duties and responsibilities.[2]

Annex B

The Administrative Reorganization of Yemen in 1872

The new administrative units were arranged as follows by *kaza*, *merkez* and *nahiye* for each *sancak*:

Ṣan‘ā’

Kaza	Merkez	Nahiye
Jabal Ḥarāz	Manākhah	Ṣa‘fān
		Mafḥaq
		‘Urr
‘Amrān	‘Amrān city	Bayt Maqdam
‘Ans		Ḥanurān
		Jahrān
		‘Utmah
Yarīm	Yarīm city	‘Amār

‘Asīr

Kaza	Merkez	Nahiye
Abhā	Manāzir	Hilla
		Sharhān
		Rafīdat al-Yaman
Ṣabyā	Ṣabyā city	Darb wa Shaqīq
		Umm al-Ḥashb
Rijāl al-Ma‘	Batīlah	—
Qunfidhah	Qunfidhah city	Dawghah
Banu Shahr	Talamīn	Bīshah
Ghāmid wa Zahrān	Raghdān	—

Ta‘izz

Kaza	Merkez	Nahiye
Ta‘izz	Ta‘izz city	Dhī Sifal
		Ḥujarīyah
Mocha	Mocha city	Khawr Shaykh Saīd
‘Udayn	‘Udayn city	—
Madīnatayn	Ibb	Makhādir
Qa‘ṭabah	Qa‘ṭabah city	Ḥawāshib

Hodeida

	Hodeida	Hodeida city	‘Abs
			Milḥān
			Ḥafash (Dhayla')
			Bura'
			Bayt al-Faqīh
			Jāzān
			Ḥays
			Zahrah
	Jabal Raymah*	al-Jabīy	Ja‘farīyah
			Kusmah
			al-Salfīyah
	Bājil*	Bājil city	—
	Zabīd*	Zabīd city	Wuṣāb (al-*aḍla*)
			Wuṣāb (al-*asfal*)

* In lieu of creating a new *liva*, these *kaza*s were attached to Hodeida under the new measures introduced following the reconquest.

Annex C

Imperial Directives for Improving the Levying and Collection of Taxes

- The *shaykh* of the tribe and the village head are to receive each year an official list of taxes due;
- levies can be farmed out in part or in whole, on grain, fruit, coffee and tribes; no deviation and no excesses are allowed; troops are to patrol the process and careful records kept;
- on vegetables, fruits, grain, yield must be estimated before amount of levy is fixed;
- levies may be farmed out by auction on cattle, but all precautions should be taken to avert abuse;
- the taxes of every locality must be carefully recorded at every administrative level, from the highest to lowest beginning with the fiscal year 1314 H/1899;
- administrative councils are to appoint assessors to make correct estimates of extraordinary levies to be collected and mayors of villages and other collecting agents to receive a maximum of 5 per cent in fees;
- the 1308/1892 order enjoining the protection of inhabitants against unfair practices is still valid and reconfirmed;
- no more abuses by *shaykh*s to be tolerated; the Maliye (Treasury) supervisor to enforce preventive measures;
- each *kaza* centre to receive a copy of instructions in Arabic, together with a copy of the record;
- the commission has authority to revise, if need be, taxation levies depending on the crop yield;
- each village *shaykh* to decide on and guarantee a fair *bedel* for a three-to-five year cycle;
- if the first two years appear too highly set, then adjustments should be made;

- taxes from non-Muslims to be recorded in separate registers;
- fees paid out to be carefully recorded;
- registers to be verified before being handed to appropriate officials.[1]

Annex D

Ibn Nuh's Report to the Sultan[1]

- When Feyzi was commandant, he sent the 28th brigade to the district of Ḥajūr, but it was defeated by the insurgents who captured its rifles and cannons. Replaced by Aptullah Paşa, he ordered six *redif* battalions against them and they too fared badly, losing rifles and cannons, and a number of soldiers were martyred.
- Rebels from Shāhil joined those at Ḥajūr posing a formidable force to overcome, even when 12 battalions were mobilized against their strongholds. The troops managed to overrun some of these, but at a heavy cost. The only workable solution in the long run was some political accommodation with them.
- Chiefs of the insurgents offered to resume obedience but on condition reforms were introduced. Aptullah proceeded to Ṣan'ā' where a meeting of military and administrative officials was held, revealing the extent of the corruption complained of. He commissioned Colonel Yusuf Beg to go to Ḥajūr and assure the chiefs that changes would be made.
- When Feyzi served as commandant, Yusuf Beg was dispatched to the area to establish a number of guardhouses; they too did not fare well given their vulnerability to attack, especially the one at Shāhil, which is presently under siege.
- As difficult as it is to storm the heights where insurgents are fortified, they must be overtaken and controlled before any terms can be reached with the rebels of the area, who have captured cannons and over a thousand rifles in previous encounters with the troops, and which must be retrieved.
- The Maḥābishah area must not be abandoned; once the inhabitants of Jill and Shāhil are brought under control and *redif* are stationed in the area — as the climate is suitable — and their expenses are met, then 300 regulars under my command could head for al-Sūdah.
- Unwise strategy and policy pursued by the commandant, in defiance of imperial orders to be fair and just in dealing with inhabitants, induced more inhabitants of the area to join the rebels, and to his being caught between two fires: Ḥajūr and Sūdah; and forced him to retreat towards Qiflah, the only route of escape after he abandoned weapons and supplies.

- The commandant sent numerous telegrams distorting the facts, which allowed the rebels to gain control of the region. Yusuf Beg led two battalions of regulars to the area seeking to appease the rebels who control fully the area, while I established myself in the *kaymakamlik* of Ḥajjah.
- With two more battalions of regulars Yusuf should be able to mitigate the influence of rebels at Ḥajūr. He is instructed to communicate by telegram the facts directly to the *seraskeriyet* and the imperial council.
- Once the rebels surrender their weapons, order can be restored; troops would have to receive more than the four-day supply they have now if their safety is to be assured and not forced to retreat.
- Careful execution of imperial directives to implement fair measures can help deflect the appeal of rebels, who are increasing their following; also one cannot conceal the reality of the situation from the imperial presence; not enough troops can be mustered to continue the military operation against them; moreover, unusual amounts of supplies would be constantly required to do so. To maintain troops for keeping order in the area requires accommodation with the insurgents and their leaders.
- As a result of reforms introduced in Ḥajūr, four of the Banī Jill and Shāhil inhabitants asked for forgiveness and they resumed their loyalty to the sultan. Some 500 to 600 rifles were surrendered in the area; over 200 were collected from the Jabal Bura' region, and several hundred from the Hodeida area, all of which proves that with the regaining of the confidence of the inhabitants, fewer troops would be required to patrol the areas of rebellion.
- The last three items dealt with the need to replace certain officers who violated the imperial orders and also the firming up of appointments to ensure against malfeasance on the part of army officers who had brutalized the inhabitants in the ongoing struggle to regain control.

Annex E

Two Messages Articulating South Arabian Positions

The first document reads as follows.

Article I: As customarily observed by kings, if one takes possession of the centre of a land, all the lands attached to it become the possession of the one who takes it;

Article II: Centres of the Arabian Peninsula consist of Ṣan'ā', Mecca, Baghdad, Damascus and Egypt, which became the possession of the imperial state [Ottoman];

Article III: After taking possession of these centres, the imperial government granted the chiefs of the tribes *berat*s over their lands;

Article IV: If any foreign state encroaches upon lands under [administrative control of] the tribal chief, it is its responsibility to inform the nature of this encroachment so it can be on the alert;

Article V: If it becomes known that interference constitutes encroachment, warning is issued to cease such interference, which is harmful to governing, in keeping with commonly observed rules;

Article VI: Every country should clearly demarcate the boundaries of its territories as a warning to other countries;

Article VII: Should a ruler grant a piece of its territory to another, its boundaries must be clearly marked to avoid harmful encroachments and disputes;

Article VIII: Should the imperial government overlook at this time the encroachment of foreigners on its territories, most of the coastal districts of Arabia will pass under their control and great harm will befall the Muslims of the Arabian peninsula, and particularly the two sanctuaries of Mecca and Medina which are in their proximity;

Article IX: Proof thereof: when France took possession from certain Arabian chiefs of land near Bāb al-Mandab [Shaykh Sa‘īd] for a certain amount of money and erected buildings thereon, the imperial government declared the sale of lands belonging to it as illegal, whereupon France immediately withdrew and left the buildings standing until today; also when it permitted Egypt to take possession of African territories, allowing it to control its ports and lands up to Ra's Hafūn (*sic*) in the face of heavy encroachment by foreigners who made monthly grants to certain chiefs, no interference by the imperial state ensued, such lands being still under Ottoman sovereignty;

Article X: As concerns Shiḥr and Mukalla, both of which are ports of Hadramawt, when the ‘Alawite *sayyid*s complained about their two chiefs to Hasib Paşa, *vali* of Hijaz and to the Sharīf Muḥammad Ibn ‘Awn, in the days of the late Sultan Abdülmecid Khan (1839–61), he prepared two armoured ships, but this took place when the sea was tempestuous; they endured great hardship; only a few soldiers landed and a skirmish took place but they were unable to anchor in the port, so they returned. Later, in the time of the late Sultan Abdülaziz (1861–76), Hasīb sent a *buyrultu* and a *nişan* to the Emir of Hadramawt. When he had received the *buyrultu* and *nişan*, the Emir of Hadramawt descended and captured Shiḥr by force from the chief who had opposed the imperial state [*al-dawlah al-‘āliyah*]. He then sought to capture the port of Mukalla. But its owner sought the aid of al-Qu‘ayṭi‘, of his own tribe, who came and laid siege to Shiḥr from the side of the sea and wrested it from the Emir of Hadramawt, who did not possess any ships. Al-Qu‘ayṭi‘ has remained until now its governor. The ‘Alawite *sayyid*s complained again to the *vali* of Hijaz and the Emir of Mecca, Aptullah Paşa, who dispatched two officials to that port of Yemen on a warship commanded by Ahmed Beg, but they returned without results. At this point, in the era of the late Abdülaziz, the *sayyid*s sent special individuals to the Sublime Porte, and an *iradé* was issued to seize the two ports. Two ships were appointed to that end during the ‘Asīri invasion of Hodeida. The imperial state ordered the retaking of Yemen by degree. We therefore entreat you to take steps to protect the Arabian Peninsula from the encroachment of foreigners. May God grant you succour and protect you against what harms you. Amen.

* * *

The content of the second message ran as follows.

An important warning to those who say in what way certain foreign countries took possession of the port of Aden. If one says by way of the *dawlah al-'āliyah* [the imperial state] or its ministers, the matter is easy; should one say it was taken by war when there was no war between the imperial state and the usurper of Aden that could decree seizure of a possession of the imperial state when that state did not aggress upon another with which it has a binding relation, or if one should say it was bought from some Arab chiefs, we respond with the fact that Aden has been one of our greatest ports in times past and a base for our soldiers, where also traces of our presence remain until today, such as buildings and cannons, and whose inhabitants and those in the surrounding area are the sons of our soldiers, deriving from the tribes known as 'Abdali and Faḍli who are descendants of Turks, following the capture of the two sanctuaries [Mecca and Medina]. All Muslims acknowledge their adherence [to the Ottoman Empire], as do the tribes and their possessions, including the two sanctuaries, from older days; their folk have defended their environs ever since we took control of its centres, as has been the custom among nations. After that there were no more kings in the Arabian peninsula, only tribal *shaykh*s, our subjects, adherents as of old to the centres, whose sale of our possessions cannot be executed, and foreign states have no right to buy from them. In our safes there are copies of *ferman*s and *buyrultu*s, which we granted to tribal chiefs when we took possession previously. If some usurp the possession of others or lay hands illegally on their lands, that does not remove the rights of our state to them because the chiefs of tribes are still our subjects, albeit killing and usurping from each other, as has been their way, should occasion warnings and punishment. As to the question of the lighthouse that was constructed on an island off Bāb al-Mandab by a certain foreign country, the facts leading to its construction can be found in the archives of the state at Hodeida. The truth can be learned through inquiry from Shaykh ibn 'Ifrīr, an inhabitant of Qishin, one of the ports of Hadramawt, concerning the alleged purchase by a certain foreigner of Socotra from ibn ‘Ifrīr.

The same can apply to the island of Bahrain. The state demands the correspondence, which went on between the foreign state [Great Britain] and Shaykh ‘Abdallah Fayṣal from the latter, to ascertain the veracity of the claim. Shaykh ‘Abdallah is an Arab chieftain, a subject of the imperial Ottoman state. Honoured Mecca is requested to search its archives for correspondence sent there when Muḥammad ‘Alī of Egypt captured Fayṣal [ibn Sa‘īd] who, when at Bahrain, had received the *kharāj* [land tax] of Muscat's ruler, and after which the agent of Muḥammad ‘Alī in Mecca received this tax. Copies of correspondence concerning this matter are preserved in the *Divan* of Egypt the protected [*al-maḥrūsah*]. This must be found lest a foreign state should claim a right of possession of parts of the Arabian peninsula by virtue of purchase from Arabian chieftains who have no right thereto [to sell]. It is feared that if they can prove some, they can then claim the purchase of other lands, and the Arabian Peninsula would thus lapse into private possession of chiefs, which is what the foreigners would like to see, especially since they have noted carefully the lands that had been neglected over the years. They reach out for the parts that are easily accessible to them and thus encourage great corruption in the Arabian Peninsula, may God protect it from their treachery and nip their evil in the bud. Ministers of the state should be careful in responding to any oral or official statement from a foreign state concerning the Arabian Peninsula. Should any obligation be incurred on the part of the Ottoman state to affirm a right to a chieftain without foundation, it is mandatory that the boundaries of the obligation be ascertained. An expert of that particular region, known for his foresight and integrity and respected by the chieftains, should be sent out to ascertain the commitment of each chieftain; if his loyalty is to the Ottoman state, then he should receive confirmation in his possession; if they claim allegiance to no one, then they should receive the rules for protecting their places from foreigners; if anyone claims foreign protection, then the limits of place must be defined in keeping with the current customs among the tribes, not by the rules of foreign states. Killing and plundering goes among them because of prevalent blood feuds and claims to rights that cannot be ended without overwhelming force, which they do not possess, which in turn allows foreigners to claim the right to protect those who have no other means of protection against the evil of rival tribes. This could lead to struggles among states, with each seeking to protect its protégés, which would render it impossible to end them. A careful enquiry into such matters is important. Concentrating on them will protect both possessions and the *ummah*.

A number of treaties and agreements were concluded between the British Resident and neighbouring tribes: a treaty with the Ḥawshabis of Hadramawt on 19 August 1878 and agreement with the Manṣūris on 17 May 1871, another with the Makhdūmis on 17 May 1871, with the ʻAṭafis on 13 May 1871, the Rijāʻis on 17 May 1871, and a treaty with the Sharīf of Mocha on 1 September 1840. Shiḥr, a vast region comprising a million inhabitants, is the country of the ʻAlawi *sayyid*s. It has numerous cities and villages. The majority of merchants of the Ḥaramayn and Yemen are from here. Its largest ports are al-Shiḥr, Mukalla and Ẓafār, which constitutes the end boundary of Hadramawt. The tribes of its cities are of the tribe of the Emir of Hadramawt.

Know this, [namely] that men who rule are of different types: there are the wise, who expend their efforts to bring benefit to their possessions. Should necessity drive one to seek gain out of ambition to enhance his interests, he seeks by tactful means to substitute trickery for use of weapons; should he fail to win by such means, he would then strive to ensure that his enemy does not have access to such an interest. Should this escape him, and another wise person expend his efforts to bring benefit to his possession short of using force and finds difficulty to achieve the desired results, he would abandon this undertaking out of inability to solve political problems. Such is the lot of worldly ambition, and it constitutes another subject.[1]

Annex F

Proposal to Develop the Red Sea Coast

A ten-point plan was proposed to such an end:

- establish civil, land and sea posts to be manned by religious, yet tough and enterprising men;
- open offices to enforce government rights and provide general services at such localities as Hodeida, Qunfidhah, Jiddah and 'Aqabah; such services might include hospitals, water and ice facilities as a favour to the inhabitants from their government;
- establish telegraphic stations to communicate with the various posts and keep officials informed of needs;
- build docking facilities to facilitate entry and departure and construct lighthouses, and plant buoys and kerosene burners to aid in the process;
- place customs officials at all such ports, not only at the major ones as at present;
- construct 500 to 600-ton boats to provision officials and military personnel at such posts, to provide postal service to them, to touch at different ports, to provide also services to merchants, and to keep an eye on smugglers in the area;
- construct blockhouses for troops to be stationed at these coastal posts in order to counter the aggressiveness of the Zarānīq, Banu Marwān, Idrīsis and tribal followers of the Ashrāfis[1] and to ensure the security of the interior;
- establish a commission of military and naval officers headed by a civil official, to meet from time to time in order to coordinate civil, military and naval activities, enforce security and prevent smuggling;
- plant armed informants at ports wherefrom smuggling takes place, from Massawa to Djibouti, who would quickly notify officials on

the other side of the Red Sea of pending smuggling activities and enable patrolling boats to interdict them, and

- patrol the coast by sea.

Annex G

Ships	*Location*[*]	*Area to Watch*
1	Bāb al-Mandab	Perim Island area
1	Bāb al-Mandab	al-Khawkhah
1	Hayish Island	Mocha to Qulayfiqah
1	Hodeida	al-Khawkhah to Ra's Kutayb
1	Kamarān	Hodeida to al-Luḥayyah
1	Midi	Ibn 'Abbās to Jāzān
1	Farasān	Midi to al-Barq
1	Qunfidhah	Shaqīq to Layth
1	Jiddah	Layth to Yunbu'
1	'Aqabah	Yunbu' to 'Aqabah

* Fuel, water and other necessities for the ships were to be provided at the above stations.

Annex H

Yaḥya's Conditions for Concluding a Peace with the Sultan[1]

- decrees issued in Istanbul should conform to the Islamic Sharī'ah;
- the imam to have the right to appoint or depose judges and interpreters of the Sharī'ah;
- the imam to punish traitors and bribers;
- judges and officials [are] to be paid sufficiently to prevent bribery;
- the *waqf*s to be turned over to the imam to promote education;
- the limits of the Sharī'ah to apply to those who commit crimes among Muslims and Israelites, a rule that was set aside by Turkish officials;
- agriculture watered by rainfall should be subject to the *'ushr*; that which is watered by well water, one half the *'ushr*; cattle, sheep and camels to be subject to the rule established by the Sharī'ah; land which produces two to four crops to be subject to half the *'ushr* after expenses are deducted;
- the chiefs to collect taxes under the supervision of the state; and those who collect more than levied, be removed from office and punished by the imam, who would have no authority to receive the imperial levies;
- the tribes of Ḥāshid, Khawlān, al-Ḥaḍā, and Arḥab to be exempted from paying expenses (a stipulation designed to keep them on his side);
- both sides to deliver to each other traitors who seek refuge with them;
- a general pardon be extended so no one can question his past (actions);
- no member of 'Ahl al-Kitāb' (Christians and Jews) should be appointed over Muslims;

- terms of this agreement to apply to Ṣan'ā', Ta'izz and their appendages;
- the government should not interfere in the affairs of 'Āns, nor to oppose the imam in appointing officials of this *kaza,* owing to the poverty of its inhabitants and the paucity of their land's yields, and in order also to avoid confrontation with officials of the government (a measure designed to win them over to his cause); and
- the government to defend this country against foreign aggression.

If these terms are acceptable, argued the imam, then good administration will ensue and conditions will improve, and all causes for outside intervention to spread dissension would end; and the government have to listen to those who do so.

Annex I

Proposed Plans for Reform

I. Kaymakam Rehmi's proposed list to effect reform:

- promote industry and commerce and prevent manipulation by foreigners;
- organize smaller *kaza*s into *sancak*s and have a full map of the land better to pinpoint obligations of tribes for taxation purposes and where to dispatch troops precisely if necessary;
- reorganize *nahiye*s — most of which are too broad and in rebellion — to effect more efficient administrative measures and police adequately;
- place temporarily army officials in charge of the strategic and critical *kaza*s until new organizational measures are put in place;
- rotate the police force every six months and limit vigil to two-hour shifts;
- natives are armed today with more modern weapons, more are killed in feuds; need to take away their arms;
- standardize taxes so extortion can be avoided, hence need to determine taxable items accurately, such as buildings and cattle, and adjust fees accurately to ensure quick and easy collection when levies are made; adjustments can be made on three- to five-year basis and pro rated;
- census is needed for army recruitment purposes; not a popular measure, hence need to have the *shaykh* of each area conduct house by house survey every year and record births and deaths; same procedure should apply to tribes;
- three million or so inhabitants in Yemen, with arms in hand can generate much unrest; disarming them is not easy task; need capable *kaymakam*s assigned to Yemen and transferred every three years;

- because of the number of *sancak*s, if proposals for modification are made and acceptable, then *mutasarrıf*s of these should, like the *kaymakam*s, be men of integrity;
- the Ministry of Education had resolved a few years ago to open a number of primary schools; these should not only be for children of notables and officials but also for those of poor tribesmen;
- new reorganization measures will increase expenditure; to limit these, it is suggested that army officers specializing in medical and engineering tasks be assigned to take care of such needs since the income of the *vilayet* is limited;
- appoint first-rate men from the inhabitants to municipality councils; none at present measure up to the standard; secretaries and directors of correspondence at every administrative level should be equally qualified, and close watch be kept over them; the poor pay up to 1000 *piastre*s in fees to have their case heard in court; it should be free for them;
- justice, criminal and civil courts had failed and were abolished. Sharī'ah courts should be given precise instructions by the *Mufti* to gain confidence of inhabitants, and process of appeal defined in order to prevent the loss of the plaintiff's case by default; and
- people of Yemen are notorious for their 'rascality'; one can not even detail the variety of feuds, rivalries, vengeance killings, aggression on each other's properties, and feuds between towns and tribes. All are subject to arbitrary and tyrannical decisions and reconciliation. The state needs to end this by defining precisely rules of settlement and punishment.

II. Ferid's commission's recommendations:

- changing Ta'izz into a separate *vilayet* to divide the Zaydi from Shāfi'i regions; keep Ṣan'ā' as is;
- collections should be conducted by authority of the councils under the supervision of a police unit accompanying the *shaykh* or *'āqil* heading the team;
- changing 'Asīr's *kaza* into a separate *vilayet,* its income never exceeds five million *piastre*s*;* it is too difficult and takes too long to reach;
- regulating and standardizing Sharī'ah laws and courts for the entire *vilayet*; the complaints submitted to courts are not uniformly acted

upon in the whole of the *vilayet*; often it is customary practices of the tribes that prevail; courts should all operate on one and the same basis, areas in which tribes are observing Jewish laws should be subject to the same regulations;

- distributing taxes fairly and evenly; this would require conducting a census and registering property; the collection of revenue should be done by *shaykh*s or *'uqqāl*s heading the teams and acting under strict authority of the *meclis*es (local councils) and accompanied by police units in order to keep order; and a respectable individual to accompany the on-collection missions; and
- establishing more schools to educate the inhabitants.

III. Council of Ministers' recommendations:

- better control over the armed forces in Yemen through the appointment of competent commanders and increase of expenditures by 20,000 to 30,000 to ensure against their bilking the natives;
- more schools, ports and improvement of the Hodeida–Ṣan'ā' road;
- punish those who defy authority, the troops to have charge of arrests;
- better control over collections of *zakah* and *'ushr* taxes;
- more responsible officials of good character;
- provide better means of communication and transportation;
- better treatment of *sayyid*s and tribal chiefs by offering them gifts and hospitality;
- consult with the *vali* of Hijaz on how to make improvements; and
- invite a delegation of two to Istanbul to discuss whether Mahmud Nedim would make a better *vali* than Feyzi.

IV. Imam's second proposal of 1907:

- the *vali* to stay at Ṣan'ā' with some troops to keep the road to Manākhah open, since the inhabitants of Ḥaymah, Bilād al-Bustān, Qaḍā' 'Ans depend on it for their livelihood and improving their lot, and do not expect to clash with Ottoman troops;
- inhabitants of Radā' and the area around Yarīm in the Qa'ṭabah country and beyond 'are savages', so defiance can be expected from them since they are in the hands of foreigners (English); no discussion will avert this (defiance);

- Ḥusayn, Khawlān, Niḥim, and Ḥāshid leaders whose source of livelihood is known, as are their ways and movements; if they are not tied to the imam, the government might be forced to deal with them harshly and more evil can be anticipated from them. If the imam prevents them from gaining a livelihood outside his administrative jurisdiction, rumours will increase;
- appointing a judge from Istanbul to adjudicate according to the Ḥanafite rite will not do since we are Zaydis and Shāfi'is and we rarely disagree with each other. In situations of misunderstanding, it is better to let the imam be the source of legal reference;
- defining carefully the subject and to whom it applies and by whom, which then can be applied judiciously once quickly revealed to the commoners and jurists;
- issuing an *iradé seniyé* (imperial decree) to cancel all *miri* tax exaction to give the inhabitants a chance to rebuild their homes, their farms and trading establishments and to define the amount to be paid, in instalments to the government, by the imam on behalf of the tribes;
- extend the period of the concession (*imtiyāz*) already granted to the imam so he can undertake constructions desired starting with *'ilmīyah* schools; and
- issuing a decree authorizing adjudication in the whole of Yemen administered directly by officials and specifying the responsibility of the imam according to the Sharī'ah, including punishment; whereby all would be equal and judges be of the ulema of the locality appointed according to their rite, the Shāfi'i for the Shāfi'is and Zaydi for the Zaydis.

V. Chamber of Deputies' recommendations:

- appointing competent and upright officials;
- resolving complaints re collection of revenue according to laws governing the process and preventing mishandling thereof;
- increasing schools and Qur'ānic learning facilities and sending those willing to military and public schools and to teacher training schools in Istanbul;
- assessing the current military force in Yemen and increasing it to the necessary level;
- improving means of control and execution of decrees;

- reviewing judicial cases in Sharī'ah courts, with the exception of those in the coastal area;
- increasing salaries to match the increase of prices and distances;
- dispatching a number of warships to patrol the coast and prevent smuggling;
- detaching the *liwā'* of 'Asīr from the *vilayet* of Yemen and erecting it into a *mutaṣarrıfīyah,* constructing a rail line between Hodeida and Ṣan'ā' to facilitate communications;
- reviewing different plans submitted so far for such a project;
- assigning administrative and legal matters of the Ṣa'dah region to the imam in order to contain the shedding of blood; and
- limiting the term of service for military officials to three years and civil officials to two years, leaving them the choice of extension.

Annex J

Terms of the Truce of Da‘ān

- the imam to select judges of the Zaydis and to inform the administration thereof;
- the headquarters of the court is to be in Ṣan‘ā’;
- a court of appeal to be organized to look into the complaints presented by the imam;
- decisions on punishment to be approved by the *shaykh*s, sent to Istanbul for approval after the judge fails to achieve reconciliation, and a decree of confirmation to be issued within four months;
- imam to have right to point out ill conduct of officials to the *vali*;
- government to have the right to appoint judges for Shāfi‘i and Ḥanafi Yemenis;
- mixed courts to be organized to look into disputes involving Zaydis and others;
- government to appoint supervisors for courts that seek to adjudicate disputes in villages of the countryside to lessen the burden of travelling to the locality of the fixed court;
- Waqfs and bequests to be under the jurisdiction of the imam;
- government to appoint Shāfi‘i and Ḥanafi judges outside mountain region;
- exempting for ten years levying and collecting taxes from the inhabitants of Arḥab and Khawlān to compensate them for their poverty, property losses and their loyalty;
- *mīri* levies to be collected according to provisions of the Sharī‘ah;
- complaints against tax collectors before the courts or government agencies should entail participation with the judges to investigate and pass necessary judgement;
- Zaydis should have the right to offer gifts to the imam, either directly or through *shaykh*s, or judges;
- the imam is obligated to surrender one-tenth of income to the state;

- due to its poverty, the region of ‘Ans, which had suffered heavy devastation due to the fighting waged there, should be exempt from taxes for ten years; and
- the imam is to free hostages held from Ṣan‘ā’ and its environ, ‘Amrān and Ḥarāz.

Notes

Introduction

1. An elitist group claiming descent from the Prophet Muḥammad.
2. For details of this campaign and its results, see Farah 1993.

Chapter 1

1. For a detailed account of this bold undertaking, see Coates 1992: 263–85.
2. For additional information, see Boxhall 1974: 102–15.
3. Bury 1915: 119.
4. Ibid., 24.
5. See dispatch from William Bruce to Henry Salt, Mocha, 16 January 1821 (FO 78/112).
6. The treaty was dated 15 January 1821 and purported to be a 'true copy' of the terms agreed on. See enclosure in Bruce to Salt, 16 January 1821 (FO 78/103).
7. Details in a copy of a memorandum prepared 5 September 1822, enclosure from B. S. Jones (secretary of the India Board) to Joseph Planta, with a copy to Lord Strangford (FO 78/112).
8. Jones to Planta of 5 September 1822 (FO 78/112).
9. B. S. Jones of the India Board to Joseph Planta of 7 September 1822 transmitting a report by Culloch of 6 September (FO 78/112).
10. Jones to Planta of 13 September 1822 (FO 78/112).
11. He wanted 600 crowns, a much larger sum than previously agreed.
12. Copy of the letter from the imam, dated July 1821 (FO 78/112).
13. This was the current appellation of Bhemjee in partnership with Nānjee Shaishkand et al., a company with headquarters in India.
14. See extract from a letter by Warden, secretary to the government of Bombay to the Resident at Mocha, 26 September 1821 (FO 78/109).
15. Dated 10 September 1822 (FO 78/112).
16. See no. 106 from Constantinople of 10 July 1822 (FO 78/109).
17. Title of the Ottoman foreign minister at this time.
18. See Strangford's no. 117 to the Marquis of Londonderry, dated 25 July 1822 from Constantinople (FO 78/109).

19. See no. 120 from Constantinople of 10 August 1822 (FO 78/109).
20. Ibid.
21. See English translation of the Porte's note of 25 July 1822 in Strangford's dispatch no. 117 (FO 78/109).
22. Strangford's dispatch no. 117 of 25 July 1822.
23. See extract of a letter from Consul General Salt to Ambassador Strangford, Alexandria, 16 August 1822, enclosure in Hamilton's dispatch to Canning from Constantinople of 25 September 1822 (FO 78/111).
24. Extract of a letter from Salt to Strangford of 17 August, enclosure no. 2 in Hamilton's dispatch to Canning of 25 October (FO 78/111).
25. Note of 10 September, translated by Chabert, 19 November 1822, no. 19 in Strangford's dispatch to the Foreign Office (with copies to Bombay and Mocha) (FO 78/111).
26. See enclosure, *Secret*, dispatch of 10 September 1822 to the governor in council at Bombay with copies to Strangford and the Resident at Mocha (FO 78/112).
27. B. S. Jones of the India Board to Planta, 2 October 1822 (FO 78/112).
28. See enclosure, copy of report from Culloch to B. S. Jones of 6 September 1822 (FO 78/112).
29. Hamilton to George Canning of 25 October 1822 (FO 78/111).

Chapter 2

1. Recourse was to Hammer-Purgstall 1827–35, vol. 5, p. 302, and vol. 6, p. 376; see Great Britain, Foreign Office (henceforth FO), vol. 88, no. 247, *Abstract of Correspondence* ..., pp. 19–20 (citations of this source hereafter abbreviated FO 881/2147, other Foreign Office references in the same fashion).
2. To do so Sinan had to reconquer Yemen in 1569/70. For details, see Farah 1993.
3. See Cevdet 1309/1891–92, vol. 9, pp. 17–18.
4. *Recueil de Firmans impériaux* ... 1934, no. 497, collection of Sha'bān 1243 (1828).
5. For their geographical distribution, see accompanying map.
6. As'ad Jābir, 'Yemen', Istanbul University Library, Turkish manuscript no. 4250, p. 353.
7. FO 78/135, Henry Salt to Foreign Office, 18 June 1825.
8. Ibid.
9. For background, see Macro 1960: 57–8.
10. See FO 78/227, no. 10, Campbell to Palmerston, 16 April 1833.
11. FO 78/228, no. 63, Campbell to Palmerston, 27 October 1833.
12. FO 78/550, no. 15, Palmerston to Campbell, 2 September 1833.
13. FO 78/550, no. 66, Campbell to Palmerston, 17 November 1833.

14. FO 78/550, no. 70, Campbell to Palmerston, 15 December 1833.
15. Jābir, 'Yemen', 356.
16. It was alleged that from Bombay he went to Baghdad, then back to Egypt, where he was seized and executed; see Jābir, 'Yemen', 356. However, he was very much alive in 1858, having been assigned to Baghdad; see Playfair 1978: 141n.
17. FO 78/257, no. 2, Campbell to Palmerston, 6 January 1835, citing letter of Captain Rose to Campbell, 29 September 1834. Rose was commander of the sloop-of-war *Coote* off Mocha.
18. FO 78/257 citing dispatch of 10 November 1834 to Clot Beg, head of the medical establishment in Egypt, from a French medical man accompanying Aḥmad Paşa.
19. Ibid.
20. For additional details, see FO 78/257, Campbell to Duke of Wellington, 16 February 1835 and, enclosure no. 2, letter from Commander Denton of India government's brig-of-war *Euphrates* to Campbell, 30 January 1835.
21. See FO 78/228, no. 24, Campbell to Palmerston, 24 July 1835, including extract of letter from agent at Jiddah to Campbell, 21 S 1251 (18 June 1835).
22. Ibid.
23. FO 78/228, no. 9, Campbell to Duke of Wellington, 18 April 1835.
24. Jābir, 'Yemen', 358.
25. FO 78/342, no. 15, Campbell to Palmerston, 27 March 1838.
26. See FO 881/2147, p. 3, citing nos 15 and 25, Palmerston to Campbell, 4 August and 8 December 1837.
27. FO 78/320, no. 38, Campbell to Palmerston, 12 July 1837.
28. FO 881/2147, p. 4.
29. See FO 881/2147, citing Bombay government to Court of Directors, 26 September 1837.
30. FO 881/2147, Bombay government to Superintendent of Indian navy, 25 November 1837.
31. FO 78/349, secret dispatch from India Board to governor general of India in Council and to Governor Council at Bombay, 30 May 1838, enclosure no. 1, political department report on the transfer of Aden to Rear Admiral Sir C. Malcolm Kirk, 20 January 1838. See also other enclosure on Haines's negotiations with the sultan and on the terms of the alleged transfer.
32. FO 78/349, Haines to Ibrahim, 3 and 6 February 1838.
33. FO 78/342, no. 15, Campbell to Palmerston, 3 March 1838, enclosing Artin Beg to Boğus Beg, 25 Zilhicce 1253 (22 March 1838).
34. FO 78/342, no. 13, Campbell to Palmerston, 20 March 1838.
35. Ibid.
36. FO 78/342, no. 15, enclosure from Artin to Boğus.

37. FO 881/2147, citing India Board to Haines, 12 December 1838.
38. Ibid.
39. FO 78/373, no. 21, Campbell to Palmerston, 8 April 1838.
40. FO 78/373, no. 21, enclosure from political department to Campbell.
41. Ibid.
42. Ibid.
43. FO 78/373, no. 21, Campbell to Palmerston, enclosing dispatch from S. B. Haines, political agent at Aden, 28 February 1839.
44. FO 881/2147, citing no. 15, Palmerston to Campbell, 12 May 1838.
45. FO 78/373, no. 21, Campbell to Plamerston, enclosing Haines to Ibrahim, 25 February 1839.
46. See FO 881/2147, p. 11, citing communication of India Board, 4 September 1839.
47. See FO 881/2147, citing no. 64, Palmerston to Lord Ponsonby, 11 May 1839.
48. See FO 881/2147, pp. 11–12, citing no. 10, Palmerston to Campbell, 11 May 1839.
49. FO 78/388, Palmerston to India Board, 13 September 1839.
50. Admiralty 1/219, Admiral Maitland to Admiralty, 7 April 1839.
51. FO 78/342, Foreign Office to Campbell, 15 June 1839.
52. See FO 78/375, no. 79, Campbell to Palmerston, 6 October 1839, for Campbell's action on his instructions from London.
53. See FO 881/2147, p. 12, citing no. 26, Colonel Hodges's communication, 22 February 1840, and India Board to Palmerston, 30 April 1840.

Chapter 3

1. The material for this chapter is mainly from the Başbakanlık Arşivi (Prime Minister's Archives) of Turkey and manuscripts housed in the Library of Istanbul University. With Yemen, like Lebanon, posing a special problem for the Ottoman state because of foreign involvement, a special dossier was prepared termed *Mesail Mühimme, Yemen Meselesi*. I have read this thoroughly and the material in this chapter often draws from it, supplemented by *iradé*s of the *Meclis-i Valâ*, *Dahiliye*, and *Ayniyat* embracing *emirname*s and other official imperial decrees. The principal manuscripts relied upon are As'ad Jābir, entitled *Yemen* (TY 5250), a thorough study by an army officer commissioned by Abdülhamid in 1909 as a result of the country's unsettled affairs; and Abdülmümin 'Alī, entitled *Mir'atü-'l Yemen*, also in Istanbul University Library, prepared by Captain 'Alī of the third battalion, 56th regiment, 7th Imperial Army. British sources are listed as utilized, deriving exclusively from the Foreign Office collection at Kew. In addition I have cited from Eric Macro's *Bibliography on Yemen and Notes on Mocha* (1960); and Cevdet's *Tarih* (1309/1891–2).

2. India Board to London, 10 December 1841, cited in FO 881/2147.
3. Report to the Secret Department, no. 66 of 1840, FO 78/3185.
4. See his no. 34 to secretary of Bombay government of 25 May 1848 (FO 78/3185).
5. See his dispatch of mid-Sha'bān (henceforth Ş) 1258/late September 1842, addressed to both the ministers and the sultan. *lef* 13 in *Mesail-i mühimme* (henceforth *Mesail*) 1797.
6. For Ottoman translations of London's and Canning's protests, see *lef* 1 in *Mesail*, 1795, also foreign minister's *tezkeré* to the *sadrazam* of 12 Muḥarram (henceforth M) 1258/23 February 1842 accompanying Canning's demand: *lef* 2 in *Mesail*, 1797.
7. Aşraf Beg was the son of Selim Sâbit, a *hacegan* (department chief) in the imperial chancery (*Divan-i Âli*).
8. See his report to the *Nizaret* (Ministry) of 18 S 1258/31 March 1842, *lef* 1 in *Mesail*, 1796.
9. For details, see viceroy's letter of 3 Rabī' al-Awwal (henceforth Ra) 1258/14 April 1842, in *lef* 1 in *Mesail*, 1796.
10. For approval and the appropriate *Emir ve Ferman* of 23 M 1259/23 February 1843, see *Mesail*, 1797.
11. For Ḥusayn's letter of 3 Jumāda al-Awwal (henceforth Ca) 1258/12 June 1842, see *lef* 5 in *Mesail*, 1797; see also a draft of the order and relevant letters together with the Sublime Porte's *ferman* to the *vali* containing instructions on this and other matters, *lef* 11 in *Mesail*, 1797.
12. For details, see the imperial *mazbata*, *lef* 1 in *Mesail*, 1797, and on Aşraf's encounter with the chief of 'Asīr, his letter to the Porte of 27 Ş 1258/2 November 1842, in *Mesail*, 1797.
13. See 'Uthmān's letter to the sultan of 15 Ş 1258/21 October 1842, *Mesail*, 1797. We have also figures 15 and 18,000 crowns.
14. See *lef* 1, *mazbata* draft, in *Mesail*, 1797.
15. See 'Uthmān's report to the sultan of 15 S 1258/28 March 1842, *lef* 13 in *Mesail*, 1797.
16. See his petition of 8 Ca 1258/17 June 1842, *lef* 10 in *Mesail*, 1797.
17. This was the *Meclis-i Valâ*'s recommendation. See *tezkeré* (p. 10 of 11 M 1259/11 February 1843, *Mesail*, 1797).
18. For text of Cruttenden's seven-point demand, see Ottoman translation dated 3 Ra 1258/14 April 1842, and the Ottoman version, *lef* 7 in *Mesail*, 1797.
19. From Lord Ripon of India Board to Aberdeen, 15 November 1843, enclosing extract of a letter from Political Agent S. B. Haines of the East India Company to the Secret Committee of 22 September 1843 (FO 78/3185).
20. See his report of 25 October 1842 enclosing a document 'in Arabic' with a Turkish statement from Aşraf forwarded to the Secret Committee (FO 78/3185).

21. Dispatch of 1 November 1842 to Secret Committee, included in Ripon's dispatch of 15 November (FO 78/3185).
22. See Rifat's memorandum to Canning of 26 July 1843 in Canning's no. 162 of 1 August to Aberdeen (FO 78/3185).
23. Aberdeen to the Queen's advocate general, transmitting correspondences from Canning and the India Board, 12 December 1843 (FO 78/3185).
24. Document signed by Hodgson at Doctor's Commons, 15 May 1844 and addressed to Lord Aberdeen in reply to his solicitation of 12 December 1843 (FO 78/3185).
25. See copy of reply from East India House of 21 September 1843 (FO 78/3185).
26. See dispatch no. 76 from Foreign Office, 20 May 1844, together with draft copy of Ripon's to Aberdeen from the India Board of 7 October 1843 in response to Canning's request for clarification of 26 August 1843 (FO 78/3185).
27. See joint *maruz* (petition) submitted by the new *vali*, Râ'if, and Muḥammad Ibn 'Awn, the Emir of Mecca, of 23 Ramaḍān (henceforth N) 1262/16 September 1846, *lef* 3 in *Mesail*, 1800.
28. See letter from Sharīf Muḥammad Râ'if, to the sultan of 19 N 1262/12 September 1846, *lef* 5 in *Mesail*, 1800.
29. Letter of 21 M 1262/21 January 1846 and the *vali*'s response of 23 N 1262/16 September 1846, *lef* 4 in *Mesail*, 1800. The article by Muḥammad Āl Zilfa, (pp. 93ff) discusses the position of the Imam Fayṣal.
30. For additional details, see his *maruz* of 13 N 1262/4 September 1846, *lef* 2 in *Mesail*, 1800.
31. For imperial endorsement of recommendations made, see *tezkeré* of 14 Ra 1262/11 March 1846 and *iradé* of 20 Ra 1262/17 March 1846, *Mesail*, 1801.
32. See report on Ḥusayn Efendi, *katib-i divan*, to the Emir of Mecca of 29 Ş 1262/24 August 1846, *lef* 5 in *Mesail*, 1804.
33. See text of the joint *maruz* from Râ'if and 'Awn to the Sublime Porte of 11 N 1262/2 September 1846, *lef* 5 in *Mesail*, 1804.
34. A subordinate of Fayṣal, of the Rashīds, who was rewarded with the hereditary governorate of Shammar for his support of Fayṣal against the Egyptians.
35. *Tezkeré* and *iradé* for full text, 27 Shawwāl (henceforth L) 1262/19 October 1846, *Mesail*, 1800.
36. See their *mazbata* of 17 L 1262/9 October 1846, *lef* 1 in *Mesail*, 1800.
37. See the account of As'ad Jābir, *Yemen*, 353–4.
38. The *vali* of Jiddah for one was convinced of this possibility. See his two letters to Muḥammad Ibn 'Awn of 9 Ş 1262/4 August 1846, *lefs* 3 and 4 in *Mesail*, 1804.

39. See the *tezkeré* of the *sadrazam* of 15 S 1263/3 February 1847, *Mesail*, 1804.
40. The *emri-i âli* was dated December 1846. Ḥusayn was officially appointed in February 1843. For the *emri*, see *lef* 1 in *iradé* of 16 Dhu 'l-Ḥijjah (henceforth Z) 1262/6 December 1846, *Mesail*, 1802.
41. See Muḥammad 'Alī's letter to the sultan of 15 M 1263/3 January 1847, *lef* 1 in *iradé* of 8 S 1263/26 January 1847, in *Mesail*, 1803.
42. For a transcript of his oral report, see *lef* 2 in *Mesail*, 1803.
43. See his *maruz* of 23 M 1263/3 January 1847, *lef* 4 in *Mesail*, 1803.
44. See his petition to the *sadrazam* of 13 M 1263/1 January 1847, *lef* 5 in *Mesail*, 1803.
45. See draft of proposed letter of reply to the viceroy, *lef* 1 in *iradé* of 2 Ra 1263/18 February 1847, *Mesail*, 1805.
46. See *tezkeré* of 6 S 1263/24 January 1847, *Mesail*, 1803.
47. See his letter to the Porte of 29 Ca 1263/15 May 1847, *lef* 2 in *Mesail*, 1807.
48. Aşraf to the Porte of the same date, *lef* 2 in *Mesail*, 1807.
49. See *maruz* of the *vali* to the *sadrazam* of 23 Jumāda II (henceforth C) 1263/10 June 1847, *lef* 1 in *Mesail*, 1807.
50. See his letter to the Sublime Porte of 27 Ca 1263/3 May 1847, *lef* 4 in *Mesail*, 1807.
51. See his letter to the *sadrazam* of 18 Rajab (henceforth B) 1263/12 July 1847, *lef* 2 in *Mesail*, 1809.
52. He reckoned it had cost him 30 purses per man to subdue them over a decade earlier; on that basis it would take the entire amount of tribute to accomplish the task again. See Murray to Palmerston from Cairo, 1 January 1847 (FO 78/3185).
53. See Murray's no. 17 of 19 January and 13 of 8 March 1847 from Cairo to Palmerston (FO 78/3185).
54. See his dispatch of 30 January 1847 to Murray (FO 78/3185).
55. See the *sadrazam*'s *tezkeré* of 17 Ş 1264/24 January 1848, *Mesail*, 1810.
56. See the imperial *iradé* of 25 S 1264/1 February 1848, *Mesail*, 1810; see also the *sadrazam*'s *tezkeré* of 11 Ra 1264/16 February 1848, *Mesail*, 1812.
57. See the imperial *iradé* of 16 R 1264/22 March 1848, *Mesail*, 1814.
58. See contents of *tezkeré* of 23 R 1264/29 March 1848 and the imperial *iradé* approving them two days later, *Mesail*, 1813.
59. *Maruz* of 2 Ca 1264/6 April 1848 to the Porte, *lef* 7 in *Mesail*, 1816.
60. See *lef* 1 in *Mesail* 1815. Macro (1960: 30), on the other hand, states that Captain Haines had rejected all offers of support from the imam.
61. See his *maruz* of 6 Ca 1264/10 April 1848, *lef* 14 in *Mesail*, 1816.
62. See his letter of 22 S 1264/29 January 1848, *lef* 20 in *Mesail*, 1816.
63. *Lef* 21 in *Mesail*, 1816.

64. Letter of 20 January 1848 (erroneously listed 13 afar of 1263 instead of 1264) to Muḥammad Ibn ʻAwn, *lef* 23 in *Mesail*, 1816.
65. Petitions were addressed to both the *vali* and the ʻShaykh of the honorable Haram', one dated 1 M (9 December) and the other 25 M (2 January) 1264/1847–8, *lefs* 22 and 24 in *Mesail*, 1816.
66. See no. 34, Captain Haines to secretary of Bombay government of 25 May 1848, enclosure in dispatch from India Board to Addington of 27 June 1848 (FO 78/3185).
67. See his letter of 15 Ra 1264/20 February 1848, *lef* 25 in *Mesail*, 1812.
68. ʻAlī, ʻMir'âü 'l-Yemen', 74.
69. See *maruz* of Ferik Mahmud to his superior of 11 Ra 1264/16 February 1848, *lef* 4 in *Mesail*, 1816.
70. See his *tezkeré* of 29 Ca 1264/3 May 1848, *Mesail*, 1815.
71. See *lef* 1 in *Mesail*, 1815.
72. See *maruz* of Aşraf, *memur-i Yemen*, Maḥmūd, *ferik-i nizamiye-i aqtar-i Hicaziye*, Sharif Muḥammad Raif, *vali eyalet-i Jidde*, and Muḥammad Ibn ʻAwn, *emir-i Mekkeyi mükerreme* of 27 Ra 1264/4 March 1848, *lef* 16 in *Mesail*, 1816. See also *lef* 18, a petition by the same parties of the same date asking for the upgrading of troop levels, additional funds, and relaying the concern of the inhabitants of Yemen over their possibly passing under non-Muslim rule.
73. For additional details, see *mazbata* draft of *Meclis*, *lef* 13 in *Mesail*, 1816.
74. See *tezkeré* of 2 Rajab (henceforth B) 1264/4 and 8 June 1848, *Mesail*, 1816.
75. See *iradé* of 14 B 1264/16 June 1848, *Mesail*, 1817.
76. *Iradé* of 21 B 1264/23 June 1848, *Mesail*, 1818.
77. Ibid.
78. *Iradé* of 2 Ş 1264/4 July 1848, *Mesail*, 1820.
79. Râğip (n.d.: 358.) makes this assertion, while a draft letter to the *vali* alleges that the imam was caught defenceless at Mocha and captured by a contingent of ʻAsīris, *lef* 4 in *Mesail*, 1821.
80. See his *maruz* of 7 S 1264/9 July 1848 (presumably to the *sadrazam*), *lef* 2 in *Mesail*, 1821.
81. See an undated Turkish letter addressed to the *vali*, *lef* 4 in *Mesail*, 1821.
82. See his *maruz* to the *sadrazam* of 27 B 1264/29 June 1848, *lef* 1 in *Mesail*, 1821.
83. *Tezkeré* of 18 N 1264/8 August 1848, *Mesail*, 1821.
84. The figure given is 18,000 crowns. For other details, see *tezkeré* of 12 Dhu ʻl-Qaʻdah (henceforth Za) 1264/29 September 1848, *Mesail*, 1822.
85. Hodeida, Mocha, al-Luḥayyah, Jadhān [Jāzān] (ports), Zabīd, Bayt al-Faqīh, Darhaymi, Bājil, Taʻizz, Zuhra, Mukhtārah, Hablaba and Ṣanʻā' (highland towns).

86. See *mazbata* (n.d.), *lef* 1 in *Mesail*, 1822.
87. Captain Haines to secretary of board of government of Bombay, no. 34 of 25 May 1848, enclosure in India Board's communication to Addington of 27 June 1848, FO 78/3185.
88. See joint *maruz* of 'Awn, Râ'if and Ferik Maḥmūd of 7 Ş 1264/9 July 1848, *lef* 1 in *Mesail*, 1824, and also reply to enquiry from the Porte of same date, *lef* 3.
89. See *maruz* of *Muhāfiz* Zayn al-'Ābidīn of 7 Ş 1264/9 July 1848, *lef* 4 in *Mesail*, 1822.
90. See his *maruz* of 11 N 1264/11 August 1848, *lef* 5 in *Mesail*, 1822.
91. *Maruz* of 19 L 1264/19 September 1848, *lef* 2 in *Mesail*, 1824, and *tezkeré* of 25 Za 1264/24 November 1848 and the imperial *iradé* of three days later, *Mesail*, 1824.
92. Jābir, *Yemen*, 360.
93. 'Alī, *Mir'atü-'l Yemen*, 76; Jabir, *Yemen*, 360–1.
94. He was appointed imam in 1246/1830–31 and deposed shortly afterwards; then again in 1262/1845, and now for the third time by Tevfik.
95. 'Alī, *Mir'atü-'l Yemen*, 77.

Chapter 4

1. Sharaf al-Dīn 1382/1963: 266.
2. See 'Arashi 1939: 74–7 for details.
3. Jirāfi 1951: 305.
4. Harris 1893: 99.
5. Wāsi'i 1366/1947: 253.
6. A faction hostile to al-Mutawakkil saw his action as a betrayal so rose and killed him. His son Ghālib laid claim to the imamate, sought vengeance for his father's death and invited the Turks back (al-'Amri 1404/1986: 19–20).
7. Citations by al-'Amri (1404/1986: 23, no. 2) from *Ḥawliyāt* (author unknown), pp. 192–3 and Zabārah 1348/1928: II, 847.
8. Al-'Amri 1404/1986: 24.
9. The authorization came after consultation with *Meclis-i Ahkâm-i Adliye* and the *Meclis-i Valâ* and after being reviewed by the sultan himself. Indeed, Hikmet Arif of the *Valâ* wanted the language checked for exact literary construction by the mufti himself and compared with the Turkish version before final approval. It was important for the language to conform to the Islamic Sharī'ah and the *fiqh* (jurisprudence) and the entire construction done at the *fetvahane* with Turkish terms employed only when no Arabic equivalent existed. The final product was to be distributed to all the *shaykh*s of Arabistan holding official posts in the *kaza*s. Details were to be worked out in consultation with the *maliye* before final approval by the *Valâ*. For relevant documents: *mazbata* of *Meclis-i Ahkâm-i Adliye* of 20 Ca 1267/24 March 1851; *arz tezkeré* dated a week later; the authorizing *iradé* of 29

Ca/3 April 1851 and the *Meclis-i Valâ*'s *maruz* of 23 R 1267/25 February 1851, all in *Meclis-i Valâ iradeler* 6534 (*dahiliye*).

10. Muḥammad 'Alī of Egypt withdrew his forces from Yemen in 1840. He chose Sharīf Ḥusayn of Abu 'Arīsh as governor and the sultan issued an imperial *iradé* appointing him *amir* over all Yemen in recognition of his loyal service (full Arabic text dated 17 B 1264/19 June 1848 in Başbakanlık Arşivi, henceforth not repeated unless documents derive from another source) *iradeler* 15133 (*Dahiliye*) of 23 R 1268/17 February 1852 (*lef* 8). Sharīf Ḥusayn governed with the rank of *paşa* and an iron hand until 1849 when Tevfik Paşa dismissed him. Shortly after returning to Abu 'Arīsh, with the help of rebellious 'Asīris and Yām tribesmen Ḥaydar ousted his brother Ḥusayn (*maruz* of Sabri of 19 Ra 1267/22 January 1851, *lef* 4 in *iradeler*, *Valâ* 6619) who lost his subsistence allowance. He went to Mecca to seek help to regain his post and some redress in keeping with his sultanic appointment (*maruz* of Abdülaziz Ağah, *vali* of Jiddah, of 28 S 1267/4 January 1851, *lef* 4 in *Valâ* 6619). Sabri wrote that Ḥusayn's allowance for his good service was 106,000 *riyal*s, when the income of his district was 120,000, and wanted to know whether he should remain in Mecca or go to Istanbul and wait until the rebels were suppressed, as decreed by military orders and the use of troops (*maruz* of Sabri of 19 Ra 1267/22 January 1851 in *Valâ* 6619). For a brief period following Tevfik's death, 'Abdallah Ibn 'Awn of Mecca governed most of the Tihāmah. He warned 'Alī Ḥamīdah of 'Asīr against pursuing aggression towards Sharīf Ḥusayn, threatening him with full Ottoman wrath if he not desist (Arabic letter from Muḥammad Ibn 'Awn to Shaykh 'Alī Ḥamīdah of 25 S 1267/1 January 1851, *lef* 6 in *Valâ* 6619). In a letter to Vali Sabri, Ḥasan stated he had received one from Muḥammad Ibn 'Awn accusing him of causing trouble on the say of his brother Ḥusayn in Mecca, which he denied (letter from al-Ḥasan ibn Muḥammad ibn 'Alī to Sabri Pasha of 9 Ra 1267/12 January 1851, *lef* 7 in *Valâ* 6619). Ibn 'Awn was not persuaded. He wrote to Sabri warning him against falling for Ḥasan's machinations, praising Ḥusayn for his loyal services and for holding many of the troublemakers in check and safeguarding the ports when his enemies were stirring 'Asiris against him. He suggested that Ḥusayn be allowed to keep Abu 'Arīsh, al-Zahrah and the surrounding areas since they were his ancestral holdings and that he be paid the allowances promised him (full text of Arabic letter dated 25 S 1267/1 January 1851, *lef* 8 in *Valâ* 6619). Only on 23 R 1268/17 February 1852, following a *Meclis-i Hass* approval, did the *dahiliye* authorize an allocation of 500 *kise*s (purses) (each containing 600 *piastre*s at this time) and grant him a monthly allowance of 30,000 *piastre*s and permission to reside in Mecca, formally appointing his brother Ḥaydar as *kaymakam* of Abu 'Arīsh, which Ḥusayn accepted (*lef* 4, *maruz* from Ḥusayn to *Meclis-i Valâ*

of 12 R 1268/ 6 February 1852). But in a subsequent undated petition to the *valâ*, Ḥusayn stated he received 50,000 from the treasury but only eight of the 24 months of subsistence promised, obliging him to face the dilemma of how to support 80 dependents left behind in Abu ʻArīsh (*lef* 9 in *iradeler, dahiliye* 15133), but his tenure was short lived.

11. See his recommendations to the *Meclis-i Valâ Adliye* of 7 L 1267/7 August 1851 (*lef* 9 in *Valâ* 6619). The *Meclis-i Hass* met on 23 Ra 1267/25 February 1851.
12. For a list of distorted observations, see Baldry (1976a: 162–3) who cites, for example, C. Doughty (1888: 4–5), who states that the Turks created a criminal government that long vexed these lands, and Wyman Bury (1915: 18) who alleged that Ottoman officialdom from the *vali* or governor to the most recent recruit to the Arab gendarme had milked the *vilayet* for all it was worth. They did so, he claimed, on behalf of the government and for private ends and blamed the Turks for the lack of agricultural development and absence of public works (Bury 1915: 126–7, 205–6). However, the archival evidence points to the contrary. To the Ottomans such development was the *sine qua non* of sustaining financially its administrative commitment in Yemen. It was largely their inability to stabilize a country so difficult to manage topographically that militated against the progress endorsed officially time and again in Istanbul.
13. *Ferman* dated 17 B 1264/19 June 1848, full Arabic text in *Dahiliye iradeler* 15133.
14. Dated only 1265/1849 from ʻAbdallah al-Manṣūr *inshā Allah* (to Mustafa Sabri). Full Arabic text, *lef* 6 in *Dahiliye iradeler* 13604.
15. *Maruz* of ʻAbdallah ibn Sharaf of 11 R 1267/13 February 1851, *lef* 1 in *iradeler* (*Dahiliye* 14332).
16. The approval came from *Daire Şevreyi Askeriyet* (24 C 1266/8 May 1850) and *Meclis-i Valâ* 21 B 1266/3 June 1850) and the *sadrazam*'s endorsement of 11 N 1266/20 July 1850, *lef* 1 in *iradeler* (*Dahiliye* 12785).
17. This was the *adliye*'s recommendation according to its *mazbata* of 2 N 1266/12 July 1850 (*lef* 5) and the *dahiliye*'s *arz tezkerési* reflecting Serasker Fethi Paşa's judgement of 15 N/25 July and the *sadrazam*'s recommendation to the sultan two days later in *iradeler* (*Dahiliye* 12785). For Sabri's *maruz* (undated), see *lef* 6; for the artillery and ordnance at Jiddah's disposal, see Ahmed Beg's list supplied to Sabri and seen by the *Meclis-i Valâ*, no. 993 of 20 C 1266/4 May 1850 (*lef* 7); for the Müsteşar Efendi's *maruz* of 20 B 1266/2 June 1850 to the *Meclis-i Valâ* (*lef* 2); for the *arz* to *Meclis-i Valâ* encompassing Muhtar Paşa (head of *tophane*) responding with only four howitzers of 29 B/11 June 1850 (*lef* 3, *Dahiliye*) and the *Meclis-i Askeri tophane*'s recommendation to Muhtar of the day before (*lef* 4) and the *vali*'s *mazbata* of 2 N 1266/12 July 1850 (*lef* 5), all in *iradeler* (*Dahiliye* 12785).

18. For relevant documents, see *adliye*'s *mazbata* of 14 Ş 1266/25 June 1850 and the *sadaret*'s endorsement of 23 Ş 1266/5 July 1850; the *vali*'s *arz tezkeréi* of 27 N 1266/8 August 1850 and the *sadrazam*'s approval two days later in *Valâ* 5292 (*maliye*).
19. He died of natural causes in the *nahiye* of 'Ubus on 21 Ra 1267/24 January 1851 according to a report submitted by 24 heads of families of the region who acknowledged that Mehmed Sırrı, the *defterdar* of the *vilayet*, was recognized as successor in accordance with the established laws of the empire. For Arabic text see *lef* 19 in *iradeler* (*Dahiliye* 13820).
20. The *sadrazam*'s recommendation is dated 14 Ca 1267/15 March 1851 and the sultan's approval the next day in *iradeler* (*Dahiliye* 13820).
21. He lists them as Sa'īd ibn Sa'īd and all other head chiefs. *Maruz* to 'Abdallah ibn Sharaf, *kaymakam* of the *sancak* of Mocha, *lef* 6 in *iradeler* (*Dahiliye* 14274).
22. *Maruz* of 'Abdallah ibn Sharaf of 15 Ca 1267/17 March 1851, *lef* 2 in *iradeler* (*Dahiliye* 14332).
23. Joint *maruz* of Sırrı and Sabri of 15 M 1267/20 November 1850, *lef* 3 in *Dahiliye* 13604.
24. For Qaşīm's Arabic petition to 'Abdallah ibn Sharaf, *kaymakam* of Mocha *sancak*, see *lef* 7 of *Dahiliye* 13064, and for Sabri's scepticism, see his *maruz* of 15 M 1267/20 November 1850, *lef* 2 in *iradeler* (*Dahiliye* 13604) with *arz tezkerési* of 20 Ra 1267/20 January 1851 and the authorizing *iradé* of 22 Ra 1267/22 January 1851.
25. *Maruz* of Mustafa Sabri of 15 M 1267/20 November 1850, *lef* 1 in *iradeler* (*Dahiliye* 13604).
26. One battalion regular, 2200 foot and mounted irregular (*başıbozuk*s), 1500 recruits from the Yām and other tribes, and four artillery pieces to be stationed at Zabīd from where the irregulars would be dispersed into the mountain region as needed. *Maruz* of Sabri of 14 M 1267/19 November 1850, in *iradeler* (*Valâ* 6619).
27. *Maruz* to *Meclis-i Valâ* of 7 C 1267/9 April 1851, *lef* 9 in *iradeler* (*Valâ* 6619).
28. The *shaykh* and his gang were defeated while heading for Mocha; 15 were killed or executed, seven went missing and four were wounded; Naci, head of the Ottoman contingent, seized Shaykh Muṭawwa'i, tore down six of his towers and left two in tact to protect the route between Ta'izz and 'Udayn where customs and levies were usually collected. Troops were stationed there to ensure the collection of levies, customs duties, *zakat* and the legal *'ushr* amounting to 2000 *riyal*s above normal income. Sabri wanted to ensure that bandit *shaykh*s, whom he threatened to subdue with his regular troops, would not jeopardize this income. He had the ulema of Zabīd's approval to do so. *Fetva* (in Arabic) signed by Muḥammad al-Mistaḥi of the

Hanafi rite (*lef* 20); *lef* 1, *maruz* of Vali Mustafa Sabri to the *Dahiliye* of 27 S 1267/4 January 1851 in *Dahiliye iradeler* 13820. He needed 12 artillery pieces (three light ones for use on *Hatt-i Yemen* with necessary supplies) four mountain pieces (he already had six); the remainder were to come with the companies (*lef* 4 in 13820). The *vali* of Jiddah responded to his request for 600 foot soldiers, tents, mountain gun, ammunition and other military supplies to put an end to scattered tribal resistance (Abdülaziz Ağah's *maruz* of 13 Ra 1267/16 January 1851, *lef* 6 in *iradeler*, *Dahiliye* 13820). Sabri's replacement, Mehmed Sırrı, promised to subdue rebel chief Abkar in Bayt al-Faqīh *kaza* once he had enough troops, for he was well fortified and Sırrı knew what had happened to the late Tevfik when he underestimated them (*maruz* of 27 Ra 1267/30 January 1851, *lef* 14 in 13820).

29. *iradeler* (*Valâ* 6619) of 11 C 1267/13 April 1851. See also *Maruz* of 27 Ra 1267/29 January 1851, *lef* 15 in 13820.
30. For specific details, see Annex A.
31. *Iradé* of 18 R 1267/20 February 1851, *iradeler* (*Dahiliye* 13708).
32. For full text, see *müsvedde* (draft), *lef* 1 (*Bahriye*) in *Dahiliye* (*iradeler* 13927) with the *arz tezkerési* of 5 C 1267/7 April 1851 and approval to finalize the draft a day later.
33. *Maruz* of Mustafa of 23 Ş 1268/11 July 1852 (*lef* 4) and the *sadrazam*'s recommendation that the *Meclis-i Mahsus* of the *Vükelâ* discuss the matter (*iradé* of 2 Za 1268/18 August 1852) in *iradeler* (*Dahiliye* 15808).
34. See Farah 1993: 1457–72.
35. *Maruz* of Sırrı of 19 N 1268/17 July 1852 (*lef* 2) and the sultan's approval in *iradeler* (*Dahiliye* 15808).
36. Mehmed Sırrı's *maruz* of 11 Ş 1268/2 June 1852, *lef* 2 in 15844.
37. *Mazbata* of 9 C 1268/2 April of 1852 in *iradeler* (*Valâ* 8060 *Teltifat*).
38. Acting on a *mazbata* from the *maliye*, the *Valâ* endorsed the recommendation that Teodor and Serafil undertake the repairs at a cost of 41,000 *piastres* provided guarantees were given. *Arz tezkerési* of 13 R 1268/7 February 1852 and *iradé* of same date in *iradeler* (*Valâ* 7912, *rüsumet*).
39. Arabic petition bearing 15 seals and dated 3 S 1267/8 December 1850 addressed to the *vali* of Jiddah, Mecca and Ethiopia (*sic*), *lef* 13 in *iradeler* (*Dahiliye* 13820).
40. Mehmed Sırrı's *maruz* of 23 Ş 1268/14 June 1852, *lef* 3 in 15844.
41. See the *sadrazam*'s *arz tezkerési* of 14 Za 1268/29 October 1852 and the sultan's authorizing *iradé* of four days later. *Iradeler* (*Dahiliye* 15844).
42. *Arz tezkerési* of 3 Z 1268/18 October 1852 and the authorizing *iradé* of two days later in *iradeler* (*Dahiliye* 15954).
43. Each *erdeb* was equivalent to about five bushels.
44. Mehmed Sırrı's *Maruz* of 11 Ş 1268/2 June 1852, *lef* 1 in *iradeler* (*Dahiliye* 15844).

45. ‘Abdallah’s *maruz* of 21 C 1267/23 April 1851, *lef* 3 in *iradeler* 14274 (*Askeriyet*).
46. ‘Abdallah stated in his *maruz* of 19 C 1267/21 April 1851 that a few days before an *arzuhal* (petition) to the sultan via the *sadaret* stated that Sırrı, then *defterdar*, took charge of Ta‘izz *sancak* temporarily after Sabri’s death and sent troops there; Qaṣīm alleged that he was put in charge as confirmed by petitions from three *shaykhs* of Khawlān and its *ḍuqqāl* (those with legal discretion in controversial matters). He judged it wise to put him in charge because he had been a loyal servant of the Ottoman state and commanded strategic towers. At the moment there were only 800 foot and 200 mounted *başıbozuk*s in the *sancak*, not enough to contain a rebellion, *lef* 1 in *iradeler* (*Dahiliye*) 14274 (*Askeriyet*) of *Gurre* N 1267/30 June 1851.
47. Known also as *aspers*; an *akçe* was a small silver piece worth about one-third of a *para*, which in turn was one-fortieth of a *kuruş*, 100 of which made one Ottoman *lira*.
48. Copy of letter from Sırrı of 15 C 1267/17 April 1851, *lef* 4 in *iradeler* (*Dahiliye*) 14274 (*Askeriyet*).
49. The *sharīf* was in a precarious situation. He was dismissed for political reasons but not for any misdeed on his part. He was authorized to go to Jiddah and wait until instructions arrived from Istanbul to say whether he would be permitted to travel there. The *sadrazam* recommended it and the sultan endorsed the permission for Ḥusayn to come to Istanbul. He was to receive an adjustment of his *maaş*, *iradeler* (*Dahiliye* 13820).
50. Vali Abdülaziz’s *maruz* of 19 Ra 1267/19 January 1851, *lef* 13 in 13820.
51. *Arz tezkerési* and imperial *iradé* of 15 Ca 1267/18 March 1851, *Dahiliye iradeler* 13820.
52. See *arz tezkerési* of 29 M 1268/26 November 1851 in *iradeler* (*Dahiliye* 14781).
53. Items requested from *tophane*: 250 tents; transport for two to three battalions of regular troops to Yemen; surplus ammunition in Jiddah to be sent to Yemen; three joiners, three blacksmiths and three supervisors to refurbish artillery and worn out carriages at Hodeida and Mocha; 50 guns firing new type of tapered bullets; and permission to use local income for repairs needed on Mocha’s fort. From the *seraskeriyet*: distinguished service medals to raise morale of troops; three doctors, ample medical supplies, a surgeon’s box and supervisor for the medical office; technical topography experts to trace locations on the *Hatt-i Yemen*. From the foreign ministry: permission to have mail transported from Suez by India ship company vessels passing through Mocha to London and back. *Irade* of 29 M 1268 quickly endorsed by *Meclis-i Valâ* the next day, *iradeler* (*Dahiliye* 14773).
54. *Lef* 1 (*Askeriyet*), no date or authorship but based on the *vali*’s *maruz* in *iradeler* (*Dahiliye* 14537) of 18 Ca 1267/21 March 1851.

55. Al-ʻAqīli, *Tārīkh al-Mikhlāf al-Sulaymāni*, 1/2, p. 563.
56. *Maruz* of ʻAbdallah ibn Sharaf, *kaymakam* Mocha *sancak*, of 19 C 1267/21 April 1851, *lef* 2 (*Askeriyet*) in *iradeler* (*Dahiliye* 14274).
57. *Maruz* of ʻAbdallah ibn Sharaf of 19 Ca 1267/22 March 1851, *lef* 4 in *iradeler* (*Dahiliye* 14332).
58. *Maruz* of Sırrı, *Vali* of *vilayet* of Yemen of 25 N 1267/25 July 1851, *lef* 5 in *iradeler* (*Dahiliye*) 14537 (*Askeriyet*).
59. For Mustafa Beg's *maruz* to Abdülaziz Ağah of 9 N 1267/9 July 1851, see *lef* 2; for the *vali*'s to the *sadaret*, see *lef* 1 (*Dahiliye*) of 9 Za 1267/7 September 1851, and for the *arz tezkerési* of the *Dahiliye* to the *sadaret* of 23 Z and authorizing *iradé* of 24 Z 1267/9 November 1851 in *iradeler* (*Dahiliye* 14660).
60. His imprisonment was reported by Sırrı on 11 Ş 1268/2 June 1852. The conspiracy is detailed in his *maruz* of 19 N 1268/7 July 1852, *lef* 1 in *iradeler* (*Dahiliye* 15808).
61. The *arz tezkerési* is dated 1 Za 1268/17 August 1852 and the *iradé* of authorization the following day in *Dahiliye* 15808.
62. Details in Mustafa Beg's *maruz* of 11 N 1267/11 July 1851, *lef* 3 in *iradeler* (*Dahiliye* 14660).
63. Translation of Yām *shaykh*'s letter to Sırrı (undated), *lef* 3 *iradé* and *arz tezkerési* in *iradeler* (*Dahiliye* 14485 *Askeriyet*).
64. *Maruz* of 21 B 1267/22 May 1851, *lef* 2 in *iradeler* (*Dahiliye* 14485 *Askeriyet*).
65. *Meclis-i Valâ iradeler* 11801 (*tophane*); promised to him by Ibn ʻAwn when he called upon him in Hodeida; *arz* and *iradé* are dated 29 Ra 1270/1 January 1854.
66. Details in its undated *takrir* (*lef* 2); authorized by its *tezkeré* of 13 S, and finalized by *iradé* a day later. The *mazbata* of the *Meclis-i valâ* of 11 S 1270/4 November 1853 bore 14 seals (*Valâ iradeler* 11543).
67. *Arz* of Mehmed Reşid of 18 M 1270/21 October 1853 to the sultan for authorization. *Dahiliye iradeler* 17675 (*Husūsî*).
68. Correspondence preserved in the Egyptian archives at ʻAbdīn and cited by Abāẓah 1979: 70–1.
69. ʻAbdīn archives, *Defter* 22, Khedive to Kâmil Beg, *kapīkehya*, no. 195, dated October 1865.
70. MAE, *Correspondence politique*, S. Marie au Ministre, no. 212, Jiddah, 24 October 1865.
71. Abāẓah 1979: 75.
72. ʻAqīli 1958: 565.
73. ʻAbdīn archives, *Sijill* 24, no. 1272 dated 11 February 1871.
74. ʻAqīli 1958: 586.
75. Wāsiʻi 1366/1947: 253.

76. 'Arashi 1939: 76.
77. Jirāfi 1951: 96.
78. He mentioned that he had at his disposal 1500 regulars — two battalions, 1000 mounted and some foot and *başıbozuk*s; not enough to pacify the land as instructed. *Maruz* of 21 B 1267/22 May 1852, *lef* 1 in *iradeler* (*Dahiliye*) 14485 (*Askeriyet*). The *sadaret* noted the legitimacy of the request but was uncertain how to respond pending the sultan's decision on the *maaş* request of Sharīf Ḥusayn for himself and family. The sultan deferred authorization until the *vilayet*'s revenues and expenses could be accurately ascertained. The *sadrazam's iradé* is dated 5 Za 1267/2 September 1851, as is the sultan's *Emr ve Firman*. *Iradeler* (*Dahiliye*) 14485 (*Askeriyet*).
79. The *maliye* set the transport expenses for the troops plus round-trip fares of Major Osman Efendi, a War Department official, and two sergeants at 24,865 *piastre*s. Report to the *Dahiliye* ministry for the attention of the *sadaret* and the sultan's endorsement of 12 L 1267/12 August 1851 in *iradeler* (*Dahiliye*) 14463 (*maliye*).
80. A purse containing between 500 (*Rumi*) and 600 *piastre*s (*Misri*) in Ottoman history.
81. Ağah's *maruz* of 23 S 1268/19 December 1851 may be suspect because of the known hostility existing between himself and 'Abdallah, *lef* 2 in *iradeler* (*Dahiliye* 15242). For Hakkı's detailed explanation of disbursements and expenditures per military and civil official in keeping with his mandate to straighten out the financial records of the *eyalet*, see *lef* 4 in *iradeler* (*Dahiliye* 15242).
82. *Maruz* of Sırrı Paşa of 25 B 1267/26 May 1851, *lef* 2 in *iradeler* (*Dahiliye*) 14528 (*Askeriyet*).
83. Recommendation dated 6 Za 1267/3 September 1851 in *Dahiliye iradeler* 14528.
84. *Lef*s 2 and 3: *Maruz* of Sırrı, both of 11 N 1267/11 July 1851 (*Askeriyet*) in 14537.
85. Transliterated from the Ottoman version. For Ghālib's petition to 'Awn of 23 Ra 1268/17 January 1851 (*lef* 2) and the other to the *paşa* of 12 Ra 1268 (*lef* 3) see *iradeler* (*Dahiliye* 16424) of 29 Ra 1269/11 January 1853.
86. The vizier's order for his appointment was dated 23 Z 1268/9 November 1852, *iradeler* (*Dahiliye*) 15997.
87. *Iradeler* (*Dahiliye*) 13820.
88. *Maruz* of the *vali* dated 26 S 1268/232 November 1851 and the *Meclis-i Valâ*'s *mazbata* of 4 Ra 1268/28 December1851, its *arz tezkerési* of 12 Ra/6 February, and the authorizing *iradé* of 14 Ra/8 February 1852 in *iradeler* (*Valâ* 7810 *Askeriyet*).
89. Emin's *maaş* was 15,000 *piastre*s a month; 'Ali's was 4000 plus 1000 in allowances (*lef* 2 in *iradeler Dahiliye* 16943 *maliye*). The *valâ*'s approval of

Emin's recommendation of 1269 (year only given: *lef* 4) of 23 B 1269/2 May 1853 included a stipulation that the position of *defterdar*ship be dissolved and a *müdürlük* position, to be occupied by 'Ali with a salary of 7500 *piastres* and the rank of *hoca*, fourth degree. The sultan approved the *valâ*'s recommendations (*Irade* of 28 N 1269/7 July 1853 in *iradeler Dahiliye* 16943).

90. Breakdown given by Emin in *piastre*s and *para*s (in brackets): Expenses of officials 3,383,280 (0); salary of cavalrymen 2,932,21 (0); foot soldiers of record 149,587 (8); Arab soldiers, as needed 216,204 (0); total sum 997340 *piastre*s (8 *para*s). *Lef* 5 in *iradeler* (*Dahiliye* 16943).
91. *Arz tezkerési* of 8 C 1270/8 March 1854 and *iradé* of the following day authorizing the *maaş* as requested for *kaymakam* and *muḥāfız*. *Lef* 1 *iradeler* (*Valâ* 12171 *Dahiliye*) acting on the *mazbata* of *Meclis-i Valâ* of 29 Ca 1270/17 February 1854.
92. Muḥammad's letter dated 13 Ra 1268/7 February 1852 to Mehmed Sırrı Paşa (*lef* 7) and Ghālib's (*lef* 8) both in *iradeler* (*Dahiliye* 15808).
93. For full text of the Arabic address to Sharīf Muḥammad Ibn 'Awn of 23 Ra 1268/17 January 1852, see *lef* 2 and, for his address to the sultan, see *lef* 3, both in *iradeler* (*Dahiliye* 16424), promised to him by Ibn 'Awn when he called upon him in Hodeida.
94. His elegantly and rhetorically embellished flattering petition to the sultan (Abdülmecid) is dated beginning of B 1268/21 April 1853. *Lef* 6 in *iradeler* (*Dahliye* 15808).
95. *Maruz* of Sırrı of 25 Ra 1268/18 January 1852. *Lef* 3 in *iradeler* (*Dahiliye* 15253).
96. *Maruz* of 23 Ş 1268/14 June 1852. *Lef* 3 in *iradeler* (*Dahiliye* 15808).
97. The *maruz* is signed by al-Ghālib bil-Lāh 'Alī ibn al-Mutawakkil and dated 5 Za 1269/10 August 1853 in *iradeler* (*Valâ* 11664).
98. The *vali*'s *maruz* is dated 5 Za 1269/10 August 1853 as is the imam's to the *vali*; the *valâ*'s *arz* is dated end of S 1270/2 November 1853 and the authorizing *iradé*, 2 Ra 1270/3 December 1853 in *iradeler* (*Valâ* 11664).

Chapter 5

1. For details of the military expedition into the highlands of 'Asīr, see accounts of Ahmed Râşid (colonel member of the *Meclis-i Hass*) entitled *Yemen ve Sana Tarihi* (1291/1875: 15–85); Atif Paşa (retired general of the military high command) *Yemen Tarihi* (1326/1908: 8–60), and Abdülmümin b. 'Ali's 'Miratü 'l-Yemen' (Istanbul Üniversitesi Kitaphanesi, Ibnülemin Kitapları, TY 6129), 87–92.
2. Kâmil 1968: 242.
3. Author of one of the major Ottoman military accounts cited here.
4. Râşid 1291/1875: 86.

5. The *dā'ī* belonged to the Makrami family of the powerful Ismā'īlī Yām tribe, who, with their reputation for ruthless bravery were often recruited by Asiri chiefs, imams and Ottomans alike to serve as mercenaries. An ancestor in the eighteenth century was preaching a reformed version of Ismā'īlism in the vast region extending from Najrān to Ḥaṣa. In 1860, when Muḥsin was imam, he granted them the emirate of Ḥaymah, Ḥarāz and Manākhah, but their tenure was short lived, for they were defeated by Muhtâr Paşa's forces and banished back to their original homeland. A few of the Makārimah remained in Ḥarāz. See Arab Bureau in Cairo, *Handbook of Yemen* (1917: 58–9).
6. Âtif 1326/1908: 63.
7. Âtif (1326/1908: 65) claimed the mountain on which the fort was built was 400–500 metres high and, from its base to the top, the fort measured 80 metres (p. 96). Râşid (1291/1875: 96) claims it was over 1000 metres high.
8. Ibid., 98–9.
9. Âtif 1326/1908: 107.
10. 'Mir'atü 'l-Yemen', 94.
11. Âtif 1326/1908: 108.
12. Impressed by the towering structure of its fort, Major Hamdi Efendi, and Kul Ağası Ismail Efendi formed a commission to enable Âtif to photograph 'Aṭṭārah and offer it to the central government.
13. Commander of the fourth company of the second battalion of the second regiment.
14. Âtif 1326/1908: 73.
15. 'Mir'atü-'l Yemen', 96.
16. Râşid 1291/1875: 115.
17. Âtif 1326/1908: 76.
18. 'Mir'atü-'l Yemen', 98.
19. Âtif 1326/1908: 75.
20. Râşid 1291/1875: 124–5.
21. Âtif 1326/1908: 81. Details given by Râşid 1291/1875: 127–9.
22. Âtif 1326/1908: 82. Râşid (1291/1875: 129–30) lists leaders of the following sub-tribes who sought and were granted quarters in writing: Dhaybān, Nihim, Sharā', Sha'b, Thilith, Ḥazm, Banu Zuhayr, and Arḥab.
23. Râşid 1291/1875: 131.
24. They and the Bakīls are referred to in the same vein but differ in origin, the former claiming descent from Ḥimyar the latter from Qahṭān but maintaining very close relations over generations. The Ḥāshids' territory stretched from north of 'Amrān to the neighbourhood of Ṣa'dah and south to Ḥajjah and al-Maḥwīt. The imams' chief strongholds, like 'Udhr, Madān, Shahārah and Qaflah, are set in the midst of Ḥāshid country, which might explain why they recruited much of their fighting force from both Ḥāshids and Bakīls. Before

the Ottoman conquest, this confederation's chief families ruled almost the whole country from north to south. When Muhtâr Paşa's troops subdued them in 1872, much resentment ensued and their chiefs were bent on regaining direct control of their lands (*Handbook of Yemen*, 60–1).

25. For the difficulties Sinan encountered in reducing Yemen's strongholds, see Farah 1993.
26. Located 12 hours from Ṣan'ā', the mountain on which Kawkabān fort stood was estimated to be 3001 metres high and highly resistant to outside forces. To reach the entrance one had to cross a natural bridge that was 20 metres wide and 15 metres high. Its length was put at two and its width at one kilometre, occupying an area of 18,000 to 20,000 square metres. A wall of 300 to 400 residences surrounded it. It rose almost perpendicularly 400 metres from Shibām to the fort on top of Kawkabān. Lining the ditch surrounding it was a wall of solid stone about half a kilometre long, topped on the natural bridge by a number of towers. For more on its description, see Âtif 1326/1908: 87–9.
27. For details of the siege and strategies used to subdue it, see Râşid 1291/1875: 136–42, Âtif 1326/1908: 95–103.
28. Râşid 1291/1875: 167. Cf. Âtif (1326/1908: 92) for discrepancies of figures given in killed and wounded and more precise detail.
29. Râşid 1291/1875: 207–8.
30. Râşid 1291/1875: 166.
31. Râşid 1291/1875: 178.
32. Âtif (1326/1908: 121) lists the following: Ḥarbi, Yadhal, Ṣabar, Ṭabar, Ḥadd al-Ḥaṣīy, Kitāf, Bura, Akmaḥ, Shaqab, Zulmāt, Jabal Faqīh, Almah, Ḥaṣūrah, Qarīyah, Shaḥr, and Qaṭa'. These must not have been of great significance as most of them do not appear in Akwa' 1404/1984.
33. Reference is to 'Adan Lā'ah in the district of Ḥajjah.
34. Ibid.
35. Author of the work cited here.
36. Râşid 1291/1875: 149.
37. Râşid 1291/1875: 170–1.
38. Râşid 1291/1875: 153.
39. Râşid 1291/1875: 146–7.
40. Âtif 1326/1908: 111.
41. Âtif 1326/1908: 113–14.
42. Râşid 1291/1875: 165.
43. He was the same Feyzi who later rose to command the entire seventh army and assume full governorship of Yemen.
44. Râşid 1291/1875: 172.
45. Râşid 1291/1875: 180; Âtif 1326/1908: 114–15.
46. Âtif 1326/1908: 116; Râşid 1291/1875: 181.

47. Âtif 1326/1908: 117; Râşid 1291/1875: 182–3.
48. For details of sovereign rights and Britain's challenge to them, see Chapter 3 above.
49. He was attached to the *Meclis-i Temyiz* (appeal) of Ṣan'ā', serving as second head, when transferred to the capital's Ministry of Justice. *Iradeler* 1289 (*Meclis-i Mahsus* 56033) of 16 Za /17 January 1873.
50. Wāsi'i 1366/1947: 256–7.
51. Abāẓah 1979: 119.
52. Wāsi'i 1366/1947: 256–7 for a list of others imprisoned or died.
53. Wāsi'i 1366/1947: 259–60.
54. Reference to the district of Shahārah in the north.
55. The presumption is that other arrangements already in place were not tampered with, namely Radā', Dhamār, al-Ṭawīlah, Ḥajjah — all part of the *sancak* of Ṣan'ā'.
56. Râşid 1291/1875: 168.
57. *Iradeler* of 1289 (*Dahiliye* 45735 *taltifat*) of 20 B 1289/23 September 1872.
58. *Iradeler* of 1289 (*Dahiliye* 45702, 3 *lefs*) of 16 B/19 September 1872.
59. *Iradeler* of 1289 (*Dahiliye* 45778) of 18 Ş/21 October 1872.
60. *Iradeler* of 1289 (*Dahiliye* 45172) of 29 S/10 April 1872 responding to *tezkeré âliye* (*dahiliye*) ordering all telegrams sent to the sultan.
61. *Iradeler* of 1289 (*Dahiliye* 45947) of 23 Ş/26 October 1872.
62. *Iradeler* of 1289 (*Tophane* 45935, 3 *lefs*) of 21 L/22 December 1872.
63. *Iradeler* of 1289 (*Teltifat* 45191) of 2 Ra/10 May 1872; other medals authorized by *Irade* 45179 (*Dahiliye*) of 4 Ra/12 May 1872; see also Râşid 1291/1875: 173.
64. Baldry (1976a: 168) claims that the imams relapsed into 'subsidized obscurity' until the general uprising of 1911.
65. For instructions on reforms authorized for 'Asīr, Hodeida, Ṣan'ā' and Ta'izz *sancaks*, see *iradeler* of 1290 (*Dahiliye* 1922) of 7 M/7 March 1873.
66. *Iradeler* of 1290 (*Maliye* 47181) of 2 Za/22 December 1873.
67. Orders for reorganization of the *sancaks* were followed by instructions to appoint necessary officials to each. See *iradeler* of 1290 (*Dahiliye* 1934, 2 *lefs*) of 16 M/16 March 1873.
68. *Iradeler* of 1290 (*Dahiliye* 2027, 2 *lefs*) of 24 L/17 December 1873.
69. *Iradeler* of 1290 (*Dahiliye* 46365) of 1 Ra/29 April 1873.
70. *Iradeler* of 1290 (*Dahiliye* 47117) of 25 L/17 December 1873.
71. For expenses of construction and staffing see *iradeler* of 1290 *Dahiliye* 47099 (*askeriyet*, 6 *lefs*) of 9 L/1 December 1873.
72. *Iradeler* of 1290 (*Dahiliye* 45490) of 14 Ca/20 July 1872 fixing cost as recommended in the Sublime Porte's commission's *mazbata* (*lef* 1).
73. *Iradeler* of 1289 (*Dahiliye* 1757 *telegraf ve posta*) of 7 M/17 March 1872, also *Dahiliye* 1813 (13 B/16 September 1872) authorizes studying

how to extend telegraph lines to the *vilayet* of Yemen and details entailed.

74. 'Mir'atü-'l Yemen', 101–2.
75. For authorization of travel expenses to him and other *vali*s being transferred, see *iradeler* of 1290 (*Dahiliye* 46450) of 17 Ra/25 May 1873. For transfer of Raûf from the *vali*ship of Baghdad to the *vali*ship of Yemen, see *iradeler* of 1290 no. 46362 of 17 Ra 1290/15 May 1873; for his appointment as commandant of police, see no. 46438 of 24 Ra/22 May 1873; for travel expenses, see no. 46450 of 27 Ra/25 May 1873; for salaries of police officers assigned to certain Yemeni *sancak*s, see no. 46683 of 2 C 1290/28 August 1873 (*zaptiye*); for cost of purchasing housing facilities for soldiers assigned to Ṣan'ā', see no. 46835 of 8 B 1290/3 August 1873 (*askeriyet*); quarantine fees for military items dispatched to Yemen were set in no. 46541 of 23 R 1290/23 June 1873; for transfer of Raûf Paşa to Council of State (*Meşveret-i Devlet*), see no. 46438.
76. *Iradeler* of 1289 (*Dahiliye* 1835) of 12 N/13 November 1872 authorizing 'Ali's appointment together with Şibli's to Mosul. Travel expenses for four *kaymakam*s assigned to Yemen and 'Asīr *sancak*s were authorized by *iradeler* (*Şura-yi Devlet* 994) of 9 M 1289/20 March 1872. Sums of money were authorized also for the payment of troops in Yemen and the method of accounting authorized. See also *Şura-yi Devlet* 1079 of 26 B 1289/29 September 1872. The Austrian Lloyd Company was contracted to transport troops; its compensation was authorized in *iradeler* of 1290 (*dahiliye* 47002 *maliye*) of 28 Ş/22 November 1873.
77. He brought back with him the medals that were exchanged and recommendations for change of rank. *Iradeler* of 1289 (*Dahiliye* 45383 *taltifat*) of 28 R/6 July 1872.
78. *Iradeler* of 1289 (*Dahiliye* 45547 *maliye*) of 2 Ca 1289/7 August 1872; for his replacement by Halil Mümtaz, see no. 45572 (*maliye*) of 9 C 1289/14 August 1872; for a special bequest to Halil, see no. 45674 (*maliye*) of 7 B 1289/10 October 1872; for other details, see Âtif 1326/1908: 123.
79. *Iradeler* of 1289 (*Dahiliye* 45771 *maliye*) of 14 Ş/17 October.
80. For orders to send troops and officers, allocate travel expenses, salaries, equipment, uniforms, supplies and cost of transport by sea through the Suez Canal and incidentals relating to military assignments, see *iradeler* of 1289/1872: authorization for 1000 winter uniforms, *Dahiliye* 45415 (*askeriyet*) of 1 Ca/7 July; expenses of troops crossing Suez Canal: no. 45371; dispatch of troops and officers: *iradeler* of 1289/1872 (*Dahiliye* 45390, 25 R/3 July); authorizing ship transport for troops: *iradeler* of 1289/1872 (*Dahiliye* 45471 *bahriye*) of 6 Ca/12 July; sending ships to Yemen and Basra through canal and other expenses: *iradeler* of 1289/1872 (*Dahiliye* 45489 *bahriye*) of 15 Ca/9 July; *mazbata* of the commission arranging passage costs:

iradeler of 1289/1872 (*Dahiliye* 45491 *bahriye*) of 22 Ca/28 July. *Iradeler* of 1289/1872 (*Dahiliye* 45673 *askeriyet*) of 7 B/10 October; sending coal from Ereğli (on Black Sea) to shores of Yemen for fuelling ships stationed there, *iradeler* of 1289/1872 (*Dahiliye* 45802 *bahriye*) of 26 Ş/29 October.

81. According to Âtif (1326/1908: 125) each area's distance in need of patrolling (measured in time) was as follows: Ṣa'dah 230 hours length and 56 hours width with 1600 square kilometres in the middle; Aden 20 hours wide and 60 hours long; with 1200 square hours from Laḥj to Hadramawt; at 50 hours long and wide is Ma'rib, which would have to be occupied to patrol it, given the inclination of the tribes there to mischief and rebellion.
82. For salaries authorized to various officials in Yemen, see *iradeler* of 1290 (*Dahiliye* 46444 *lef*s 1 and 2) of 26 Ra/24 May; for regulations issued to the three *mutasarrifliks*: Ṣan'ā', Hodeida and Ta'izz, see *Dahiliye* 46445 (*lefs* 1, 2 and 3) of 26 Ra/24 May.
83. Aptullah Efendi was chosen for the post attached to the *sancak* of Ṣan'ā'; see *iradeler* of 1290 (*Dahiliye* 47245 *adliye*) of 7 Za/27 December 1873.
84. The authorization for negotiating cost and construction in *iradeler* of 1290 (*Dahiliye* 46455 *askeriyet*) 27 Ra/25 May 1873.
85. Description of the encounter in the newspaper *'Ibret*, issue no. 69 of 10 L 1289/11 December 1872.
86. Telegram to the Seraskeriyet published in *Basiret*, issue no. 807 of 20 L 1289/21 December 1872.
87. Âtif 1326/1908: 130.
88. Âtif 1326/1908: 132.
89. Râşid 1291/1875: 209.
90. Râşid 1291/1875: 210.
91. Yıldız Tasnifi. Sadaret Husûsî Marûzat (henceforth YSHM) 165/74/2.91297 (1879) and YSHM 165.
92. YSHM 165/16/10 Ş 1297 (1879).
93. YSHM 180/31/1 S 1302 (1885) and YSHM 180.
94. YSHM 164/61/21 Ca 1297 (1880).
95. For a list of these, see Râşid 1291/1875: 242–7.
96. Interview with *La Turquie*, 11 (95) of 26 April 1884. His enthusiastic support of Abdülhamid induced the sultan in 1908 to appoint him to a special commission to come up with solutions after the British continued their drive for influence in the south.

Chapter 6

1. Such was the will of the imperial government as stated in an *iradé seniyé* of 23 R 1300/29 February 1883. Bāb-i Āli Evrâk Odası: Dâhiliye Nezaret Gelen Giden (henceforth BEO.NGG) 87/846.
2. Memorandum from Izzet approved by the *Meclis-i Husūsî* of the *sadrazam*

on 21 R 1302/9 February 1885 in Yıldız Tasnîfî. Mütenevi Marûzât (henceforth YMM) 17/16.

3. 'Ali Riza to the *seraskeriyet-hususiye* summarizing report of Feyzi for the attention of the sultan dated 15 L 1303/17 July 1886 in YMM 21/146.
4. Vali Aziz Paşa report of 27 Ş 1304/22 May 1887 and *tezkeré* to the *seraskeriyet* of 18 L 130/11 July 1887 (YMM 21/39).
5. *Mazbata* of the *Şura-yi Devlet* of 10 Ra 1302/28 December 1884. *Iradé* authorizing appointment dated a week later (BEO.NGG 88/961).
6. *Iradé seniyé* issued in accordance with the *mazbata* proposing changes dated 11 Ra 1302/5 January 1885 and the imperial *buyrultu* of seven days later (BEO.NGG 88/951).
7. Memorandum of 22 C 1302/10 April 1885 (BEO.NGG 54/32 *âmadi*).
8. *Iradé* of 27 Ca 1306/29 January 1889 (BEO.NGG 89/1508).
9. Authorization signed by three ministers on 24 Za 1306/22 July 1989 (YMM 45/54).
10. *Iradé seniyé* of 1 Ra 1302/28 December 1884 (BEO.NGG 88/566). Names mentioned — Hasan 'Ali, Mustafa, Ahmed, Ḥusayn, Necip and Sherif — suggest they were from Yemen itself. No reference to appointments being made from Istanbul except as stated above.
11. *Tezkeré* of 4 L 1300/8 August 1883; also communications from the *serasker* 512/3 *lefs*; *muhabere Dahiliye* 193, and *Dahiliye* to the *seraskeriyet* 2 *lefs* (BEO.NGG 87/826).
12. *Iradé seniyé* of 10 B 1302/7 April 1886 (BEO.NGG 88/147).
13. *Iradés* of 7 and 15 B 1302/11 and 19 April 1886 (BEO.NGG 88/147 and 161).
14. *Iradé seniyé* 849 of 15 L 1303/7 July 1886 (BEO.NGG 53/510 *âmadi*).
15. BEO.NGG 89/660.
16. Imperial confirmation on 8 L 1303/10 July 1886 (BEO.NGG 88/420).
17. Dated 1 July 1886 (BEO.NGG 88/410).
18. BEO.NGG 88/451.
19. BEO.NGG 89/83 and 358.
20. He was apparently displeased with the post because as soon as he arrived in Yemen he asked to be transferred out. Petition of 16 R 1305/3 January 1888 (BEO.NGG 89/1263).
21. Dated 24 Ca 1305/8 February 1888 (BEO.NGG 89/1437).
22. *Buyrultu âli* of 22 S 1305/10 October 1887 (BEO.NGG 89/1045).
23. *Buyrultu âli* of 29 L 1305 (BEO.NGG 89/471).
24. *Buyrultu âli* of 12 R 1305/28 December 1887 (BEO.NGG 89/1261).
25. BEO.NGG 89/581.
26. *Buyrultu âli* of 7 R 1304/5 January 1887confirming *iradé seniyé* of 4 R 1304 (BEO.NGG 89/1094).
27. Appointment dated 20 Ş 1305/3 May 1888 (BEO.NGG 89/236).

28. *Buyrultu âli* of 18 Z 1305/26 August 1888 (BEO.NGG 89/653).
29. Some 15 letters attached to *mazbata*, one dispatched to the *dahiliye nezaret* and confirmed 12 April 1888 dispatched to the *Şura-yi Devlet* June 23 (BEO.NGG 89/149).
30. *Buyrultu âli* confirming *tezkeré* submission of 13 M 1306/19 September 1888 (BEO.NGG 89/811).
31. *Tezkeré* of 9 N 1305/20 May 1888 (BEO.NGG 89/295).
32. *Buyrultu âli* of 3 M 1303/12 October 1885 endorsing the appointment (BEO.NGG 88/751).
33. *Iradé seniyé* of 27 Ra 1304/24 December 1886 supported by an imperial order three days later (BEO.NGG 89/1071).
34. Person in charge of tithe collectors.
35. *Iradé* of 29 N 1304 endorsed by *buyrultu* of 4 L 1304/26 June 1887 (BEO. NGG 89/415).
36. *Buyrultu âli* 9 L 1304/2 July 1887 (BEO.NGG 89/442).
37. Dated 1 C 1306/2 February 1889 (BEO.NGG 89/1516).
38. *Tezkeré* dated 6 L 1304/28 June 1887 (BEO.NGG 89/429).
39. *Mazbata* of *Şura-yi Devlet* and endorsement by a *buyrultu âli* of 14 S 1306/20 September 1888 (BEO.NGG 89/971).
40. *Iradé seniyé* of 21 L 1304/14 July 1887 (BEO.NGG 89/495).
41. *Buyrultu âli* of 7 Ra 1305/23 November 1887 (BEO.NGG 89/1111).
42. *Tezkeré* of *Divan-i Muhasebat* with its 19 *lef*s of 28 Ca 1302/13 March 1885 (BEO.NGG 88/9).
43. *Tezkeré* of 16 C 1302 and the imperial *buyrultu* of 22 C 1302/10 April 1885 enclosing the list (BEO.NGG 88/117).
44. Memorandum re situation in Yemen submitted to his government in 1885. Yıldız Esas Evrâkı (henceforth YEE) 239, *kısım* 14, *zarf* 126.
45. Decree of 2 M 1305/20 September 1887 (BEO.NGG 54/364).
46. *Meclis-i Vükelâ Mazbataları* (henceforth MVM). *Defter* 45/20 of 12 Za 1306/10 July 1889.
47. MVM, *defter* 38/8 of 30 N 1305/11 June 1888.
48. YMM, *dosya* 37 *sıra* 73 of 7 C 1307/4 July 1889.
49. *Dahiliye Siyasiye* (henceforth DS) 33/4.
50. *Buyrultu âli* of 1 Ş 1302/14 July 1885 (BEO.NGG 54/116 *âmadi*).
51. *Mazbata* and *buyrultu âli* 894 of 28 Ca 1302/13 February 1885 (BEO.NGG 88/741).
52. Assessment by Austrians in *Neue Freie Presse*, Vienna, 19 January 1887.
53. Feyzi's telegram was dated 27 February 1891 and the *sadrazam*'s no. 7 of 1 March in YIHM 256/110. Similar report in YIHM 256/110 of 28 B 1309.
54. YIHM 67 of 13 B 1319.
55. *Yıldız Tasnifi. Sadâret Resmi Marûzâti Evrâkı* (henceforth YSRM), 124/79 of 5 March 1904.

56. The commission consisted of Marshal Darwiş Paşa, Mehmet Şâkir Paşa (*ferik* of the palace) and Osman Nuri Paşa (division general and former governor of Yemen) according to a report in *La Turquie*, 24 (283) of 7 Ca 1308/18 December 1890. A *mazbata* of the *sadaret* of 30 Z 1308/7 August 1891, which member's of the sultan's commission approved, recommended promoting 'Ali Beg to major for his loyal service and giving a higher salary to Hussein Efendi, both serving in Yemen (in YSHM 256/62).
57. YSHM 252/62 of 15 B 1309.
58. Sadrazam ve Yaver Cevad to *Divan-i Hümayun*, no. 1, *mazbata* of 15 B 1309/15 February 1892 (YSHM 256/62).
59. Instructions of 24 Ra 1300/1 March 1883 (BEO.NGG 87/749).
60. MVM. *Defter* 64/25 of 6 N 1308/ 15 April 1891.
61. MVM. *Defter* 74/92 of 16 L 1310/4 May 1892.
62. MVM. *Defter* 48/55 of 21 Ra 1306/25 November 1888.
63. MVM. *Defter* 48 of 3 Ra 1307/28 October 1889.
64. *Iradé seniyé* approving the *tezkeré* of submission and the accompanying *buyrultu âli* of 20 S 1305/8 October 1887 (BEO.NGG 89/1030).
65. Yıldız Tasnifi, *Sadâret Resmi Marûzâti* (henceforth YSRM) 69/2/3 B 1311 and four enclosures.
66. It was reported that foreign ships were loading very old items at Birkat al-Jamād between Qunfidhah and Hodeida. YT. *Idâret Hususi Maruzat Evrâkı* (henceforth IHME) 251/174 of 28 S 1309.
67. MVM. *Defter* 56/33 of 2 M 1308/18 August 1890.
68. YT.MME, *dosya* 31, *sıra* no. 26 of 26 C 1305/7 July 1888.
69. YT.MME, *dosya* 31, *sıra* no. 51 (two pieces). 10 B 1305/17 June 1885.
70. YT.MME, *dosya* 31, *sıra* 68 (six enclosures) of 24 B 1305.
71. Reported to Istanbul (YT.IHME, 252/56 of 13 Ra 1309).
72. YT.MME, *dosya* 31, *sıra* no. 64 of 22 B 1305/1 August 1888.
73. According to intelligence reports relayed to the Aden Residency, he was one very rich Sayyid Yūsuf al-Rifā'i, who was stationed at Farasān.
74. For relevant correspondence see, 'German–Ottoman complicity to establish a coal depot in the Red Sea', no. 137; telegram of de Bunsen to Salisbury, Constantinople, 22 October 1900, no. 138; de Bunsen to Salisbury (no. 362 *Confidential*), Therapia, 19 October 1900, no. 187; de Bunsen to Lansdowne (no. 420 *Confidential*), Constantinople, 30 November 1900, no. 174; de Bunsen to Lansdowne (no. 399 *Confidential*), Constantinople, 19 November 1900; enclosure in 183 'particulars regarding the acquisition of Farsan by the German government', and no. 210; de Bunsen to Lansdowne, Constantinople, 24 December 1900 with enclosure; extract from the *Levant Herald* of 19 December 1900 (FO 416/4).
75. BEO: Dahiliye Nezareti Giden 88/1125.
76. *Buyrultu âli* of 12 R 1302/29 January 1885.

77. *Tezkeré* and *buyrultu âli* of 32 C 1306/24 February 1889 (BEO: Dahiliye Nezareti Giden 89/1525).
78. Arrest order *(zapt)* 1 of 24 C 1302/12 April 1885 (BEO: Dahiliye Giden 88/715).
79. YT.MME, *dosya* 27, *sıra* no. 98 of 19 Z 1304/17 January 1887.
80. *Iradé* of 9 M 1306/15 September 1888 (Dahiliye Nezareti Giden 89/772).
81. Notification of 11 N 1303/13 June 1886 (Dahiliye Nezareti Giden 88/1040).

Chapter 7

1. At Quṣayr, Egypt in 1829; Perim in 1799 and 1837, but it had no water; Jiddah was unfriendly; Kamarān in 1837, but it was declared useless; then at Socotra in 1829 and 1833, finally occupied in 1835, but it too was declared unsuitable. They put coal in the Maldives in 1833, but it was too reef bound, thus useless; Mukalla in Hadramawt was used for coaling in 1829, but the monsoons put an end to that. Mocha seemed suitable; Americans, Dutch, French and British trading establishments had factories there and it had a good jetty, but the harbour silted up and fell into disuse after 1839. Aden now proved the most suitable of all.
2. From a presentation by E. Macro at the Arabian seminar conference on 14 July 1981 at Cambridge, England.
3. 'Arashi 1939: 176.
4. 'Arashi 1939: 177.
5. 'Arashi 1939: 178.
6. The tribes and their fighting strength: 'Abdali (2000); Faḍli (2000); Ḥawshabi (3000); Sharjabi (4000); Yāfi' (15,000); 'Awlaqi (7000); 'Ud/Budfān (2000); Amir (4000); 'Alawi (600); Dathīn (2000) and Raṣṣās (4000), a substantial reduction of the numbers of fighting men from earlier estimates. See 'Notes on the Political and Military Conditions of Aden', by James Outram in his 12 September 1855 report to Bombay. Aden. R20/A/133, vol. 165.
7. Report by P. Badger from Aden, 21 July 1854.
8. Maria Teresa dollars.
9. The term stood for common property, free to all, before it was discovered to be profitable in supplying the harbour of Aden with sweet water. At this point the Sultan of Laḥj contracted out the supplying of water to a native of Aden and to another who acquired the rights to the wells.
10. The recommendation came from Ottoman Ambassador Musurus to the under-secretary for foreign affairs who relayed it by order of Lord Granville to the under-secretary for India (London, 17 December 1873). The reply from the India Office of 12 January 1874 was negative. See Secret from India Office, no. 20 of 13 February 1874. The Ottomans never accepted Britain's attempts to deny them sovereignty over a part of Yemen they (the British) had wished

to exploit for themselves ever since they had gained control of Aden through the devious tactics of Captain Haines back in the 1820s.

11. India Office, London, no. 102, Goldsmid, secretary to government of Bombay, to Captain S. B. Haines, Bombay Castle, 12 April 1851 (Aden R/20/A1A/96 file 79).
12. These are stated as: (1) murdering a seaman of the *Auckland*, for which the Sultan of Laḥj could give no satisfactory answer, with Captain Haines, in his bullish way, demanding the destruction of Bīr Aḥmad fort in retaliation; (2) wounding sepoy sentries at the barrier gate, December 1850; (3) murdering Captain Milne, March 1851, the murderer taking refuge out of reach with the Faḍli and Haines again recommending the destruction of Bīr Aḥmad fort; (4) attack from Bīr Aḥmad in 1851, aiming to kill Haines but dangerously wounding Lieutenant Delliser of HM 78th Highlanders on the public road instead. Haines retaliated by stopping payment of stipend to the Faḍlis. Report from Aden of 12 September 1855 to the government of India detailing relations with the tribes.
13. No. 1257, Sir Henry Elliot, secretary, to Goldsmid, secretary to the government of Bombay, 21 April 1851.
14. No. 187 of 1851, Malet to Haines.
15. No. 423 of 1851. A. Malet Esquire, chief secretary to the government of Bombay, to Captain S. B. Haines of 3 December 1851 (Secret Department) acknowledging Haines's no. 58 of 15 November 1851. In his no. 425 of 3 December, Malet relays information on the stipend's restoration once the parties named in Haines's no. 55 had been punished.
16. Brigadier Acting Political Resident and Commandant James Outram made the report on 12 September 1855 in R20/A/133, vol. 165.
17. Duke of Argyll of the India Office to Earl of Granville of 9 January 1874, referring to a telegram of 6 January stating that the son was still being held hostage. Copy requesting the release was sent to the chargé at Constantinople (no. 2010) FO, 22 January 1874.
18. Apparently, Sir Bartle Frère was assigned the task of suppressing the slave trade; he argued it would not be possible if the Ottomans were allowed to occupy the coast on the grounds that the 'Turkish flag would be flown by maritime tribes engaged in slave traffic'. A copy of the letter was sent to the government of Bombay, India Office, 28 November 1873, to the under-secretary of state of the Foreign Office (no. 396) to the Earl of Granville.
19. This 'occupation', with Britain's tacit approval, led to the suppression of the tribes and paved the way for them to move in and occupy Aden in 1839.
20. For details of the episode, see Aden 220/A/120, no. 444 of 1854. Colonel James Outram, political Resident at Aden to H. S. Anderson, political secretary to the government of Bombay, 10 August 1854.
21. A1A 643 R/20/17/418, no. 239 (*Secret*) Secretary (Duke of Argyll) India

Office, 28 November 1873 to secretary of government of India, foreign department, FO of 17 November 1873 to under-secretary of state of India Office from secretary of state for foreign affairs, relaying the telegram from Sir H. Elliot of 15 November 1873. Another telegram from him of 16 November states that the Porte did instruct its governor to withdraw.

22. A1A 643 R/20/17/418, no. 396, Therapia, 7 November 1873 to Earl of Granville (reference to Dispatch 388 of 30 October).
23. Subsequent events are detailed in Lord Tenterden's memorandum of November 1873.
24. Foreign Department (*Secret*) from India Office, no. 20 of 13 February 1874, responding to FO London's of 17 December 1873 relaying by order of the Earl of Granville, under-secretary for foreign affairs, copy of a dispatch from the British ambassador in Constantinople with respect to Musurus's proposal to the Porte.
25. Ibid.
26. With the 'Abdalis in June 1839, 11 February 1843, 'Abdali Bond of 20 February 1844, treaty of 7 May 1849, engagement of 16 December 1873 and treaty of 7 February 1882. With the 'Awlaqis in bond of 30 May 1872. With Faḍlis in treaty of June 1839, May 1876, 6 May 1872. With the Ḥawshabis in slave treaty of 17 November 1873. Other treaties and a variety of agreements extended into the 1890s, all of which may be termed infringements of Ottoman sovereignty. For details of these and other treaties, see *Leases and Treaties in Aden* (4/20/A/1108, no. 49).
27. See Annex E.
28. Abāẓah 1979: 141.
29. Harris 1893: 115.
30. Report of Vali Hilmi of 3 October 1899 to chief secretary of sultan's *mabeyn* no. 231 forwarding report dated 1 August 1899 of tobacco official sent secretly to investigate, as well as of police assistant who confirmed rumours in his report dated 26 September 1899 (YMM 194/131, no. 2).
31. Memorandum of Granville submitted by the chargé of the British embassy to the Ottoman foreign ministry whose translation bureau submitted the Ottoman version to the Sublime Porte, dated 7 February 1883 (YMM 212/168, no. 4).
32. John W. Schneider was the last Resident of Aden, 1872–78. The secretary of state for India was the highest authority overseeing the India Office. The India Office in turn supervised the secret committee and other committees constituting the government of India, which in turn administered the Bombay government, to which the Indian navy, the Persian Gulf political agent, the Resident of Aden and other agents assigned to Arabia reported in the first instance.
33. No. 352, Foreign Office, 19 November 1873, to the Earl of Granville in Aden (R/20/A/418).

34. Aden, R/20/A/418, vol. 643 of 1874: *Secret Compilations*, 'Affairs of Yemen', no. 352. Foreign Office of 19 November 1873 to Earl of Granville.
35. Resident at Aden to secretary of India Office of 8 March 1874, referring to reply of 11 March and his again of 18 March.
36. No. 379, Political Department, Bombay Castle, 30 June 1874 in reference to the Resident's no. 114–437 of 9 June 1874.
37. No. 10 of 1874, Government of India, Foreign Department (*Secret*) to the Duke of Argyll, secretary of state for India, Fort Wilhain, 6 February 1874 in Aden R/20/A/418, vol. no. 643 of 1874, *Secret Compilations*: *'Affairs of Yemen'*.
38. The documents cited above derive from the collection entitled Turkey, no. 1 (1874), *Correspondences respecting Turkish proceedings in the neighbourhood of Aden presented to both Houses of Parliament.*
39. Âtif Paşa, 1326/1908: 126.
40. Reference to no. 340 of 6 November 1882 from London to the Ottoman foreign ministry in response to Granville's no. 142 in YMM 212/168, no. 2.
41. *Iradé hususiye* 129/41/21 L 1322 (*defter kısmındadir*, no. 12775). See also 129/65/15 Za 1322.
42. *Iradé hususiye* 130/1/1 M 1323 (four enclosures).
43. *Iradé hususiye* 128/90/15 N 1322 (four enclosures).
44. *Iradé hususiye* 127/80/1 B 1322 (five enclosures).
45. *Iradé hususiye* 124/91/18 Z 1321, *mazbata* in *defter* 12068; also 124/107 of 21 Z 1321, *iradé seniyé* in *defter*s 12078, 12082. For other exchanges with the British over this district, see *iradé hususiye* 128/71 of 5 N 1322.
46. Telegram from Curzon, Vice-Raj of India to Major General Mason from Mahableshwar (*sic*) of 21 November 1904 and from Bombay Castle, 14 November 1905 insisting the emir sign the treaty before leaving Aden. Enclosures 5 and 6 in no. 133, signed in Aden on 28 November (FO 406/21).
47. Major Merewether wrote to Colonel Davies from al-Ḍāli' on 29 October 1904 (*Confidential*) that he disagreed with the under secretary's letter to the India government's foreign department of 22 September saying it was inadvisable to grant a subsidy to the Kutaybis who are nominally dependents of the emir of al-Ḍāli'. The fact is, he argued, they do not acknowledge his suzerainty and would clobber him were it not for the presence of British troops. 'He is avaricious, cruel and treacherous, and has estranged practically all the tribes under him. He would accede to a Kutaybi subsidy because he has no power to resist if we say do so. We lost considerable prestige for supporting our Amir, [who is] universally detested by Arabs. Why give him 100 dollars more? He has not kept up any troops at all, is saving money, not so with Sultans of Lahaj and Mukalla. We would have to secure the route Dthala–Sulek (*sic*) where outrages are often. From the date he signed the agreement (1888) he had no intention to abide by it; indeed,

he is the one preventing Koteibis from reconciling with the British — Koteibis originally are lower Yāfi'ʻs and on good terms with their Sultan Abdallah b. Muhsin. If the Koteibis rise, what can our 1200 men do against an alliance of 25,000 armed with French rifles from our supply and two camel battery guns?' (Enclosure 4 in no. 133 from the India government to Brodrick of 9 March 1905). India Office to Foreign Office of 18 April 1905 enclosing copy of revised treaty with the amir and ratified by the viceroy and governor general in Council (*Secret*) FO 406/21 (*Confidential*).

48. Enclosure in no. 4, Mr Brodrick to the government of India, India Office, 2 January 1905 and no. 4 India Office to the Foreign Office, telegram of 3 January 1905 (FO 406/20).
49. No. 37, Lansdowne to Townley, Foreign Office, 18 January 1905, no. 27 *Confidential* (FO 406/20).
50. Aden Resident's report of 25 February 1906. Enclosure in no. 35 (18432) India Office to the Foreign Office of 29 May 1906 enclosing a memorandum received in April 1906 re external affairs of Arabia.
51. Political Resident at Aden to government of Bombay, 18 March 1906 (*Confidential*). Enclosure 2 in no. 39 (India Office to Foreign Office of 31 May 1906 enclosing (*Confidential*). Government of Bombay to government of India, Bombay Castle, 5 April 1906 (FO 406/28).
52. Captain Hancock (for the political Resident at Aden) to Shaykh Shāhir b. Sayf, Aden Residency 26 January 1906. Enclosure 17 in no. 52, India Office to Foreign Office of 21 March 1906 (10068). FO 406/27. Enclosure 18: similar letter addressed to Sayyid al-Hāshimi and Shaykh Saʻīd al-Jirāfi of 26 January 1906.

Chapter 8

1. These were Taʻizz, Ṣanʻā', ʻAsīr, and Hodeida.
2. See Annex A for details.
3. As Harold Jacob, the British Resident in Aden saw it, the Ottomans its entirety to the Imam of Sana [*sic*] and retained merely their own suzerainty. Their weakness prompted half measures, and so two kingdoms were set up one in the hills and the other in the lowlands of Yemen. See Jacob 1923: 68. His perspective was in keeping with British aims to cultivate closer ties with the imam and keep the Ottoman off balance in the highlands.
4. Wavell 1912: v.
5. Report titled 'Yemen ahvaline dair' (concerning conditions in Yemen) of 11 S 1325/26 March 1907 to the sultan's government (*Yıldız* 37, 14/293).
6. Hilmi's report, *Yıldız* 37, 14/293: 3–4.
7. Wāsiʻi 1366/1947: 293.
8. 'Arashi (1939: 84) states this as one of the reasons why Aptullah was replaced by Tevfik Paşa.

9. The 1902 episode, when four major Italian warships commanded by an admiral bombarded and levelled Midi after the ultimatum they had addressed to the Ottoman authorities at Hodeida expired, left no doubt that Italy would aggressively defend its interests in the Red Sea. Despite the Ottoman government's very conciliatory attitude and the intercession of the German foreign office on its behalf, the Italian government was undeterred. For details see PAA, *Türkei*, 165 no. 2.
10. Details in Memduh (former minister of the interior) 1324/1908: 2–5.
11. FO 195/2126 as cited by Baldry 1975a: 173, n. 1.
12. Considered an Arabophile, Nedim allegedly paved the way for Izzet Paşa in 1911 to come to terms with the imam by smoothing over differences with the Ottoman government, Jacob 1923: 69.
13. *Yıldız* 37, 'Yemen hakkında Mahmut Nedim imzalı lâyıha', 14/330.
14. For British reports on Italian activities, see FO 195/2148, 2126, 2128 (p. 51), FO 195/2254 (p. 52), and FO 195/2286 (p. 54) by Baldry 1976b: 51–4.
15. Cited by Bidwell 1983: 47.
16. Bidwell 1983: 9, 51.
17. He is listed as Privat dozent, resident of Munich with a number of works on South Arabia. Fück (1955: 256) mentions him briefly and there is a biographical entry for him in the *Deutsche Rundschau* of 1889. In the 1880s he worked in Yemen on deciphering Sabaic-Himyaritic script.
18. The Memduh Commission report summarized previous recommendations made by other officials sent to Yemen. It came out in 1904. For an analysis of it, see Mandaville 1985: 20–7.
19. For details of Glaser's mission and recommendations, see Farah 1994: 43–58; also KPA II (*zarf* 126, *kutu* 7) for Glaser's memorandum, its translation into Ottoman and the *sadaret*'s *husûsi tezkerési* in response to it.
20. For full text of this report, see Yıldız 37, 14/241.
21. Jacob 1923: 86.
22. Jacob 1923: 92.
23. See 'Les Pays arabes aux Arabes' circulated by Ligue de la Patrie arabe's Comité supérieur. Annex to Political Report no. 48 from German consulate general in Cairo to Reichskanzler von Bülow (PAA, no. 6454 in *Türkei*, 165, vol. 20). See also 'Eine Englische Einmischung in Arabien?' (unsigned) in *Berliner Tageblatt*, 19 May 1905 and 'Die groβen türkischen Bestrebungen in Arabien und der Aufstand in Yemen' by Karl Tigdor in *Neue Freie Presse*, 22 May 1905 (PAA, nos 8546 and 8786 in *Türkei*, 165, vol. 21).
24. Article by Henri Moreau in *L'Europe coloniale*, cited by *The Pioneer*, 20 July 1905, dismissing his views as a 'farrago of nonsense' (annex to Political Report no. 446 from A. Quadt of the German consulate general at Calcutta, 24 July 1905 to von Bülow (PAA, *Türkei*, 165, vol. 21). *The Times of India* (17 January 1905) in an article entitled 'The Revolt in

Yemen and the Position of the Turks' denounces more strongly allegations of British complicity either in arms smuggling or in rendering assistance to the imam's forces against the Turks. With reference to the implications of the revolt, see also *The Times* (London), 15 May 1905. Annex to Political Report no. 600 from German embassy in London to von Bülow of same date (PAA, *Türkei*, 165, vol. 21). Speculation on the demise both of Ottoman power and German influence can be seen in a report by Gervais Courtellement in *Le Temps*, 27 January 1905, under the title 'L'Allemagne et la Révolution arabe', which was cited also by the *Morning Post*, 27 June 1905, in an article entitled 'The Arab Rising, International Aspect', sent by the German embassy in London to Berlin (annex to Political Reports of 27 and 30 June 1905, See nos 449, 764, and 11314 in *Türkei*, 165, vol. 21).

25. It is interesting to note in this regard that Kaiser Wilhelm II was genuinely concerned when notified from Istanbul that the British were pressing the sultan's government not to allow Germany to proceed past Basra with the rail line. They sought the exclusive right to build the segment from Basra to Kuwait. In this manner the British would control the access to the Gulf that German commerce sought and influence completely the German character of the railroad. See Bülow (1929: 157–8) referring to telegram 123 from Kaiser Wilhelm. See also article in *L'Echo de Paris*, 17 July 1905, on expanding British influence in Arabia, especially with Shaykh Mubārak of Kuwait. Annex to political report no. 579 of 17 July 1905 from German embassy in Paris to von Bülow (PAA, no. 12693 in *Türkei*, 165, vol. 21).
26. See issue of 19 February 1907, report by 'special correspondent', dateline Constantinople. See also follow-up article by same unknown correspondent. Annex to Political Report no. 50 from Freiherr von Grünau to Fürsten von Bülow, of 27 February 1907, requesting clarification on Burckhardt's mission (PAA, no. 3324 in *Türkei*, 165, vol. 27).
27. Von Bülow's reply to von Grünau, Berlin, 8 March 1907 (PAA, no. 3795 in *Türkei*, 165, vol. 27).
28. Chargé of the German consulate general in Cairo to Fürsten von Bülow, of 24 March 1907. Grünau had received this intelligence directly from Burckhardt (PAA, *Türkei*, 165, vol. 27).
29. Burckhardt (PAA, *Türkei*, 165, vol. 27). He cites directly from Burckhardt's letter to Dr Moritz.
30. Ever since they occupied Eritrea, the Italians had been actively expanding their economic influence in Yemen. It was alleged that they had planned at one time to occupy the Yemeni port of Mocha and use it as a trading outlet. See Eduard Glaser, 'Unruhe in Yemen', *Neue Freie Presse*, 18 January 1887 (PAA, no. 8044 in *Türkei*, 165, vol. 1). Indeed, in 1910 they sent their own engineers to Yemen to study the technical feasibility of such a line (Baldry 1976b: 54).

31. The *Berliner Tageblatt*, 27 December 1909, reported under the heading 'Der Europäermord in Yemen', based on a telegram from a correspondent in Rome, that Arabs had killed Herman Burckhardt along with an Italian companion who had sought to defend him. The article hinted that he was on a secret mission. The Turkish authorities at Ibb had buried him and Benzoni (the companion). The *Giornale d'Italia*, which first reported the incident, expressed surprise because the people there were regarded as generally peaceful. It alleged that Burckhardt had claimed that he was 'on an important mission'. Benzoni had gone along to investigate trading possibilities and to acquire the same privileges accorded to Germany in Yemen (PAA, no. 21254 in *Türkei*, 158, vol. 11).
32. In the 18 January 1887 issue of *Neue Freie Presse* of Vienna, he answers statements appearing in the English press denying unrest in Yemen. He gives a cursory survey of British expansion northward from Aden under the guise of establishing security in areas they influenced and to check Ottoman activities among border tribes inimical to British protégés. He also ventures the opinion that south Arabia held greater promise for Britain than India and parts of Africa (PAA, no. 8044, *Türkei*, 165, vol. 1).
33. Jirāfi 1951: 211–15.
34. Reference is made here to tribes in the south and southeast adhering to the Sunni Shāfi'i rite as contrasted with the Shiite Zaydis and Ismā'īlīs.
35. His report to the Sublime Porte in PAA, no. 8044, *Türkei*, 165, vol. 1: 3.
36. Ibid., p. 4. It is important to note that the Ottomans had no direct authority over any of this critical area east and north of Ṣan'ā', including Ma'rib, Ṣa'dah, Najrān, Shahārah, Qafalat Ma'rib 'Adhar or over the tribes who lived there. Nor did they control the nine protectorates in lower Yemen, which were tributaries of the Aden administration. See article by Aḥmad Waṣfi Zakarīyah in *al-Muqtaṭaf*, vol. 90, no. 1: 80, as cited by Sālim 1984: 38, n. 2.
37. It is interesting to note here that when the dam was finally rebuilt (1983–86) after 1500 years, it was by a Turkish construction company.
38. Glaser Report (PAA, no. 21254 in *Türkei*, 158, vol. 11), p. 6.
39. Ibid., pp. 5–6.
40. Ibid., p. 6.
41. Ibid., p. 7.
42. Ibid.
43. Ibid., pp. 8–9.
44. Ibid., p. 9.
45. Ibid., p. 10. The reference is most presumably to Count Carlo Landberg, a known linguist with whom Glaser had an ongoing rivalry.
46. As the bombardment of the Yemeni coast by their fleet proved. Moreover, Germany was concerned about the possibility of an Anglo–Italian understanding in the lower Red Sea that might induce Italy to support British

obstruction to the Baghdad Bahn (Monts of the German embassy in Rome to von Bülow, 22 January 1907, and Berlin to Rome of 31 January 1907. See nos 1344 and 1737 in *Türkei*, 76, vol. 10).

47. Members of the Arab nationalist party boasted of a branch in Ṣan'ā'. The platform of *La Ligue arabe* boasted of the movement's intention to liberate all Arab provinces from Ottoman control. When the imam's forces defeated Rıza Paşa in April 1905, Yaḥya threatened to march to Mecca, liberate it and proclaim himself caliph. Syrian troops were refusing to fight in Yemen. A nationalist spokesman claimed that Arabs could mobilize 150,000 armed men against the Ottomans. See 'La révolte arabe', PAA, no. 8492 (dated 18 May 1905) in *Türkei*, 165, vol. 21.
48. Glaser's report (PAA, no. 8044, *Türkei*, 165, vol. 1), p. 10.

Chapter 9

1. Reformist ministers of the centre in Istanbul who opted for Western style models over the prevailing Islam-based laws derived from the Sharī'ah.
2. From the preliminary draft of a paper by J. Kelly Dixon entitled 'Power and Legitimacy: the Imamate and the 'Ulama', p. 1.
3. Such was the will of the imperial government as stated in an *iradé seniyé* of 23 R 1300/29 February 1883 (BEO.NGG 87/846).
4. Memorandum from Izzet approved by the *Meclis-i Husūsî* of the *sadrazam* on 21 R 1302/9 February 1885 in YMM 17/16.
5. YMM. *Dosya* 31, *sıra* 64 of 22 B 1305/1 August 1888.
6. *Zapt* 1 of 24 C 13202/12 April 1885 (BEO.NGG 88/715).
7. YT.MME. Dosya 27, sıra no. 98 of 19 Z 1304/17 January 1887.
8. Iradé of 9 M 1306/15 September 1888 (BEO.NGG 89/772).
9. Notification of 11 N 1303/13 June 1886 (BEO.NGG 88/1040).
10. 'Ali Riza to the *seraskeriyet-hususiye* summarizing Feyzi's report for the sultan's attention dated 15 L 1303/17 July 1886 in YMM 21/146.
11. *Mazbata* of the *Meclis-i Vükelâ* of 27 L 1304/18 July 1887. *Defter* 22, *belge* 8.
12. *Meclis-i Mahsus zabt varakası* of 22 Ra 1303/29 December 1885 (MVM, *defter* 7, *sıra* no. 48).
13. MVM, decision of 15 Ca 1302/2 March 1885. *Defter* 1, *belge* 47.
14. Reported in the newspaper *Tarik*, 27 February 1886.
15. The *Meclis-i Vükelâ* recommended the appointment of an official to supervise it at a salary of £600 sterling annually. Dated 5 C 1307/28 December 1889 (*Mazbata* in *defter* 50, *belge* 57/1 and 2).
16. *Serasker*'s *tezkeré* 116 of 25 M 1303/4 November 1885 sent to the minister of interior three days later (BEO.NGG 53/115 *âmadi*).
17. Correspondence of 11 Ra 1303/18 December 1885 (BEO.NGG 53/1202 *âmadi*).

18. Some 19 letters were submitted to the *dahiliye* on 25 M 1303/4 November 1885. For replies, see BEO.NGG 53/627 (*âmadi*).
19. Jirāfi 1951: 207.
20. This was the name the Turks used for al-Mutawakkil Muḥsin ibn Aḥmad.
21. 'Arashi 1939: 80.
22. Jirāfi 1951: 209.
23. Wāsi'i 1366/1947: 268.
24. Wāsi'i 1366/1947: 270.
25. Telegram summary submitted to the *seraskeriyet* on 23 M 1302/13 November 1884. See *buyrultu âli* 792 sent 30 M 1302/21 November 1884 (BEO.NGG, *defter* 53/796 *âmadi*).
26. Reply of 8 S 1302/27 November 1884 (BEO.NGG 53/828 *âmadi*).
27. Nuri n.d.: 949.
28. Encoded telegram from Ismail Hakkı, commandant of seventh army to the *seraskeriyet* of 24 October 1306/1888 and war command's reply of 18 June 1307/1889 stating steamship *Hasan Pasha* was on its way with a battery of cannons and 709 troops and officers (YEE 65/34, no. 34).
29. Telegram of 21 May, received 24 May 1890 in the *seraskeriyet* (YEE 65/34. no. 5).
30. According to Nuri (n.d.: 950) 6700 new troops arrived in Yemen in May 1895 to boost the 9753 present, including 15 battalions of irregulars.
31. Serasker Riza relayed the contents of the telegram to the *sadaret* in a brief *mazbata* of 14 Ş 1310/24 August 1890 (YMM 66/93).
32. MVM, *defter* 74, *belge* 105 of 23 L 1310/1890.
33. Wāsi'i 1366/1947: 264.
34. Abāẓah 1979: 122.
35. The *Meclis-i Vukulâ*'s special consultative sessions and their *mazbata* of 23 Z 1303/23 September 1886.
36. Authorization of 26 Za 1303/26 August 1886 (YMM 11/88).
37. Wāsi'i 1366/1947: 262.
38. A'ẓami 1349/1931: 245.
39. Wāsi'i 1366/1947: 263.
40. Wāsi'i 1366/1947: 464.
41. Wāsi'i 1366/1947: 263.
42. Wāsi'i 1366/1947: 264.
43. The same Nuri (n.d.) cited in this text.
44. Wāsi'i 1366/1947: 265.
45. YMM, *dosya* 43, *sıra* 116, 25 L 1307/20 November 1889, *tarihi* (three enclosures).
46. Nuri n.d.: 266.
47. Harris (1893: 95–6) made these observations during a visit to Yemen in 1892. Details also in Abāẓah 1979: 131–2.

48. YMM. *Dosya* 50, *sıra* 97 of 29 L 1308, *tarihi*.
49. Bury 1915: 35.
50. YMM, *dosya* 41, *sıra* 18.16.3.1307, *tarihi* (9April 1890).
51. Among them were 'Abd al-Wahhāb ibn Rāji', head of the Arḥab, Muqbil ibn Yaḥya Abu Fāri', head of Ḥāshid, Muqbil Dāhish, head of the Banu Ḥarith, Sayyid Muḥammad al-Shuwayyi', head of Ḍila', and Shaykh 'Alī ibn Muḥammad al-Balīli, head of Ṣan'ā' (Wāsi'i 1366/1947: 273).
52. Wāsi'i 1366/1947: 273.
53. Specifically from Ḥāshid, Bakīl, Dhu Muḥammad, Dhū Ḥusayn, Barat, all known for their boldness and hatred of Ottoman Turks (Abāẓah 1979: 134).
54. Detailed description by Harris 1893: 102–3.
55. Detailed description in Wāsi'i 1366/1947: 274–5.
56. Harris 1893: 105.
57. On 20 September the *Standard* (London) reported the fall of the city and the Ottomans rushing troops from the Hijaz to stem the tide. German newspapers picked up the account and Berlin sought confirmation from the Ottoman foreign ministry, which denied the report, spread also by *The Times*, and instructed the *Standard*'s reporter in Istanbul to deny the report, allegedly obtained from a reliable source. In August 1891 the *Wiener Abendblatt* had reported that rebels shouting 'no Abdülhamid, no Istanbul' had attacked Ottoman troops and forced them to take refuge in Mocha and Hodeida. The ministry issued another set of instructions to its correspondent to deny the report. No, 124 of the Foreign Publications Section and Sadrazam Cevâd's *mazbata* to *Divan-i Hümayun* (imperial chancery) in YSHM 251/16; also YSHM 251/127 for telegram from Berlin to foreign ministry of 22 September 1891 requesting that an official denial be issued.
58. YMM, *dosya* 51, *sıra* 5 of 2 Za 1308, *tarihi*.
59. Harris 1893: 101.
60. YMM, *dosya* 58, *sıra* 9 of 3 C 1309 *tarihi* (four pieces).
61. Rīḥānī 1930: 212–13.
62. Wāsi'i 1366/1947: 276.
63. Harris 1893: 96.
64. Wāsi'i 1366/1947: 272.
65. Report in conjunction with the arrival of French Ambassador Cambon in Istanbul and satisfaction with Kâmil Paşa as grand vizier. See *Journal des Débats* of 19 October 1891.
66. *Marûz* of the *seraskeriyet* of 22 Z 1309/18 July 1892 signed by Kaymakam 'Ali Riza, Miralay Ömer Kâmil and Ferik Ibrahim Ethem (deputy chief of staff), endorsed by the chief secretary of the sultan at Yıldız on 23 Z 1308/ 21 July 1892 (YMM, *dosya* 6, *sıra* 82 of 22 B 1309).
67. YMM.53/20 of 5 M 1309 (two pieces).
68. YMM.53/29 of 8 M 1309.

69. YMM, *dosya* 54, *sıra* 80 of 19 S 1308, *tarihi*.
70. Issue of 29 September 1899.
71. YMM, *dosya* 64, *sıra* 82 of 2 S 1309, *tarihi* (two pieces).
72. Reference is to the well-fortified two mountains, one nearly inaccessible, near Zabīd. See Akwa' 1404/1984: vol. 2, 450–1.
73. YT.MM, *dosya* 6, *sıra* 93 of 14 S 1310, *tarihi* (two pieces).
74. YMM, *dosya* 62, *sıra* 97 of 24 L 1309, *tarihi* (four pieces).
75. YMM, *dosya* 5, *sıra* 16 of 5 Z 1308, *tarihi* (nine pieces).
76. YMM, *dosya* 52, *sıra* 63 of 21 Z 1308, *tarihi* (three pieces).
77. Encoded telegraphic report from Feyzi to the *sadrazam* of 16 October 1891 (252/66).
78. YMM, *dosya* 70/182 of 29 R 1310 (three pieces).
79. YMM, *dosya* 75/51 of 9 Ş 1310.
80. YMM, *dosya* 75/107 of 15 Ş 1310.
81. Harris 1893: 111.
82. *Mazbata* of that date forwarded to the imperial chancery for action (YSHM 252/66).
83. It seems that Harris's presence was tolerated until Feyzi became convinced he was a spy for Britain, so he had him arrested and imprisoned, with his entourage, and was only released when he contracted a strong fever in prison, whereupon he was allowed to depart to avoid an incident. Harris had voiced his admiration for Feyzi's military ability, but criticized his harsh methods, which might account also for his arrest (Abāẓah 1979: 140).
84. Harris 1893: 15–16.
85. *Mazbata* of the *Bahriye Nezareti* of 9 R 1316/27 August 1898 signed by the *nazir* himself in YMM 181/34.
86. Correspondence Bureau of the *vilayet*, no. 113 to the *mabeyn*'s head correspondent from Vali Hussein Hilmi of 6 Z 1317/17 May 1899 addressed to the sultan. YMM 191/28 no. 1 (two pieces).
87. *Mazbata* of 13 Ra 1320/20 June 1902, passed by the *Meclis-i Mahsus* and endorsed by all ministers, the *şeyhülislam*, *serasker* and Sadrazam Saïd and forwarded to the sultan for endorsement (YSRM, *defter* 10665).
88. Report of the minister of the navy of 2 B 1319/15 October 1901 (YMM 222/4).
89. Report no. 289 from the *vali* to the chief of correspondence of the sultan's mabeyn of 12 B 1317/16 November 1899 (YMM 197/2. no. 2).
90. For the clash with the ʻAsīri party, see YMM 196/48, no. 1.
91. Extract dated 28 October 1899, enclosure no. 164 (10 to the Foreign Office of 23 November 1899) Konfidential (sic) (FO 416/1).
92. Report from Taʻizz of 24 Ra 1317/2 August 1899 (YMM 192/149).
93. Relayed by Vali Hussein Hilmi to the sultan on 21 Ca 1317/26 September 1899 (YMM 194/131. no. 1).

94. Mazbata of Meclis-i Mahsus of 9 C 1319/24 August 1901 YSRM (defter 9727).
95. Report to Serasker Riza of 21 Ca 1319/6 September 1901 (YMM. 221/117, no. 2).
96. Nuri n.d.: 948.
97. For his biography, see Zabārah n.d.: 48–9.
98. Descendant of a line of imams settled in Wādi'ah around Khamir. See Akwa' 1404/1984: vol. 4, 761 for lineage and settlement in land of Ḥāshid.
99. For text of the letter and comments, see document no. 14 in Sālim 1982: 137–41.
100. Wāsi'i 1366/1947: 277.
101. Ibid.

Chapter 10

1. We see evidence of this in a letter to Shaykh 'Abdallah ibn Yaḥya al-Wāsi'i dated 1312/1894, full text and comments in Sālim 1982: 133–41.
2. Vali Hussein's chief secretary's no. 217 to the *mabeyn-i hümayun*'s chief secretariat of 16 Ca 1317/22 September 1899 (YMM 194/71, no. 1).
3. Ibid.
4. Abāẓah 1979: 145.
5. Wāsi'i 1366/1947: 279.
6. See journal stating the exile and the question of how to deal with those exiled. YMM 138/5 of 4 L 1313/1895 (two pieces).
7. Wāsi'i 1366/1947: 282.
8. According to Wāsi'i (1366/1947: 281–2), the tax farmer responsible for tobacco cornered the whole procedure allowing no one he did not authorize to collect fees; no trader could purchase except from him; if he were to do so, the *multazim* would confiscate it and in this manner he accumulated enormous wealth. When the Yemenis complained to the sultan about the tax farmer's excesses and when orders were issued to dismiss him, he only increased his pressure on the inhabitants, forcing his way into their homes. He had aides at all entrances to the city and in all parts of the country to control traffic (Abāẓah 1979: 147).
9. Plural of *waqf*.
10. Plural of *'āmil*, the one who under Islamic law was responsible for collecting the tithe (*zakah*).
11. Wāsi'i 1366/1947: 283–4.
12. Jirāfi 1951: 210.
13. YMM 145/149 of 17 Ra 1314/1896.
14. YMM 133/84 of 13 B 1313/1895 (three pieces).
15. Wāsi'i 1366/1947: 289.
16. YMM 1/1/44 of 11 Ş 1315/1897 (six pieces).

17. Feyzi's report by telegram, no. 992 to the *seraskeriyet* in YMM 171/44 together with the chief secretariat of Yıldız's summary report, no. 5443 of 11 N 1313/23 December 1895. Included also is the official complaint of the attendant against the *ferik* of 21 and 23 October 1895. See *mazbata* to the sultan dated 11 N 1315/23 December 1313 (*sic*) in YMM 17/44.
18. By order of the department of religious affairs, the programme of instruction in elementary schools was to consist of the Koran, its recitation as well, *'ilm*, Turkish names, mathematics, dictation, ethics, handwriting and grammar (instructions to Correspondence Bureau of Yemen YMM 195/34, nos. 1 and 2).
19. When one of them, Muḥammad Efendi ibn 'Alī, displayed bad conduct and the authorities were seriously considering sending the lot of them back to Yemen, the superintendent of Yemeni tribal affairs petitioned the *mabeyn* on 27 February 1902 not to send them all back, as did also the colonel of the imperial band, the imperial *yaver-i harp*, and Ferik Süleiman, commandant of imperial music, suggesting that the offender be separated instead from the rest and sent back to Yemen or to one of the schools of Teşra (YMM 256/123).
20. Wāsi'i 1366/1947: 291.
21. The sultan's government had newly pursued a policy of centralization and, to institute a system of checks and balances and to prevent the concentration of power in one or other top official, had separated the administrative from the military post hitherto concentrated in one person.
22. Wāsi'i 1366/1947: 292.
23. Enclosure 26, Ponsonby to O'Conor relayed to Salisbury in London, no. 15. Constantinople, 12 July 1899 (FO 416/1).
24. Nuri n.d.: 949.
25. *Iradé* of 21 R 1316/10 September 1898 and the *serasker*'s *mazbata* of two days later in YMM 181/98.
26. 'Arashi 1939: 83.
27. Brigadier General Creagh to the government of Bombay, Aden Residency, 7 January 1900. Enclosure 1 in no. 32 (10 to FO of 26 January) FO 416/2.
28. Brigadier General O. M. Creagh to Bombay government, Aden Residency of 26 January 1900. Enclosure 1 in no. 88, India Office to FO of 19 February 1900 by under secretary of state at direction of Lord Hamilton (FO 416/2).
29. Report from Ṣan'ā' of 17 September 1899. Enclosure in no. 10 (*Confidential*) of 8 November 1899 to Foreign Office (FO 416/1).
30. Report of 28 December 1899. Enclosure in no. 64 from Brigadier General Creagh to the government of Bombay of 16 January 1900 (*Confidential*) (FO 416/2).
31. Dispatch from Simla to the India Office and the quartermaster general in India, intelligence branch. Enclosure in no. 4 (10 to the Foreign Office) of 3 January 1900 (FO 461/2).

32. Enclosure 2 in no. 2 from Brigadier General Creagh to the government of Bombay. Aden, 18 November 1899 (FO 416/2).
33. Sir Julian Panefote stated Britain's position in a letter of 19 November 1887 when discussions took place to conclude protectorate agreements with tribes near Aden. Secret agreements were reached with Ubayhis and Falist 'Aqrabīs (Sir A. Godley's letter to Foreign Office of 2 July 1890) and similar agreements with Ḥawshabis, 'Alawīs and lower Yāfi' tribes (letter to Foreign Office of 21 November 1895; with the 'Abdalīs, as early as 1849, modified 6 February 1882). Lord Hamilton instructed India Office in telegram of 29 December 1899 (enclosure in no. 185) to notify the Foreign Office that the Bombay government had grounds to insist the Porte lay off Amīri country, referring to Lord Granville's notification to Sublime Porte in Sir H. Elliot's dispatch of 13 May 1873, which was never withdrawn. In 1895 the Aden Resident told home authorities that the British would suffer no interference with the nine tribes (including the Amīris) *but have no record of this*. The *vali* of Yemen allegedly did not object to the Resident referring to their independence (Atchison, vol. xi, no. 68). Hence his recommendation that the British formally declare a protectorate to resist annexation by the Ottomans and avoid loss of prestige to Britain, though it may have involved boundary disputes with the Ottomans. The country was valuable because of the important caravan routes and sanatorium (no. 184. India Office to the Foreign Office, signed by Horace Walpole, 28 December 1899, FO 416/1).
34. Enclosure no. 121 from India Office to Foreign Office of 14 March 1900 forwarding telegram of 13 March from Resident to Lord G. Marquis of Salisbury cabled (no. 21 of 17 March) Sir N. O'Conor (British ambassador in Istanbul) to demand the Turkish government withdraw troops in keeping with treaty with Ḥawshabi chiefs in his no. 390 of 3 December 1895 and copy of report from Captain Wahab from Aden forwarded to embassy in August 1893 with map attached. In his no. 37, A. Godley of India Office communicated to Foreign Office on 21 March 1900. Hamilton instructed O'Conor to tell the 'Sublime Porte to refrain from interfering within all territories of the tribes whose independence was affirmed in Lord Granville's dispatch no. 111 to Sir H. G. Elliott of 15 May 1873' and communicated to the Ottoman government on 30 May 1873 (FO 416/2).
35. No. 56 (telegram) O'Conor to Salisbury, Constantinople, 19 May 1900 (no. 39, FO 416/3).
36. Telegram from the government of India to Lord Hamilton, 10 January 1901 (FO 416/5).
37. Hamilton to India government, 7 June 1901, enclosure in no. 220 (FO 416/5).
38. The Resident's telegram stated that when the British troops got there they met with great resistance from the fort's defenders, which included 100 Ottoman troops. Lansdowne urged O'Conor to get the sultan's government

to withdraw its force. See his no. 69 to Ahthopoulo Pasha, FO July 290, 1901. FO 416/6 (*Confidential* 7887) Part VI.

39. No. 144 from Therapia of 13 August 1901 (no. 30) FO 416/6.
40. No. 253 to O'Conor, Foreign Office, 30 September 1901 (no. 226) FO 416/6.
41. No. 72, Constantinople, 22 May 1900 (no. 179) FO 416/3.
42. No. 78 of 7 June 1900 (FO 4516/3).
43. No. 80 (telegram), O'Conor to Salisbury, Constantinople, 10 June 1900 (no. 46).
44. *Iradé seniyé* of 28 Za 1318/17 March 1901 and the response of two days later (YMM 212/168. no. 1).
45. No. 54, FO to India Office, 25 October 1901 (FO 416/7).
46. No. 69, Lansdowne's telegram to O'Conor, Foreign Office, 30 October 1901 (no. 153) FO 416/7.
47. YMM 233/150, 236/104, 241/86 (exchanges between Ottomans and British on establishing a joint commission) and 251/69 (no. 8 is a draft of a proposed map showing areas of dispute for drawing north–south boundary line).
48. Enclosure in no. 165, political Resident to Sir W. Lee-Warner, Aden, 6 November 1901 (FO 416/7).
49. No. 31, Lansdowne to O'Conor, FO, 15 October 1901 (no. 236) Aden delimitation (FO 416/7).
50. Enclosure 1 in no. 100 (India Office to Foreign Office 26 June 1900). W. T. Morrison, acting secretary of the government of Bombay to the government of India, Bombay Castle, 9 May 1900, responding to 27 January request of the Resident at Aden (FO 461/3).
51. Enclosure in no. 82 of 11 June 1900 (FO 416/13).
52. No. 185, telegram by Turkish ambassador in London (FO 416/3).
53. No. 186, Foreign Office (T. H. Sanderson) to India Office of 3 December 1900, Lansdowne directs Hamilton to investigate and report back. Enclosure in no. 193, Hamilton to governor of Bombay, India Office, 5 December 1900 seeking the truth, and no. 201 from Godley of 12 December 1900 denying the *vali*'s allegations (FO 416/3).
54. Enclosure 3 in no. 32, Brigadier General Creagh of Aden Residency to Bombay government, 8 January 1900 (*Confidential*) appending a translation of a letter to him from the sultan of Laḥj re his interview (FO 416/2).
55. 'Arashi 1939: 82–4.
56. No. 15, O'Conor to Salisbury, Constantinople 12 July 1899 relaying Ponsonby's to O'Conor (enclosure no. 26) of 3 July 1899 (FO 416/1).
57. Enclosure 2 in no. 1, substance of the letter dated 20 Ca 1317/23 September 1899 from 'Abdallah al-Manṣūr bil-Lāh to Ahmad Faḍl ibn Muḥsin, sultan of Laḥj, offering to divide the country, north of Makhādir for himself, south of it for the British except for the parts belonging to the sultan of Laḥj, paying taxes to the latter in return for

an annual stipend in exchange for a treaty. The condition the imam set was that the British were to prohibit the import of arms, ammunition and stores into Yemen for the Turkish military. The imam alleged that he did not fear Turkish attacks, which he was confident he could defeat. Godley's no. 10 to Foreign Office of 1 January 1900 repeating information to Salisbury in a dispatch of 5 December 1899 by General Creagh, vice consul to the government of Bombay (F 416/2).

58. Dispatch by cipher to the chief of correspondence at Yıldız. The commission on reform recommended approval. Signed by Hafzi, Zehdi and Hussein, 19 June 1900 (YMM 203/19).
59. Telegram from the commandant of the seventh army to Serasker Riza of 16 N 1327/18 January 1900 (YMM 198/68).
60. Telegram from commandant in Yemen to Serasker Riza of 16 N 1317/18 January 1900 (YT.MME 198/67, no. 1).
61. Report of 11 Ca 1319/25 August 1901 requested that Serasker Riza notify the *vali* and commandant of Tripolitania accordingly (YMM 220/78).
62. Dispatch by *yaver* of Commandant Aptullah Paşa to the *mabeyn-i hümayun* of 14 Ca 1319/28 August 1901 (YMM 220/104). Nos 1 and 2, translation of *fesadname* to Naqīb al-Mujāhid Rājiḥ ibn Ḥusayn, 'Alī ibn 'Alī al-Sarājị, Naqīb al-Mujāhid Mrshid ibn 'Abdallah al-Jindi, and al-Ḥājj Muḥammad ibn Ahmad al-Farmati dated 28 R 1319/16 August 1901. Another appeal to arms, undated, is addressed to al-Ḥājj 'Abdallah ibn 'Alī Rāshid.
63. Enclosure in no. 54, O'Conor to Lansdowne (no. 58), Constantinople, 11 February 1901 relaying report of Acting Vice Consul Husain to Consul Devey, Hodeida, 18 January 1901 (FO 416/5).
64. No. 97, O'Conor to Lansdowne, Constantinople, 7 May 1902 (FO 416/9).
65. Riza Efendi, secretary of the regiment, to the *serasker* by cipher telegrams of 2 and 3 December 1902 (YMM 269/67, nos 2 and 3).
66. Encoded telegrams to Serasker Riza from the *mutasarrif* of Ta'izz of 6 December 1902 (YMM 269/86) and from Hodeida's Alay Emini Riza Efendi of 14 December 1902 (YMM 269/199).
67. Report of commandant of seventh army to Serasker Riza, and the latter's *mazbata* of 3 M 1320/12 April 1902 recommending the additional 15,000 troops requested and forwarded by Sadrazam Saïd to the sultan following the endorsement of the *Meclis-i Mahsus* of the *Vükelâ* on 7 M 1320.
68. No. 18, Lieutenant Colonel Maunsell to O'Conor, Constantinople, 21 May 1902, enclosure in no. 153, O'Conor to Lansdowne, 21 May 1902 (*Confidential*) FO 416/9.
69. Per diem costs in terms of expenses, clothing and pay were estimated as follows: steamer cost of transport 3,368,520 *piastres*; Hodeida to Ṣan'ā' transport 60,000; monthly pay while serving in Yemen 645,120 *piastres* (7,741,420 per year); and clothing 860,118 *piastres* (YSRME 116/2).

70. No. 20, Vice Consul Massey to O'Conor from Adana, 25 April 1901, enclosure in no. 162, O'Conor to Lansdowne, Constantinople, 6 May 1901 (no. 169).
71. Enclosure in no. 214 (India Office to Foreign Office, 4 June 1901) FO 416/5.
72. Enclosure 1 in no. 240 of Vice Consul Richardson at Hodeida to Consul Devey, no. 292 from de Bunsen to Lansdowne, Therapia, 25 June 1902 (FO 416/5).
73. Appeal to the *seraskeriyet* by encoded telegram received 20 June 1902 (YMM 2361/111, no. 2).

Chapter 11

1. For chronological details, see Danişmend n.d.: 351–8.
2. Cf. Baldry 1976b: 51, where he reports that the British, to the contrary, were alarmed by Italian activity in the Red Sea. He cites *A Report on the necessity of consular establishments in the Red Sea* (FO 195/1375) to help prevent the extension of Italian influence.
3. Report from Consul General Sola at Hodeida to Ministry of Foreign Affairs of 28 March 1906. Enclosure 1 in no. 42, memorandum from Italian embassy of 7 June 1906 to Foreign Office (19549) FO 406/28.
4. KPA II 81/38, no. 3742 (undated draft).
5. YSRM 81/11 of 4 Ra 1314 (two enclosures).
6. YSRM 71/4 of 4 M 1312 (four enclosures).
7. YSRM 118/41 of 13 B 1320 (*defter kismsindadir* 10665).
8. A 1344, Monts of the German embassy in Rome to Chancellor von Bülow in Berlin, Rome, 22 January 1907. Politisches Archiv (henceforth PA) of Bonn, *Türkei*, 76, vol. 10.
9. PA at Bonn, A 1737, Berlin, 31 January 1907 to German embassy in Rome, *Türkei*, 76, vol. 10.
10. No. 137, Bunsen's telegram to Salisbury, Constantinople, 22 October 1900 (FO 416/4). Reference here is to the Boxer rebellion and the European expedition to quell it.
11. No. 138, de Bunsen to Salisbury (no. 362 *Confidential*) Therapia, 19 October 1900 (FO 416/4).
12. No. 174, de Bunsen to Lansdowne (no. 399 *Confidential*) Constantinople, 19 November 1900 (FO 416/4).
13. The report of 10 November by Brigadier General H. E. Benton, political Resident at Aden, stated that about two months earlier Captain Karapouf of the *Marie* came from Lisbon to Kamarān, took on a native Arab pilot, sailed for Farasān, and 'got himself intentionally grounded by taking the wrong course, where he landed 53 tons of coal, gave the Resident a gold watch, and sailed back to Kamarān within five days'. The Resident allegedly wired the *vali* who dispatched a telegram to the commodore at Hodeida, which the *vali* relayed to

Istanbul. The sultan reportedly said that the coal should be taken back on board or confiscated. But three days later a telegram from Constantinople stated that the Turks and Germans were friends, so should be permitted a facility to store up to 5000 tons of coal on Kumh island, six miles from Farasān, at the *tersane* where the Turkish flag flies and a small gunboat is kept, and where all German warships will now coal; eventually the facility could be expanded to handle 10,000 tons. The *vali* sent an engineer, a municipal commissioner, the commodore of Hodeida, and a mason to survey and report on the feasibility of such a facility (enclosure in no. 138, 'Particulars regarding the acquisition of Farasān by the German government' (FO 416/4).

14. No. 187, de Bunsen to Lansdowne (no. 420 *Confidential*) Constantinople, 30 November 1900 (FO 416/4).
15. Enclosure in no. 210, extract from the *Levant Herald* of 19 December 1900, in no. 210, de Bunsen to Lansdowne (no. 445), Constantinople, 24 December 1900.
16. YMM, *dosya* 31, *belge* 51, report of 10 B 1305/1889.
17. On troop mobilization authorization by the Ottoman government, see a series of reports to Istanbul in YMM, *dosya* 31, *belge* 68 (six enclosures) and the authorization order of 14 B 1305/1889.
18. Baldry (1976b: 51) citing Richardson to Grey of 25 June 1913 (FO 195/245 of 3/1896).
19. See *maruzat* to the *sadaret* of 2 B 1319/15 October 1901 in YMM, *dosya* 222 and the enclosures: telegrams from the Ottoman naval command in the Red Sea urging reinforcements and the authorization for them by minister of marines, Hussein Paşa of 7 S 1320/16 May 1902 (YMM, *dosya* 230/39).
20. FO 195/2060, 2083, 2148 and 2126 as cited by Baldry 1976b.
21. See YMM, *dosya* 105, no. 14, a petition from the ministry of marine to the *sadrazam* of 16 Ra 1312/1897. See also request to the ministry to increase gunboat patrol in the Red Sea of 19 R 1316/1898.
22. MVM, *defter* 22, *belge* 8, decision of 27 L 1304/18 July 1887.
23. MVM 64/25, *mazbata* of 6 N 1308/17 March 1890.
24. The *Meclis-i Vükelâ* authorized contracting it with a foreign company for the sum of 7264 French francs; they recommended also the appointment of a supervising official to the department of post and telegraph at an annual salary of £600 sterling. Decision of 5 C 1307/14 January 1887.
25. A decade later Muḥammad 'Alī Thābit, a resident of Massawa, said in a letter to the *vali* of Djibouti that his father had sold the property the French took over to them and now wished to retrieve it. Sadrazam Mahmud Nedim, through the *vali* of Yemen, told İzzet Paşa, *mutasarrif* of Ta'izz, to be on the alert against renewed attempts by France to use this as a pretext to reoccupy Shaykh Sa'īd. He emphasized the military value and strategic location of Shaykh Sa'īd to the Ottomans. The war ministry was to take appropriate measures to reinforce it

militarily. See report of *sadrazam* to minister of the interior of 13 L 1328/1910 and the minister's reply in *tezkeré* 2674 of 11 Za 1330, followed three days later by an imperial response of 17 Z 1330/14 November 1910.

26. See dispatch of Münir Paşa the foreign ministry and of 21 S 1319/1901 and the decision of the special council (*encümani mahsus*), *tezkeré* of the *sadrazam* to the sultan for his review and reply (YSRM 124/79).
27. MVM, *defter* 7, no. 48, summary of Italy's control of the port's impact on revenue and the decision to demand that customs duties be levied on goods leaving that port after clarifying the status with Egypt by telegraphic dispatch, *mazbata* and decision of the *meclis* dated 22 Ra 1303/29 December 1885.
28. MVM, defter 1, *belge* 47, decision of 15 C 1302/2 March 1885.
29. YIHM, *mazbata* of the *sadrazam* dated 15 B 1309/2 February 1889.
30. MVM, *defter* 74, *belge* 92, *mazbata* of 16 L 1310/4 May 1890.
31. Enclosure in no. 164 to the Foreign Office of 23 November 1899 (*Confidential*); extract from *Yemen (Sanaa) News* dated 28 October 1899 announcing the return of the *mutasarrif* (FO 416/1). For the Ottoman account, see Yemen Vali Ḥussein Ḥilmi to the *baş kitabet* of the *mabeyn-i hümayun*, no. 289 of 1 B 1317/3 Za 1315/16 November 1899 (YMM 228/7).
32. Ottoman foreign minister, instructions to his *husūsiyet* (*Confidential* staff) of 8 B 1317/31 L 1315/12 November 1899 (YMM 196/25).
33. YIHM, *bölüm* 251/174 of 28 S 1309/1891.
34. This small flat-bottomed boat was manoeuvrable and elusive when chased.
35. Telegraphic communiqué from the *sadaret* (prime ministry) of the Ottoman government to the *vali* of Yemen dated 28 L 1318/1900. Republic of Yemen, Centre for Documentation and Research, document 50690.
36. *Pall Mall Gazette*, 28 February 1885.
37. Ibid. For details of the struggle, see PA, *Acta-Türkei*, vols 1–4 (1858–85).
38. For details see PA, *Acta-Türkei*, vol. 5 of 4–14 February 1885.
39. PA, *Acta-Türkei*, vol. 7 (20 March and 1 June 1885).
40. Incidents reported to Berlin by German ambassador in Rome (PA, A 15856, *Türkei* 165 no. 2).
41. Constantinople, 29 October 1902 (PA, no. 144 in A 15865). Given the strained relations between Istanbul and Rome, Berlin was used as the centre for communicating Ottoman responses to Rome, the underlying assumption being that Italy would listen to Germany.
42. PA, A 1192, Rome, 18 January 1911 to Berlin, *Türkei*, 76, vol. 10.
43. Turkey, Başbakanlık Arşivi. Telegrams of Lieutenant Colonel Rüşdü and Colonel Riza relayed to *sadrazam* in Aptullah Paşa's telegram of 28 October.
44. Telegram of Riza Beg of 17 L 1318/1902 from Ṣan'ā' (PA, A 15993, *Türkei*, 165, no. 2).
45. PA, Annex to 15993.
46. PA, A 16091, *Türkei* 165, no. 2.

47. Report in the *Frankfurter Zeitung* of 22 October 1902 (PA, A 15430 in *Türkei* 165, no. 2).
48. PA, Annex to A 15993.
49. PA, telegram 392 of 6 November 1902, A 16213, *Türkei* 165, no. 2.
50. Communiqué from the sultan's government, Pera, 18 October 1902, to the German embassy (PA, A 15266 in *Türkei* 165, no. 2).
51. PA, Berlin, 21 October 1902 (A 15369 in *Türkei* 165, no. 2).
52. Telegram from Constantinople of 20 October published in the *Frankfurter Zeitung* the next day (PA, A 15387 in *Türkei* 165, no. 2).
53. Article in the *Daily Mail* (5 November 1902) under the title 'Action of the Italians' and reprinted in the *Neue Preussische Zeitung* (11 November) under the heading 'Aus England' (copy in PA, A 16327 in *Türkei* 165, no. 2).
54. Alphonse Humbert's 'Facheux Rapprochement', in *L'Eclaire*, 9 November.
55. Report from Aden (15 March 1908) relaying Ottoman concern over the diversion of trade from Hodeida to Aden and the loss of customs revenue, especially in coffee and tobacco.
56. Article in *The Globe*, 11 December 1902, under the heading 'Italy and the Yemen: Important Action Pending' relaying a report from Rome of 9 December (copy in PA, Ad to 18060, *Türkei* 165, no. 2).
57. See Baldry n.d.: 148–97; and 1976b: 51–65.
58. Report titled 'Recommendations for effecting particular reforms in Yemen' submitted to the Ottoman sultan by former *kaymakam* (deputy governor) of Mocha, Mehmed Riza of 27 Ca 1307/1889 in YEE 437, *kısım* 14, *zarf* 126, second of two.
59. See YEE 330, *kısım* 14, *zarf* 126 for details.
60. Exports were valued at 1,610,000 *lira*s and imports at 340,000, most of it from India and Persian Gulf ports. See Nedim's report (pp. 14–15) for breakdown of import–export items.
61. Entitled 'Yemen ve Hicaz Savahilinin inzibat ve bahren muhafazası hakkında mütalâat'. Deniz Müzesi Kütühanesi elyazması, 167.
62. For specific provisions see Annex F.
63. For proposed locations see Annex G.
64. Ottoman bridges had either round arches or wide-based pointed arches. The 'eye' intended here is the round one.
65. R20/A4F2 as cited by Baldry 1976b: 54.
66. Feyzi, former commander-in-chief, was retired; Necip Paşa became *mutasarrıf* of Hodeida, and Mahmud Emin Efendi his *naip*.
67. Richardson's report (11855) on the revolt of the Zarānīq and Ottoman operations against them was relayed by Lowther in his no. 70 to Earl Grey (no. 212), 24 March 1909 (FO 4243/218).

Chapter 12

1. Rīḥānī 1954: vol. 1, 147.
2. Abāẓah 1979: 155.
3. Brémond 1937: 71.
4. Report to the *Times of India* cited by *The Times* (London), 30 May 1905.
5. Most famous and bravest of the tribes in the Tihāmah; they had been exposed to numerous outside attacks on account of their strategic location on a coastal stretch of land 60 kilometres wide and 70 kilometres long, with their base at Bayt al-Faqīh; they rose against the Ottomans often but were the last to submit to the imam's rule. See Washīli 1402/1982: 78, n. 1.
6. No. 103, G. A. Richardson to Aden Protectorate of 12 August 1904.
7. No. 130 *Confidential* (no. 8, Townsley to Lansdowne, Constantinople, 28 February 1905 (FO 406/21 *Confidential*).
8. *Iradé husūsiye* 1322, *genel* 1251, *husūsi*, 34, 10 Za 1322/16 January 1905.
9. *Serasker* to the *sadaret*, 15 and 16 July 1905 (YMM 276/96).
10. Wāsi'i 1366/1947: 197–8 and Jirāfi 1951: 219.
11. Indeed, German diplomats were convinced that the British were behind the rising. See below.
12. No. 2 in YMM 269/106. Serasker Riza to the *sadrazam* relaying urgent message from the *vali* of Ṣan'ā' of 14 L 1322/22 December 1904.
13. Telegram in cipher to the *seraskeriyet* of 12 Z 1320/1904 (YMM 269/201). Serasker Riza passed the information on to the *sadrazam* for deliberation and action on 2 January 1905.
14. 'Condition in the Yemen', *The Times*, 13 March 1906, p. 10, column 3.
15. Ambassador O'Conor dispatched a summary of events from the renewed outbreaks to 14 March 1905 to Lansdowne (no. 170), enclosure in no. 52 (FO 406/21 *Confidential*).
16. *Seraskeriyet* of 14 S 1323/19 April 1905 (YMM 273/78).
17. Authorization of Serasker Riza of 5 S 1323/10 April 1905 (YMM 273/22). See also YEE 86/27–/2671 of 1 M 1324.
18. Letter no. 2603 of 2 May 1905 in IOR, R/20/A/1220: AIA/ C/53: '1905 Yemen-Arabia: Revolt of the Arabs under the Imam of Yemen against the Turks'.
19. There are conflicting dates for the surrender of the city. Abāẓah claimed it was on 20 March; British reports place it on 30 April. See 'The Yemen Revolt', *The Times*, 30 May 1905, p. 14, column 3.
20. *Confidential*, no. 39, Richardson to Mason of 5 June 1905 in IOR R/20/A/1220.
21. 'The Yemen Rising: Fall of Sana' (*sic*), *The Times*, 29 April 1905, p. 7, column 4.
22. For details of his official function, see 126/79/19 R 1322 (*defter kısmındadir*, no. 12380).

23. Enciphered telegram to the *serasker* of 14 March 1905 (YMM 273/58).
24. Vice Consul Richardson from Hodeida to Mason, no. 30, *Confidential* of 21 March 1905.
25. No. 13, Townley to Lansdowne (no. 5), Constantinople, 3 January 1905. Enclosure 1, Consul Devey to Sir N. O'Conor from Jiddah, 15 December 1904, forwarding G. A. Richardson's dispatch to him (enclosure 2 in no. 13) FO 406/20 (*Confidential*).
26. He was *vali* of Monastir when the Russian consul was shot there in 1903, after which he was transferred to Tripoli.
27. No. 178 (no. 73, O'Conor to Lansdowne, Constantinople, 21 March 1905 (FO 406/21 *Confidential*).
28. *Maruz* of 3 L 1322/13 October 1904, no. 2. The *serasker* passed it on for quick action (YMM 266/55, no. 1).
29. *Iradé hususiye* 130/65/28 S 1323 (five enclosures); also 130/82/16 Ra 1323 (two enclosures).
30. *Iradé hususiye* 130/99/5 Ra 1323 (*defter kismsindadir*, no. 13064).
31. *Iradé hususiye* 131/13/7 R 1323 (*defter kismsindadir*, no. 13146).
32. Feyzi first served in Yemen in 1873 as captain, rising to the rank of major general in 1887. He conducted successful campaigns against Ibn Saud. For seven years he served as *vali* and commander-in-chief in Yemen. He repelled the attacks on Ṣan'ā' in 1892 and recaptured most of the towns seized by the former imam (*Confidential* no. 53, Richardson to Mason of 5 April 1905).
33. No. 10 (enclosure in no. 23, Consul General Richards to Townsley, Damascus, 21 February 1905 (FO 406/21 *Confidential*).
34. *The Times*, 10 May 1905, p. 5, column 4.
35. No. 178 (no. 73, O'Conor to Lansdowne, Constantinople, 21 March 1905 (FO 406/21 *Confidential*).
36. It is difficult to verify the exact number of troops being assembled for the relief expedition. Lieutenant Colonel Maunsell, British military attaché in Istanbul, reported to Ambassador O'Conor (no. 4) that he had held conversations with the Ottoman war minister on 3 July 1905 who told him that the relief expedition led by 'Ali Riza reached Hodeida on 5 March and that with eight battalions (5000 men) was pushing on. The expedition apparently was also to comprise 24 Syrian battalions, but due to the urgency of the situation he left before the rest could arrive. The Adana relief brigade had been waiting at Qunfdha's coast since November 1903 to take part in the pacification of the 'Asīr region. It was now ordered to join the relief expedition. Four battalions of Syrian *redif* were still waiting at 'Aqabah with four more on the railway from Ma'an, but, according to the minister, transport difficulties had not been fully overcome; government marines were unable to transport troops so were calling on private maritime

companies to fill the need. Besides, if all troops converged on 'Aqabah they would comprise the fifth Syrian corps of 25,000 troops in addition to another 5000 recruits from Adalia and the Syrian coast to form the *nizam* battalions (enclosure in no. 1. *Arabia Confidential* of 13 March 1905, section 6).

37. No. 7 (enclosure in no. 48, Lieutenant Colonel Maunsell to O'Conor, Constantinople, 13 March 1905 (FO 406/21 *Confidential*).
38. Dated 22 Za 1322/28 January 1905 (YMM 270/128).
39. For the various requests and authorizations by the central government for meeting the expenses of paying, provisioning and dispatch of troops see *Iradé hususiye* 131/15/7 R 1323; 131/17/10 R 1323; 131/25/1323/4/17; 131/39/24 R 1323 (five enclosures); 131/62/13 Ca 1323 (four enclosures); 132/41/25 C 1323 (three enclosures); 132/100/27 B 1323; 134/24/ 20 L 1323 (eight enclosures); 136/37/18 S 1324 (two enclosures); 136/80/ 15 Ra 1324 (three enclosures); 137.48/5 Ca 1324 (two enclosures); 139/4/1 Ş 1324 (in *defter*, no. 1410), and 139/19/15 Ş 1324.
40. 'The Revolt in Yemen', *The Times*, 8 May 1905, p. 5, column 2, from Istanbul, 6 May.
41. Figures British military attaché Maunsell submitted to O'Conor were: eight *nizam* from Yanina and western Greek frontiers; eight *redif* brigades from Elbasan (Albania); eight *redif* brigades from Rize (eastern Black Sea coast); and eight *redif* brigades from Isbarta (west central Anatolia). no. 19, Constantinople, 5 February 1905, in *Arabia Confidential*, 8 May, Section 3.
42. Enclosure in no. 1, Vice Consul Richardson to Consul Devey, Hodeida, 6 December 1905, *Arabia Confidential*, 3 July, Section 2.
43. Though 75 miles by road.
44. No. 105, Richardson to Consul Devey, Camaran (Kamarān) 20 December 1904 (enclosure in no. 31) (FO 406/20 *Confidential*).
45. No. 3 (enclosure in no. 73, Walter Townsley to Lansdowne (no. 80) Constantinople, 31 January 1905.
46. Riza Efendi, commandant of the Hodeida regiment, to the *serasker* by enciphered telegram of 16 December 1904, no. 2 in YMM 269/142.
47. No. 29, Townsley to Marquess of Lansdowne from Constantinople, 10 January 1905, relaying the consul's dispatch of 24 December 1904 from Damascus (FO 406/20 *Confidential*).
48. No. 7 (enclosure in no. 116) Consul Richards to Townsley from Damascus, 7 February 1905 (FO 406/20 *Confidential*).
49. Townley to Marquess of Lansdowne, Constantinople, 2 May 1905 and enclosure 1: no. 4, Consul W. S. Richards from Damascus of 24 January 1905 in *Arabia* (Yemen) *Confidential*, 13 February, section 2.
50. 'Insurrection in Yemen', *The Times*, 28 February 1905, p. 5, column 5, based on a report from Constantinople of 26 February.

51. 'The Yemen Rising', *The Times*, 2 March 1905, p. 5, columns 5–56.
52. As follows: original garrison (20,000); Adana relief brigade sent in November 1903 (6000); first reinforcement from Syria, 24 battalions (17,000); recruits from Konya district (5000); second reinforcements on way after fall of Ṣan'ā (28,000). No. 1, O'Conor to Lansdowne, Constantinople, 9 May 1905, enclosure in no. 22, Maunsell to O'Conor of 7 May 1905, *Arabia Confidential*, 15 May, section 4.
53. O'Conor to Lansdowne of 9 May.
54. 'Yemen Insurrection', *The Times*, 11 March 1905, p. 7, column 6 based on a report from Istanbul dated 9 March.
55. Report of 29 March 1905, p. 5, column 4 in ibid.
56. *The Times*, 7 June 1905, p. 7, column 2 reporting from Hodeida.
57. KPA II, 86/23 through 86/29, November 1904 to May 1906.
58. 'The Yemen Revolt', *The Times*, 13 July 1905, column 5.
59. Report from Aden to *The Times*, 1 August 1905.
60. Reports in *The Times* of 21 and 28 August 1905.
61. Reports from Istanbul to *The Times*, 14, 17, 21 and 18 August 1905.
62. Enclosure in no. 16, Colonel Surtees to O'Conor, Constantinople, 25 January 1906 (no. 3), news from Turkish source (FO 406/27).
63. Jirāfi 1951: 220. See also O'Conor's report of 4 January confirming these reverses. Enclosure in no. 6 B (12490, received in Foreign Office, 11 April 1906) FO 406/28.
64. The imperial Ottoman embassy in London cabled Reuters to claim that the two reports by its correspondent from Perim about Feyzi's retreat were lies, alleging that Feyzi and his troops were moving freely around the region (*The Times*, 2 March 1906, p. 5, columns 5–6).
65. Reports by Reuters, published in *The Times*, 12 and 26 February 1906 under the titles 'Rising in Yemen' (p. 6 column 2) and 'Turkish Retreat', Perim, 26 February (p. 6 column 2).
66. For instructions to reform commission, see *Sadaret resmi tezkeré* in YEE, *kısım* 13, no. 112 K 6; and for inspection team sent out, see *mahsus talimat* (special instructions), *zarf* 12, *karton* 6 of *kısım* 13, no. 112/26.
67. No. 45, O'Conor to Earl Grey, Constantinople, 28 February 1906 (no. 132 *Confidential*) in reference to O'Conor's 120, *Confidential* of 26 February 1906.
68. 'The Yemen', *The Times*, 4 January 1906, p. 8, columns 2–3, from a correspondent.
69. 'The Yemen Rising', *The Times*, 14 March 1906, p. 5, column 5.
70. Enclosure in no. 22 (no. 6) Colonel Suntee to O'Conor, Constantinople, 30 January 1906 (FO 406/21 *Confidential*).
71. Wāsi'i 1366/1947: 205–6.
72. O'Conor to Earl Grey, no. 40. Constantinople, 25 February 1906 (7709) (no. 120 *Confidential*) (FO 406/27).

73. No. 8 (1904) O'Conor to Edward Grey, Constantinople, 9 January 1906, no. 14 (FO 406/21 *Confidential*).
74. False information of British Residency at Aden. The imam wanted the British to intercede on his behalf with the sultan in Istanbul because he feared that his own letter (dated 29 R 1323/7 March 1905) to the Sublime Porte never arrived. No. 90, Vice Consul Richardson to Consul Devey, Hodeida, 15 July 1905, enclosure in no. 12, O'Conor to Lansdowne, Therapia, 8 August 1905. Arabia, *Confidential*, 14 August, section 2. The possibility was strong because Ferid Paşa, the *serasker*, was known to favour fighting the imam until he was defeated with no truce or compromises.
75. India Office, 11 October 1905 from Under Secretary of State Walpole of the Foreign Office, IOR. R/20/A/1220: AIA/C/53, '1905 Yemen-Arabia: Revolt of the Arabs under the Imam of Yemen against the Turks'.
76. Telegram of 5 June 1907 to Istanbul headlined 'Desperate Situation', in *The Times*, 11 June 1907, purportedly from a private source.
77. 'Reported Turkish Defeat', *The Times*, 7 June 1907, columns 3–4 as reported from Constantinople.
78. Report by correspondent of the *Egyptian Gazette*, Cairo, 27 April 1906.
79. 'Turkey and Arabia', *The Times*, 19 October 1906, p. 3 column 5, from its correspondent in Cairo. It is worth noting that Istanbul no longer welcomed British correspondents, hence the shift to Cairo for news.
80. 'Turkish Reinforcements for Yemen', *The Times*, 8 May 1906, p. 5, column 3.
81. 'Mutiny of Turkish Troops', *The Times*, 2 July 1906, p. 5, column 5, based on a report from Aden of 30 June.
82. Report from Cairo dated 4 October in *The Times* under the heading 'Turkey and Arabia', 11 October 1906, p. 4, column 1.
83. Report from Beirut by special correspondent of *The Times*, 11 July 1907, appearing on 25 July, p. 4, column 2.
84. Report from Constantinople to Berlin, *Frankfurter Zeitung*, 17 July 1907.
85. 'The Yemen Rising', *The Times*, 24 October 1906, p. 5, column 6.
86. No. 1, memorandum 'Respecting the State of Affairs in Arabia' submitted by the General Staff, War Office, 23 May 1905.
87. 'The Menace to Mecca', *Spectator*, 1 July 1905, forwarded same day from German embassy in London to Reichkanzler Fürsten Bülow (*Türkei* 165).
88. Ibid.
89. *The Times*, 18 July 1905.
90. There is no concrete evidence that the imam openly challenged the Ottomans for the caliphal role; most observers claim it was a British ploy to strip it from the sultan and hand it to an Arab whom they could manipulate and that the imam appeared a suitable candidate through descent from the Prophet's family. The article was forwarded to Berlin from Paris, in *Türkei* 165.

91. See Farah n.d.
92. See von Bülow's 'An den Staatssekretär des Auswärtigen Amtes von Schoen', Berlin, 14 November 1907, in Bülow 1929: 157–8.
93. 'Eine englische Einmischung in Arabien?' 19 May 1905 (annex to political report 8546, in *Türkei* 165). A similar article by Karl Tigdor entitled 'Die grosstürischen Besrehungen in Arabien un der Aufstand in Yemen' of 22 May 1905 (annex to political report 8786 of 22 May 1905, in *Türkei* 165).
94. 'Die Ursachen des english-türkischen Konfliktes', Vienna, 10 May 1906, in *Neue Freie Presse*, 11 May 1906 (A8636, in *Türkei* 165).
95. Petition dated 18 Ş 1320/1904 (YEE 1390, *kısım* 15, *zarf* 74).
96. He described himself as a servitor of the Khawlān tribe and a descendant of the Prophet.
97. KPA II, 86/32–/3117/9 B 1325.
98. It is alleged that he had spent half his life serving and battling in Arabia.
99. KPA II, 86/32/3117.
100. 'The Situation in Yemen', *The Times*, 16 April 1906, p. 3, column 6, based on a report from its correspondent in Istanbul of 10 April from letters sent home by Turkish officials.
101. Reported in *al-Muqtabas* of Damascus, no. 416 of 29 C 1328/7 July 1910.
102. Quite clearly accurate assessments were not published in Istanbul newspapers. The account was published in *Sabah* and reproduced in *al-Muqtabas*, year 1, no. 101 of 27 Ra 1327/17 April 1909.
103. Richardson to Lowther, 19 March 1909, enclosure in no. 52 (15565) Lowther to Grey, Constantinople, 15 April 1909 (FO 424/219).
104. Senni 1326/1908: 166, 168.
105. The 1902 episode, when four Italian warships commanded by an admiral bombed and levelled Midi after the ultimatum they had given the Ottoman authorities at Hodeida expired, left no doubt that Italy would defend its interests in the Red Sea. Despite the Ottoman government's conciliatory attitude and the German foreign office's intercession on their behalf, the Italian government was undeterred. For details, see PAA, *Türkei*, 165 no. 2.
106. Details in Memduh (former minister of the interior) 1324/1908: 2–5.
107. No. 70 (11855) Lowther to Grey (no. 212) of 24 March 1909 (FO 424/218).
108. Reported in *al-Muqtabas* on the basis of a report from Istanbul, year 1, no. 98 of 23 Ra 1327/13 April 1909.
109. He was appointed *vali* and commandant of Yemen shortly afterwards. For his instructions, see KPA II, *kısım* 123, *zarf* 112, *kutu* 6.
110. A series of enciphered telegrams from the Ottoman *mutasarrıf*, Muḥammad 'Ali, in Hodeida of 25 May, 5 June, 28 June and 10 August 1911 to the *dahiliye* (interior ministry) in Istanbul all in *Dahiliye Siyasiye*, 40/18.
111. *The Times*, 4 July 1911, based on dispatch from Constantinople of 26 June, p. 5, column 6.

112. See *Dahiliye Siyasiye*, 40/6 for reports sent to Istanbul on him.
113. 'Murder in the Yemen', *The Times*, 25 December 1909, p. 3, column 4. Report from correspondent in Rome of previous day.
114. KPA II, 86/32–/3150/30 Ra 1326 (2).
115. Sublime Porte's reply to the *serasker*'s *maruz* of 22 Ra 1323/29 May 1905 (no. 1), no. 2 in YMM 274/117.
116. Numbers 370, 371 and 372 all dated 23 April 1908.
117. Reported in *Tasvir-i Efkâr*, no. 225 of 15 January 1910 under special report entitled 'A criminal incident in Yemen'.
118. Report from Richardson to Lowther forwarded to Grey. Enclosure in no. 66 (32105) to the Foreign Office of 25 August 1909, by telegram also from the government of India by Viscount Morley (FO 424/220).
119. *The Times*, 26 October 1909, p. 5, column 3, based on 23 August report from Constantinople.
120. 'The Yemen and the Sultan', *The Times*, 9 October 1909, p. 3, column 6.
121. *The Times*, 25 August 1909, p. 3, column 4; and *al-Muqtabas*, year 1, no. 224 of 22 Ş 1327/7 September 1909.
122. *Al-Muqtabas*, no. 122 of 15 N 1327/30 September 1909.
123. *Al-Muqtabas,* citing Istanbul newspapers, year 1, issue 227 of 26 Ş 1327/11 September 1909.
124. *Iradé hususiye* 340/4/9 L 1327.
125. *Iradé hususiye* 347/10/11 L 1327 and 351/12/15 L 1327 (two enclosures each).
126. *The Times*, 19 February 1910, p. 6, column 1, from its correspondent in Istanbul, dispatch of 13 February.
127. *Dahiliye* to Izzet Paşa, overall commandant of Yemen forces dated 20 Z 1329/12 December 1911 (*Dahiliye Siyasiye*, 37/3).
128. Sadrazam Saïd to minister of the interior, no. 2308 of 20 Z 1329/12 December 1911 (*Dahiliye Siyasiye*, 37/3).
129. Dated 1 Ca 1331/8 April 1913 and endorsed by the *sadrazam* two days later (*Dahiliye Siyasiye* 37/16, no. 4).
130. Instructions from the *sadrazam*'s counsellor to the minister of interior, *tezkeré* no. 586 of 16 B 1331/21 June 1913 in *Dahiliye Siyasiye* 27/4.
131. No. 60 of 14 B 1331/19 June 1913 in *Dahiliye Siyasiye* 96/1, no. 63.
132. Vali Nedim to the Ministry of Interior of 7 L 1331/9 October 1913 in *Dahiliye Siyasiye* 27/21, no. 4.
133. *The Times*, 23 January 1911, p. 5, column 4, dispatched by correspondent in Constantinople.
134. *Tasvir-i Efkâr,* article on conditions in Yemen in no. 507 of 19 S 1329/19 February 1911.
135. One document alone had 160 enclosures on meeting salary deficiencies (*Dahiliye Siyasiye* 96/1).
136. *The Times*, 20 February 1911, p. 5, column 2, Reuters from Istanbul.

137. Report from Jiddah of 2 March, *The Times*, 3 March 1911, p. 5, column 6.
138. *Al-Murāqib* of Jurji Shāhīn 'Aṭīyah, year 3, no. 108 of 15 and 28 January 1911, pp. 88–9.
139. Cited in the newspaper *Iqdām* and reproduced in *Al-Murāqib*, no. 109 of 4 February 1911, p. 165.
140. *Al-Murāqib*, no. 113, of 4 February 1911, pp. 99–100.
141. *Tasvir-i Efkâr*, issues 511 and 516 of 23 and 28 February 1911.
142. *Tasvir-i Efkâr*, nos. 522 and 524 of 5 Ra 1329/6 March 1911 and 524 of 7 Ra 1329/8 March 1911.
143. *The Times*, 16 February 1912, p. 5, column 3.

Chapter 13

1. For text of his petition, see KPA II, 86/34 no. 3303.
2. KPA II, 86/34/3379/10 Ra 1327.
3. Petition by Ẓāhir, son of Faḍl Paşa Zadé, dated 28 Z 1326/22 January 1909. KPA II, 86/34, no. 3315; see also 86/40/3951 (undated) which surmised that the Arabs would take control of Yemen if no real changes were introduced; the government consulted Sharīf 'Abdallah, son of Hussein of Mecca being held in Istanbul as surety, about the situation and needed reforms in Yemen and the rest of Arabia; see KPA II, 86/37/3618 (undated).
4. KPA II, 86/34/3315/28 Z 1326.
5. *The Times*, 24 October 1906.
6. The Porte's representatives were Sharīf 'Abdallah ibn Ḥusayn and Sharīf Muḥammad ibn 'Abdallah (both of the Meccan sharifate) who had submitted their views on Yemen (KPA II, 86/37/3618, n.d.); Sayyid 'Abdallah ibn Ibrahim, Muḥammad ibn Aḥmad al-Shāmi, and Qāḍi Sa'd ibn Muḥammad al-Sharqi represented the imam to the Porte; five accompanied the Ottoman delegation, seven the imam's, signed by *memur* and *muḥāfiz* of seventh Ottoman army, 55th regiment, third battalion's Colonel Ahmed Şevki Efendi (KPA II, 86/37 no. 3632). See 'The Unrest in Yemen', *The Times*, 28 March 1906 (p. 3 column 2) and 8 April 1908 (p. 3 columns 3–4).
7. KPA II, 86/34/3303/15 S 1326.
8. See Annex H for specific demands.
9. Clearly expressed in his *mahzara-yi hümayun*, KPA II, 2617, *kısım* 9, *zarf* 72, no. 41.
10. Same type of inquiry applied to Tripolitania, where similar problems prevailed. Members suggested the following financial compensation for each: Refik Beg, *defterdar* of Aydin, 15,000; Ferik Hayri Paşa, commanding officer of *redifs* at Bursa, 15,000; Feyzullah Efendi of *Umur-i Adliye*, 7500; Miralay Ibrahim Muhyiddin Beg, 7500 for salary plus per diem from the *maliye naziri*. *Tezkeré* of *sadaret* submitted by Cevad on 16 S 1312/20 July

1894 to sultan in keeping with the *mazbata* of the *divan* of 11 days earlier (YSRM 2 S 1312).

11. *Tezkeré* of Cevad of Ş 1312/3 February 1895 (YSRM of 5 S 1312).
12. *Mazbata* of 18 B 1309/18 February 1902 (YSHM 256/77).
13. *Mazbata* of the Başkitabet embodying *tâlimat* from Yıldız of 28 Z 1315/20 May 1898 (YRE of 28 Za 1315 92/50).
14. 'Aẓm 1938: 158.
15. See Annex A.
16. One and a half in the capital; one in 'Asīr, half each in Ta'izz, and Hodeida; if order were established, the need would be reduced to four altogether, argued Hilmi.
17. For more on him, see above.
18. Hussein Hilmi's memorandum on Yemen of 23 August 1891 (KPA II, 437, *kısım* 14, *zarf* 126).
19. YSRM, 1309, no. 59/16.
20. YMM 183/93 of 17 C 1316 and 184/66 of 17 B 1316.
21. Enciphered telegraph from Hilmi re recommendations to improve conditions in Yemen of 4 N 1316/16 January 1899 (KPA II, 1341, *kısım* 14, *zarf* 126).
22. YSRM 123–92.
23. Hussein Hilmi's memorandum of 11 S 1325/26 March 1907 in KPA II, 293, *kısım* 14, *zarf* 126.
24. For details of the Memduh mission, see Mandaville 1985: 20–33.
25. Sadrazam Ferid approved the decision in his *tezkeré* of 11 N 1321/1 December 1903 (YSRM 123–64).
26. YSRM, 12 Ca 1320, no. 117/84.
27. See above, Chapter 12, n. 109.
28. *Arz tezkeré* of the *sadaret* dated 25 Z 1324/10 January 1907 (KPA II, 241, *kısım* 14, *zarf* 126).
29. See Annex I, I and II for specific provisions.
30. For the imam's memorandum, see KPA II, 86/34/3303 of 15 Z 1326.
31. See Annex I, III for their recommendations.
32. For details, see KPA II, 86/34/3315 of 28 Z 1236.
33. For specific provisions of his recommendations, see Annex I, III and *arz tezkeré* of 24 M 1325/7 March 1907 (KPA II, 294, *kısım* 14, *zarf* 126).
34. For details see Annex I, IV.
35. Dated 13 S 1324/10 April 1906. Terms spelled out by Wāsi'i 1366/1947: 207–9.
36. Report by Reuters correspondent from Constantinople in *The Times*, 3 September 1907, p. 3, column 4.
37. Report of 28 August from Constantinople, *The Times*, 30 August 1907, p. 3, column 4.
38. From *Egyptian Gazette* correspondent in Aden, *The Times*, 14 December 1907, p. 5, column 4.

39. Appeal of their spokesman Sayyid Sulaymān 'Abd al-Bārī published in *al-Ittiḥād al-'Uthmāni*, no. 23, 12 April 1909.
40. 'The Yemen Rebels', *The Times*, 13 April 1909, p. 3, column 5, report from Constantinople correspondent of 12 April.
41. Dated 15 Z 1326/9 January 1909.
42. 'Turkish deserter' from Kawkabān garrison to the British Resident at Aden, reported to India Office and to the Foreign Office. Enclosure in no. 35 (18432) 29 May 1906 (FO 406/28).
43. Vice Consul Richardson to Lowther, Hodeida, 1 March 1909. Enclosure in no. 71 (11857) Lowther to Grey (no. 214) of 24 March 1909.
44. No. 64 (43483) Lowther to Grey, Pera, 8 December 1908 (FO 424).
45. 'Reforming Yemen', *al-Ittiḥād al-'Uthmāni*, 1 (15) 15 February 1909, p. 13. For specific provisions, see Annex I, V.
46. Specifically (1) determine number of military forces in Yemen and what required number should be; (2) replace bad with good officials; (3) reorganize police; (4) place lawsuits other than those on the coast in Sharī'ah courts; (5) eliminate malpractices in tax collection by implementing regulations in force and restore to legitimate course, leaving no room for complaints; (6) enforce reform measures, increase local schools, advance institutions of learning, and send to military schools in Istanbul the more competent sons of notables and to teachers' training college pupils to be employed later as teachers in local schools; (7) since it is not possible always to send money from here, local expenses should be defrayed from the revenue of the *vilayet*; for now the treasury is authorized to send TL 60,000 to provide for two months' pay and allowances for civil functionaries and military officers and men; (8) due to high prices and distance, local salaries should be proportionally increased; (9) to police the coast and prevent smuggling, the ministry of marine is to send a few ships; (10) being far from Ṣan'ā', the *liwā* of 'Asīr should be detached and erected into a separate *vilayet*; (11) civil and religious administration in the district where he resides be delegated to 'Sherif Yahya who claims the imamate', to end bloodshed; (12) recently arrived notables from Yemen, Sharīf 'Abdallah ibn Ḥasan and his companions, sent by the imam, to await the decision of the government on the conclusion of their efforts; and (13) longer service of three years to be made after the two-year mandated service for military and civil officials, is an option to be made at the end of the second year.
47. Signed only D. K., issue of 7136 under the title 'Yemenin Tarz-i Idaresi' (Format for Yemen's Administration).
48. See al-Sayyid Sulaymān ibn 'Abd al-Bārī's appeal in *al-Muqtabas*, 1 (23) 12 April 1909, p. 5.

49. *Tasvir Efkâr* (Portrayal of Ideas), no. 282 of 1 Ra 1328/23 March 1910.
50. According to a letter appearing in *Ahwal*, issue of 9 Ş 1327/26 August 1909 and appearing in issue 7201 of *Sabah* of 11 October 1909.
51. Article appearing in *al-Waṭan*, no. 453 of 20 January and 2 February 1911, p. 302.
52. Ibid.
53. Editorial in *Sabah*, issue 7187 of 27 September 1909.
54. *Sabah*, issue 7213 of 23 October 1909 and 7232 of 11 November 1909.
55. *Tasvir-i Efkâr*, no. 116 of 9 N 1327/24 September 1909.
56. *Tasvir-i Efkâr*, no. 117 of 10 N 1327/25 September 1909.
57. *Tasvir-i Efkâr*, no. 118 of 11 N 1327/26 September 1909.
58. Senni 1326/1908: 168.
59. *Tasviri Efkâr*, no. 120 of 13 N 1327/28 September 1909.
60. The need to change currency was mentioned in 1902 when the newspaper *Iqbāl* noted in its first year that 10,000 Ottoman *lira*s and 100,000 *mecidiye*s were sent to Yemen to exchange for the foreign coins being used by Yemenis (see no. 12 of 1 N 1320/1 December 1902). The same issue alluded to the appointment of Muṣtafa Paşa al-ʻĀbid as *mutasarrıf* of the *liva* of al-Karak. He was the brother of ʻIzzet Paşa al-ʻĀbid.
61. YMM 231/107 for details.
62. Senni 1326/1908: 160–1.
63. *Sabah*, no. 121 of 14 N 1327/29 September 1909.
64. *Sabah*, no. 126 of 19 N 1327/4 October 1909.
65. According to Burckhardt's report as condensed and sent under Max von Oppenheim's signature to Chancellor von Bülow in Berlin, no. 372, Cairo, 23 April 1908 (Bonn: Auswertiges Amtes PA, *Orientalia generaralia* 9, no. 1, Bd. 10).
66. Issue no. 49 of 6 M 1328/18 January 1910.
67. For Arab membership of the *Mebusan*, see Prätor 1993: 213–24.
68. Reproduced in *Sadayi Millet*, no. 79 of 7 S 1328/17 February 1910.
69. *Sabah*, no. 7187 of 27 September 1909.
70. See Birru 1960: 153.
71. See *Dahiliye Siyasiye* 33/4 for the full agreement.
72. Full text reproduced in Wāsiʻi 1366/1947: 320; see Annex J for the terms.
73. Sadrazam Saïd referred the decision to the *Mebusan* for advice 30 Z 1329/21 December 1911 (*Dahiliye Siyasiye* 37/6).
74. See Sālim 1984: 184 *et seq.* for details; however, his assertion about the revolt and the truce coinciding with it is was not entirely true, for Idris had commenced his aggressive activities more than a year earlier.
75. Wāsiʻi 1366/1947: 246.
76. Enclosure in no. 8 (30458/ME 44) political resident at Aden to Earl Curzon, Aden, 6 February 1919, signed by Major-General J. M. Stewart (FO 406/42).

Annex A

1. Each *yuk* equalled 100,000 *piastres*.
2. Six-point proposal of Sırrı of 11 N 1267/11 July 1851 in petition form to the *Sadaret*. *Lef* 4 (*Askeriyet*) in 14537.

Annex C

1. Approved by the Council of State and head of the finance bureau, endorsed by the *Sadrazam* and Council of Ministers on 2 S 1317/13 April 1899 (YSRM 101/4 of 2 S 1317).

Annex D

1. Report to the imperial council's chief secretary of 4 August 1899 (YMM 192/160, no. 2).

Annex E

1. Both documents are preserved in the Başbakanlık Arşivi in Istanbul under Yıldız *Esas Evrakı*, *kısım* 18, *evrak* no. 553/182 in *zarf* 93, *karton* 35.

Annex F

1. Powerful clans who attribute their descent to the Prophet Muḥammad and enjoyed both prestige and power in the lower Yemen.

Annex H

1. KPA II, 86/31–/3092/2.12.1324 for the imam's list of complaints.

Glossary of Turkish and Arabic Terms

ahl al-bayt	Prophet's family
akçe	small silver piece worth about one-third of a *para*
âmadi	incoming
'amāmah	headgear
aman	safety, quarter
'āmil	person under Islamic law responsible for collecting the tithe (*zakah*)
amir	commander-emir
arz tezkeré	as below
arz tezkerési	writ of grand vizier submitted to sultan
arzuhal	petition
âşàr	collectors of tithes
âşâr	tax levy on cattle
ashrāf	Descendants of Prophet Muḥammad
askeriyet	military department
asper	same as *akçe*
awqāf	plural of *waqf*
Ayniyat	bureau supervising property
bahriye	naval ministry
Bahriye Nezareti	ministry of the navy
bandar	port
baş kitabet	chief secretariat
başıbozuk	irregular troop levies
bedel	fee in lieu of military service
belge	document, certificate
berat	patent of authorization
bölüm	part, division
bustān	garden
buyrultu	official order
buyrultu âli	imperial rescript
da'wah	summon to faith

dahiliye	interior
dahiliye nezaret	interior ministry
Dahiliye Siyasiye	interior political
dā'i	missionary
Daire Şevreyi Askeriyet	Military Consultative Bureau
da'wah	mission, summons to faith
dawlah	Same as *dola*
defter kısmındadir	section in a register
defterdar	'holder of the book', keeper of fiscal records
defterdarlık	office of director of finances of a province
divan	council of state
Divan-i Âli	imperial chancery
Divan-i Hümayun	imperial chancery
Divan-i Muhasebat	bureau of accounts
Divan-i Temyiz	supreme court of appeals
dola	title of imam's administrator in the south
dosya	file
dragoman	professional interpreter or guide
drang nach norden	push to the north
ḍaqīl	singular of *ḍuqqāl*
ḍuqqāl	those possessing legal discretion in controversial matters
emir-i hac	commander of the pilgrimage caravan
emir-i ümera	commander of commanders
emirname	royal decree
emr-i âli	imperial decree
encümani mahsus	special council
erdeb	grain measure of about five bushels
erkan harp	war command
erkân-i harbiye	general staff
eyalet	province
fakih (faqīh)	Islamic jurist
ferik	division general
ferman (firman)	imperial edict
fesadname	mischief register
fetva	legal opinion
fetvahane	office dealing out *fetva*s
fiqh	jurisprudence
fuqahā'	legal consultant
genel	general
gümrük	customs duty
gümrükcü	customs official

Gurre	beginning of month in Islamic calendar
hacegan	department chief
Hamidiye	military unit named after Sultan Abdülhamid
haram	holy city
Hatt-i Yemen	line of communication to Yemen
hilat	robe of honour
hoca	Muslim teacher
hocalik	master
husūsi	private
husûsi tezkerési	private memorandum
husūsiye	same as *husūsiyet*
husūsiyet	special feature
huswa	fall in value
ḥasharāt	insects
'ilm	religious knowledge
iltizām	farming out of revenue collection
imam	spiritual and administrative supreme leader of Zaydi Shi'ites
iradé	order, decree
iradé seniyé	exalted will, namely of the sultan
iradeler	plural of *iradé*
istabl	imperial equerry
ittihad-i Osmani	Ottoman unity
jabal	highland
jamadār	surrogate official for British Residency, an Indian title
janbiyāh	weapon
jawāri	pulse
jawli	reed used for building houses
kāfir	infidel
kapicibaşi	head of the palace doorkeepers
kapīkehya	chief gatekeeper
kapudan	admiral of the Ottoman fleet
kapudan paşa	grand admiral
kapukehya	representative before the Sublime Porte
kaput	military cloak
karakol	sentry post
karton	carton, box
kasaba	same as *kasabah*
kasabah	borough
Kat	a nut chewed by Yemenis
kaymakam	deputy, head official of a district

kaymakamlık	district of a *kaymakam*
kaza	administrative district
kaza	township
kaza müdürü	district administrator
kethüda	aide-de-camp
khalīfah	caliph
khatt	line of communication
kise	purse
Kise akçe	purse of small silver coins
kısım	part, piece
kiswah	cover of the *Ka'bah* in Mecca
konak	halting place, stage
Kul	slave, janissary
kuruş	one-hundredth of an Ottoman *lira*
kutu	small box
Lef	enclosure
liva	administrative area/major-general
liwa	brigade
maaş	subsistence allowance
mabeyn	entourage/sultan's private camarilla
mabeyn-i hümayun	imperial private quarters for receiving viziers
mahdi	messianic type leader
mahsus talimat	special instructions
mahsusa	special
mahzara-yi hümayun	imperial presence, judicial decree
mal katipi	financial recorder
mal müdürü	financial administrator
maliye	treasury
maliye naziri	supervisor of finance
Maliye Nezareti	treasury department
maruz	petition
maruzat	plural of *maruz*
mashāyikh	elders, chiefs
maydān	open courtyard
mazbata	official report, protocol
Mebusan	Chamber of Deputies
mecidiye	coin named after Sultan Abdülmecid
meclis	consultative body
Meclis-i Hass	cabinet meeting
Meclis-i Husūsî	same as *Meclis-i Mahsus*
Meclis-i Mahsus	special cabinet session
meclis-i temyiz	appeal court

Meclis-i Valâ	court dealing with high officials, Supreme Council
Meclis-i Vükelâ	cabinet of ministers
medrese	religious school
mektupçu	chief secretary, censor of publications
memur	official
merkez	administrative capital
Meşveret-i Devlet	Council of State
mikhlāf	province of Yemen
minbar	pulpit, dais
miralay	colonel
miri	belonging to the government, public
mîr-i mirân	commander-in-chief
mirliva	major general
Misri	Egyptian
mudīrīyah	canton
müdür	supervisor, manager
müdür-i tahrirât	chief of correspondence
müdüriyet	office of a manager
müdürluk	head office of a directorate
mufti	chief expounder of Islamic law
muhabere	correspondence
muḥāfiz	commander of a fort, warden of an administrative district
muhasıpçı	accountant
muḥiqq	just person
muhtar	mayor
multazim	contractor of tax farming
munshi	secretary, clerk
muqaddam	rank of someone placed before
müşür	field marshal
müsvedde	draft
mutamahdi	claimant to the mahdiship
mutasallim	lieutenant governor
mutasarrıf	*sancak* governor
mutasarrifiye	prefecture
mutasarriflik	post and jurisdiction of a *mutasarrıf*
mütevekkil	deputy in charge
nā'ib	deputy
nahiye	subdivision of a *kaza* or district governed by a *müdür*
naip	same as *nā'ib*
naqīb	warden

narguila	water pipe
nazir	overseer
nişan	decoration
nizamiye	regular troops
nişan-i âli	medal of high rank
nişan-i emaret	medal of leadership
nizam	order, system, method
nizamiye	new levies, regular troops
nizaret	ministry
öşür	tithe
padişah	sovereign, sultan
para	currency, one-fortieth of a *kuruş*
paşa	pasha
piastre	Turkish monetary unit worth one-hundreth of a *lira*
Porte/Sublime Porte	seat of administrative government or ministries
qāḍi	judge
qāfilah	caravan
qalami	pertaining to an office
qat	see *kat*
rahīn	surety
redif	Irregular troops
Reis Efendi	secretary for foreign affairs
resmi	official
riyal	main unit of currency in Yemen
Rumi	Pertaining to a Greco–Roman term
Rüşdiye	high school under late Ottomans
rüsumet	official duties or fees
ruzalā	mischief makers
sadaqah	charity
sadaret	grand vizierate/prime ministry
sadr	chief minister
sadrazam	equivalent of prime minister
salname	almanac, year book
sancak	principal subdivision of an administrative province
sarsevari	head of cavalry
sayyid	notable of Yemen who claims descendance from Prophet's family
Sayyid al-Khilāfah	lord of the successorship/caliphate
senet	note
serasker	commander in chief
seraskeriyet	central military headquarters in Istanbul
seraskeriyet-hususiye	special to military headquarters

şethiye	small, two- to three-mast boat
şeyhülislam	chief legal spokesman of Islam
shal	cashmere shawl
Sharī'ah	fundamental law of Islam, its constitution
sharīḍah	Islam's fundamental law
sharīf	descendants of the Prophet, noble
shaykh	sheikh
shaykh mashāyikh	chief of chiefs
sherifate	pertaining to *sharīf*
sipahi	mounted guard, warrior
sıra	path, row, rank
sunbūq	small boat
Şura-yi Devlet	Consultative Council of State
ta'dīb	teaching a lesson
takrir	official note, deposition
takvim-i vekâyi	official almanac
tâlimat	instructions
taltifat	favours granted as recompense
tarihi	pertaining to date
telegraf ve posta	post and telegraph
tersane	maritime arsenal
tezkeré	memorandum
tezkeré âliye	imperial memorandum
tezkere samiye	lofty memorandum
tezkerési	pertaining to *tezkeré*
thaler	currency, Austrian word for dollar
tophane	artillery depot
ulema	body of Muslim scholars or religious leaders
'ummāl	plural of *'āmil*
Umur-i Adliye	judicial affairs
'uqqāl	wise men, custodians of the faith
'urfi	kind of decree
'ushr	see *öşür*
üşriye	pertaining to *'ushr* or tithe
'uzlah	subdistrict of a *nahiye*
Valâ	high court
vali	governor of province
vaqīl	agent, proxy
vekalet	ministry
vergi	tax, tribute
vergi rüsumet	taxes, charges, customs
vilayet	province

Vükelâ	ministers
Wahhābi	fundamentalist sect of north Arabia
wakil	deputy
waqf	mortmain
waṣāya	bequests
yaver	aide-de-camp
yaver-i harp	colonel of the imperial band
yavur kaymakam	aid deputy
yi Ahkâm-i Adliye	judicial ordinances
yuk	equivalent of 100,000 *piastre*s
zabt varakası	paper issuing restraining order
zakah	customary tax/tithe
zaptname	restraining order
zapt	order for arrest
zaptiye	police
zarf	receptacle, container

Bibliographical References

Documentary Sources

EGYPT
Recueil de Firmans imperiaux addresés aux Vali et aux Khédives d'Egypt 1006 H–1332 H (1597–1904), Cairo, 1934.

FRANCE
Ministère des Affaires étrangérs (Paris)
Correspondences politiques.

GERMANY
Politisches Archiv des Auswertiges Amtes (Bonn)
Abteilung A. Akten:
Acta-Türkei I.A.B.q. 76, vols 1–4.
Türkei, 76, vol. 10. 'Südarabisches Litoral des Rothen Meeres'.
Türkei, 158: 'Das Verhältnis Deutschlands zur Türkei'
Türkei, 165: 'Arabien'.
Türkei, 165 nr 2: 'Italienisch-Türkischer Konflikt wegen das Seeräuberunwesens im Roten Meere'.

GREAT BRITAIN
Arab Bureau (Cairo)
Handbook of Yemen, Cairo: Government Press, 1917.

India Office (London)
Bombay Government
Bombay Political and Secret Consultations, 1820–37.
Bombay Secret Consultations, 1837–57.
Bombay Secret Letters and Enclosures, 1857–66.
Letters from Aden and Muscat, 1864–66.
Letters from Aden, 1872–77 (copies in Foreign Office files).

Aden
R 20/AIA96. File 79.
R 20/A/120. vol. no. 146.
R 20/A/133. vol. no. 165.
R 20/A/173. vol. no. 222.
R 20/A/188. vol. no. 244.
R 20/A/418. A1A. vol. 6453 of 1874: *Secret Compilations: 'Affairs of Yemen'.*

Public Records Office (Kew Gardens)
Turkey
Correspondence respecting Turkish proceedings in the neighbourhood of Aden presented to both Houses of Parliament.
FO 78/2753 – FO 78/2756: Yemen, Sovereignty Question 1873–77.
FO 78/3185 – FO 78/3189: Egypt, Claims to Sovereignty in the Red Sea, Africa and Arabia, 1827–77.
FO 78/135; 78/228; 78/320; 78/257; 78/318578/342; 78/349; 78/373; 78/375; 78/388; 78/550;
Foreign Office (Confidential) *Abstract of Correspondence and Memorandum Respecting the Right of the Porte to the Sovereignty over the Yemen, and other Points Connected with that Question* (FO 881/2147).

TURKEY
Başbakanlık Arşivi (Istanbul)
Iradeler Tasnifi of 1288, 1289, 1290 of the Sadâret's Meclis-i Mahsûs and Dahiliye, authorizations to Adliye, Askeriye, Bahriye, Maliye, Meşveret-i Devlet, Şura-yı Devlet, Teltifat, Posta ve Telegraf, and Zaptiye ministries and departments.
Mesail-i Mühimme–Yemen, 1803.
Yemen Meselesi dair, 1795–1805.

Yıldız Tasnifi
1. Yıldız 37:
Kısım 14, no. 241: 'Yemen hakkında Dr Glazer'in lâheyasi ile tercümesi vaki olan Beyanat-i Seniye'. Zarf 126, Karton 7.
Kısım 14, no. 293: 'Yemen ahvaline dair Husein Hilmi Paşanin 11 Safar 1325 tarihili arize-i müfassale'. Zarf 126, Karton 7.
Kısım 14, no. 330: 'Yemen hakkında Mahmut Nedim imzalı lâyeha', *zarf* 126, *karton* 8.

Idaret Husûsi Marûzât Evrâkı (YIHM)
Yıldız Esâs Evkerâı (YEE)
Yıldız Mütenevvi Marûzât (YMM)
Yıldız Sadâret Resmi Marûzât Evrâkı (YSRM)
Sadaret Husûsi Marûzât Evrâkı (YSHM), 164, 165, 180.
2. Kâmil Paşa Evrâkına Ek. II (KPA II)
3. Meclis-i Vükelâ Mazbataları (MVM)

Deniz Müzesi Kütüphanesi (Istanbul)
El yazması #167 13s. 'Yemen ve Hicaz Savahilinin inzibat ve bahren muhafazasi hakkinda mütalaat.'

YEMEN
Documents housed in Centre for Yemeni Studies and Research in Ṣan'ā'.

Manuscripts

Abdülmü'min b. 'Ali, 'Mir'atü-'l Yemen', Istanbul Üniversitesi, Ibnülemin Kitapları, TY 6129.
Jābir, As'ad, 'Yemen', Istanbul University Library, TY 4250.
Ziya, Ahmed, *Mufassal Yemen Coğrafyası*, Istanbul Üniversitesi Kitaphane, Ibnülemin Kitapları, Y 4254 (author was army inspector in Yemen in 1307/1889–90).

Secondary references

Abāẓah, Fārūq 'Uthmān (1979) *'Al-Ḥukm al-'Uthmāni fī 'l-Yaman 1872–1918*, Beirut: Dār al-'Awdah.
'Abdali, Aḥmad Faḍl ibn 'Ali Muḥsin al- (1932) *Hadīyat al-Zaman fī Akhbār Mulūk Laḥj wa 'Adan*, Cairo: Salafīyah.
Akwa', Ismā'īl ibn 'Ali al- (ed.) (1404/1984) *Majmū' Buldān al-Yaman wa Qabā'iluhu* (compiled by al-Qādi Muḥammad ibn Aḥmad al-Ḥajari al-Yamāni, 4 vols Ṣan'ā': Ministry of Information and Culture.
'Amri, Ḥusayn ibn 'Abdallah al- (ed.) (1404/1986) *Fitrat al-Fawḍah wa 'Awdat al-Atrāk ila Ṣan'ā'* (part II of al-Ḥarāzi's *Riyāḍ al-Rayyāḥīn* 1276–1289/1859–1872) Ṣan'ā': Dār al-Ḥikmah and Damascus: Dār al-Fikr.
— (1985) *The Yemen in the 18th and 19th Centuries: A Political and Intellectual History*, London: Ithaca Press.

Anonymous (1840) 'A descriptive and historical notice of Aden lately captured by the British', in *United Service Journal*, part II (May).

Anonymous (1848) A *Historical and Statistical Sketch of Aden in Arabia Felix*, Madras: Twigg.

Anonymous, 'The Occupation of Aden' (1843) *Blackwoods Magazine*, vol. LIII (April).

'Aqīli, Muḥammad ibn Aḥmad 'Īsa, al- (1958 and 1961) *Ta'rīkh al-Mikhlāf al-Sulaymāni aw al-Junūb al-'Arabi fi 'l-Ta'rīkh*, 2 vols, vol. I. Riyād: Local Press, vol. II, Cairo: Dār al-Kitāb al-'Arabi.

Arab Information Center (1958) *British Imperialism in Southern Arabia*, New York: Research Center.

'Arashi, al-Qāḍi Ḥusayn b. Aḥmad al (edited by Revd Anastas al-Kirmili) (1939) *Bulūgh al-Marām fi Sharḥ Misk al-Khitām fi man tawalla Mulk al-Yaman min Malik wa Imām*, Cairo: al-Bartīrī and Beirut: Dār al-Nadwah al-Jadīdah.

Âtif Paşa, *Yemen Tarihi* (1326/1908) vol. II, Dar-i Saadet: Manzume-i Efkâr Matbaâsı.

A'ẓami, Aḥmad 'Izzat al- (1349/1931) *al-Qaḍīyah al-'Arabīyah*, 2 vols, Baghdad: Maṭba'at al-Sha'b.

'Aẓm, Nazīh Mu'ayyad al- (1938) *Riḥlah fi Bilād al-'Arabīyah al-Sa'īdah*, Cairo: 'Īsa al-Bābī al-Ḥalabi.

Baldry, John (1976a) 'Al-Yaman and the Turkish Occupation 1849–1914', *Arabica*, 23, 156–96.

— (1976b) 'The Turkish–Italian War in the Yemen, 1911–12', in R. B. Serjeant and R. L. Bidwell (eds) *Arabian Studies*, III, London: C. Hurst & Company, 1976: 51–6.

— (n.d.) 'British Naval Operations Against Turkish Yeman 1914–1919', *Die Welt des Islam*, XIX 1–4: 148–97.

Barakāti, Sharaf 'Abd al-Muḥsin (1330/1912) *Al-Riḥlah al-Yamānīyah lil-Sharīf Ḥusayn Bāsha, Amīn Makkah al-Mukarramah*, Cairo: al-Sa'ādah.

Bidwell, Robin L. (1983) *The Two Yemens*, London and Boulder: Longman and Westview Press.

Birru, Tawfīq 'Ali (1960) *Al-'Arab wa 'l-Turk fi 'l-'Ahd al-Dustūri al-'Uthmāni (1908–1914)*, Cairo: Ma'had al-Dirāsāt al-'Arabīyah.

Boxhall, Porter (1974) 'The Diary of a Mocha Coffee Agent', *Arabian Studies*, I: 102–15.

Brémond, E. (1937) *Yémen et Saoudia*, Paris: Charles-Lavauzelle.

Bülow, Fürsten Bernhard von (1929) *Deutschland und die Mächte vor dem Krieg in amtlichen Schriften der*, vol. 2, Dresden: Carl Reissner.

Bury, George (1915) *Arabia Infelix or the Turks in Yemen*, London: Macmillan Company.

Cevdet, A. (1309/1891–92) *Tarih*, vols 9 and 11, Istanbul: Osmania.

Coates, Timothy (1992) 'D. Joao de Castro's 1541 Red Sea Voyage in the Greater Context of the Sixteenth Century', in Caesar E. Farah (ed.) *Decision Making and Change in the Ottoman Empire*, Kirkville (Mo.): Thomas Jefferson University Press, 263–86.

Danişmend, I. H. (n.d.) *Izahlı Osmanlı Tarihi Kronologisi*, 4, Istanbul: Yayınevi.

Deutsche Rundschau für Geographie und Statistik, 1889.

Doughty, Charles (1888) *Travels in Arabia Deserta*, Cambridge: Cambridge University Press.

Farah, Caesar (n.d.) 'Beginning of Imperial Rivalries in the Persian Gulf', *Anatolia Moderna*, VI: 179–90.

— (1983) 'Anglo–Ottoman Confrontation in Yemen: The First Mocha Incident, 1817–22', in R. L. Bidwell and G. R. Smith (eds) *Arabian and Islamic Studies: Articles Presented to R. B. Serjeant*, London, 214–24.

— (1993) 'Organizing for the Second Conquest of Yemen', *X. Türk Kongresirst'nden ayrıbasım*, Ankara: Türk Tarih Kurumu Basımevi, 1457–72.

— (1994) 'A German Plan of Reform for Ottoman Yemen', in VII CIEPO Sempozyumu'ndan ayrıbasım, Türk Tarih Kurumu Basımevi, Ankara.

— (1998)'Ottoman Return to the Highlands of Yemen', *Proceedings of the Seminar for Arabian Studies*, vol. 28, 49–60.

— (1998)'The British Challenge to Ottoman Sovereignty in Yemen', *The Turkish Studies Association Bulletin*, vol. 22, no. 1 (Spring): 36–57.

Fück, Johann (1955) *Die arabischen Studien in Europa*, Leipzig: Otto Harrasowitz.

Glaser, Eduard (1884) Interview in *La Turquie* of Istanbul, 11th year, no. 95 of 26 April.

Haines, Captain Stafford B. (1845) 'Memoirs on the South and East Coast of Arabia', *Journal of the Royal Geographic Society*, vol. XI.

Hammer-Purgstall, Joseph von (1827–35) *Geschichte der osmanischen Reiches* (10 vols) vols V and VI, Budapest.

Harris, W. B. (1893) *A Journey through the Yemen, and Some General Remarks upon that Country*, London.

Helfritz, H. (1958) *The Yemen: A Secret Journey*, Published in German in 1956 and translated into English by M. Heron, London: Allen and Unwin.

Ḥibshi, ʻAbdallah M. al- (ed.) (1400/1980) *Ḥawlīyāt Yamānīyah*, Damascus.

Hunter, Major F. M. (1886) *An Account of the Arab Tribes in the Vicinity of Aden*, Bombay: Government Central Press.

Jacob, Harold (1923) *The Kings of Arabia*, London: Mills & Boon Ltd.

Jirāfi, ʻAbdallah ʻAbd al-Karīm al- (1951) *al-Muqtaṭaf min Ta'rīkh al-Yaman*, Cairo: al-Ḥalabi.

Kâmil, Mahmûd (1968) *Al-Yaman: Shimāluhu wa Junūbuhu wa 'Ilāqātuhu al-Duwalīyah*, Beirut: Dār Beirut lil-Ṭibāʻah wa ʻl-Nashr.

Macro, Eric (1960) *Bibliography on Yemen and Notes on Mocha*, Coral Gables, Florida: University of Miami Press.

Mandaville, Jon (1985) 'Memduh Pasha and Aziz Bey: Ottoman Experience in Yemen', in Brian Pridham (ed.) *Contemporary Yemen*, London: Croom Helm, 20–33.

Marston, Thomas (1961) *Britain's Imperial Role in the Red Sea Area 1870–1878*, Hamden, Conn.

Memduh (1324/1908) *Yemen Kıtasında hakkında bazı mütalaat*, Istanbul.

Muḥyi b. al- Ḥusayn b. al-Qāsim b. M. b. ʻAli, in Saʻīd ʻAbd al-Fattāh 'Ashūr and M. Ziyādah (eds) (1968) *Ghāyat al-Amāni fi Akhbār al-Qaṭr al-Yamāni*, Cairo: Dār al-Kātib al-'Arabi.

Nuri, Osman (n.d.) *Sultan Abdülhamid Sâni ve Devri Saltanati*, Istanbul.

Playfair, Captain R. L. (1978) *A History of Arabia Felix or Yemen ... including an account of the British Settlement of Aden*, Bombay: Government Printing by Education Society Press, Byculla, 1859; reprinted by Documentary Publications, Salisbury NC.

Prätor, Sabine (1993) *Der arabische Faktor in der jungterkischen Politik*, Berlin.

Râğıp (n.d.)*Yemen*.

Râşid, Hacci Ahmed (1291/1875) *Yemen ve Sanaa Tarihi*, vol. II, Istanbul: Basirat Matbaâsı.

Rāzi, Aḥmad ibn ʻAbdallah (1981) *Ta'rīkh Madīnat Ṣanʻā'* and its *Dhayl* by al-'Arashi (ed.) Ḥusayn al-ʻAmrī, Damascus.

Reilly, B. (1960) *Aden and the Yemen*, London: Her Majesty's Stationery Office.

Rīḥāni, Amīn al- (1954) *Mulūk al-'Arab*, 2 vols, Beirut: 'Ilmīyah.
— (1930) *Travels in Yemen*, London: Constable & Co. Ltd.
Sa'īd, Amīn (1959) *Al-Yaman, Ta'rīkhuhu al-Siyāsi mundhu Istiqlāluhu fi al-Qarn al-Thālith al-Hijri*, Cairo: Dār Iḥyā' al-Kutub al-'Arabīyah.
Sālim, Sayyid Muṣṭafa (1982) (ed.) *Wathā'iq Yamanīyah*, Cairo.
— (1984) *Takwīn al-Yaman al-Ḥadīth*, 3rd edn, Cairo: Madbūli.
Senni, Abdülğani (1326/1908) *Yemen Yolunda*, Istanbul: Ahmed Ihsan & Company.
Sharaf al-Dīn, Aḥmad Ḥusayn (1382/1963) *Al-Yaman 'Ibr al-Ta'rīkh*, Cairo: al-Sunnah al-Muḥammadīyah.
Ubeidoullah Essad (ed.) (1327/1912) *Resimli Kitap*, vol. 5, no. 29 (April) pp. 378–9, 384.
Washīli al-Tihāmi al-Ḥasani, al- (1402/1982) in M. ibn M. al-Shu'aybi (ed.) *Nashr al-Thanā' al-Ḥasan (Tihāmah wa 'l-Mikhlāf al-Sulaymāni 12587–1356 H/1868–1927*), Ṣan'ā': al-'Aṣrīyah.
Wāsi'i, 'Abd al- (1366/1947) *Ta'rīkh al-Yaman al-Musamma 'Furjat al-Humūm wa 'l-Ḥuzn fi Ḥawādith wa Ta'rīkh al-Yaman*, Cairo.
Wavell, A. J. B. (1912) *A Modern Pilgrim in Mecca and a Siege in Sana*, London: Constable & Company Ltd.
Zabārah, M. b. M. Yaḥya (n.d.) *A'immat al-Yaman*, 2nd edn, Cairo.
— (1348/1928) *Nayl al-Waṭar min Tarājim Rijāl al-Yaman fi 'l-Qarn al-Thālith 'Ashar*, vol. I, Cairo: al-Maṭba'ah al-Salafīyah.
— (1979) *Nuzhat al-Naẓar fi Rijāl al-Qarn al-Rābi' 'Ashar*, 2 vols, Ṣan'ā': Markaz al-Dirāsāt wa 'l-Abḥāth al-Yamānīyah.

Newspapers and journals

Arabic language
Al-Ittiḥad al-'Uthmāni
Al-Liwā'
Al-Manār
Al-Mu'ayyad
Al-Murāqib
Al-Muqtabas
al-Muqtaṭaf
Al-Waṭan

Turkish and Ottoman
Ahwal

Iqbal
Iqdam
Sabah
Saday-i Millet
Tanin
Tasvir-i Efkâr

Western languages
Daily Mail
Egyptian Gazette
Frankfurter Zeitung
Globe
Journal des Débats
L'Echo de Paris
L'Eclaire
L'Europe Coloniale
Matin
Morning Post
Neue Freie Presse
Pall Mall Gazette
Pioneer
Spectator
Standard
The Times (London)
Times of India
Wiener Abendblatt
Yemen News

Index